Pierre Batiffol, Atwell Mervyn Yates Baylay

History of the Roman Breviary

Pierre Batiffol, Atwell Mervyn Yates Baylay
History of the Roman Breviary
ISBN/EAN: 9783744774338
Printed in Europe, USA, Canada, Australia, Japan
Cover: Foto ©ninafisch / pixelio.de

More available books at **www.hansebooks.com**

HISTORY

OF THE

ROMAN BREVIARY

By PIERRE BATIFFOL, Litt.D.

TRANSLATED BY

ATWELL M. Y. BAYLAY, M.A.

VICAR OF THURGARTON, NOTTS

WITH A NEW PREFACE BY THE AUTHOR

LONGMANS, GREEN, AND CO.

89 PATERNOSTER ROW, LONDON

NEW YORK AND BOMBAY

1898

All rights reserved

PRÉFACE

DE

L'ÉDITION ANGLAISE

—⋄—

Notre *Histoire du Bréviaire romain*, que le zèle si soigneux et si éclairé de M. Baylay a pris la peine de traduire en anglais, a paru en français dans les premiers jours de 1893, et six mois plus tard une seconde édition en fut donnée par nous, qui différait de la première en ce que les pages 193-208 avaient été intégralement refondues. C'est cette seconde édition qui est actuellement encore dans le commerce, et que la présente édition anglaise reproduit.

Toutefois, depuis 1893, des critiques qui m'ont été adressés, des recherches que j'ai pu faire, des travaux d'autrui qui ont été publiés, il y avait quelque fruit à retirer dont la présente édition anglaise était en droit de profiter. Sur mes indications M. Baylay a bien voulu corriger un certain nombre d'erreurs matérielles, et je dois à son acribie de m'en avoir signalé plusieurs qui m'avaient échappé. La *Geschichte des Breviers* de Dom Bäumer, parue en 1895, m'a fourni peu de chose : la raison en est que cet ouvrage avait paru pour une bonne part en articles de revues antérieurs à mon livre même, articles que je connaissais quand j'écrivis mon *Histoire du Bréviaire romain*; pour une autre part la *Geschichte des Breviers* dépend de mon propre livre ; pour une troisième part elle le contredit et le critique. Mon intention ne saurait être de transformer cette histoire en controverse, surtout en controverse contre un religieux dont je m'honore d'avoir été l'ami, et dont la mort prématurée m'a été un deuil sensible. Il me suffira de dire que sur les points capitaux où mon opinion diffère de celle de l'érudit Bénédictin de Beuron, sur ceux-là surtout où il qualifie mon sentiment de ' neue Theorie,' ses raisons ne m'ont nullement converti au sentiment qu'il défend. Pour la présente édition anglaise, j'emprunterai à la *Geschichte des Breviers* quelques indications concernant les réformes du XVIe siècle, indications que Dom Bäumer a été le premier à produire. Je crois que pour la période qui va du concile de Trente à Benoît XIV l'histoire du bréviaire est maintenant bien connue. Pour le moyen âge, je salue avec joie la publication de M. Ehrensperger, *Libri liturgici Bibliothecae Apostolicae Vaticanae manuscripti* (Fribourg-B. 1897), comme le commencement de cette inventaire critique des manuscrits liturgiques, qui sera le travail préparatoire indispensable à mener à bon terme avant de pouvoir entreprendre une histoire définitive de la liturgie romaine de l'office divin. Je salue aussi la grande œuvre scientifique que nos Bénédictins français de Solesmes poursuivent avec tant de zèle, leur *Paléographie Musicale* ; on y voit que l'archéologie musicale est encore à sa première période, 'la période des fouilles et des coups de pioche,' comme les Bénédictins le disent eux-mêmes ; mais déjà que d'indications heureuses et de trouvailles de détail ! Je salue enfin la promesse que nous font les mêmes Bénédictins de nous donner bientôt un *Auctarium*, où nous trouverons édités en une série complète les anciens livres liturgiques, à commencer par les livres milanais. Ce sont là autant d'entreprises de bon augure, et qui permettent d'espérer bien des progrès pour les historiens qui reprendront dans quelque vingt ans l'histoire des sources du bréviaire romain.

Puisse mon livre, provisoire comme il est sur tant de points, faire du moins aimer notre antique liturgie romaine. Et puisqu'il est traduit en anglais en cette mémorable année où d'un cœur également ému catholiques anglicans et catholiques romains nous célébrons le centenaire de la venue de Saint Augustin en Angleterre, le centenaire aussi de l'initiation de l'Angleterre à la liturgie de Saint-Pierre, puisse-t-il porter avec lui l'écho de cette unanimité des anciens jours, et contribuer dans son humble mesure à l'intégrale restauration d'un passé qui nous est si cher.

P. B.

Paris, 25 *décembre*, 1897.

TRANSLATOR'S NOTE

It has been my effort, throughout this translation, without any straining after literalness, to give the author's meaning fully and faithfully, and, in so far as I have failed, I can only beg forgiveness both of him and of my readers. I have not felt it my business to put forward my own opinions on any part of the subject.

As will have been seen in the foregoing Preface, this translation is no *mere* reproduction of the second French edition : it incorporates, in fact, a great deal, both in the way of recasting and expansion, newly contributed by M. BATIFFOL, of whose kindness, not only in so willingly giving permission for the publication of an English translation of his work, but in manifesting the warmest and most unwearied interest in its progress, I cannot speak too gratefully.

The references and notes are M. BATIFFOL's, except a few marked A. B. I have ventured to add English versions of the principal Latin passages quoted, as I hope the book will be read with interest by many of my countrymen who are not better acquainted with Latin than with French.

My best thanks are due to the Revs. E. G. Wood and C. F. G. Turner for many valuable hints, and to my old friend Mr. Lacey for allowing me to avail myself throughout of his well-known learning and acumen.

I hope that some of my readers, not hitherto familiar with the Breviary, will be led to desire its better acquaintance: I am sure that those who know and love it already will love it all the more.

PREFACE

TO

THE FIRST FRENCH EDITION

THE author of this Manual, while calling it a History of the Roman Breviary, has been far from supposing that so great a subject could be exhaustively treated in so few pages. His object has been to summarise, and on some points to state more precisely, and with all possible clearness, the results reached or led up to by such learned writers as Cardinal Bona, Cardinal Tommasi, Thomassin, Dom Guéranger, and Monsignor de Roskovány. In summarising these results, he has in every case verified them by reference to their original sources, being determined that, though his work was to popularise the subject, it should be work at first hand, and give direct information. He has even been led to revise them, not considering himself forbidden to make researches on his own account, to classify in accordance with his personal observation, and to draw conclusions on his own responsibility and at his own risk. But in thus treating this vast subject it has not been possible for him to avoid seeing how many unexplored countries are still to be found in that ancient continent. We are still without a critical edition of the *Liber Responsalis* of the Roman Church; we have no collection or scientific classification of the most ancient *Ordines Romani*; no catalogue of the Roman liturgical books from the eighth to the thirteenth century; no catalogue or classification of monastic breviaries of dates anterior to the thirteenth century, or of breviaries, whether Roman or non-Roman, from the thirteenth to the fifteenth century; we have not even a descriptive account of *printed* Roman breviaries! Not to speak of documents which might be published relating to the various reforms of the Roman Breviary in the sixteenth, seventeenth, and eighteenth centuries. A man might gladly devote years to such researches, but then, the book he would write would not be a Manual: a collection such as the *Analecta Liturgica* of Mr. Weale would be none too large. So one must needs restrain oneself, and be content simply to strive to keep in the right track, and guide others along it.

The author has endeavoured to avoid those practical questions of ritual which depend either on moral theology or on the decisions of the Congregation of Rites; and still more to keep clear of the prejudices which, in France at least, have too long embittered such questions. His aim has been to treat the subject from the standpoint of Christian archaeology and the history of Christian literature. More fortunate than some liturgical writers of the last generation, we are now able to speak of 'liturgy' without being influenced by external considerations; we can criticise and we can admire without reference to any other matter; taking for the guiding principle of our appreciation those admirable words, worthy of S. Gregory, though they are not his, *non pro locis res, sed pro rebus loca nobis amanda sunt*.[1]

Newman, while still an Anglican, could write this remarkable passage :

'There is so much of excellence and beauty in the services of the Breviary, that, were it skilfully set before the Protestant by Roman controversialists as the book of devotions received in their Communion, it would undoubtedly raise a prejudice in their favour, if he were ignorant of the circumstances of the case, and but ordinarily candid and unprejudiced.'[2]

It is this excellence and beauty of the Roman office which I have endeavoured to express, just as I have myself been sensible of it. And as to the 'circumstances of the case,' alluded to by Newman, I have considered it my duty to analyse them just as they are, without attempting to minimise them, being well convinced that they would not tend to diminish the general impression of esteem and admiration which the Roman Breviary must produce, whether considered as regards its contents or the sources from which they are drawn. It is the impression

---

[1] ['We are not to love things for the sake of the place where we find them, but places for the sake of the good things we find there.' S. Gregory's letter to S. Augustine, as given by Bede, i. 27.—A.B.]

[2] *Tracts for the Times*, No. 75, 'On the Roman Breviary,' p. 1.

I have experienced in tracing back from the sixteenth century to the thirteenth, from the thirteenth to the seventh, the traditions of the Roman Liturgy; in studying in their authentic text the most ancient *cursus* of the Roman basilicas, and of the Vatican basilica above all; in transplanting myself, as it were, into ancient times, and becoming like one of those Anglo-Saxon clerks of the seventh century, who came on pilgrimage to the tomb of the Prince of the Apostles, and who, at once influenced by the authority and enthralled by the mystic beauty of the *Ordo Romanus* and the Gregorian chant, asked of S. Peter that he would teach them to pray, themselves repeating to him the *Doce nos orare* of the Gospel. May the Roman Church pardon me if my predilection for these ancient forms of her liturgy has made me too severe or less judicious a critic of those which are more modern, or if that predilection has sometimes betrayed itself in what I have written.

Paris: *November* 11, 1892.

CONTENTS

	PAGE
Préface de l'Édition Anglaise	v
Translator's Note	ix
Preface to the First French Edition	xi

CHAP.
- I. THE GENESIS OF THE CANONICAL HOURS 1
- II. THE SOURCES OF THE ROMAN *ORDO PSALLENDI* . . . 89
- III. THE ROMAN CANONICAL OFFICE IN THE TIME OF CHARLEMAGNE 90
- IV. THE *MODERNUM OFFICIUM* AND THE BREVIARIES OF THE CURIA 158
- V. THE BREVIARY OF THE COUNCIL OF TRENT . . . 229
- VI. THE PROJECTS OF BENEDICT XIV. 289
- CONCLUSION 351

APPENDICES

		PAGE
A.	EXTRACTS FROM THE *ORDO* OF MONTPELLIER	357
B.	EXTRACTS FROM THE *ORDO* OF S. AMAND	360
C.	EXTRACTS FROM THE ANONYMOUS LITURGICAL WORK PRINTED BY GERBERT	365
D.	TRANSLATION OF SOME PASSAGES IN THE EXTRACTS	377
E.	LIST OF M. BATIFFOL'S OTHER CONTRIBUTIONS TO THE HISTORY OF THE BREVIARY	384
	INDEX	385

HISTORY
OF THE
ROMAN BREVIARY

―•◦•―

CHAPTER I

THE GENESIS OF THE CANONICAL HOURS

THE Roman canonical Office, of which the Roman Breviary is an adaptation, dates from the end of the seventh century or the beginning of the eighth. But this Roman canonical Office is not by any means a creation, formed in all its parts at a given date, by some Pope whose name is unknown to us. It is a composite work: various ages have contributed to it; some of the materials which find a place in it have come from far: it is like the basilica of St. Peter in the days of Pope Adrian the First.

In the second chapter we shall have to analyse the materials furnished by Rome herself to this work of her canonical Office, but we have in the first place to deal with those which it owes to the common tradition of all the Churches. To Rome belong its Kalendar, its apparatus of antiphons and responds, its chant, and the actual order of its psalmody; to Catholic usage belongs the prescription of the various hours of prayer: that is to say, the

B

principle of the Office itself, a principle whose origin and primitive developments it is important to determine, in order to be in a better position for understanding the independent application which was made of that principle by the Roman Church.

I

The principal element in the Divine Office may be, at all events conjecturally, regarded as being connected with one of the very earliest Christian ideas.

Our Saviour Jesus Christ died forsaken by His own disciples, condemned by the Jews, crucified between two thieves. He rose again the third day, He ascended into Heaven; but was that the whole of the triumph which the prophets had foretold for the Messiah, the Son of David? No! and what had been wanting to Him in His passage through this world, that royal glory of the Conqueror, so clearly promised by so many prophets, was yet to be realised in a return which was near at hand, and which would, in fact, be His accession to His Kingdom.

Christ was going to return in triumph to judge the world; the first generation would not pass before His glory and His royal justice would manifest themselves in the Holy City and to the whole world; or rather let us say, that first generation and many more would pass away without the loyal children of the new faith losing aught of their hope and dread of that return, always close at hand.

Moreover, if the year of His return was uncertain, if as the Synoptic Gospels testified, its very season was unknown, the impression was easily formed at an early date that, as the night of the Holy Saturday which ushered in the first Easter was that on which the Saviour came forth alive from the tomb, on such a night also would He reappear, like the destroying angel who on the night of the first passover had smitten the first-born of Egypt and avenged the children of Israel. On that night, then, it was meet that none should sleep, but watch and pray till dawn, awaiting the coming of the Lord.

So, from the evening of Holy Saturday to cock-crow on Easter morning the faithful remained gathered together in prayer. This explanation of the origin of the vigil of Easter is very ancient. S. Isidore of Seville (*d.* 636), who mentions it,[1] borrowed it from Lactantius[2] (*d.* 325); S. Jerome alludes to it as an Apostolic tradition.[3] The

---

[1] *Etymolog.* vi. 17.   [2] *Divin. Instit.* vii. 19.
[3] *Comment. in Matt.* iv. 25:

'Traditio Iudaeorum est Christum media nocte venturum in similitudinem Aegyptii temporis, quando Pascha celebratum est et exterminator venit, et Dominus super tabernacula transiit, et sanguine agni postes nostrarum frontium consecrati sunt. Unde reor et traditionem apostolicam permansisse ut, in die vigiliarum Paschae, ante noctis dimidium populos dimittere non liceat, expectantes adventum Christi. Et postquam illud tempus transierit, securitate praesumpta, festum cuncti agunt diem. Unde et Psalmista dicebat, *Media nocte surgebam ad confitendum Tibi super iudicia iustificationis Tuae.*'

'The tradition of the Jews is that Christ will come at midnight, as at the time of the going forth from Egypt, when the Passover was celebrated, and the destroying angel came; when the Lord passed over our dwellings, and our door-posts were hallowed by the blood of the lamb. Whence also I think that the Apostolic tradition has survived, of not allowing the people to be dismissed before midnight on the vigil of Easter, in expectation of the coming of Christ. But after that hour has passed, all, with confidence of safety, celebrate the festival. Whence the Psalmist also said, "At midnight I will rise to give thanks unto Thee, because of Thy righteous judgments" (Ps. cxviii. [cxix.], 62).'

vigil of Easter was, to use S. Augustine's expression, 'the mother of all the holy vigils.'[1]

The Paschal observance being the prototype of the observance of the Sunday, just in the same way as Easter had its great night vigil, each Sunday had its night vigil. The institution of this vigil is as old as the institution of the Sunday itself. It has been remarked that it already makes its appearance in the letter of Pliny about the Christians, where we read: 'The Christians affirm that their crime or their error consists in nothing more than this, that they are accustomed to meet together on certain fixed days before sunrise; to sing together a hymn to Christ as God;. . . . which being done, they separate, and meet again afterwards to take a repast in common.'[2] This meeting before sunrise on a fixed day, a meeting distinct from the Eucharistic assembly, and devoted to the singing of a hymn to Christ, can be nothing else, so it is conjectured, but the Sunday vigil.

In strictness, the Sunday vigil, like that of Easter, ought to have lasted all night, and hence came its ancient Greek name of παννυχίς. But, as a general rule, the Sunday vigil only began at cock-crow, an hour varying with the season, but always after midnight. In order, however, to remain faithful to the primitive idea of the vigil, Christians devoted to prayer the beginning of the night, the time just after sunset, when the first lamps were lighted. This hour was called in Greek λυχνικόν, in Latin *lucernare*, or, as S. Ambrose somewhere says, *hora incensi*, 'the hour of incense.' So what we call Vespers was, in its origin, the first part of the night vigil. It is true, this

[1] *Serm.* ccxix.   [2] Plin. *Epist.* x. 97.

idea of its original oneness with the night vigil was early lost. But Methodius (d. 311) is mindful of it, when he compares the life of virgins to a vigil, which, like all vigils, had three periods : the evening watch, the second watch, and the third watch (*vigilia vespertina, secunda, tertia*), representing youth, middle age, and old age.[1] So John Cassian, at the beginning of the fifth century, preserves the same tradition when he includes the office of Vespers and that of the cock-crowing under the one title of night-office.[2] This, then, is my idea of the origin of the 'liturgy of prayer.' Is there any need for me to call attention to the fact that everything so far is of necessity uncertain? Let us pass on rapidly to firmer ground.

The programme of the vigil office comprised three different exercises : the psalmody, the reading of Holy Scripture, and the prayers or collects. Tertullian, when speaking of the Sunday observances, distinguishes these three constituent parts : *in ecclesia, inter Dominica solemnia . . . psalmi canuntur . . . scripturae leguntur . . . petitiones delegantur.* Psalms, lessons, prayers : such is the composition of the vigil office.[3]

[1] *Sympos.* v. 2. [2] *Coenob. Institut.* iii. 8.
[3] Speaking of a prophetess of his sect, the Montanists (*D˘ Anima*, 9):

'Est hodie soror apud nos revelationum charismata sortita, quas in ecclesia inter dominica solemnia per ecstasin in spiritu patitur. . . . Iamvero prout Scripturae leguntur, aut psalmi canuntur, aut adlocutiones proferuntur, aut petitiones delegantur, ita inde materiae visionibus subministrantur.'

'We have now among us a sister gifted with revelations, which she receives in spirit, in an ecstasy, while the Sunday observances in church are proceeding. For according as the Scriptures are being read, or the Psalms sung, or addresses delivered, or prayers offered up, so from each is matter for her visions supplied to her.'

The number of those who knew how to read was small, and books were scarce : the psalmody was not executed by all the congregation together, but as a solo, by a cleric (whether deacon or reader), or by a chanter, styled *hypoboleus* or *modulator*, who was not a cleric. He chanted the psalm to a musical phrase, sometimes simple, like a recitative, sometimes more ornate. Custom was divided, in different places, between these two modes of rendering the psalmody. At Alexandria, as also at Carthage and at Rome, the simple chant was preferred to the more ornate. S. Athanasius ordered that the reader of the psalms should use such slight inflexions of the voice that he might seem rather to say than to chant them : '*Tam modico flexu vocis faciebat sonare lectorem psalmi ut pronuncianti vicinior esset quam canenti.*'[1] Meanwhile the congregation listened in silence to the soloist as he proceeded with the chant of the psalm. But the psalm always ended with a fixed phrase set to a well-known chant, which the congregation sang all together. Such, for instance, is the origin of the doxology *Gloria Patri.* Even in the course of the psalm they interpolated similar fixed phrases, which the congregation were to chant all together, after each verse or pair of verses. Such a formula was called ἀκροστίχιον.[2] The chant of the Invitatory as still used with the *Venite*, or the refrain of the hymn *Gloria laus et honor*, will give some idea of the psalmody then called *Psalmus Responsorius*. Sozomen, relating the translation of the body of S. Babylas at Antioch in the time of Julian the Apostate, speaks of chanters singing psalms to which the multitude responded 'Confounded

---

[1] S. August. *Confess.* x. 33.   [2] *Constit. Apost.* ii. 57.

be all they that worship carved images' (Ps. xcvi. [xcvii.], 7).[1] So again : ' I took my place on the throne,' writes S. Athanasius, 'and ordered a deacon to say a psalm, and the congregation to respond "For his mercy endureth for ever."'[2] And S. Augustine : ' Evodius took the psalter, and began to chant a psalm, to which we responded all together "My song shall be of mercy and judgment: unto Thee, O Lord, will I sing"' (Ps. c. [ci.], 1).[3] This simple form of psalmody had been borrowed by the Christians from the custom of the Jews (Euseb. *H. E.* ii. 17, 22).

We are assured by John Cassian that the monastic communities of Egypt at the end of the fourth century remained faithful to this severe and ancient form of psalmody. The office of the evening and that of the night, the two portions of the night office, as Cassian calls them, were each taken up with the recitation of twelve psalms. And this number appears to have been fixed at a very early period, for the Egyptians loved to assert that it dated back to S. Mark, their first bishop. These twelve psalms were executed as a solo by a reader, or rather by four readers who relieved each other, each of them having to recite only three psalms in succession. If the psalm was long, a short pause was made after every ten or twelve verses. There was no Doxology at the end of the psalm, but simply a prayer, and at the end of the twelfth psalm an Alleluya. Then they went on to the reading of the Scriptures, which comprised two lessons, one being from the Old Testament and the other from the New, on every day but Saturday and Sunday, when both were

[1] Soz. v. 19.   [2] *Apol. de Fuga*, 24.   [3] *Conf.* ix. 12.

from the New Testament. During the whole time occupied by the psalmody and lessons the monks remained in absolute silence: they were forbidden to spit, to cough, or even to sigh in an audible manner; nothing was to be heard but one voice; there seemed to be as it were but one soul, so rapt was the attention of the congregation. The two lessons being ended, the congregation, who had hitherto been seated, knelt down to thank God in silence. Then, all standing up, the officiant recited a prayer aloud.[1]

In the Syrian churches, during the first half of the fourth century, the vigil offices presented an aspect in which one easily recognises the same features as in Egypt, with some important differences. The vigil had already ceased to be composed, as it was in Egypt, of two offices of equal length, the evening and the night office, and consisted of three unequal offices, the evening, the night, and the morning. In the evening the bishop assembled the faithful in the church; the psalms of the vesper office having been said, the deacon recited a prayer for catechumens, for the possessed, and for penitents. Then, these classes of persons having been dismissed, he said, 'Let us, the faithful, pray,' and the congregation, standing up, asked of God silently a quiet night without sin. The bishop, in his turn, rose, recited a prayer, and blessed the faithful, after which the deacon dismissed the congregation. The night office, which was concluded in the same way,[2] was in itself much what it was in Egypt: they rose for it at midnight; there was a psalmody of a fixed number of psalms with a prayer after each; every group of three psalms was followed by

---

[1] Cassian, *Coenob. Instit.* ii. 4-12   [2] *Constit. Apost.* ii. 59.

THE GENESIS OF THE CANONICAL HOURS 9

an Alleluya; after the psalmody came the lessons. But, as soon as the sun appeared, an office was recited, composed, like the vesper offices after this time, of invariable psalms, known as the psalms of the dawn (ὀρθρινοί)—viz. the *Deus Deus meus, ad te de luce vigilo* (Ps. lxii. [lxiii.]), the *Benedicite*, and the *Gloria in excelsis*.[1] Thus to the night office was added a morning psalmody, corresponding to that of the evening; it is the origin of what we call ' Lauds.' But, everything being considered, the trilogy of Vespers, Nocturns, and Lauds was by no means a development foreign to the idea of the primitive vigil; it formed, on the contrary, its harmonious expression, and recalled the three periods which Methodius in his definition distinguished as entering into the composition of every vigil.

We have just seen that in Syria, in the first half of the fourth century, the *Gloria in excelsis* was reckoned as one of the *psalms* of the morning office. In the same way they reckoned among the vesper psalms the following little hymn:

> We praise Thee, we hymn Thee, we bless Thee for Thy great glory, O Lord our King. O Father of Christ the Lamb that was slain and hath taken away the sin of the world, to Thee be praise, to Thee the hymn, to Thee the glory, to Thee Who art God, even the Father, through the Son, in the Holy Ghost, for ever and ever. Amen.[2]

These are two curiosities of euchology. They are what used to be called ' private psalms ' (*psalmi idiotici*). This sort of Christian psalm had been, in the second and

---

[1] Pseud.-Athanas. *De Virginitate*, 20.
[2] *Constit. Apost.* vii. 47.

third centuries, in great favour both with Catholics and heretics. In a fragment of an anonymous Roman treatise, 'Against the Heresy of Artemon,' quoted by Eusebius, the controversialist opposes to the unitarian innovations of that heresiarch of the end of the second century the authority of the Popes Victor and Zephyrinus, who had condemned him, as also of S. Justin Martyr, S. Clement, S. Irenaeus, and Melito, who had so clearly affirmed the Divinity of Christ . . . . ' and so great a number of Christian psalms and hymns, composed by the faithful from the very beginning of the Church, wherein they celebrate Christ, the Word of God, proclaiming Him to be God Himself.'[1] Paul of Samosata, who was Bishop of Antioch from 260 to 270, had suppressed ' the psalms which were chanted there in honour of our Lord Jesus Christ.' Such is the expression used by the bishops in giving sentence of deposition against Paul. And what pretext had the latter alleged in justification of this suppression? 'These psalms,' he had said, 'were not the ancient psalms of David: they were new, and the work of new men.'[2]

The names of some authors of new psalms of this sort are known. S. Basil mentions Athenogenes, a martyr of the time of Septimius Severus, as the author of a psalm, still famous in the fourth century for the remarkable expression of the dogma of the Trinity which it is said to have contained.[3] The fragment of Muratori testifies that Marcion, in the second half of the second century, put in circulation a book of psalms of his own

---

[1] Euseb. *H. E.* v. 28, 5.   [2] *Ib.* vii. 30, 10.
[3] Basil, *De Spiritu Sancto*, 73.

way of thinking. S. Dionysius of Alexandria (d. 265) speaks in praise of 'the numerous psalms, so dear to a vast number of the faithful,' composed by Nepos, an Egyptian bishop of the first half of the third century.[1] Valentine, the great Roman Gnostic of the time of Antoninus (138-161), had also composed psalms, which were known to Tertullian.[2] Bardesanes, one of his disciples (A.D. 223), was the author of a collection of 150 psalms, which were widely used in Syriac-speaking churches; it was an entire psalter, and a Gnostic one.[3] More than one specimen of these psalms has come down to us, especially in the apocryphal Acts of the Apostles, which are in great part Gnostic works of the second half of the second century or the first half of the third; and we find these anonymous works distinguished sometimes by a lofty style of poetry. Such are the Gnostic hymns in the *Acta Iohannis* and the *Acta Thomae*. Here is a hymn of the kind, of Catholic origin, composed in the time of Clement of Alexandria.[4]

EVENING HYMN

O Jesu Christ, joyful Light of the holy glory of the Immortal Father, the Heavenly, the Holy, the Blessèd: now being come unto the setting of the sun, and beholding the light of evening, we bless the Father, the Son, and the Holy Spirit of God.

Worthy art Thou at all times to be praised with holy voices, O Son of God that givest Life.

Therefore doth all the world glorify Thee.

---

[1] Euseb. *H. E.* vii. 24, 4.
[2] *De Carne Christi*, 17; cf. *Philosophum.* vi. 37.
[3] Soz. iii. 16.
[4] Wilh. Christ and M. Paranikas, *Anthologia Graeca Carminum Christianorum*, Leipzig, 1871, p. 40; cf. Clem. Alex. *Paedag.* iii. 12 (Christ and Par. *op. cit.* p. 37). [Routh, *Rel. Sacr.* tom. iii, 515.]

Thus in the second and third centuries an original Christian lyric poetry was developed. It was its misfortune to be made all too easily the medium of Gnostic and Marcionite ideas, and it became, later on, an instrument in the hands of worse heretics. In the fourth century the Donatists and Arians made use of similar psalms to propagate their doctrines. Arius composed to new melodies 'songs for sailors' and 'songs for travellers,' which insinuated his pernicious teachings into simple hearts through the charm of their music.[1] It was quite enough to discourage the Catholic Church from the use of such psalms. The metrical hymns of S. Gregory Nazianzen were never honoured with a place in the liturgy. By that time, the second half of the fourth century, the *psalmi idiotici* had been banished from Catholic liturgical use. Yet they have not entirely perished. The beautiful evening psalm quoted above still forms part of the canonical Office of the Greek Church. The morning psalm, *Gloria in excelsis*, banished from the office of Lauds, found, before the sixth century, a place in the Roman *Ordo Missae*. And the *Te Deum*, still sung at the end of Nocturns, is nothing else than a *psalmus idioticus*.

The vigil office, which originally was peculiar to the observance of Sunday, was early introduced into the observance of the festivals of martyrs. Each such anniversary, or *natale*, as it was called, was observed, like the Lord's Day, with a Eucharistic assembly preceded by a vigil (*coetus antelucanus*). The antiquity of these anni-

[1] Philostorg. li. 2; Socrat. vi. 8.

versaries is attested by a document of the year 155: I mean the encyclical letter of the faithful at Smyrna, announcing the martyrdom of S. Polycarp. It mentions, as an already established custom, the idea of celebrating the *natale* of a martyr by the assembly of the faithful at the place where his body reposes.[1] It is the same custom to which allusion is made in the 'Passion of S. Cyprian,' when it is mentioned as a providential circumstance that the people of Carthage were celebrating a vigil on the night which preceded the martyrdom of their bishop: '*Concessit ei tunc Divina bonitas . . . ut Dei populus etiam in sacerdotis passione vigilaret*'[2]: as if God had caused the *natale* of the saint to be celebrated even before his death. And the author of the 'Passion of S. Saturninus of Toulouse' has described this custom in excellent terms, writing thus: 'The anniversaries of the days on which the martyrs were crowned in Heaven we celebrate by vigils and by a Mass.'[3] These vigils of martyrs were not celebrated in city churches, but outside the walls, in the cemetery where the martyr was buried. 'Assemble yourselves,' say the 'Apostolic Constitutions' in the fourth century, 'in the cemeteries, to read the Holy Scriptures and sing psalms over the bodies of the martyrs who sleep there, and to offer there the Eucharistic sacrifice.'[4]

[1] *Martyrium Polyc.* 18.
[2] Ruinart, *Acta Sincera*, p. 186: 'The divine bounty granted to him that the people of God were keeping vigil at the very time of the passion of their Priest.'
[3] *Ib.* p. 109: 'Illos dies, quibus in Dominici nominis confessione luctantes, beatoque obitu regnis caelestibus renascentes . . . coronantur, vigiliis, hymnis, ac sacramentis etiam solemnibus honoramus.'
[4] *Const. Apost.* vi. 30.

Moreover, the Sundays and the anniversaries of the martyrs were not the only solemnities which in the early Church had their vigils—'*nocturnae convocationes*,' as Tertullian calls them.[1] The 'station days' were added to them at an early date. Just as the Jews fasted 'twice in the week,' so did the Christians. The 'Teaching of the Apostles,' at the end of the first century, mentions these two fasting days. The 'Shepherd' of Hermas, at the beginning of the second century, also speaks of them, and gives them for the first time the name of 'stations.' In the third century the stations on Wednesday and Friday were a matter of Catholic custom. And every station involved a vigil. '*Die stationis, nocte vigiliae meminerimus*,' writes Tertullian.[2]

II

Sunday vigils, station vigils, vigils in cemeteries, each comprising a triple office—evening, night, and morning. The literature of the first three centuries affords no trace of any other assemblies for prayer than these. It is not until we come to the fourth century that we see the service of public prayer undergoing modification, and it does so under the influence of new causes.

The fourth century witnessed the birth of Christian ecclesiastical architecture. The poor and narrow limits within which Christian worship was so long confined, owing to the smallness of the earliest churches, such as those of Mount Syon at Jerusalem, or the old churches of S. Theonas at Alexandria and S. Theophilus at

---

[1] *Ad Uxorem*, ii. 4.
[2] *De Orat.* 29: 'On the station day let us not fail to keep vigil by night.'

Antioch, were suddenly expanded in accordance with the magnificence of the basilicas of the age of Constantine, such as the '*Basilica Aurea*' of S. John Lateran, the '*Dominicum*' of Alexandria,' the '*Anastasis*' of Jerusalem, the Church of the Holy Apostles at Constantinople, and many others. What religious joy must these beautiful buildings have inspired in the hearts of the faithful! At Alexandria they were so impatient to begin their assemblies in the *Dominicum* that, in the midst of Lent, A.D. 354, they implored their bishop, S. Athanasius, to open it for worship, though it was not yet consecrated, or even completed; nor was the saint able to withstand their entreaties.[1]

And was it only at rare intervals that they were to assemble in such a beautiful house of the Lord? Were its grand and holy aisles to stand silent and prayerless for hours and days together? Were there not pious souls ready to carry on there a never-ceasing service of prayer?

True, one could no longer reckon upon the whole body of the faithful. With increased numbers the Christian community had been far from growing more fervent. They were beginning to neglect even the Eucharistic assembly on the Sunday, to the great grief of their pastors.[2] But, just in proportion as the Church in extending itself had grown colder, there had taken place within its bosom a drawing together of those souls which were possessed with the greatest zeal and fervour. These consisted of men and women alike, living in the world and without severing themselves from the ties and obligations of ordinary life, yet binding themselves by private

[1] S. Athan. *Apol. ad Constant.* 14.
[2] Chrysost. *Homil. IV. in Annam*, 1; *Homil. de Bapt. Chr. et de Epiph.* 1; S. August. *Serm.* Append. ix.

vow or public profession to live in chastity all their life, to fast all the week, to spend their days in prayer. They were called in Syria *monazontes* and *parthenae*—ascetics and virgins. They formed, as it were, a third order—a confraternity without a hierarchy and without organisation; a connecting link between clergy and laity, the ascetics not having any of the powers of the clergy, but only duties more strict than those of the laity. The religious life properly so called was in fact only a development of this secular institution. In the first half of the fourth century we find these associations of ascetics and virgins established in all the great Churches of the East—at Alexandria, Jerusalem, Antioch, Edessa.

Well then, their rule of life imposed on these ascetics and virgins the duty of daily prayer. They were not to be contented with the appointed vigils of the Church, but were to celebrate privately daily vigils. Their life was, in fact, to be a perpetual vigil. In the treatise '*De Virginitate*' which has been ascribed to S. Athanasius, but which is in reality a hyperascetic and perhaps Cappadocian work of about the year 370, virgins are told to rise every night for prayer, an office entirely private, but which is nothing else than the vigil office made a daily exercise.[1] A similar exercise is recommended by Clement of Alexandria to his 'Gnostic.'[2] Soon this exercise became public. S. John Chrysostom, speaking of the ascetics of Antioch, writes: 'Scarcely has the cock crowed when they rise. Scarcely have they risen when they chant the Psalms of David; and with what sweet harmony! Neither harp

[1] Pseud.-Athan. *De Virginitate*, 20; cf. *Römische Quartalschrift*, tom. vii. (1893), p. 286.
[2] Clem. Alex. *Paedag.* ii. 9.

nor. flute nor any other instrument of music can utter a melody comparable to that which is heard to rise, in the silence of that lone hour, from the lips of these holy men. And so with the angels—with the angels, I say, they sing "*O praise the Lord of Heaven*," while we men of the world are still asleep, or, it may be, half awake, and even then thinking of nothing but our own miserable affairs. Not until daybreak do they take any repose, and scarcely has the sun appeared when they once more betake themselves to prayer, and perform their morning service of praise.'[1]

S. John Chrysostom and the author of the treatise *De Virginitate* both go on to say that, not only every morning at cock-crow and at the hour of dawn do the ascetics and virgins devote themselves to united psalmody, but yet again, every day, at the third, sixth, and ninth hour. So ancient a custom is it for Christians to consecrate by prayer the times we call *Terce, Sext,* and *None*. The faithful took delight in associating the commemoration of Christian mysteries with these three points of time, which divided the day into three stages: at the third hour (9 A.M.), the commemoration of the condemnation of the Saviour; at the sixth hour (noon), of His crucifixion; at the ninth (3 P.M.), of His death.[2] And each of these hours, as it sounded, was to recall to the faithful their obligation, not to allow their hearts to lose their hold on the mysteries of the faith; as says Tertullian[3]: '*Tres*

---
[1] Chrysost. *Hom. in* 1 *Tim. XIV.* 4.
[2] *Const. Apost.* vii. 34.
[3] *De Ieiun.* 10 : 'Just as these three hours are reckoned as more important in the affairs of this world, since they are publicly sounded and divide the day into its parts, so let us understand that they are more especially to be observed with prayer to God.'

istas horas ut insigniores in rebus humanis, quae diem distribuunt, quae negotia distinguunt, quae publice resonant, ita et solemniores fuisse in orationibus divinis [intellegamus].' But what was for the faithful of the third century nothing more than a counsel [1] had become for the ascetics and virgins of the fourth century a rule. They prayed at Terce and Sext and None, and they united in psalmody at each of these hours, just as they united at the cock-crowing or at the hour of the *lucernarium*.[2]

One step yet remained to be taken: namely, that the Church should offer the hospitality of its aisles to these ascetics and virgins, and that the clergy should undertake the direction of these exercises, which had been originally voluntary and private. This step was taken towards the middle of the fourth century. All the passages that we see quoted from authors previous to the fourth century mentioning the daily observance of exercises of common prayer morning and evening, or at Terce, Sext, and None, testify to the existence of voluntary and private exercises, and nothing more. The first occasion on which we meet with the mention of the daily observance of a *public* exercise of common prayer—and even then nothing more is mentioned than the morning office at the cock-crowing and the evening office at sunset—is to be found in a document of the middle of the fourth century, and of Syrian origin, the second book of the 'Apostolic Constitutions.' There we see the faithful urged by the bishop to come to the church on the Sunday and Saturday—'*praecipue die Sabbati et die Dominica studiosius ad ecclesiam accurrite*'

---

[1] Clem. Alex. *Strom.* vii. 7.

[2] Chrysost., see note 1, p. 17; and Pseud.-Athan., see note 1, p. 16.

THE GENESIS OF THE CANONICAL HOURS   19

—but the point is the sanctification of the Saturday, which was still a liturgical innovation towards the end of the fourth century[1]; and, moreover, whether as regards Saturday or Sunday, the passage so far does not allude to anything beyond the *Eucharistic* assembly. However, the bishop is also, to the utmost of his power, to encourage the faithful to come to the church every day, morning and evening, to take part in the psalmody and prayer conducted by the clergy: '*singulis diebus congregemini mane et vespere psallentes et orantes in aedibus Dominicis.*'[2] And in fact we find a Syrian bishop, Zeno of Maiuma, who died, a hundred years old, just at the end of the fourth century, praised for having made a point of never failing to be present at the morning and evening service.[3]

This custom of throwing open the church every morning and evening to the more zealous among the faithful, in order that they might there, under the direction of the clergy, celebrate their devotional exercises —that is, the daily vigils—had been inaugurated at Antioch in the time of the semi-Arian bishop Leontius (344-357), a charitable but inconsistent prelate, very unfortunate in finding himself at the head of a Church where the partisans of the Nicene faith were numerous and zealous. The ascetics of the place formed the main body of the Nicene party, which had for its heads two laymen of high rank, Flavian and Diodorus. The potent influence which an association led by such men was able to bring to bear on Leontius induced him to make concessions. In 350 he banished the Arian Aetius, a man whom he himself had had the weakness to ordain deacon

[1] Funk, *Apost. Konst.* (1891), p. 93.   [2] *Const. Apost.* ii. 59.
[3] Soz. vii. 28.

and receive into the Church of Antioch. He did more. Just as the guest-houses (*xenodochia*) were administered by lay prefects appointed by the bishop, so he decided that the brotherhoods (*asketeria*) should be governed by prefects of his choosing, and he advanced Diodorus to that office. This event must be dated between 350 and 357, and most likely nearer to 350, the year when Aetius was banished. And it is with this appointment that the introduction of the daily office into the Church service is connected. For Leontius had no intention that the confraternities should meet without the clergy, or in irregular sanctuaries: their meetings were to take place in the principal basilica of Antioch.

In twenty years' time the reform carried out at Antioch under the episcopate of Leontius established itself in all the Greek-speaking Churches of the East. S. Basil introduced it at Caesaraea (A.D. 375), in spite of the opposition of a party among the clergy, disturbed in their customs by this liturgical innovation.[1] At Constantinople S. John Chrysostom imposed it on his clergy, and an old author tells us that they were very much put out at not being allowed to sleep all the night as had been their wont.[2] At Milan, S. Ambrose, a personal friend of S. Basil, having become bishop in 374, introduced the Oriental custom of daily vigils. 'At this time,' writes Paulinus, his biographer, 'the vigils first began to be celebrated in the Church of Milan.'[3] At Jerusalem, where the ascetics and virgins were more numerous than anywhere else, this daily public office assumed a still greater solemnity.

[1] S. Basil. *Epistul.* ccvii. 2-4.   [2] Pallad. *Dial. Hist.* 5.
[3] Paulin. *Vita Ambr.* 13.

S. Silvia, a Gallo-Roman lady, who visited the Holy Places about A.D. 385-388, and whose travelling-journal has come down to us [1]—a hundred pages of very queer Latin, forming one of the most precious jewels of early Christian literature—has given us a detailed description of the daily service of prayer in the Anastasis, the cathedral church of Jerusalem.

Here is her account of the vesper office:

'At the tenth hour—the hour which they call here *licnicon*, and which we call *lucernare*—the people crowd into the Anastasis. All the candles are lit, and the illumination is brilliant. Then they chant the evening psalms (*psalmi lucernares*), psalms with long antiphons.[2] At the appointed moment word is sent to the bishop. He comes into the church, and seats himself on his lofty throne, with the priests in their places round him. When the chanting of the psalms and antiphons is finished, the bishop rises, and stands in front of the balustrade of the sanctuary,[3] while a deacon reads out the names of all those who are to be prayed for, and the *pisinni*, or children, of whom there are great numbers, respond at each name, "*Kyrie eleison.*" You hear as it were the sound of innumerable voices. The deacon having finished the list, the bishop recites a prayer. It is the prayer for all the congregation, and all, both the faithful and the catechumens, bow their heads. Then the bishop recites the prayer for the catechumens, and these alone bow their heads. Lastly the bishop says the prayer for the

[1] *S. Silviae Peregrinatio ad Loca Sancta*, Rome, 1887, p. 76 *sqq.*; cf. Dom Cabrol, *Les églises de Jérusalem* (1895), p. 31 *sqq.*

[2] ['*Dicuntur etiam psalmi lucernares, sed et antiphonae diutius.*' —A.B.]

[3] ['*Stat ante cancellum, id est, ante speluncam.*' —A.B.]

faithful, who, in their turn, bow down themselves for the episcopal benediction. So ends the office: everyone departs, after kissing the bishop's hand. It is already dark night.'

Next we have the description of Nocturns and Lauds:

'Every day, before cock-crow, the doors of the Anastasis are opened, and forthwith the *monazontes* and the *parthenae* come in; nor only these, but lay folk besides, men and women, who desire to keep vigil.[1] From that time to sunrise they sing psalms.[2] At the end of each psalm a prayer is recited. These prayers are said by priests and deacons, who are appointed for each day, to the number of two or three, to come and conduct the office of the *monazontes*.' (Nothing is said about any lessons.) 'But at the moment when the day dawns they begin singing the morning psalms (*matutinos ymnos*). At this time the bishop arrives with his clergy, and, standing *within* the balustrade,[3] he says the prayers, "for all," for catechumens, and for the faithful. He then retires, everyone having gone up to kiss his hand and receive his benediction. It being now daylight (*iam luce*), the congregation is dismissed.'

Then for Sext and None:

'At the sixth hour the faithful again assemble in the same manner at the Anastasis. The psalms and antiphons are said. This being duly signified to the bishop, he comes, and, without sitting down, remaining standing within the balustrade, as in the morning, he recites the

---

[1] ['*Qui volunt maturius vigilare.*'—A.B.]
[2] ['*Psalmi responduntur.*'—A.B.]
[3] ['*Ingreditur intro speluncam, et de intro cancellos primum dicet,*' &c.—A.B.]

prayers as before. He then retires, everyone having gone up to kiss his hand. At the ninth hour the same office is performed as at the sixth.' S. Silvia says nothing of any assembly for psalmody at the third hour.

Such was the daily office when introduced, along with the ascetics and virgins, into the public service o the basilicas. Do we wish to see how it was combined there with the ancient observance of the Sunday vigil? S. Silvia shall tell us:

'On Sunday, before cock-crow, a multitude, as numerous as if it were Easter (not merely the ascetics and a certain number of devoutly disposed laity), assembles at the Anastasis, in front of the church, by the light of certain lanterns. The faithful begin coming even long before the time, fearing to arrive after the hour of cock-crowing. They sit down, and psalms and antiphons are sung, each psalm being followed by a prayer said by a priest or deacon, for there are always priests and deacons present. It is the custom that the doors of the basilica should not be opened before the first cock-crowing. But as soon as this is heard, the bishop comes, the doors are thrown open, the crowd enters; the basilica sparkles with a thousand lights; the Sunday vigil properly so called is about to begin. When the people have come in, a priest says a psalm, to which the congregation respond; after the psalm, a prayer. Then a deacon says a second psalm, followed by a prayer. Then some cleric says a third psalm, followed by a third prayer. Then follows the commemoration of those to be prayed for, with the three prayers, just as before at Vespers. These being ended, the censers are brought in; the basilica is filled with their perfume. At this point the bishop takes the Gospel-book and reads from it[1]; after which he blesses the faithful, and the office is over. The bishop retires; the faithful go home to rest. But the *monazontes* remain in the basilica until daybreak, to sing psalms and antiphons, each psalm being followed by a prayer said by some priest or deacon. Some of the laity also remain, whoever may wish to do so, whether men or women.'

In this full and graphic description one sees clearly the superposition of one liturgy on another: first, that which belonged to the whole body of the faithful, the Sunday vigil at cock-crow, then the liturgy of the ascetics and virgins, or daily vigil, from cock-crow to sunrise; the first comprising a fixed number of psalms and collects, with a lesson, the second an indeterminate number of psalms and collects, without any lesson. And these two liturgies succeed one another on Sunday in such wise that the first is of obligation, attended by the whole clergy and all the faithful, while the second, though it follows immediately, remains optional, and is attended only by the more fervent among the laity, and a few of the clergy, who preside over it.[2] Such was the liturgical custom at

---

[1] [' *Et tunc, ubi stat episcopus intro cancellos, prendet Evangelium, et accedet ad hostium et leget Resurrectionem dominus episcopus ipse. . . . Lecto ergo evangelio exit episcopus, et ducitur cum ymnis ad Crucem, et omnis populus cum illo. Ibi denuo dicitur unus psalmus, et fit oratio. Item benedicit fideles et fit missa. . . . Mox autem recipit se episcopus in domum suam. Etiam in illa hora revertuntur omnes monazontes ad Anastasim, et psalmi dicuntur et antiphonae usque ad lucem.*'—A.B.]

[2] Compare with the account given by S. Silvia that presented in the Life of S. Melania (*Analecta Bolland.* 1889, p. 29), which relates to the custom at Jerusalem thirty years later than the pilgrimage of Silvia; also S. Jerome, *Tract. de Ps. cxix.*, ap. Morin, *Anecdota Maredsolana*, tom. iii. pt. ii. p. 229.

Jerusalem, and—setting aside the public observance of Sext and None, which I have not found to be general at this period, and remembering to add the anniversary commemorations of local martyrs, which at Jerusalem seem to have been exceptionally little regarded—one may say that such was then also the liturgical custom of all the Greek-speaking Churches of the East, and in all parts of Gaul as well. As the biographer of S. Ambrose says, '*Cuius celebritatis devotio . . . non solum in eadem ecclesia* [*Mediolanensi*] *verum per omnes pene Occidentis provincias manet.*'[1]

The daily observance of vigils was not the only innovation due to the ascetics and virgins of Syria. To them the Church owed also a thorough transformation of her psalmody.

We have already seen what the early chant of the psalms was like—the chant of the *psalmus responsorius*; and one cannot bear in mind too carefully the description of it given by S. Augustine when speaking of S. Athanasius: 'He caused the reader to use such slight inflexions, that he seemed to say the psalms rather than to sing them.' But if a chant of this kind sufficed to fix the attention of a congregation of limited numbers, closely packed together, and to fill a small church, it could not be the case when there was a great crowd of people in a vast basilica. Under such conditions the slender voice of a single reader was unable to make itself heard above the confused murmur of the people. A bishop of the fourth century observes what difficulty

[1] Paulin. *Vita Amb.* 13.

there was in procuring due silence when the lessons were being read.[1] In congregations which the same author compares to a tossing and murmuring sea, there was need for a chant of greater power—powerful itself as the noise of mighty waters. And so, for the psalm said as a solo was substituted psalmody rendered by a choir.

'Antiphony,' writes S. Isidore, 'means the chant of two choirs which respond to one another—not one repeating what has been sung by the other, but taking up successive verses' (*in antiphonis versibus alternant chori*).[2] No more solos; all the congregation takes part in the chanting, being divided into two choirs or 'systems,' one of which sings the first verse of the psalm, the other the second, and so on. S. Isidore adds that this kind of psalmody came from the Greeks, and this is fully borne out by other testimonies, which with one consent agree in attributing to Diodorus the first introduction of antiphonal chanting in the Church of Antioch.

If we may believe Theodore of Mopsuestia, who was well placed for knowing accurately how things were at Antioch, having passed his youth in the brotherhoods presided over by Diodorus, antiphonal chanting was borrowed by the latter from the Syriac-speaking Churches. S. Basil confirms this testimony, writing that, in his time (A.D. 375) the Churches of the Euphrates valley performed their psalmody in two choirs, like the Greek Churches of Palestine and Syria.[3] At Antioch, somewhat later, they desired to make out a more native and a

---

[1] S. Amb. *In Ps. i. Enarr.* 9: '*Quantum laboratur in ecclesia ut fiat silentium cum lectiones leguntur; si unus loquatur obstrepunt universi.*'

[2] S. Isid. *Etymol.* vi. 19.   [3] S. Basil. *Epistul.* ccvii. 3.

more glorious origin : they said that antiphonal chanting dated back to S. Ignatius, who, having seen in vision the angels chanting in this fashion the praises of the Holy Trinity, realised the heavenly vision in his church at Antioch. This legend is related by the historian Socrates, who is usually more circumspect.[1]

Being thus introduced at Antioch at the same time as the daily observance of the divine office, the antiphonal chanting of the psalms soon established itself in all the great Churches of the East. S. Basil, in the same letter which we have already repeatedly quoted, defends himself against the criticism of certain of the clergy, who charged him with having introduced a singularity of his own devising in the Church of Caesaraea by establishing there this mode of chanting. 'This new psalmody,' he writes, 'has nothing singular about it, for at this very day [A.D. 375]· it is practised in all the Churches of God. The clergy who are disposed to break with me on this ground, must on the same account break with the Churches of Egypt, Palestine, Syria, and the Euphrates valley.' We find antiphonal chanting established at Constantinople in the time of S. John Chrysostom, at Jerusalem in the time of S. Silvia, at Milan in the time of S. Ambrose and by his means, at Toledo from the year 400.[2]

More than this, the antiphonal chant, which, in its original simplicity had been nothing more than a sufficiently monotonous musical phrase, became all at once a melody as varied as it was expressive. Thus the psalm-chant, having begun by being a simple recitative, assumed

[1] Socrat. vi. 8. [2] Mansi, tom. iii. p. 1000.

the form of an elaborate piece of music like a gradual. In 387, when Flavian, bishop of Antioch, went to Constantinople to beg for mercy for the inhabitants of his city, who were threatened with the anger of Theodosius, in order the more effectually to touch the heart of the Emperor, he asked the young singers who were wont to furnish music at the royal table to sing the psalmody of supplication used at Antioch—apparently some kind of litany. Theodosius was overcome by the expressive character of this religious music, which was new to him; tears of emotion fell into the cup which he was holding in his hand.[1] When S. John Chrysostom became Bishop of Constantinople he introduced this music into his Church, giving the direction of the choirs into the hands of a eunuch of the Empress's household, the chief singer at her court.[2]

Antiphonal chanting took a similar development at Milan to that which we have remarked at Antioch. S. Ambrose, in order to increase the attraction of the daily vigils in his Church, caused the psalms to be executed there after the Eastern fashion (*secundum morem orientalium partium*). And the innovation spread rapidly to ' almost all the Churches of the West.' ' How have I wept,' writes S. Augustine not long after, 'at the sound of this psalmody, moved by the voices that rang so sweetly through the church ! '[3] Yet the same Augustine is inclined to consider this elaborate musical rendering of the psalmody as a disturbing invasion of Art into the ancient and severe simplicity of worship. ' Yes,' he

[1] Soz. vii. 23.   [2] *Ib.* viii. 8.
[3] '*Quantum flevi* . . . *suave sonantis ecclesiae tuae vocibus commotus acriter.*'

continues, 'I have wept at the sound of those voices, and I have found sweetness in my tears. But—pardon my severity if it is a fault—I have often wished I could banish from my ears, and from the ears of the Church itself, all the sweet melody of those chants with which the psalms of David are now performed.' And it is in this connection that he recalls the direction of S. Athanasius, that the reader should make use of such moderate inflexions as to seem to say the psalms rather than to chant them, adding that it is safer to follow Athanasius.[1]

It is no part of my design to enter on any inquiries as to what this musical rendering of the psalmody may have been like, whether at Antioch or at Milan. But we cannot help noticing the mistake into which even a mind so great as S. Augustine's fell. He regretted the primitive simplicity of psalmody, forgetting, it would seem, that such simplicity was no longer suited to the pomp of Christian worship in its triumph. Christian art of every sort was budding forth: architecture, painting, ceremonial. For these multitudes of the faithful, assembled under the marble arches and sparkling mosaics of the Anastasis or the Church of the Holy Apostles; for these long trains of clergy vested in robes of dazzling white, there was needed the attraction and the prestige of a powerful and ornate choral music, on a level with the eloquence of S. John Chrysostom or S. Ambrose. It is not desirable that the arts, when they put themselves at the service of the Church, should be cut off from participation in the advance of culture and taste. Most of

---

[1] S. Aug. *Conf.* ix. 6-7, x. 33.

all is this true of music, which is an art so eminently living and progressive. S. Augustine was in the wrong as against S. Ambrose and S. John Chrysostom, just as in our days plain-chantists would be wrong if they were to desire to impose on us the chant of the seventh century as the final expression of Christian music, saying in their turn, 'Safer to follow S. Ambrose,' or 'Safer to follow S. Gregory.'

III

The liturgical work of the fourth century is accomplished. It has consisted in the organisation of a double service of psalmody for every day: on the one hand, the nocturnal *cursus*, comprising Vespers, the night office at cock-crow, and Lauds in the early morning; on the other, the diurnal course, comprising psalmody at the three hours of Terce, Sext, and None, these two courses being celebrated in church by confraternities of virgins and ascetics under the direction of the clergy, and celebrated, as regards music, with a quite new degree of pomp and dignity—'*antiphonarum protelatos melodiis et adiunctione quarumdam modulationum*'—as says John Cassian.[1] This liturgical revolution has been carried out under the influence, we might almost say under the pressure, exerted by these confraternities.

But now, dating from the reign of Theodosius and the time when Catholicism became the social religion of the Roman world, comes the moment when a deep cleavage in religious society manifests itself. These ascetics and virgins, who till now have lived mingled

---

[1] *Coenob. Institut.* ii. 2: 'Long drawn out with antiphonal chant and added melodies.'

with the common body of the faithful, abandon the world and go forth into the wilderness. The coenobitic life, mere attempts at which have hitherto been seen, establishes itself as a distinct Christian society by the side of, and one might even say outside, the Catholic body. The Church of the multitude is no longer a sufficiently holy city for these pure ones; they go forth to build in the deserts the Jerusalem for which they crave.

Henceforth we shall find a double *Ordo psallendi*: that of the monastic communities, and that of the churches under the immediate direction of the bishops.

And in no such church shall we find the Office as it was celebrated in the Anastasis at Jerusalem in the time of S. Silvia; Terce, Sext, and None will for a long time to come form no part of the public office of the clergy. 'We desire,' says a constitution of Justinian, dated 529, 'that the whole clergy established in each church do themselves sing Vespers, Nocturns, and Lauds.' 'For,' adds the Emperor, 'it is absurd that the clergy, on whom rests the duty of executing the psalmody should hire people to sing in their stead; and that the large number of lay folk, who for the good of their souls show diligence in coming to church to take part in that psalmody, should be in a position to see that the clergy who are specially appointed for that office do not fulfil it.' And the Constitution accordingly enacts that the clergy of each church shall be required by the bishop of the place and the *defensor* (or treasurer) of the particular church to take part in the psalmody: those who show themselves negligent of this service are to be expelled from the clerical body.[1] Thus we see that in the

---
[1] *Cod. Iustin.* i. 3, 4.

Greek-speaking East, at the beginning of the sixth century, each church had its *nocturnal* course : viz. the offices of evening, night, and early morning—at which the faithful still loved to assist, and over which it was the duty of the clergy to preside—but no public *diurnal* course.

The custom in all parts of Gaul was similar, the rule for the office to be performed by the clergy not differing from that which the Constitution of Justinian cited above lays down for the Greek-speaking East. 'We ordain,' says the second Council of Braga in 561, 'that there shall be but one and the same *ordo psallendi* for the evening and morning offices : and we reject the monastic uses, which it is sought to mingle with those which according to rule obtain in our churches.'[1] It would be impossible more strongly to express the distinction between the monastic and clerical offices. And we find the Spanish custom to be the same as in Gaul : 'We ordain,' says the fourth Council of Toledo in 633, 'that there shall be but one *ordo psallendi* for Spain and Gaul in the evening and morning offices.'[2] Such was the mind of the Council of Agde in 506, when it pronounces that there shall be in the Narbonnaise, 'just as everywhere else' (*sicut ubique fit*), an office chanted every day in the morning, and also an office chanted every evening, at which the clergy are to assist, with the bishop at their head.[3] All these

---

[1] Mansi, tom. ix. p. 777 ; '*Placuit omnibus communi consensu ut unus atque idem psallendi ordo in matutinis vel vespertinis officiis teneatur et non diversae et privatae, neque monasteriorum consuetudines cum ecclesiastica regula sint permixtae.*'
[2] Mansi, tom. x. p. 616.
[3] Mansi, tom. viii. p. 329.

passages agree in making the canonical Office of the clergy consist of two exercises,[1] that of the evening, or Vespers, and that of the dawn, or Mattins, this last corresponding to the two offices of Nocturns and Lauds. And if in some churches—as, for instance, at Arles, in the time of S. Caesarius—mention is made of the performance in the cathedral of a diurnal course (Terce, Sext and None), we are at the same time duly informed that this monastic exercise exists only for the benefit of penitents, or those of the faithful who are distinguished by an extraordinary degree of fervour.[2]

Such was the *ordo psallendi* of the clergy in the sixth century.

As to the anniversaries of martyrs, to which were now added the anniversaries of translations of martyrs, of

[1] A canon of the Council of Tours in 567 gives us some instruction as to the composition of this double office. At Vespers, which the clergy of S. Martin's call 'the twelfth hour,' twelve psalms are invariably recited, without any other antiphon than Alleluya. At Mattins the number of psalms varies with the season: from Easter to September (*i.e.* in summer), twelve psalms are sung, with an antiphon to every two—six antiphons altogether; in September, fourteen psalms, seven antiphons; in October, twenty-four psalms, but only eight antiphons—one to every three psalms; in November, twenty-seven psalms, nine antiphons; from November to Easter, thirty psalms, ten antiphons. If anyone has leisure to sing *more* psalms, he is to be by all means encouraged to do so; but one who at times may not be able to go through so long a psalmody at Mattins is to do as much as he can (*ut possibilitas habet*), it being understood that he must never recite at Mattins less than twelve psalms, on pain of being condemned, as a penance, to fast until evening, and even then to take no other refreshment than bread and water (Mansi, tom. ix. p. 796). Compare with this canon the indications given in the *De Cursu Stellarum* of Gregory of Tours. (*Mon. Germ. Scriptores Rerum Merov.* tom. i. p. 870–872.)

[2] Bolland. *Acta Sanct. August.* tom. vi. p. 67: *Vita S. Caesar.* i. 13.

saints other than martyrs, and of dedications of churches, it would be an error to suppose, with respect to any such anniversary, that because it is found in martyrologies it was therefore observed throughout the Catholic world: the number of such 'Catholic' festivals, the fixed feasts of our Lord, or the festivals of Apostles, is as yet very small. They would seem to consist of Christmas, Epiphany, and the festivals of S. Stephen, S. James, S. John, S. Peter, and S. Paul.[1] As a general rule, it was only at the place where was the 'confession' of a saint (*i.e.* his tomb), or where some relic of a saint was enshrined, that his *natale* was observed; and so the festival had always some connection with a certain *place*, just as it had with the *time* when it was originally celebrated in the actual cemetery. Hence it is that the monastic communities, such as John Cassian describes, kept no festivals of saints; and it was a new feature in the Benedictine rule[2] that it introduced into the monastic liturgy the *natalitia sanctorum*, which had hitherto been the peculiar privilege of the ancient Christian Churches, rich in local martyrs, or enriched with relics brought from elsewhere. At Tours, the *natale* of S. John Evangelist was celebrated in the basilica of S. Martin; that of SS. Peter and Paul in the basilica of those saints; those of S. Martin, S. Brice, S. Hilary, all in the basilica of S. Martin; of S. Litorius, in his own basilica; and the festival of Christmas was kept in the cathedral.[3]

Meanwhile, at the same period, the *ordo psallendi* of the monks had reached its full development. The

[1] S. Greg. Nyss. *In Laudem Frat. Basilii*, 1; cf. Jaffé, 255.
[2] *Bened. Reg.* 14.   [3] Greg. Turon. *Hist. Franc.* x. 31, 6.

monks of Palestine had in this matter exercised a preponderating influence. As for those of Egypt, at all events in the time of John Cassian, their only common exercise was the night office, and that in the archaic form we have already described. They had no *diurnal* course: when once the *antelucanae orationes*, as Cassian in old-fashioned phrase somewhere calls them, were finished, the Egyptian coenobites went off to their manual labour, and whatever prayers they said in the course of the day were the freewill offering of each individual (*voluntarium munus*).[1] Their practice also was an archaic form of Christian euchology. But the monks of Palestine, on their part, had preserved the office in the form in which it was practised by the ascetics and virgins at Jerusalem in the time of S. Silvia: the night course, comprising Vespers (*vespertina solemnitas*) at sunset; Nocturns (*nocturna solemnitas*) and Lauds in the early morning; and the diurnal course, comprising Terce, Sext, and None.[2] Moreover, these customs of the Palestinian monks before long established themselves in Egypt as well.[3]

However, the monks of Palestine, or, to speak more precisely, those of Bethlehem, had added one more office to the diurnal course. The institution of it was not of early date, since John Cassian witnessed its introduction at the time of his stay at Bethlehem (390-403). The monks of Palestine, like those of Egypt, originally did not take any repose when the office of Nocturns and Lauds was ended, and this point of their rule appears exceedingly severe. Accordingly it was thought more

[1] Cass. *Coenob. Instit.* iii. 2.   [2] *Ib.* iii. 3.
[3] *Vita S. Eupraxiae*, 18; Bolland. *Acta Sanct. Mart.* tom ii. 730.

humane to allow the monks to take some rest after Nocturns and Lauds; but as the day of a man of God could only begin with prayer, the monks of Bethlehem, on rising, assembled for the purpose of singing an office of three psalms—similar, therefore, to the office at the other three day hours. It was called Prime.[1]

Just as the early morning office of Lauds no longer synchronised with the beginning of the day, so neither did the office of Vespers coincide with its end. After Vespers came the evening meal, then bedtime. Could the day of a man of God finish otherwise than with prayer? That is an ancient idea indeed—an idea, rather, whose beginning no one can pretend to date—that we must end the day by thanking God for His mercies, and commending ourselves to Him for the night on which we are entering. S. Basil speaks of this last evening prayer as a thing handed down by tradition.[2] In the West, S. Benedict was the first, so it is said, to give it a place in the series of daily offices, giving it at the same time the name it has ever since retained, of Compline —*completorium*, the completion.

And now the cycle of the monastic office was complete.

Here one might pause to study in detail the description of this office given by S. Benedict in his 'Rule': but we will not now linger over it. The Benedictine Office is a composite work, the result of an adaptation carried out by one individual. 'Our intention,' says the saint by way of conclusion, 'is that, if anyone does not approve this apportionment of the psalter which we have made, he should take such order in the matter as he

[1] Cass. *Coenob. Instit.* iii. 4.   [2] S. Basil, *De Spiritu Sancto*, 73.

THE GENESIS OF THE CANONICAL HOURS 37

judges to be more convenient.'[1] He left to his disciples the same liberty which he himself had exercised. Some elements of the Benedictine Office came from Rome, some from Milan. In its entirety, this Office was only to exercise a remote and long-deferred influence on the formation of the Roman Office, of which it may rather be regarded as an offshoot.

But from the point at which we have arrived, we take in at one view the whole process in which is found the genesis of the canonical hours. A Christian idea—that of the return of Christ—created the primitive vigil, viz. the evening, night, and early morning office of Sunday. The celebration of this office was extended by the Church to the station days and the anniversaries of the martyrs. The confraternities of ascetics and virgins caused it to become of daily observance. The disposition on the part of the more devout to do more than they were bound to, suggested and produced the offices of Terce, Sext, and None—offices which throughout the whole of Christian antiquity remained peculiar to the monks, who from mere private devotions had made their observance part of the liturgy. Of more recent date are the offices of Prime and Compline, originating in the conditions of monastic life, and destined to continue for a longer time than the rest peculiar to the rites observed in monasteries. We recognise in these broad features of the canonical Office the parts respectively due to the primitive Church and to monasticism—parts which remained separate until the sixth century.

It remains for the seventh and eighth centuries to fuse together these differing elements, and to effect that

[1] *Bened. Reg.* 18.

liturgical incorporation of them which is represented by the canonical Office of the time of Charlemagne. But even in the very mention of liturgical incorporation we touch upon what was peculiarly the work of the Roman Church, and the moment has come for us to enter on the study to which all that precedes has conducted us.

CHAPTER II

THE SOURCES OF THE ROMAN *ORDO PSALLENDI*

WE have seen how it was in the Catholic Church that the liturgy of the hours of prayer was originated and developed. We have studied its formation and development outside the Roman Church, in order to be in a better position for distinguishing, in the customs in use within that Church, that which is due to local tradition from that which is derived from Catholic tradition. Henceforth our work lies at Rome. By the help of the documents anterior to the eighth century with which Roman literature supplies us, we have to describe the development of the liturgy of the hours of prayer at Rome, the successive stages through which it passed before becoming fixed in that *Ordo psallendi*, partly original, partly borrowed from elsewhere, which formed the canonical Roman Office of the time of Charlemagne.

The special interior organisation of the Roman Church conditions the whole history of the Divine Office in that Church. Four sorts of churches are found at Rome. First, those which were subsequently known as patriarchal churches—the Constantinian basilica of the Lateran, which takes rank by itself; the Liberian basilica, or

S. Mary the Greater; the Sessorian [1] basilica, or Holy Cross in Jerusalem; the Constantinian basilicas of the Vatican, of S. Paul without the Walls, and of S. Lawrence without the Walls; and lastly, the latest in date, the basilica of S. Sebastian *ad catacumbas*. All these are churches of exceptional importance, some of which (viz. those within the city, like the Lateran, the Liberian, and the Sessorian) were to Rome what the 'great churches' were to Alexandria, Antioch, and Carthage, while the others (those in the suburbs) were the renowned and venerated temples which enshrined and commemorated the great Roman martyrs. Secondly, the 'titles' (*tituli*): of these there were twenty-seven in the sixth century, and this number, which seems to have remained stationary since the fourth century, rises eventually to twenty-eight, but only by the eleventh century. These titles, scattered over the whole space enclosed within the walls of Rome, were like parish churches—'*quasi-dioeceses*, as the '*Liber Pontificalis*' says: they maintained the service of God as regarded Holy Baptism, the dealing with penitents, and the burial of the faithful. Each title had a priest over it, who in time came to be called a Cardinal Priest, and this priest had under his orders a hierarchy of inferior clergy, readers, acolytes, exorcists, and interrers of the dead. Thirdly, there were the deaconries. From the third century Rome was divided into seven ecclesiastical districts, each having a deacon over it. These seven deacons, afterwards called the Cardinal Deacons, were not originally attached to any church: they administered, each in his own district, a kind of charitable

[[1] On the site of the Sessorium, an ancient law-court.—A. B.]

institution, and their duties included the management of the hospitals for the poor and for pilgrims, and the distribution of alms. Later—that is to say, after the fifth century, but before the end of the seventh—while the number of districts remained unchanged, the number of deaconries was gradually extended to sixteen; under Pope Adrian I. it reached eighteen. And by this time each deaconry had a church belonging to it, which bore the name of the deaconry. These deacons also had under them a hierarchy of inferior clergy, subdeacons and acolytes, who formed the body of district clergy. Finally, a fourth class of churches and oratories consisted of the various sanctuaries in the suburban cemeteries, the serving of which belonged to the clergy of the 'titles.'[1] Thus the Roman clergy was divided into two hierarchies, the clergy of the titles and the clergy of the districts: hierarchies which are both of them distinct from that to which at a later time were entrusted the duties of the Apostolic Chancery, and which we call the 'Curia.' The execution of the Divine Office at Rome, at all events from the fourth to the eighth century, was in the hands of these two hierarchies, and the distinctive character of the Roman Office is owing to the part which they took respectively in its performance.

But first we have to go back to the very origin of this Roman Office.

I

The document of earliest date which throws any light upon the liturgical customs of the Roman Church is that

[1] *Liber Pontificalis* (ed. Duchesne), tom. i. pp. 165 and 364; cf. Mabillon, *Musaeum Ital.* tom. ii. p. xi *sqq*.

collection of thirty-eight canons in Greek, which has come down to us bearing the name of S. Hippolytus, but which in reality is rather a Roman synodical document contemporary with Pope Victor (190-200). These *Canones Hippolyti* bear the following testimony to the discipline of the Roman Church in the closing years of the second century.[1]

We observe in them the ancient distinction between the *liturgical* assembly, devoted to the celebration of the sacred mysteries (*oblatio*), and the *euchological* assemblies employed only in praising God (*oratio*). Whenever the liturgical assembly is celebrated, the bishop assembles his deacons and priests, vested in robes of dazzling white, more beautiful than those of the people. He assembles also his readers, wearing their festal attire. These take their place at the ambo, where first one reads and then another, until the whole congregation is assembled. Then the bishop recites a prayer, and proceeds to the celebration of the Liturgy. Here we have the programme and the ceremonial surroundings of the Roman Mass at the end of the second century: the celebration of the sacred mysteries, preceded by a series of lessons and a prayer said by the bishop.[2] The euchological assemblies have a different programme and ceremonial. Nothing is said of the presence of the bishop, but only of his clergy, deacons, and readers. Nor is anything said about festal vestments. The euchological assembly is celebrated at cock-crow, and in church; but it is not a matter of daily observance, for these same canons provide for days when there is no such morning assembly

---

[1] Cf. *Revue Historique*, tom. xlvii. (1892), p. 384 *sqq*.
[2] *Can. Hipp.* (ed. Achelis), 37.

at the church, on which the faithful are to supply its place by private exercises of devotion, each one for himself: '*Quocunque die in ecclesia non orant, sumas Scripturam ut legas in ea: sol conspiciat matutino tempore Scripturam super genua tua.*'[1]

On certain days, then, but not daily, they assemble at the church at the hour of cock-crow. This assembly is of obligation for the clergy. The cleric who absents himself without grave reason is to be excommunicated: '*De clero autem qui convenire negligunt, neque morbo neque itinere impediti, separentur.*'[2] And this assembly at cock-crow is devoted to three exercises, the psalmody, the reading of the Holy Scriptures, and the prayers: '.... *vacentque psalmis et lectioni Scripturarum cum orationibus.*'[3]

If we compare these passages with those which we have quoted in the preceding chapter, especially with those from Tertullian, it is easy to recognise, in these euchological assemblies prescribed on certain days at cock-crow, the vigils of the Sundays and the station days. But, further, we remark that nothing is said about the vesper office. At Rome, at the end of the second century, the vigil begins at cock-crow; the public vesper office, celebrated by the Churches of the East, is here unknown. And unknown it will remain for many years yet to come. Finally, if the Canons of Hippolytus prescribe prayer at Terce, Sext, and None, and at Sunset, 'because

---

[1] *Can. Hipp.* 27: 'On each day when there is no prayer in church, take the Scripture and read in it: let sunrise find the Scripture spread open upon your knees.'

[2] 'As for the clergy who neglect to attend, not being hindered by sickness or absence from home, let them be put apart.'   [3] *Ib.* 21.

that is the end of the day,'[1] such prayer is put exactly on a level with those private and individual exercises by which, in the early morning, a Christian was to compensate for the absence of the solemn assembly at the church. And while the canons 'put apart' the cleric who without grave reason fails to assist at the vigils in church, indicating thereby that those are matters of precept and not of mere counsel, no canonical obligation attaches to the observance of Terce, Sext, and None, any more than of private prayer, morning and evening.

It was still the same at the end of the fourth century With S. Jerome the observance of Terce, Sext, None, and Vespers is, in the case of a Roman lady like Paula Eustochium, or Laeta, a private and individual exercise At precisely the same date at Jerusalem, on the one hand, S. Silvia was attending the basilica of the Anastasis, to take part in the solemn and public daily celebration of Terce, Sext, None, and Vespers; while at Rome, on the other, it was in the solitary seclusion of her mother's house that the daughter of Laeta had to practise these devotional exercises along with her *virgc veterana* (her governess, as we might call her), who was always with her: '*Assuescat . . . . mane hymnos canere, tertia, sexta, nona hora stare in acie quasi bellatricem Christi, accensaque lucernula reddere sacrificium vespertinum.*'[2] In fact, beside Mass, there was no other public

---

[1] *Can. Hipp.* 27.

[2] 'Accustom her to sing hymns every morning; to stand in the ranks of Christ as a faithful warrior at the third, sixth, and ninth hour, and to offer her evening sacrifice at the time when the lamp is lit.'—S. Hier. *Epistul.* xxii. 37, and cvii. 9; cf. Pelag. *Epist. ad Demetriadem*, 23.

office at which she had to assist, except the vigils. But at these solemn vigils, both of the Sunday and of the stations, which were celebrated in this or that church, and in which the Roman clergy took part, all the faithful attended. The crowd was considerable, the attraction very great, and sometimes there was deplorable disorder.[1] S. Jerome advises Laeta not to allow her daughter to go without her; he tells her to keep her close by her side when there: '*Vigiliarum dies et solemnes pernoctationes sic virguncula nostra celebret, ut ne transverso quidem ungue a matre discedat.*'[2] And he thus lets us see that it was not without some ground that Vigilantius demanded the suppression of the nocturnal office of the vigils, on account of the scandals that arose from it. But that would have been to make a very foolish concession to the perversity of a few libertines (*culpa iuvenum vilissimarumque mulierum*), and so the Roman Church condemned Vigilantius, thus showing how great a value she put upon these solemn nocturnal vigils.

Yet we must not suppose that at the end of the fourth century these solemn vigils at Rome, however well attended they were, possessed the same attractions as the vigils which were celebrated daily in other places, as, for instance, at Constantinople in the time of S. John Chrysostom, or at Milan in the time of S. Ambrose. The Greek style of music (*canendi mos orientalium partium*), as S. Augustine called it when speaking of the Ambrosian

---

[1] S. Hier. *Contra Vigilant.* 9.
[2] *Epistul.* cvii. 9: 'Let our young damsel keep the days of the vigils with their solemn night-services; but so that she depart not so much as a finger's breadth from her mother.'

vigils, that *melos cantilenarum* which gave so thrilling a charm to the daily nocturnal office of the basilicas at Milan, was an innovation as yet unknown at Rome.

The psalmody was executed there, as at Alexandria in the time of S. Athanasius, in solo, and with such simple inflexions of the voice that the chant was as nearly as possible the same as that of the lessons: '*sic cantet servus Christi, ut non vox canentis sed verba placeant quae leguntur.*'¹ In the time of Pope Damasus and S. Jerome there is no sign of psalmody rendered by two choirs: nothing, it would seem, more than *psalmi responsorii*, psalms executed in the same way as litanies. To the deacons appertained the duty of thus executing the psalmody; and in many instances the epitaphs of deacons allude to the skill they possessed in this sort of chant. Thus, that of the deacon Redemptus, an inscription of the time of Damasus, in the cemetery of Callixtus:

> . . . Redemptum
> Levitam subito rapuit sibi regia caeli :
> Dulcia nectareo promebat mella canore,
> Prophetam celebrans placido modulamine senem :
> Haec fuit insontis vitae laudata iuventus. ²

The 'ancient prophet' is of course, no other than David. In the epitaph of another deacon, contemporary with Redemptus, we read :

¹ S. Hier. *Comm. in Eph.* v. 19 : .' So should the servant of Christ chant, that not the voice of the singer but the words which he recites may cause delight.'

² De Rossi, *Roma Sotterranea*,' tom. iii. p. 239 : 'Suddenly did the Palace of Heaven catch up to itself the Levite Redemptus : with honeyed accents was he wont to set forth sweetness, in gentle melody uttering the words of the ancient Prophet : praiseworthy for innocence of life was his youth.'

Hic levitarum primus in ordine vivens
Davidici cantor carminis iste fuit.[1]

We see that the chant of the psalms of David was in the time of Damasus executed as a solo by the Roman 'levites,' and that in a style sufficiently severe to be described as *modulamen placidum*. They were still a long way off choral psalmody rendered antiphonally.

At what date did the *canendi mos orientalium partium*, the antiphonal choral psalmody, reach Rome? It is impossible to determine this point with precision. The '*Liber Pontificalis*' attributes this innovation to Pope Coelestine (422-432): he, we are there told, caused the hundred and fifty psalms of David to be chanted before the sacrifice of the Mass, a custom unknown previously. This is the reading of the most ancient text of the book. The second edition, which dates from the sixth century, adds that the chanting instituted by Coelestine was antiphonal.[2] So in the sixth century choral psalmody was regarded at Rome as having been instituted by Pope Coelestine. The evidence furnished by the '*Liber Pontificalis*' is, as a matter of fact, very slight, and I attach the less importance to it because this unlucky passage has been found to lend itself to the most contradictory interpretations.

The establishment at Rome of daily vigils is a matter of greater interest. With S. Hippolytus, or even with

[1] De Rossi, *op. cit.* p. 242 : 'Famous was he while he lived, among the order of Levites, as a chanter of the song of David.' Cf. De Waal, 'Le Chant liturgique dans les Inscriptions Romaines du IVme au IXme Siècle,' *Comptes Rendus du Troisième Congrès Scientifique International des Catholiques*, Bruxelles, 1894, f. ii. p. 310 *sqq*.

[2] L. P. (Duchesne), tom. i. p. 280 : '. . . *Constituit ut psalmi David CL ante sacrificium psalli* antephanatim ex omnibus, *quod ante non fiebat.*'

S. Jerome at the end of the fourth century, there was no question of anything more than vigils for Sundays and station-days (*festivae dies*). That was the old *régime* as regards liturgy. Ordinary days, called in the fifth century *privatae dies*, 'private days,' were not, up to that time, furnished with vigils. It is only in the course of the fifth century that they began to have them at Rome. The most ancient mention to be found of daily vigils at Rome is in the Rule of S. Benedict. Having to settle the programme of the vigils for 'private days,' S. Benedict ordains that at these one of the canticles of the Old Testament shall be chanted every day, 'as does the Roman Church,' '[*privatis*] *diebus canticum unumquemque die suo ex prophetis, sicut psallit ecclesia Romana, dicantur.*'[1] Here we observe that at the end of the fifth century the Roman Church had a daily canonical Office, or, in other words, vigils for 'private days.' The Roman Church was late in falling in with the *régime* adopted a century before at Jerusalem, Antioch, Constantinople, and Milan. But the innovation adapted itself, nevertheless, without difficulty to the previously existing Roman customs.

The vigils of the station-days were arranged in connection with the Mass of the station; with it they were celebrated in a specified basilica, the whole Church being supposed to take part in the celebration, the Pope, the clergy of the seven ecclesiastical districts or the particular district specified for the occasion, and the general body of the faithful.[2] The daily vigils, on the other hand, stood in a similar relation to the private Mass celebrated daily

---

[1] *Bened. Reg.* 13.   [2] S. Leo, *Epist. IX.*, 2.

in each presbyteral 'title'; and just as this private Mass was celebrated by the priest of the title, assisted only by his acolytes, and with no other than a voluntary congregation—some of the faithful of the neighbourhood and perchance some pilgrims—so the daily vigils were celebrated in each presbyteral title only by the clergy attached to that title, and the congregation was composed of such of the layfolk of the neighbourhood as might be disposed to attend.

These daily vigils, inaugurated in the fifth century, were destined for a long time to form the chief part of the office of the Roman clergy. Let us proceed to follow up such few traces as they have left in history and canon law.

The '*Liber Pontificalis*' furnishes us with some interesting information when it relates that Pope Hormisdas (514–523) '*composuit clerum et psalmis erudivit.*'[1] If this had meant that he instructed the clergy in the knowledge of Holy Scripture, mention would not have been made of the Psalms alone. The reference is to chanting the psalms. Here, then, this chanting of the psalms is spoken of as a duty in which it was necessary to instruct, or to the performance of which it was even necessary to compel, the clergy: *erudivit . . . composuit*. We may, in fact, see in these efforts of Pope Hormisdas the same intention which the Emperor Justinian expressed at about the same date in his Constitution of A.D. 529, when he recalled the clergy to the duty of chanting the psalms at the daily vigils of the churches to which they were attached.

[1] *L. P.* (Duchesne), tom. i. p. 269: 'He set in order the clergy, and instructed them in psalms.'

A much more definite expression of the same duty appears in a fragment of a Decretal incorporated in the work of Gratian. It bears in the manuscripts sometimes the name of Pope Gelasius, sometimes of a Pope Pelagius. One cannot be certain to whom it ought really to be assigned, but we may certainly see in it an authentic document of the second half of the sixth century at latest. And what do we read in it? A suburbicarian [1] bishop had given a pledge to the Holy See that he would cause the office of the daily vigils to be performed by his clergy. But the latter, deeming the obligation too onerous, have not responded to the call of their bishop, who therefore refers the matter to the Pope, and the Pope replies that the bishop is to recall his clergy by every means in his power to their liturgical duty, which he thus defines: '*ut cottidianis diebus vigiliae celebrentur in ecclesia.*' [2]

One would like to know what was the programme of these daily vigils, which thus in the fifth and sixth centuries formed the entire office recited by the Roman clergy. Well, a document closely connected with the fragment of Decretal which I have just quoted will tell us. Here is a form taken from the '*Liber Diurnus*'—the actual form of that pledge which the suburbicarian bishops gave to the Pope on receiving consecration from him. This form describes the liturgical office to which these bishops bound themselves in their own name and

---

[1] The suburbicarian Churches, says Canon Bright, were probably those of Picenum Suburbicarium, Campania, Tuscia and Umbria, Apulia and Calabria, Bruttii and Lucania, Valeria, Sicily, Sardinia and Corsica.—A. B.]

[2] Friedberg, tom. i. p. 316.

SOURCES OF THE ROMAN *ORDO PSALLENDI* 51

that of their clergy. It is the most ancient *Ordo* of the Roman Office which we possess:

> Illud etiam prae omnibus spondeo atque promitto, me omni tempore per singulos dies, a primo gallo usque mane, cum omni ordine clericorum meorum vigilias in ecclesia celebrare, ita ut minoris quidem noctis, id est a Pascha usque ad Aequinoctium XXIV^a die mensis Septembris, tres lectiones et tres antiphonae atque tres responsorii dicantur; ab hoc vero Aequinoctio usque ad aliud vernale Aequinoctium et usque ad Pascha, quatuor lectiones cum responsoriis et antiphonis suis dicantur; Dominico autem in omni tempore novem lectiones cum antiphonis et responsoriis suis persolvere Deo profitemur.[1]

Thus, at all times of the year, every day, from the first cock-crowing to sunrise, the whole clergy, with the bishop at their head, assembled at the church to celebrate the vigils. On every Sunday in the year these vigils comprised psalmody with antiphons, nine lessons and their responds. Daily there was psalmody with antiphons, lessons and responds, varying in number according to the season: three lessons from Easter to September the 24th, four lessons from then to Easter. Let us study the passage point by point.

(1) Each day there is a vigil office. The anonymous Decretal quoted by Gratian told us this, but the '*Liber Diurnus*' is more precise: it shows us that this office is to be performed on every day in the year, at whatever season; that it begins at the first cock-crowing; and that it is obligatory for the whole body of clergy. Such was also the state of things contemplated by the Spanish and Frankish councils of the sixth century.

(2) This vigil office is distinct from the early morning

---

[1] *Liber Diurnus*, iii. 7.

office which we call Lauds. The vigil office is celebrated *a primo gallo usque mane*—from the first cock-crowing to sunrise; the office of Lauds at sunrise, *i.e.* just after the vigil office properly so called. It is true that the '*Liber Diurnus*' does not mention this office of Lauds, but S. Benedict (who, in accordance with monastic custom both in the Greek- and Latin-speaking Churches, prescribes the observance of Lauds at sunrise, at the end of the nocturnal vigil office) gives us to understand that such was also the custom of the Roman Church.

(3) On the other hand, the '*Liber Diurnus*' says not one word about the office of Vespers. Nor does the Decretal quoted by Gratian. We are thus led to recall the fact that, while the Spanish and Frankish councils of the sixth century, in common with Byzantine law at the same period, distinguish clearly between the evening and morning offices—the *missae vespertinae* and the *missae matutinae*—there was at Rome at the same date no such distinction; at Rome nothing but a nocturnal vigil.

(4) The vigil office from Easter to September 24, when the nights are shortest, comprises three lessons, three responds, three antiphons; from September 24 to Easter, when the nights are longest, it has four lessons; but on all Sundays, without exception, nine lessons. It appears that the number of antiphons in the three specifications above is meant to correspond with the number of lessons, just as is the case with the responds; but what relation has the number of antiphons with the number of psalms? In other words, how many psalms were chanted at an office of three, of four, or of nine lessons respectively? I am unable to say.

(5) The lessons, whether three or four or nine in

number, will all have been from Holy Scripture. It is, however, certain that, in the time of S. Gregory (590-604) they were also taken from other than canonical writings. 'It has been reported to me,' he writes, 'that our very reverend brother and fellow-bishop Marinianus uses our commentary on Job for reading at the vigils. I am not pleased at this, for that work is not composed for the people. . . . Tell him to substitute for it our commentary on the Psalms (*commenta psalmorum legi ad vigilias faciat*), as that is more suited for the instruction of the minds of the laity in right conduct' (*Epistul.* xii. 24).

In fact, we find that this *Ordo*, the most ancient we possess of the Roman Office, is not very explicit. It nevertheless furnishes us with some precious materials for the purpose of comparison, sufficient to enable us to show by-and-by how that which was to be definitively the canonical Roman Office was eventually formed, on a different plan, after the opening of the seventh century.

We have said that the vigils of the 'private days'— the ferial vigils—were the province of the priest and clergy attached to each 'title' or parish church. Among these inferior clergy we must assign a special place to the *readers*. They belonged to the titles, not to the districts. Inscriptions of the fourth century mention a *lector tituli Pallacinae* (S. Mark's), a *lector tituli Fasciolae* (SS. Nereus and Achilles'), a *lector de Pudentiana*. In an inscription of the seventh century we find mention of a *lector tituli Sanctae Caeciliae*.[1] There is one important detail to be remarked here, viz. that in the fourth century

[1] De Rossi, *Bullettino*, 1883, p. 20.

the readers of Rome were not only grown-up men, but of ripe age: the reader of the basilica of Pudentiana is twenty-four years old; he of the basilica of Fasciola is forty-six. But in the seventh century, on the contrary, the readers are children: the reader of the basilica of S. Caecilia is twelve years old. Thus between the fourth and seventh centuries the condition of the Roman readers was completely changed, and that because the Roman chant itself was completely changed. They had broken with that ancient and severe style of chanting the psalms which an inscription of the time of Damasus, as we have seen, characterised as *modulamen placidum.* Choral psalmody had at last gained its foothold in the Roman city. That is why these clerks, with their grave and manly tones, had given way to choirs of children with flexible young voices, as had already been the case elsewhere for a considerable time: in Africa, for example, where we come across the twelve little clerks of Carthage —*infantuli clerici, . . . strenui atque apti modulis cantilenae*—whose touching martyrdom is related by Victor Vitensis.[1] To children now belonged the principal part in the liturgical chant. The epitaph of Pope Deusdedit (615-618) records that he started on his clerical career as a reader:

Hic vir ab exortu Petri est nutritus ovili,

and that his duty as reader was to chant at the vigils:

Excubians Christi cantibus hymnisonis.[2]

---

[1] Vict. Vit. *De Persecut. Vand.* v. 10.
[2] De Rossi, *Inscrip. Christ.* tom. ii. p. 127: 'He from his birth was nourished up in the fold of Peter . . . keeping watch by night in hymns of praise to Christ.'

In the same way it is recorded of Pope Leo II. (682-683), that in early youth he had been instructed in the science of psalmody and chanting (*cantilena ac psalmodia praaecipuus*); of Pope Benedict II. (684-685), that he had distinguished himself from his childhood in chanting (*in cantilena a puerili aetate*); of Pope Sergius (687-701), that when quite young he had been entrusted to the prior of the chanters for instruction, because he was industrious and had a talent for chanting (*quia studiosus erat et capax in officio cantilenae priori cantorum pro doctrina est traditus*).[1] Thus we see appear in the seventh century the Roman *chant*, and straightway with the chant comes forth a school for chanters.

Each title had its readers. It was thought good that the two great basilicas of Rome, those of the Vatican and the Lateran, should have their readers gathered together in a sort of college, like those *Scholae Lectorum* which already existed at Milan, at Lyons, at Rheims, at Constantinople.[2] The two colleges of readers thus founded, and destined to bear in common the name at first of *Orphanotrophaeum*,[3] afterwards of the *Schola Cantorum*, formed two distinct establishments: the one built in front of the great staircase of S. Peter's, the other situated on the groundfloor of the palace of the Lateran. At all events, such was the case in the ninth century[4] under John VIII. (872-882), at the time when John the Deacon wrote the Life of S. Gregory, to whom he attributes the foundation of the *Schola Cantorum*.

[1] *L. P.* (Duchesne), tom. i. pp. 350, 363, 371.
[2] De Rossi, *Bullettino*, 1883, p. 19.
[3] *L. P.* (Duchesne), tom. ii. p. 92.
[4] *Ib.* tom. ii. p. 86; cf. p. 102, note 18.

One cannot but be struck with this fact: the simultaneous appearance at Rome of the chant and the school for chanters dates back to the age of S. Gregory. Yet I cannot believe that in reality the *Schola Cantorum,* such as we find it in the ninth century, was instituted by that great Pope. John the Deacon, it is true, positively affirms it.

> Like a wise Solomon, knowing the compunction which is inspired by the sweetness of the music in the house of the Lord, S. Gregory compiled for the advantage of the chanters the collection which we call the Antiphonary, which is of so great utility. So also he instituted the school for chanters, whose members still execute sacred song in the holy Roman Church according to the instructions received from him. To this school he assigned property, and built for it two dwelling-houses, one at the foot of the steps of the basilica of the Apostle S. Peter, the other close by the buildings of the patriarchal palace of the Lateran. They still show there the couch on which he rested while giving his lessons in chanting; and the rod with which he threatened the children of the choir is still preserved there, and venerated as a relic, as is also his original Antiphonary. By a clause inserted in the act of donation, he directed under pain of anathema that the property given by him should be divided between the two parts of the *Schola* as a remuneration for their daily service.[1]

But the testimony of John the Deacon merely represents the opinion of the ninth century, by which time the name of S. Gregory was too glorious for an institution such as the *Schola* not to be somewhat tempted to appropriate it. And his assertion is not corroborated by any other author of the same or any earlier date. The '*Liber Pontificalis,*' whose notice of S. Gregory is of the seventh century, says not a word of this alleged foundation of the *Schola Cantorum.* More than that, we have

---

[1] Ioann. Diac. ii. 6.

the constitutions of a council held at Rome by S. Gregory in 595, which have been inserted by Gratian in his *Decretum*: and what is the substance of what we read there? 'In the holy Roman Church there is a custom of old standing, but most reprehensible, of having the chanting done by deacons and other persons who are engaged in the ministry of the holy altar: whence it comes about that, in advancing persons to the order of deacon, less attention is often paid to their conduct than to the quality of their voices: a grave abuse, for which a speedy remedy is to be found by forbidding the deacons to act as chanters, and confining their duties to those of the sacred ministry; as for the chanting, it is to be performed by the subdeacons, or, if necessity requires, by those in minor orders' (*Psalmos vero ac reliquas lectiones censeo per subdiaconos vel si necessitas fuerit per minores ordines exhiberi*).[1] Observe the *si necessitas fuerit*; the psalms and lessons are in the holy Roman Church the province of the subdeacons by right, and only by way of exception belong to the readers, when no other arrangement can be made. It is certainly a singular settlement of the question which this regulation of S. Gregory's proposes, and its effect does not seem to have been lasting; but so far as it goes the regulation is quite against the hypothesis of the foundation by S. Gregory of a college of readers, or even of simple chanters, intended to undertake the very office which he here regards as reserved generally for the subdeacons.

If the idea of the institution by S. Gregory of the *Schola Cantorum* is a tradition of late origin, to which we

---

[1] Migne, *Patr. Lat.* tom. lxxvii. p. 1335.

find no testimony earlier than the very end of the eighth
century, and which is traversed by documents of the
seventh, what are we to say to the tradition which
attributes to this pontiff the creation of the Roman chant—
in other words, of the actual music of the antiphons and
responds of the Divine Office? Fervent partisans of the
theory of the Gregorian origin of plain-chant have
laboured to collect together all the passages which make
S. Gregory the author of this music,[1] and in them I see
one thing very clearly, viz. that, just as the *Ordo* of the
Mass was attributed to S. Gregory, so the authorship of
the pieces of music which found a place in that *Ordo* was
assigned to him; the authenticity of the Gregorian
Sacramentary suggested that of the Antiphonary. Such
was the view taken by Egbert, Bishop of York (732-766),
the earliest author who witnesses to the Gregorian origin
of the Antiphonary. Speaking of the Embertide fast, he
says: ' It is S. Gregory who in his Antiphonary and his
Missal has marked the week which follows Pentecost as
that in which the Church of England ought to observe
this fast; it is not only our Antiphonaries which attest
this, but also those which, with the Missals which belong
to them, we have consulted in the basilicas of the holy
Apostles Peter and Paul ' (*Nostra testantur antiphonaria,
sed et ipsa quae cum missalibus suis conspeximus apud
Apostolorum Petri et Pauli limina*).[2] Whatever authority
there is for assigning the Sacramentary to S. Gregory, the
same there is for attributing to him the Antiphonary, and

---

[1] Dom Morin, *Les véritables Origines du Chant Grégorien*, Maredsous, 1890, pp. 7-33 (cf. Gevaert, *Les Origines du Chant liturgique de l'Eglise Latine*, Ghent, 1890).

[2] Morin, p. 28.

no more: and everybody knows what a limited right the Sacramentary has to be called 'Gregorian,'[1] being in fact partly more ancient, partly more modern, than the time of S. Gregory. And even were the Sacramentary absolutely Gregorian, and the Antiphonary no less so, we should still have no right to say that the composition of the antiphons and responds of the Divine Office is due to S. Gregory. For, in fact, in the language of the eighth century, the word 'Antiphonary' designates the collection of music sung at Mass—what we now call the Gradual, *Liber Gradualis*—and not that sung in the Divine Office, the *Liber Responsalis*. And therefore the whole question of the authorship of this collection of antiphons and responds, this *Liber Responsalis*, stands entirely apart from the question of the origin of the Gregorian Antiphonary.

Much better founded was the opinion of that anonymous liturgical author of the end of the seventh century, an earlier writer, therefore, than John the Deacon or Egbert of York, and more familiar also, it would seem, with the traditions and usages of the Vatican basilica, who attributes the creation of the Roman chant of the antiphons and responds, not to any one pontiff, but to many: S. Leo (440-461), Gelasius (492-496), Symmachus (498-514), John I. (523-526), Boniface II. (530-533), and only finally to S. Gregory. Nor was it at the hands of S. Gregory that it received its full development: the work went on being perfected by the labours of Pope Martin I. (649-653), and by others after him, unknown to fame, whose names are recorded for us by this same

[1] Duchesne, *Origines*, p. 117.

author, men of the latter part of the seventh century, Catalenus, Maurianus, and others.[1] And thus what was called in the seventh century the Roman chant has no right to bear distinctively the name of S. Gregory.

II

We have seen that each presbyteral 'title' had a daily vigil office, celebrated by the clergy who served the title,[2] a custom inaugurated in the fifth century, and, as we have seen, flourishing in the sixth. Now while the office connected with the station-days was not destined to undergo any development, this of the daily vigils, on the contrary, was going to lend itself to changes full of influence on the future: and it is here that for the first time in the history of the Roman liturgy monastic influence makes itself apparent. It seems to have been a tradition with the Roman clergy in the fourth, fifth, and sixth centuries to evince a persevering ill-will towards monastic institutions. We all know what sort of reception they gave S. Jerome, the first who undertook the advocacy of monachism at Rome: he has taken good care to let us hear of it, and, indeed, to give his adversaries as good as they gave.

Less well known are certain prefaces of the Leonine Sacramentary,[3] which M. Duchesne believes may be dated back to the latter part of the fourth century, and which on no supposition can be later than the first half of the sixth, in which Roman priests do not shrink from expressing their grievances even in the Liturgy. 'They are

---

[1] Anon. ap. Gerbert, v. 6; see App. C.   [2] See above, p. 48.
[3] Migne, *Patr. Lat.* tom. lv. pp. 28, 64, 65, 74.

regular diatribes against the monks. . . . The attention of the Almighty is called to the fact that nowadays His Church contains false confessors mingled among the true; much is said about enemies, calumniators, proud ones who deem themselves better than others and tear them in pieces—who present an outward appearance of piety, but who are set on doing harm. The need of guarding against them is asserted.'[1]

If such utterances as these are to be understood of the monks (as has been conjectured, though perhaps on insufficient grounds), and if they are to be considered as expressing the feeling of at least one section of the Roman clergy, we are not saying too much when we speak of the animosity against itself which was excited at Rome by monachism. And perhaps with this state of animosity was connected the lost Constitution of Pope Innocent (401–417) *De regulis monasteriorum*.[2] In spite of all this, monachism took root in Rome and endured. For one moment, in fact, there seemed reason to believe that it would become a power, a political force to be reckoned with; in 556 the election of Pope Pelagius was held in check by the opposition of the Roman monks. Under S. Gregory the favour shown to them was extreme. But this flourishing state of Roman monachism towards the end of the sixth century was of short duration; the favour which it had met with, and which it owed particularly to the protection of S. Gregory, ceased immediately after the death of that Pope in 604: a sensible reaction followed, and the clerks who edit this

[1] Duchesne, *Origines*, p. 135.
[2] *L. P.* (Duchesne), tom. i. p. 220; cf. Jaffé, 494 and 496, where the severity of S. Leo towards monks is set forth.

part of the '*Liber Pontificalis*' betray in more than one passage the feeling of joy, not entirely disinterested, which was inspired in them by this change of feeling. We find them commending Pope Sabinian (604-606) for having, in his short pontificate, and evidently in contradiction to his predecessor, S. Gregory, filled the Church with clerks, and Pope Deusdedit (615-618) for having restored to them the offices and revenues they had formerly possessed—a great mark of affection for the clergy.[1] What had happened at the election of Pelagius did not occur again after the close of the sixth century. But, on the other hand, if there was need of missionaries for the wildest and most remote countries of the West, or of men to serve the most forlorn and neglected sanctuaries in the outskirts of Rome, it was to monachism that the Bishops of Rome looked to supply the want. The Roman idea was that the monks should render an unacknowledged and unrewarded, though devoted, service, and to this state of things the Roman monks resigned themselves with all submission. Their establishments at Rome, far from resembling some of the monasteries at Constantinople, for instance, were those of communities which possessed an existence almost always obscure and precarious, and for the most part quite ephemeral. There was but one occupation which proved for them a lasting one, and in which they unmistakably made their mark. No one, perhaps, would have dreamt, in the sixth century and the early part of the seventh, of entrusting to monks the daily vigil office of the presbyteral titles at Rome. But there was in other localities a custom, already

---

[1] *L. P.* (Duchesne), tom. i. pp. 303, 312, 315, 319.

ancient, of honouring the tombs of the martyrs and certain rich sanctuaries by the perpetual chanting of psalms, and of entrusting this service to monastic communities.[1] This custom had been introduced at Rome itself in the fifth century, under Sixtus III. (432-440), who entrusted to certain monks the care of the cemetery *Ad Catacumbas* on the Appian Way, the place where the basilica of S. Sebastian was afterwards erected.[2] His exact object it is not easy to discover: was it to secure the serving of the sanctuary as regards liturgy, or merely the proper care of it? One cannot say. On the other hand, the idea of S. Leo (440-461), his immediate successor, is more easy to determine. He established a monastery at S. Peter's.[3] It is not permissible to say that these monks were put there to attend to the catechumens and the penitents, for such service belonged to the priests of the district. Nor can we suppose that their office was to take care of the basilica, and more especially of the 'Confession' of the Prince of the Apostles, for that had been entrusted by a Constitution of S. Leo himself to clerks of a particular sort, the *cubicularii*. The monks, then, were set there for the carrying on of public worship—*i.e.* probably the office of the daily vigils—and their monastery, supposed to be identical with that of SS. John and Paul at the Vatican, was a *manécanterie*— a song-school—as was also that founded by Pope Hilary (461-468) at S. Laurence without the Walls.[4]

The three monasteries mentioned above are all

---

[1] Greg. Turon. *Hist. Franc.* iii. 5, *Glor. Mart.* 74, *Vit. Patr.* vii. 2; Sozomen, viii. 17.

[2] *L. P.* (Duchesne), tom. i. p. 234.   [3] *Ib.* p. 239.

[4] *L. P.* (Duchesne), tom. i. p. 245.

attached to basilicas *extra muros*—S. Sebastian's, S. Peter's, S. Laurence's. Within the walls of Rome, the clergy still sufficed for the maintenance of the vigil office in their titles. After this, if we go by the information supplied by the '*Liber Pontificalis*,' these basilican monasteries of the fifth century seem to have been very little further developed in the two centuries that followed, even if it be granted that they did not cease to carry on their functions. In the time of S. Gregory one hears for the first time of a monastery at the Lateran.[1] Are we to suppose that this monastery, attached to a basilica within the walls, continued to exist under S. Gregory's successors? Who can say? Only at the end of the seventh century, and still more during the eighth, do we see these basilican communities develop themselves, and become a really important factor in the service of the Roman Church.

Outside the walls, the basilica of S. Pancras has its monastery, *Monasterium S. Victoris*, restored by Pope Adrian I. (772-795), mentioned in the time of Leo III. (795-816).[2] S. Laurence's now has two: S. Stephen's, mentioned above as being founded by Pope Hilary, and S. Cassian's, of more recent date; both mentioned as existing under Leo III.[3] S. Paul's has two: S. Caesarius' and S. Stephen's, both ancient, for Pope Gregory II. (715-731) did no more than restore them.[4] Both these are mentioned under Leo III., and were destined to last on into the middle ages.

Within the walls, the basilica of the Holy Apostles

---

[1] S. Greg. *Dial.* II. Prolog.
[2] *L. P.* (Duchesne), tom. i. p. 508; tom. ii. p. 23.
[3] *Ib.* tom. ii. p. 23.   [4] *Ib.* tom. i. p. 397.

possesses the monastery of S. Andrew, the existence of which is attested in the time of Leo III., and again under Stephen V. (885-891).[1] Attached to the basilica of S. Peter's Chains is the monastery of S. Agapitus, of the time of Leo III. and his successor Stephen IV. (816-817).[2] S. Pudentiana's has the monastery of S. Euphemia. S. Prisca's has the monastery of S. Donatus. S. Bibiana's has a '*Monasterium S. Vivianae.*' The three preceding monasteries are all mentioned under Leo III.[3] The basilica of S. Caecilia is furnished by Pope Paschal (817-824) with a monastery '*SS. Agathae et Caeciliae.*'[4] The basilica of S. Praxedis also receives from the same Pope a monastery, which is given to a community of *Greek* monks.[5] Gregory III. (731-741) founds the monastery '*SS. Stephani, Laurentii, et Chrysogoni,*' attached to the basilica of S. Chrysogonus, and this establishment is also mentioned under Leo III.[6] Not one, but three monasteries are found grouped round S. Mary's the Greater. Of these, S. Andrew's, called '*Cata Barbara Patricia,*' or '*In Massa Iuliana,*' is a foundation of date anterior to Gregory III., to whom is due its restoration. It is mentioned under Leo III.,[7] as is also the monastery of S. Adrian's, at the same basilica; while the third, SS. Cosmas and Damian, which in the time of Gregory II. (715-731) had been nothing more than an almshouse for aged men, is by this time a monastery.[8] Three monasteries, again, are attached to the Lateran.

[1] *L. P.* (Duchesne), tom. ii. pp. 23, 195.
[2] *Ib.* pp. 12, 24, 49.
[3] *Ib.* p. 24.
[4] *Ib.* p. 57.
[5] *Ib.* pp. 55, 57.
[6] *Ib.* tom. i. p. 418, ii. 23.
[7] *Ib.* tom. i. p. 397, ii. 23.
[8] *Ib.* tom. ii. p. 23; cf. tom. i. p. 397.

(1) S. Stephen's, which does not appear to have been in existence in the days of Adrian I., is spoken of under Leo III. as *juxta Lateranis*, and is said to be close to the papal palace.[1] (2) S. Pancras', of earlier foundation than the time of Gregory III., was restored by him, and supported by Adrian I. and Leo III.[2] It was situated exactly where the cloisters of the canons now stand.[3] (3) The '*Monasterium Honorii*' (also called the monastery of SS. Andrew and Bartholomew) was founded, according to a gloss in the '*Liber Pontificalis*,' by Pope Honorius (625-638) in his own ancestral house, on the site now occupied by the Hospital of S. John, near the baptistery of the Lateran; but having soon fallen into extreme desolation through the neglect of its inhabitants, it was reconstructed and reformed by Adrian I. It was still in existence in the time of Leo III.[4]

Finally we come to S. Peter's, where we find, not three monasteries, as at the Lateran and Liberian basilicas, but four. (1) S. Stephen's the Less, the latest in date, was founded by Pope Stephen II. (752-757). It was built round the oratory of S. Stephen '*de Agulia*'—that is to say, on the site of the present sacristy of S. Peter's.[5] (2) S. Martin's, mentioned for the first time under Gregory III., was close to the apse of the basilica. Between 847 and 855, S. Martin's, being in danger of crumbling under the weight of years (*longo senio casurum*),

[1] *L. P.* (Duchesne), tom. i. p. 506, ii. p. 22.
[2] *Ib.* tom. i. pp. 419, 506, ii. p. 22.
[3] On the conjectural identification of this establishment with the *Lateranense Monasterium* mentioned in the *Dialogues* of S. Gregory (ii. Prolog.), see Mabillon, *Annales O. S. B.* tom. i. p. 177.
[4] *L. P.* tom. i. p. 506, ii. p. 22.
[5] *Ib.* tom. i. p. 451; *de Agulia*—*i.e.* of the Obelisk; see p. 163.

was restored by Leo IV., out of affection to the monastery where he had passed his childhood.¹ (3) S. Stephen's the Greater was situated on the site of the present College of *San Stefano de' Copti*, by the apse of the basilica. This monastery, reformed by Adrian I. and rebuilt by Leo III., bore also the name of ' *Cata Barbara Patricia*,' or ' *Cata Galla Patricia*.' It seems to have been originally a convent of women, and as such may have existed from the time of S. Gregory.² (4) The monastery of SS. John and Paul was situated where now stands the Sistine chapel. Its foundation, as we have already remarked, dates back to the pontificate of S. Leo.

Summing up the information given above, we observe that the principal part in the foundation and development of these monasteries within the city belongs to Gregory II., Gregory III., and so forth, the Popes of the first half of the eighth century; and further, that among the whole body of monasteries, whether within or without the walls, there is one group which takes rank by itself, both for its antiquity and for its importance in the eighth century— the four monasteries of the Vatican.³

It would be a mistake to suppose that these basilican monasteries of the eighth century were similar in character to monasteries in the strict sense of the word, such as those of the Benedictines. *Monastery*, at Rome, implied simply a body who lived in community. When, in the seventh century, the *deaconries* are spoken of, the documents mention a *monasterium diaconiae* attached to

---

¹ *L. P.* (Duchesne), tom. i. p. 417, ii. pp. 106, 130, 133.
² *Ib.* tom. ii. p. 28, i. p. 501.
³ See the ' Acta ' of the Roman Synod of 732, in Duchesne, *L. P.* tom. i. pp. 422-423.

each; these 'monasteries' are charged with the performance of various charitable offices which used to belong to the deacon of the district and his clergy. Each such establishment has at its head a Rector, who bears the title of *Dispensator* or *Pater*, and who has priests under his command.[1] One can see from these features how far such a *monasterium diaconiae* resembled a monastery on the Benedictine plan! It is much the same with the monasteries attached to basilicas. In an independent monastery the community governs itself, elects its abbot, administers its goods, and we find such monasteries at Rome at the period we are speaking of [2]; but with the basilican monasteries it is quite otherwise. No doubt the basilican monastery is exempt from the authority of the priest of the title to which it has been attached,[3] but the appointment of the Rector or *Pater* belongs to the Pope; the community accepts him without having elected him. More than that, this abbot nominated by the Pope is not a professed monk, but as it were a prelate of the *carriera*. During the last years of the eighth century, under Leo III., the office of abbot of the monastery of S. Stephen the Greater, one of the four monasteries attached to S. Peter's, having become vacant, whom does the Pope nominate to it? A clerk educated in the Lateran, in the papal palace, the priest Paschal, destined to succeed Pope Stephen IV. in 817.[4]

[1] *L. P.* (Duchesne), tom. i. p. 365.
[2] Jaffé, n. 2346 (speaking of the Monastery of SS. Stephen and Sylvester, founded by Paul I. in 761).
[3] *L. P.* tom. i. p. 418 : '[*Monasterium*] *segregatum a iure potestatis presbiteri praedicti Tituli*' (speaking of the basilican Monastery of SS. Stephen, Laurence, and Chrysogonus, founded by Gregory III.). [4] *Ib.* tom. ii. p. 52.

And these monks themselves—monks under the government of a secular abbot—are not monks in the strict sense of the word. Stephen III. (768–772), having come from Sicily to Rome quite young, was placed by Pope Gregory III. in his monastery attached to the basilica of S. Chrysogonus, where he became clerk and monk (*illicque clericus atque monachus est effectus*); and while being a monk there is no doubt as to his being in Holy Orders as well, for we find Pope Zachary (741–752) taking him from his monastery and attaching him to the service of the Camera (*in Lateranensis patriarchii cubiculo esse praecepit*), after which he becomes priest of the title of S. Caecilia.[1] S. Chrodegang founded his Canons Regular (*clerici canonici*) at Metz on exactly the same footing, taking as his model, so Paul the Deacon assures us, the state of things he had seen in practice at Rome.[2]

And now, what is the office of these Roman basilican monks of the eighth century? To instruct young clerks in the ecclesiastical way of life and the knowledge required in it, in co-operation with the *vestiarium* of the pontifical palace? To lodge the pilgrims who come to

---

[1] *L. P.* (Duchesne), tom. i. p. 468, ii. p. 52.

[2] Paul. Diac. *Gesta Episc. Met.* (Migne, *Patr. Lat.* tom. xcv.), p. 709 : '*Hic [Chrodegangus] clerum adunavit, et ad instar coenobii, intra claustrorum septa conversari fecit. . . . Ipsumque clerum, abundanter lege Divina Romanaque imbutum cantilena, morem atque ordinem Romanae ecclesiae servare praecepit.*'—' Chrodegang collected the clergy together, and caused them to live within the enclosure of their cloister as in a monastery. And having thoroughly instructed them in the law of God and the Roman chant, he commanded them to observe the use and order of the Roman Church.' In the Life of Pope Gregory IV. (827–844) the title of *monachi canonici* is given to the Roman basilican monks (*L. P.* [Duchesne], tom. ii. p. 78).

visit the Apostolic sanctuaries? No doubt. But the *principal* office of these monks is to sing the Divine Service. And, being both clerks and monks, this office of theirs is a double one. As clerks, they take part in the daily office of the clergy—I mean the vigils. As monks, they add to these the diurnal office peculiar to monks: Terce, Sext, and None. Speaking of the refounding by Gregory II. (715-731) of the monasteries attached to S. Paul's without the Walls, the editor of the Pontifical Archives writes:

> Monasteria que secus basilicam S. Pauli Apostoli erant ad solitudinem deducta innovavit; atque ordinatis servis Dei monachis, congregationem post longum tempus constituens, ut *tribus per diem vicibus* et *noctu matutinos* dicerent, &c.

And again, as if afraid we might not ascribe to these words their full meaning, he repeats them soon after, indicating still more clearly the canonical character of the office:

> Monasterium iuxta [ecclesiam S. Dei Genetricis ad Praesepe] positum S. Andreae, . . . ad nimiam deductus desertionem, in quibus ne unus habebatur monachus, restaurans, monachos faciens, ordinavit, ut *tertiam sextam* et *nonam* vel *matutinos* in eadem ecclesia S. Dei Genetricis cotidianis agerent diebus; et manet nunc usque pia eius ordinatio.[2]

In other words, the monks at S. Paul's and S. Mary's the Greater sing in their basilicas by night the vigil office

---

[1] *L. P.* (Duchesne), tom. i. pp. 397, 398. The two passages quoted may be Englished as follows: 'He restored the monasteries belonging to the basilica of S. Paul, which had been brought to desolation, setting there, after a long interval, a congregation of monks, servants of God, that they might say their office three times a day, as well as the Mattins by night.' 'Restoring the monastery of St. Andrew by the Church of the Holy Mother of God at the *Praesepe*, which had been brought to the utmost desolation, so that

(*noctu matutinos*) and besides this, by day, Terce, Sext, and None (*tribus per diem vicibus*). This is early in the eighth century: a few years later, and it is no longer a question of Terce, Sext, and None only, but of Prime and Vespers as well. This is how the '*Liber Pontificalis*' speaks of Pope Adrian I., towards the end of the eighth century:

> Hic ... dum per almissima exquisitione sua repperuisset monasterium quondam Honorii papae in nimia desolatione per quandam neglegentiam evenire, divina inspiratione motus, a noviter eum aedificavit atque ditavit; et abbatem cum ceteros monachos regulariter ibidem vita degentes ordinavit. Et constituit eos in basilica Salvatoris, quae et Constantiniana, iuxta Lateranense patriarchio posita, officio celebrari, hoc est, *matutino, ora prima* et *tertia, sexta* seu *nona*, etiam et *vespertina*, ab uno choro qui dudum singulariter in utrosque psallebant, monachi monasterii S. Pancratii ibidem positi, et ab altero choro monachi iamfati monasterii SS. Andreae et Bartholomei, qui appellatur Honorii papae, quatenus piis laudibus naviterque psallentes, hymniferis choris Deique letis resonent cantibus. ...[1]

not a single monk remained there, and setting monks in it, he ordained that they should say in the same church every day Terce, Sext, None, and also Mattins; and this his pious foundation yet remains.'

[1] L. P. (Duchesne), tom. i. p. 506: 'He, finding by benevolent inquiry that the monastery of Pope Honorius had through negligence come to great desolation, being moved by God, rebuilt and enriched it; and set there an abbot and monks to live duly according to rule. And he appointed them to celebrate the Divine Office in the basilica of the Saviour, which is that founded by Constantine, by the palace of the Lateran: that is to say, Mattins, the First, Third, Sixth, and Ninth hours, and also Vespers; the same to be performed by one choir which hitherto had sung the offices alone, viz. the monks of the monastery of S. Pancras, founded at that basilica, and by a second choir composed of the monks of the above-named monastery of SS. Andrew and Bartholomew, which is also called that of Pope Honorius, so that rendering devout praise with all assiduity, they might with hymning choirs make joyful songs resound to God.'

The passage specifies that the monks of these two monasteries attached to the Lateran are to chant the office in choir in the basilica, the same comprising the nocturnal office of the vigils and the day office of Terce, Sext, and None, to which, now and henceforth, we find added Prime and Vespers.'[1]

We detect in these passages some indication of the process of liturgical evolution which took place at Rome between the end of the seventh century and the middle of the eighth, under monastic influence: I mean the daily juxtaposition of the traditional vigil office of the clergy and the monastic hours of prayer. Nay, is there not something more than this juxtaposition? Has not the vigil office of the clergy, as it was set forth in the '*Liber Diurnus*' at the beginning of the seventh century, undergone a complete transformation? Was not that arrangement of the psalms and lessons in the vigil office at Rome at the end of the eighth century which we are about to examine in the next chapter—an arrangement so perceptibly different from what it had been at the beginning of the seventh, judging from the '*Liber Diurnus*'— brought about by the basilican monks?

And further, whatever development of the liturgy of the Roman basilicas took place, it was due to the preponderating influence of the Vatican basilica. It is certain that in the time of Gregory III. (731-741) the

---

[1] Similarly, of the monks attached to the basilica of S. Mark: '*Constituit ut in titulo B. Marci . . . officium fungerent, id est, matutino, hora prima, tertia, et sexta, atque nona, seu vespera psallerent.*' And of the convent of women belonging to the basilica of S. Eugenia: '*Constituit ut iugiter illuc Deo canerent laudes, videlicet hora prima, tertia, sexta, nona, vespera et matutino.*' (*L. P.* [Duchesne], tom. i. pp. 507, 510.)

monks of the three monasteries then existing in connection with that basilica were already wont to sing Vespers every day before the 'Confession' of the Prince of the Apostles. We know this from the following passage taken from the Constitutions of a Roman synod of the year 732:

> Tria illa monasteria quae secus basilicam Apostoli sunt constituta, SS. Ioannis et Pauli, S. Stephani, et S. Martini, id est, eorum congregatio, omnibus diebus, dum *vesperas* expleverint ante Confessionem . . .[1]

And the same Pope, when founding the monastery attached to the basilica of S. Chrysogonus, which has been already mentioned several times, specifies that the monks of the said monastery are to sing the praises of God in the basilica, not only by night, but also by day, according to the custom of the basilica of S. Peter:

> Constituens monachorum congregationem, ad persolvendas Dei laudes in eundem titulum diurnis atque nocturnis temporibus ordinatam, secundum instar officiorum ecclesiae B. Petri Apostoli.[2]

So also he restores and reorganises the monasteries of the Lateran:

> Congregationem monachorum . . . constituit ad persolvenda cotidie sacra officia laudis Divinae in basilica Salvatoris . . . diurnis nocturnisque temporibus ordinata, iuxta instar officiorum ecclesiae B. Petri Apostoli.[3]

S. Peter's, the site of the Confession of the Prince of the Apostles! It was the sanctuary pre-eminent in

---

[1] The Constitution in question, made at a synod of the clergy of Rome, was engraved on marble tablets in the basilica of S. Peter, and these tablets are still partly preserved. See the whole passage in M. Duchesne's edition of the *Liber Pontificalis*, tom. i. pp. 422–424.

[2] *L. P.* (Duchesne), tom. i. p. 418.   [3] *Ib.* p. 419.

holiness, and the liturgy used at S. Peter's could not but form the model of all liturgy. The monasteries which served this basilica were also the most ancient in Rome, going back to the time of S. Leo: their customs constituted a tradition which, even in Rome itself, possessed an exceptional authority. Their abbots or rectors, who were, as we have seen, clerks, added to their functions as abbots the still more important office of chief chanters of S. Peter's; they were the leading authorities on liturgy for the Roman Church. The anonymous Frankish writer on liturgy whom I have already mentioned, and of whom I shall have more to say anon, has preserved for us the names of three of these rectors, whom he places after the Popes Leo, Gelasius, Symmachus, John, Boniface, Gregory, and Martin, as the masters of liturgy and ecclesiastical music in the Roman Church who were in his time the most recent in date and of the greatest authority:

> Post istos quoque Catalenus abba, ibi deserviens ad sepulcrum S. Petri, et ipse quidem anni circuli cantum diligentissime edidit.
> Post hunc quoque Maurianus abba, ipsius S. Petri Apostoli serviens, annalem suum cantum et ipse nobile ordinavit.
> Post hunc vero domnus Virbonus abba et omnem cantum anni circuli magnifice ordinavit.'[1]

Nor was it only at Rome that this authority was recognised and followed. S. Peter's was pre-eminently the sanctuary venerated by the whole of Latin Catholicism, and the tomb of the Apostle the corner-stone of the Western Church. The eyes of all were turned towards that august 'Confession.' Pilgrims came thither every

[1] Anon. ap. Gerbert. v. 6; see App. C.

day from the furthest corners of Britain, just as much as from the valleys of the Loire and the Rhine. And these regarded in an especial degree the liturgy in use at S. Peter's as the absolute canon of what liturgy should be. Benedict Biscop, the famous abbot of Wearmouth, the teacher of Bede (628-690), was one of these pilgrims of the seventh century, so full of devotion to the tomb of the Prince of the Apostles: five times did he make the pilgrimage from England to Rome. It was at Rome that he asked as to the plan of his abbey at Wearmouth. In memory of Rome he determined that it should bear the name of S. Peter. At Rome he bought the books for his monks. From Rome he derived the office and the chant they were to use. Finally he asked Pope Agatho (678-681) to supply him with some Roman clerks, who might come to Wearmouth to instruct the Anglo-Saxon monks in the customs of the monks at Rome. And, in granting his request, to whom did the Pope entrust this commission? To 'the venerable John, chief chanter of the Church of the Apostle S. Peter, and abbot of the Monastery of S. Martin,' one of the four Vatican monasteries. And Benedict Biscop brought the said Abbot John into Britain, 'in order that he might teach the monks in his monastery to sing the office as it was sung at S. Peter's at Rome.'[1]

[1] Bed. *Hist. Anglor.* iv. 18: 'Accepit et praefatum Ioannem abbatem Britanniam perducendum, quatenus in monasterio suo cursum canendi annuum, sicut ad S. Petrum Romae agebatur, edoceret; egitque abba Ioannes ut iussionem acceperat pontificis, et ordinem videlicet ritumque canendi ac legendi viva voce praefati monasterii cantores edocendo, et ea quae totius anni circulus in celebratione dierum festorum poscebat etiam litteris mandando : quae hactenus in eodem monasterio servata, et a multis iam sunt circumqua-

It is a fact full of instruction, and not hitherto sufficiently dwelt on, that the basilica of S. Peter with its corporation of monks as chanters, its *Schola Cantorum*, and its chief chanters, was in the strictest sense the fountain-head of the Roman canonical Office. This state of things came about in the third quarter of the seventh century, thanks to that irresistible movement of devotion and admiration which induced monks from beyond mountains and seas no longer to look upon as truly *Roman* anything but the clerico-monastic office used at S. Peter's; and to borrow from that office the distribution of the psalter, the order of the lectionary, the words of the antiphons and responds, and the cycle of the feasts of the Church seasons. Such was the renown and such the authority of the rule of Divine Service in use in the basilica of S. Peter, even at a time when it was not yet definitely fixed, either as regards words or music, for the Abbot John, we are told, taught it at Wearmouth without

que transcripta. Non solum autem idem Ioannes ipsius monasterii fratres docebat, verum de omnibus pene eiusdem provinciae monasteriis ad audiendum eum qui cantandi erant periti confluebant, sed et ipsum per loca, in quibus doceret, multi invitare curabant.'—'And he took the aforesaid Abbot John and brought him to Britain, that in his monastery he might teach the annual *cursus* of singing Divine Service, as it was observed at S. Peter's at Rome: and Abbot John did in accordance with the commandment of the Pontiff, both teaching the chanters of the monastery aforesaid by word of mouth the order and rite of singing and saying the service, and writing down all that was required for the celebration of the festivals throughout the year; which writings are yet preserved in the said monastery, and have been copied by many persons from divers places. Moreover, not only did the same John teach the brethren of the said monastery, but those who were skilful in chanting came together to hear him, from almost all the monasteries of that province, and many of them were careful to invite him to come to their own localities that he might teach there.'

book, by word of mouth, and had to set about writing it out for the greater convenience of the Anglo-Saxon monasteries. As soon as the office of S. Peter's was codified, and those *libri responsales* and *antiphonarii* were published which, though bearing the name of S. Gregory, were in reality simply the books in use at S. Peter's, they carried the Roman basilicas by storm, even as very shortly they were destined to make a conquest of the Churches of the Franks.

But before considering this success of the Roman basilican office, we have to explain how it befell, that, alongside of the Sunday and station-day office of the clergy, the daily vigil office of the titles, and the diurnal office of the basilican monasteries, there was formed and developed the office of the cemetery churches—in other words the *Sanctorale* of the Roman Church—and how, at a wonderfully late date, and as it were by accident, it found a place in the office of the Roman basilicas.

III

The festivals of the saints, at Rome as in all other Christian Churches, were originally the anniversaries of local martyrs. And it is thus that the history of the Roman saints' days is bound up with that of the cemeteries and cemetery churches in the outskirts of Rome.

The churches within the walls did not at first bear the names of Saints. The 'titles' or presbyteral churches were named after the Pope or other Christian at whose cost they had been founded. Thus, in the fourth and fifth centuries people spoke of 'the title of Vestina,' 'of Lucina,' 'of Fasciola,' 'of Damasus,' 'of Pudens,' 'of

Clement,' by way of designating these parish churches. It was only in the latter part of the sixth century and during the seventh, that the Churches of the Deaconries were founded, and received the names of saints ; among these we find, within the walls, the basilicas of SS. Cosmas and Damian, S. Adrian, SS. Sergius and Bacchus, S. Lucy, &c., and they are thus named in imitation of the suburban basilicas, which had been built over the actual tombs of the martyrs and on that account were called by their names.

It was only in these suburban cemeteries that the anniversaries of the martyrs were originally celebrated, just as were those of the departed members of each family. A passage in the '*Liber Pontificalis*,' not particularly clear, attributes to Pope Felix (269-274) the institution of Eucharistic assemblies at the tombs of the martyrs ;[1] but, as M. Duchesne remarks, this passage in reality testifies to nothing more than the contemporary custom at Rome, at the time when this text of the '*Liber Pontificalis*' was edited—*i.e.* the beginning of the sixth century. Nevertheless, thanks to Prudentius, we know that such a custom existed at the beginning of the fourth century : viz. that on the anniversary of the death of a martyr Mass was celebrated, either at the altar of the cemetery church which had been built over the tomb, or at the very spot where the body rested in the catacomb itself (if that was still in existence), at an altar erected by the tomb. This Mass *ad corpus*, with its necessarily restricted number of worshippers, was, by force of circumstances, *quasi* private ; but the other, on the

---

[1] *L. P.* (Duchesne), tom. i. p. 158.

contrary, celebrated as it was in a building often of great size, or even in the open air on the *area* of the cemetery, was a public Mass;¹ the people could assist at it in crowds. Speaking of the anniversary of S. Hippolytus on the Tiburtine Way, Prudentius distinguishes carefully between the crypt, where the body of the martyr reposes, and the faithful come every day to pray by themselves—

> Haud procul extremo culta ad pomoeria vallo
> Mersa latebrosis crypta patet foveis. . . .
> Ipsa illas animae exuvias quae continet intus
> Aedicula argento fulgurat ex solido—

and the basilica (in this case that of S. Laurence) erected on the level of the ground above, whither, on the anniversary, the people of Rome, and pilgrims from afar, come in crowds to assist at the Eucharistic solemnities:

> Iam cum se renovat decursis mensibus annus
> Natalemque diem passio festa refert, . . .
> Urbs augusta suos vomit effunditque Quirites. . .
> Exultat fremitus variarum hinc inde viarum. . . .
> Stat sed iuxta aliud quod tanta frequentia templum
> Tunc adeat, cultu nobile regifico. . . .
> Plena laborantes aegre domus accipit undas,
> Arctaque confertis aestuat in foribus.²

---

¹ De Rossi, *Roma Sotterranea*, tom. iii. pp. 488-494.

² Prud. *Peristephanon*, xi. 153 *sqq.*: 'Near where the rampart's edge touches on the garden spaces which border it, the crypt opens its mouth amid the dark shadows of deeply excavated pits: the shrine itself, containing the mortal garment that wrapped the martyr's soul, shines with massive silver.' 'And now, when the months have fled, and the year come round, bringing back the festal memory of his glorious death, the imperial city pours forth its citizens; on every side the din of numbers rises from the roads. Lo! nigh at hand another temple, dight with royal splendour, into which even so vast a crowd may enter. Yet scarcely can its full halls contain the struggling waves of people, and its thronged porches overflow with their numbers.'

But in these lines, and indeed in the whole poem of Prudentius, it does not appear that there is any question of keeping the anniversary feast of S. Hippolytus otherwise than by the celebration of a Mass. On the other hand, the author of the treatise *De Haeresi Praedestinatorum*, who wrote in the fifth century, gives us to understand that the cemeteries of the martyrs had their vigils. He is telling us about the basilica of SS. Processus and Martinian, at the second milestone on the Aurelian Way, being recovered out of the hands of the heretic sect of the Tertullianists, who had established in it their form of worship (392-394). The latest date that can be assigned to their expulsion is that of the pontificate of Innocent I. (401-417). Well, our author uses the following expression: '*Martyrum suorum Deus excubias Catholicae festivitati restituit.*'[1] Now, *excubiae* is a recognised synonym for *vigiliae*.

If we may be allowed to have recourse to the customs of lands beyond the Alps for an explanation of Roman customs, we shall find an excellent commentary on the above passage in the description given by Sidonius Apollinaris of the vigils celebrated at Lyons at the tomb of Justus, on the anniversary of that martyr. 'We went,' says he, ' to the tomb of S. Justus before daylight, to keep his anniversary (*processio antelucana, solemnitas anniversaria*). The crowd was enormous, so that the basilica, and the crypt, and the porches together, could not contain it. First, the vigils were celebrated, the psalms being chanted by alternate choirs of monks and clerks (*cultu peracto vigiliarum, quas alternante mulcedine*

[1] Migne, *Patr. Lat.* tom. liii. p. 617: 'God restored to Catholic observance the vigils of His martyrs.'

monachi clericique psalmicines concelebraverunt). After the vigils, everyone walked about as he pleased, taking care not to go too far away, for it was necessary to be back by the hour of Terce for the solemn Mass (*ad tertiam praesto futuri, cum sacerdotibus res divina facienda*). It was,' he adds, 'a delightful moment; we came panting out of that basilica crowded to suffocation and blazing with lights, and found ourselves in the open country, in the cool of a night which still retained the softness of summer, but just touched with the refreshing keenness of an autumn dawn.'[1]

At Rome, in the course of the fourth century, not only had the historic vaults of the catacombs been arranged for worship of this nature, but basilicas had been built on the *area* of most of the cemeteries. I have mentioned S. Laurence's on the Tiburtine Way, and many more might be added; such as S. Sylvester's in the cemetery of Priscilla, SS. Nereus and Achilles in the cemetery of Domitilla, and, above all, S. Peter's at the Vatican and S. Paul's on the Ostian Way. The care which we see taken in the most ancient Roman Kalendars, such as that of the date A.D. 354, to record the *Locus Depositionis* of each saint whose feast is kept, is a proof that these feasts were celebrated at the actual place of sepulture.

[1] Sidon. Ap. *Epistul.* cvii. 9. Compare the very important and characteristically Roman passage in the Latin 'Life of S. Melania' relating to the vigil of S. Laurence, *Analecta Bolland.* 1889, p. 23: '*Occasio venit ut et dies solemnis et commemoratio B. Martyris Laurentii ageretur. Beatissima . . . desiderabat ire in S. Martyris basilicam et pervigilem celebrare noctem; sed non permittitur a parentibus,*' &c.—'It happened that the solemn commemoration of the Blessed Martyr Laurence was kept. This blessed lady desired to go to the basilica of the Martyr, and keep the night-long vigil there; but her parents did not permit it.'

What is called the Leonine Sacramentary, which is the most ancient Roman Missal we possess—it is certainly anterior to the time of S. Gregory, and some parts may be as old as the end of the fourth century—marks, in the case of all the festivals of saints included in it, the place where they are celebrated or the *locus depositionis*, and it is always in a suburban cemetery that the meeting place for the faithful is appointed:

> III. non. Augusti, natale S. Stephani, in cymiterio Callisti, via Appia.
> VIII. id. Augusti, natale S. Xysti, in cymiterio Callisti; e Felicissimi et Agapeti, in cymiterio Praetextati, via Appia, &c.

In the later Sacramentaries, the places of observance are indicated just in the same way, and one may gather indications to the same effect from the homilies of S. Gregory; in fact, setting aside the homilies preached on station-days, if we find this Pope preaching to the people on the *natale* of a martyr, we may be sure it is in the cemetery basilica belonging to that martyr, *i.e.* in some church without the walls. Such was the state of things at the beginning of the seventh century.

But in ceasing, after the taking of Rome by Alaric and his Goths in 410, to be the ordinary cemeteries of the Roman parishes, and so becoming mere places of pilgrimage, the catacombs lost many of their visitors, and suffered a corresponding diminution in the number of those who attended to them. In the fifth century the grave-diggers (*fossores*) disappear from the scene. The custom of celebrating, in these ancient cities of the dead, private anniversary Masses for the departed became extinct in the following century, when we find Pope John III. (561-574) endeavouring to restore this devotion, and obliged to defray himself the moderate expense of keeping up even a Sunday celebration of the Holy Mysteries in the ancient cemeteries. Thus, with the sixth century commenced the period of gradual ruin and neglect. To this the siege of Rome by the Goths in 537 contributed more than anything else: '*nam et ecclesiae et corpora martyrum exterminatae sunt a Gothis*,' writes the editor of the Life of Pope Sylverius (536–537).[1] Nor were the Lombards, in the seventh and eighth centuries, enemies at all likely to refrain from such sacrilegious acts.

In the midst of all these panics and disasters, what was to become of the cultus of the martyrs? When the *locus depositionis* was no longer available for worship, would the festival of the saint cease to be kept? Was it not possible for the *Cultus Martyrum* to migrate into the interior of the city of Rome, and find a shelter within her walls?

This migration coincides with, and is marked by, the period when the churches of the Roman 'titles' began to be designated by the names of saints. The churches of the deaconries, founded in the latter part of the sixth century and in the course of the seventh, had, as we have seen, been all along so designated. And about the same time the presbyteral titles assume the names of martyrs: the title of Pudens becomes S. Pudentiana's; the title of Prisca, S. Prisca's; the title of Anastasia, S. Anastasia's; the title of Clement, S. Clement's. This transformation of the names of the basilicas was completed in the eighth century. The same idea which led to the names of saints foreign to Rome being bestowed on the churches of the deaconries, had, even in the fifth century caused

[1] *L. P.* (Duchesne), tom. i. pp. 305, 291.

the consecration of basilicas within the walls of Rome under the invocation of the Virgin Mary and the Holy Apostles. The anniversary of the dedication of these urban churches most often coincided with the date set down in the martyrologies as the anniversary of the saint whose name the particular church bore. Thus it was that the festivals of non-local saints were the first to establish themselves in the churches within the walls of Rome. Then, in the seventh century, the relics of martyrs began to be translated from the suburbs into the basilicas of the town—those of SS. Primus and Felicianus in 648, from the fifteenth milestone on the Nomentan Way; those of SS. Simplicius, Faustinus and Viatrix,[1] in 682, from the fifth milestone on the road to Porto. In the eighth century, after the siege of Rome by Astolphus and the Lombards in 756, the bodies of the principal martyrs were translated even from the catacombs themselves to churches within the walls, and their cultus followed them thither.[2]

While the festivals of the saints thus ceased to be observed in the cemeteries, they did not as yet lose their strictly *local* character. Where the relics of the saint reposed, there was observed his festival; and now also, by analogy, to the church which bore the *name* of any

[1] This is the more accurate form of the name; she appears in the kalendars as Beatrix.

[2] De Rossi, *Roma Sotterranea*, tom. i. p. 221. In the time of Gregory III. the anniversaries of the martyrs were still observed with vigils in the catacombs. See *L. P.* (Duchesne), tom. i. p. 421: '*Disposuit ut in cimiteriis circumquaque positis Romae, in die natalitiorum eorum luminaria ad vigilias faciendum . . . deportentur.*'—'He provided that lamps should be carried to the cemeteries on every side of Rome, for the purpose of holding vigils on the anniversaries of the martyrs.'

saint belonged the keeping of the festival of that saint. Thus the feasts of the Virgin Mary were kept at S. Mary's the Greater; of SS. Cosmas and Damian at their own basilica; of SS. Simplicius and Faustinus at the basilica of S. Bibiana; and so with others. In the Roman *Ordo* in the library of Montpellier, which is of the eighth century, occurs the following rubric: the archdeacon at the pontifical High Mass, before giving the Communion to the faithful, is to give notice of any approaching 'station' as follows: 'Such a day is the anniversary of such a saint, martyr, or confessor, which will be kept at such or such a place;' which proves that the festivals of the *Sanctorale*, even when celebrated within the walls, remained merely local feasts. There is another proof of the same fact in the Life of Pope Gregory III. (731–741), He constructed in the basilica of S. Peter an oratory 'in honour of the Saviour, the Virgin Mary, the Apostles, Martyrs, Confessors, and all the Just'; and ordained that every day, after Vespers had been said before the Confession of S. Peter, the monks of the three monasteries attached to the basilica (SS. John and Paul, S. Stephen's, and S. Martin's) should proceed to the new oratory and sing there three psalms, followed by a lesson taken from the Holy Gospels, in honour of the saints whose anniversaries fell on that day (*quorum natalitia fuerint*). In other words, since the daily office did not make any commemoration of the saints whose festivals were marked in the Roman Kalendar, Pope Gregory III. established a commemorative office by itself, in order that these saints, whose festivals were kept elsewhere, should not be forgotten in the basilica of S. Peter.[1]

[1] *L. P.* (Duchesne), tom. i. p. 422.

Commenting on this passage in the Life of Gregory III., M. Duchesne observes: 'This liturgical foundation of Gregory III. is not mentioned in the Lives of the Popes who succeed him, nor in any other passage, so far as I know. Probably the monks soon shook themselves free from a somewhat burdensome service.'[1] May it not rather be the case that this foundation or ordinance of Gregory III. was transformed into another, whose existence was more lasting? And what would this be but the extension to all the urban basilicas of the custom of celebrating the anniversaries of all the martyrs and confessors in the Roman Kalendar?

In the absence of more direct proof, the coincidence of dates is striking. In 741 the anniversaries of martyrs are still localised at the *locus depositionis* or *locus tituli*; in 756 comes the siege of Rome by the Lombards, and then the translation within the walls of the bodies of the principal martyrs from the catacombs; in the time of Pope Adrian I. (772–795) the general *Sanctorale* finds a place in the order of the office at S. Peter's:

> Passiones sanctorum vel gesta ipsorum usque Adriani tempora tantummodo ibi legebantur ubi ecclesia ipsius sancti vel titulus: ipse vero a tempore suo rennuere iussit, et in ecclesia S. Petri legendas esse constituit.

Thus we read in the *Ordo* of the Vallicellan Library published by Tommasi.[2] This, indeed, amounts to no

---

[1] *L. P.* (Duchesne), tom. i. p. 423.

[2] Tommasi, tom. iv. p. 325: 'The passions or mighty deeds of the saints were, up to the time of Adrian, only read in that place where was the church or title of each saint: but he ordered that from henceforth . . . they should be read in the Church of S. Peter also.' [The word *rennuere*, or *renovere*, as it is otherwise given in the MS., I am not able to explain.—A. B.]

more than a hint : what is more than a hint is the fact that the Carolingian liturgists, when introducing into France the Roman canonical Office, are not aware of any other state of things than that referred to above. The *Sanctorale*, after having been so long considered as something outside of the canonical Office, has become an integral part of it.[1]

For the time came—and, another significant coincidence, it came with the pontificate of the immediate successors of Gregory III.—when the Office used at S. Peter's was to establish its rule over the Frankish Churches; when the same sentiment which at the end of the previous century had made popular in England the *cursus* and the chant of S. Peter's was to lead to the adoption of the same chant and office by the Frank bishops; when there would be no longer only basilicas at Rome like that of S. Chrysogonus, but distant cathedrals such as those of Metz and Rouen, where the Divine Office would be henceforth celebrated *iuxta instar officiorum ecclesiae B. Petri Apostoli*. In France, as in England a hundred years before, this adoption of the Roman Office was spontaneous: the Holy See co-operated in it, but did not suggest it. The Roman liturgy attracted affection to itself for the sake of S. Peter, and also by reason of its own inherent beauty. S. Chrodegang, like Benedict Biscop, was deeply penetrated by devotion to the customs of Rome and S. Peter's. On his return from a pilgrimage to the tomb of the Prince of the Apostles in 754, being desirous of securing the regular performance of the offices, both nocturnal and diurnal, in the cathedral

[1] Amalarius, *De Ord. Antiph.* 28.

of Metz, he founded a college of clergy, on the model of
the monastic communities attached to the basilicas at
Rome, and gave them for their observance the Roman
Ordo of the office, and the Roman chant.[1] Before
the death of the great Bishop of Metz, his example had
been followed by Remigius, Archbishop of Rouen: he
also was returning from a pilgrimage to Rome when he
brought to Rouen, in 760, by the permission of Pope
Paul, the second in command—the vice-principal, as we
might say—of the *Schola Cantorum*, to initiate his clergy
into 'the modulations of the Roman method of chanting.'
Then, this Roman chanter being obliged within a short
time to return to Rome, Remigius sent his clerks to
finish their instruction at Rome itself, in the *Schola
Cantorum*.[2] He wished to have at Rouen, as Chrodegang
had wished to have at Metz, the pure and genuine *Ordo*
and chant of S. Peter's. Then, in his turn, Pepin extends
to all the Frankish Churches the reform inaugurated at
Metz and Rouen, commanding all the Frank bishops to
give up the Gallican *Ordo*, to learn the Roman chant, and
to celebrate the Divine Office henceforth in conformity
with the custom of the Holy See:

> Ut cantum Romanum pleniter discant et ordinabiliter per
> nocturnale vel gradale officium peragatur, secundum quod beatae
> memoriae genitor noster Pippinus rex decertavit ut fieret, quando
> Gallicanum tulit, ob unanimitatem Apostolicae sedis et sanctae
> Dei ecclesiae pacificam concordiam.

Such are the terms used by the Emperor Charlemagne
in remaking, in 789, the decree of Pepin le Bref.[3]

---

[1] See above, p. 69.   [2] Jaffé, No. 2371.

[3] See Duchesne, *Origines*, p. 97: 'That they shall fully learn the
Roman chant, and that the offices be performed in due order, by

The conclusion, then, which we must draw from all these important facts is, that by about the middle of the eighth century the Roman Office is already codified, and supplants the old Gallican office. What is called the Antiphonary or Responsoral of S. Gregory—in reality the Antiphonary of S. Peter's—is now written down and completed. And, in fact, about the year 760, we have Pope Paul I. sending to King Pepin a copy of the 'Liber Responsalis,' or collection of the antiphons and responds of the Roman Office.[1] A similar collection had been brought by S. Chrodegang to Metz in 756, just as, soon after, we find Wala, Abbot of Corbey, bringing one to his abbey.

It is this liturgical work, thus for the first time codified—or at all events making its appearance in a codified form—in 756, which we have now to describe in detail, reconstructing, so far as our historical resources permit, that Roman Office by which our forefathers, the pilgrims of the eighth century, were so powerfully attracted that they did not hesitate to renounce in its favour the liturgical traditions which belonged to their own Churches.

means of the books for Divine Service and the Mass respectively, according to the decree made by our father King Pepin of blessed memory, when he suppressed the Gallican *Ordo* with a view to the maintaining of due agreement with the Apostolic See, and the peace and concord of the Holy Church of God.'

[1] Jaffé, No. 2351.

CHAPTER III

THE ROMAN CANONICAL OFFICE IN THE TIME OF CHARLEMAGNE

WE have now reached the culminating point of the whole historical development which our subject includes. First the archaic period, extending over five centuries; then a century of more immediate preparation; then the golden age, embracing two centuries, the seventh and the eighth, during which, in the basilica of S. Peter, the *cursus* took shape which, in the case of the Anglo-Saxon monks of the seventh century, triumphed over the Benedictine, and, in the case of the Carolingian princes, over the Gallican; and which eventually became the rule for the whole of Latin Christianity. It is the supreme moment of its success and perfection, the moment for studying and analysing it to the best advantage.

The documents we have to draw upon for this purpose are numerous and explicit. If, as a matter of fact, we do not possess any of the Roman *Libri Responsales* of the eighth or ninth centuries, we have at all events the work of the Frankish liturgist Amalarius,[1] born at Metz in the last quarter of the eighth century, a disciple of Alcuin, deputed by Charlemagne, at the request of

---

[1] Migne, *Patr. Lat.* tom. cv. pp. 985 *sqq.*; Mabillon, *Vetera Analecta* (ed. 1723), pp. 93-100.

Leidrad, Archbishop of Lyons, to organise the proper performance of the canonical Office in that Church in conformity with the use adopted at the emperor's palace. It is believed that Amalarius had already visited Rome in the time of Leo III. (795–816) before his journey thither as the messenger of Louis le Débonnaire, in the pontificate of Gregory IV. (827–844). There he applied himself to the study of liturgical manuscripts, and the observation of the ceremonial of the basilicas, especially that used by Archdeacon Theodore and his clergy at S. Peter's. He even asked the Pope to give him an authentic copy of the *Liber Responsalis* of the Roman Church, but Gregory, not being in a position to grant his request, merely referred him to the copies which Pope Eugenius II. had given to Wala for the abbey of Corbey. On these researches Amalarius founded two works, which are still extant: first the *De Ecclesiasticis Officiis*, finished in 823, secondly the *De Ordine Antiphonarii*, published between 827 and 834. Between the appearances of these two works he had published what we may call a standard edition of the Roman *Liber Responsalis* as used in France, and it is this edition which he defends and explains in his *De Ordine Antiphonarii*.

The information given by Amalarius, and his remarks, enable us to verify the antiquity of a ceremony or of some passage in the liturgy. The text itself of the liturgy must be sought in the manuscripts of it which exist. Two of these will be of special service to us. First, the *Liber Responsalis*, published as S. Gregory's by the Benedictine editors of his works (Dom Denis de S. Marthe and Dom Guillaume Bersin), from a manuscript of the end of the ninth century, which is now in the *Bibliothèque Nationale* at Paris (Ext. 17438). As the Benedictine editors have observed, this manuscript gives the text of the *Liber Responsalis* as adapted to the use of a particular church, a non-monastic church in France. In it appear the proper offices of saints of the north-east of France, such as S. Vedast, S. Medard, S. Denis, S. Quintin. But setting aside these, we have undoubtedly before us, in this manuscript, a text distinctly Roman, and one whose rubrics in many instances have been very clumsily altered in order that they might not remain inapplicable to any but the Roman clergy.[1] Our second manuscript is of more recent date by far, being of the twelfth century, but it is from a distinctly Roman source—nay, more than that, it was written for the use of the basilica of S. Peter's itself, among the archives of which it is still preserved (B. 79). This text of the *Liber Responsalis* was published by Cardinal Tommasi,[2] who observes that both as regards its texts and its rubrics it agrees with what Amalarius tells us of the text and rubrics of the Roman Office in the ninth century.[3]

In the next place, we are able to draw a further body of information from the *Ordines Romani*, at all events from those which are the most ancient, and most purely Roman, such as the *Ordo* of S. Amand, or that of

---

[1] This *Liber Responsalis* of S. Cornelius' is reprinted in Migne, *Patr. Lat.* tom. lxxviii. pp. 726-850.

[2] *J. M. Thomasii Opera Omnia* (Romae, 1749), tom. iv. pp. 1-169.

[3] *Ib.* p. xxxii.: '*Illa propemodum omnia, eoque fere ordine digesta, in eo reperiuntur, quae de Romano antiphonario tradidit Amalarius, unde cuique constare potest nostri antiphonarii ritus saeculo XII. usurpatos ab illis non distare qui in moribus Romanorum erant saeculo IX.*'

Einsiedeln, which have been published of late years,[1] or the *Ordo Primus* of Mabillon in its original portions,[2] or lastly, the *Ordo* published by Dom Gerbert, so necessary for a right acquaintance with the monastic uses founded on that of S. Peter's.[3]

From these sources, then, we proceed to draw the materials for that reconstruction of the Roman Office in the time of Pepin and of Charlemagne, which we propose to make.

I

We have first to consider the ordinary Office of the Season, and we start with the nocturnal course, which comprises Vespers, Nocturns (properly so called), and Lauds.

The office of Vespers begins with the versicle *Deus in adiutorium* (O God, make speed), intoned by the officiant—and its response—and then follows *Gloria Patri*. Lauds begin in the same way, as do also the hours of the diurnal course, and this uniform commencement is prescribed as early as the Rule of S. Benedict. The psalmody of Vespers has invariably five psalms: the Rule of S. Benedict only prescribed four. The psalms allotted to Vespers are the 'Gradual Psalms' (cxix.–cxxxiii. [*i.e.* cxx.–cxxxiv. in Book of Common Prayer]). But as these fifteen psalms were insufficient, other short psalms not allotted to the other hours were.

---

[1] De Rossi, *Inscriptiones Christianae*, tom. ii. pp. 34, 35; Duchesné *Origines*, pp. 439–463.

[2] Mabillon, *Musaeum Italicum*, tom. ii. pp. 9–40.

[3] Gerbert, *Monumenta Veteris Liturgiae Alemannicae* (1777–79), tom. ii. pp. 168–185.

added: the same kind of arrangement is made in the Rule of S. Benedict, to which the Roman vesper office owes much, Vespers being at Rome a late introduction borrowed from monastic custom. '*Quotidianus usus noster tenet ut quinque psalmos cantemus in vespertinali synaxi . . . hos quinque psalmos antiphonatim cantare solemus,*' says Amalarius:[1] the psalmody at Vespers is antiphonal. But antiphonal psalmody at Rome in the eighth century does not mean what is implied by the same term in the language of S. Ambrose and S. Augustine. Antiphony, as far as Amalarius is concerned, means the intercalation, after every verse or pair of verses of the psalm, of a short phrase, unconnected with the general course of the psalm. By an easy transition, this short phrase itself receives the name of *antiphon*. It has its musical notation, and in accordance with the Mode in which the music of the antiphon is composed the whole psalm is chanted. '*Antiphona inchoatur ab uno unius chori; et ad eius symphoniam psalmus cantatur per duos choros . . . Cantores alternatim ex utraque parte antiphonas levant.*'[2] It is not absolutely stated in this passage of Amalarius that the antiphon is to be repeated after each verse of the psalm, but it is nevertheless most probable that such was the genuine Roman custom in early times. In Frank countries the traces of this are few, as of a custom which was on the point of disappearing; but at the end of the ninth century the canons of

[1] Amal. *De Eccl. Off.* iv. 7, *De Ord. Antiph.* 6.

[2] Amal. *De Eccl. Off.* iv. 7: 'The antiphon is begun by one chanter on one side of the choir, and in accordance with its Mode the psalm is sung by the two sides of the choir alternately. The antiphons for successive psalms are begun by chanters on the two sides alternately.'

S. Martin's at Tours still repeated the antiphon after every verse of the psalm: '*unamquamque antiphonam per singulos psalmorum versus repetendo canebant,*' as we read in the Life of S. Odo of Cluny.[1] On the other hand, at the *beginning* of the same century, we find a clerk of Ratisbon complaining that his fellows sing the office without devotion, getting through the psalms as fast as they can, and, in order to be off to their other concerns the sooner, leaving out the antiphons—*sine antiphonis*—forgetting the very *raison d'être* of these repetitions, instituted of old by holy doctors for the consolation of souls:

> Nesciunt quia sancti doctores et eruditores Ecclesiae instituerunt modulationem in antiphonarum vel responsoriorum repetitione honestissima, quatenus hac dulcedine animus ardentius accenderetur.[2]

So the canons of Tours were behind their time; even at Rome the custom of suppressing these repetitions soon prevailed. But the rubrics prescribing them were not for all that suppressed: in the twelfth century, for solemn feasts, such as Christmas, we still find the direction that 'in Nocturns, the antiphons are to be repeated, at the beginning of the psalm, in the course of the psalm at the points marked for the purpose, at the end of the psalm, after the *Gloria Patri*, and finally after *Sicut erat.*'[3] This rubric is taken from the *Liber Responsalis* of S. Peter's mentioned above. We can see from it the great importance assigned to the antiphon in the Roman psalmody of the eighth century, and how, instead of being, as it is now, a parasitic prelude to the psalm, it was

---

[1] Migne, *Patr. Lat.* tom. cxxxiii. p. 48.
[2] *Ib.* tom. cxxix. p. 1399.   [3] Tommasi, tom. iv. p. 87.

the most characteristic element of the chanted psalmody at Rome.[1]

After the five vesper psalms and their antiphons were finished, the officiant read a short lesson from Holy Scripture :—'*Sequitur lectio brevis a pastore prolata.*' [2] This short lesson was followed by a versicle and response, such as *Vespertina oratio ascendat ad Te, Domine,* &c.,' or '*Dirigatur oratio mea sicut incensum,* &c.,' which, instead of being chanted, were read, like the lesson. Immediately after this versicle and response the *Magnificat* with its antiphon was sung. At the end of Vespers there was no *Dominus vobiscum,* but *Kyrie eleison,* said all together, and as final prayer the *Pater noster,* which all said aloud, as is still prescribed by the rubric of the ferial office. The most solemn place of all was thus given to the Lord's Prayer, as being the prayer of all prayers—a religious and primitive thought which unhappily was afterwards lost: in fact, even in the eighth century, the *Pater noster* was on festivals, Sundays, and station-days, supplanted by the collect for the day. This

---

[1] It sometimes even happened that a psalm had, not one, but two antiphons : ' *Si duae antiphonae notantur sub uno psalmo, prima antiphona cantatur in principio et in fine psalmi et post* Gloria *et post* Sicut erat, *secunda antiphona cantatur intra psalmum tantum ubi invenitur*' (Tommasi, *loc. cit.*). The first antiphon served for the beginning and end, the second was sung at intervals in the course of the psalm. [A survival of the psalm with antiphon after every verse is found in the *Venite* as sung on Epiphany in the third nocturn ; as also in the *Nunc dimittis* on Candlemas, in the distribution of candles, where the antiphon, as it happens, has the same melody. For other examples see the Ascension psalm, xlvi. [xlvii.] and the Assumption psalm, xliv. [xlv.], in *Variae Preces,* Solesmes, 1892, pp. 149, 192. The last example has the antiphon after every *pair* of verses.—A. B.]

[2] Amal. *De Eccl. Off.* iv. 7.

substitution is later than the time of S. Benedict, who was unaware of any other custom than the ancient one of saying the *Pater noster* at the end of the psalmody. This vesper psalmody most often ended when it was getting dark, having been begun at the twelfth hour (about six p.m.); a fact which gives occasion to Amalarius to remark, with more justice than he is aware of, that Vespers belong to the night office (*vespertinum officium ad noctem pertinet*).[1]

To the vesper office as we have just described it—and also to the office of Lauds which we shall describe presently—there was added a short euchological office,[2] the same, in fact, which now bears the name of *preces feriales*. These week-day prayers in the form in which they are still recited in the ferial office, are mentioned by Amalarius: they were of Roman monastic prescription. In them we pray for the faithful who are present and for ourselves (*Ego dixi, Domine miserere mei*—'I said, Lord, be merciful unto me' . . . *Fiat misericordia Tua Domine super nos*—'O Lord, let Thy mercy be shewed upon us' . . .): for the whole ecclesiastical state (*Sacerdotes tui induantur iustitiam*—'Let Thy priests be clothed with righteousness' . . .): for the community (*Memento congregationis Tuae*—'O think upon Thy congregation' . . .): for the dead (*Oremus pro fidelibus defunctis*—'Let us pray for the faithful departed' . . .): for those absent (*Pro fratribus nostris absentibus* . . .): for captives and those in distress (*Pro afflictis et captivis* . . .): and finally, for the common salvation (*Exurge Christe, adiuva nos*—'O Christ, arise, help us' . . .). This series of

---

[1] Amal. *ib.*   [2] *Ib.* iv. 4.

prayers is spoken of by S. Columbanus in the seventh century; it is called by S. Benedict *Supplicatio litaniae*, and it is in reality a litany of a euchological type sensibly more antique than the Roman Office.[1] In the eighth century this litany followed not only Lauds and Vespers, but also Terce, Sext and None.[2]

Compline, of which it seems natural to speak in this place, was no part of the nocturnal office, nor of the day office either; it was a purely conventual exercise, having nothing to do with the liturgy of the basilicas. It was simply the prayer of the monks at bed-time. When supper was over, the basilican monks of the eighth century did not go back from their refectory to the basilica to sing Compline there: they went straight from the refectory to the dormitory, and there they said Compline: '*Canuntur completorio ubi dormiunt in dormitorio*,' says Gerbert's anonymous liturgical writer in his dog-Latin.[3] But Compline, in the Liturgy of Amalarius, has already become a less private and informal office; and just as the monastic *ordines* of the ninth century speak of Compline as sung in chapter,[4] Amalarius does not indicate any other place for its recitation than in choir. At the beginning of Compline he places a short lesson, a feature not shared by any other office. This short lesson, in fact, represents the conclusion of the reading or *collatio* which had just been carried on in the refectory during supper: '*Ante istud officium conveniunt in unum fratres*

---

[1] Bäumer, *Geschichte*, pp. 602-614.

[2] [It continued to be so prescribed in the Sarum Breviary down to the Reformation.—A. B.]

[3] Anon. ap. Gerbert, iv. 2; see App. C.

[4] Migne, *Patr. Lat.* tom. lxvi. p. 941.

ad lectionem'; and in another place, '*In isto consumitur* [i.e. *consummatur*] *esus, potus et collatio.*'[1]

The psalmody of Compline is composed of four psalms, a number not found at any other canonical hour, and these psalms are invariable, being the same still recited in this office. Then comes the canticle *Nunc dimittis*, followed, without *Kyrie eleison*, by a collect—'*Tantummodo postulatio pro custodia deprecetur.*'[2] And after this prayer, Amalarius adds, complete silence follows; or, as Gerbert's anonymous writer says: '*Et tunc vadant cum silentio pausare in lectula sua.*'[3] Everything, as one sees, is peculiar in this office of Compline, and this is so because Compline is the hour of prayer which longest continued to be of private observance only.

The nocturnal office properly so called began *nocte media* at ordinary times; for the most solemn occasions the middle of the night was somewhat anticipated. At the sound of the bell,[4] all the pious company of clerks and monks came together to the basilica. The office began with the versicle and response *Domine labia mea aperies* ('O Lord, open Thou, &c.'), the officiant saying the verse; then followed *Gloria Patri*. The verse *Deus in adiutorium* ('O God, make speed') would have been regarded as useless repetition along with the *Domine labia mea*, and it therefore found no place at the beginning of this office.

Immediately after the *Gloria Patri* came the Invitatory

---

[1] Amal. *De Eccl. Off.* iv. 8: 'Before this office the brethren assemble for the reading.' 'With this office eating, drinking, and reading are brought to an end.'

[2] 'Let nothing more than the prayer for God's protection be said.'

[3] 'And then let them go in silence to rest, each one in his bed.'

[4] On the bell for vigils, see *L. P.* (Duchesne), tom. i. p. 454.

psalm *Venite exultemus*. This beautiful feature of the liturgy deserves careful attention. It is not, though it has often been said to be, 'a remnant of the ancient method of using what we call antiphons';[1] it rather represents the ancient way of singing the *psalmi responsorii*; and therefore the Frank author of the seventh century, known by the title of *Magister anonymus*, to whom we owe the most ancient commentary on the Rule of S. Benedict, has very justly given to the Invitatory psalm the name of '*Responsorium orationis.*'[2] In it, a soloist first sings the invitatory verse (which is not really an antiphon but an *acrostichion*), and the choir repeat it all together. After this, it is not the choir that sing the psalm, but the soloist, while the choir does nothing but repeat, after every two verses, the *acrostichion*, as at the first. Here we have the true primitive ecclesiastical psalmody.

After the *Venite exultemus*, the chanting of the psalms begins. The nocturn comprises twelve psalms, not furnished with antiphons, like those of Vespers, but sung continuously (*in directum*). After every four psalms, however, a *Gloria Patri* was inserted.[3] The version of the psalter in use at Rome was not the same as that used by the Frankish Churches. The Roman Church had preserved—and we find her continuing to do so until the fifteenth century—her own ancient version, that of which S. Jerome, in 383, at the request of Pope

[1 The *Venite* in the third nocturn on Epiphany *is* such a remnant, and may be contrasted with the same psalm as commonly used with Invitatory.—A. B.]

[2] Migne, *Patr. Lat.* tom. lxxxviii. p. 1006.

[3] Amal. *De Eccl. Off.* iv. 2.

Damasus, made a revision in accordance with the Septuagint, but hasty and incomplete.¹ At Rome the psalms were sung from this version of 383, while in Gaul, from the time of Gregory of Tours, there had been adopted S. Jerome's second version of the psalter, which we consequently call Gallican, a translation made by him at Bethlehem, between 387 and 391, with corrections from the Hebrew and the Hexapla, and now used by the whole of the Catholic Church.²

As to the distribution of the psalms of the psalter to the Nocturns of the different days of the week, that also was peculiar to Rome. At what date was it fixed? In the seventh century, at earliest. A liturgist of the middle ages gives the following excellent account of it: 'We must observe that the psalter has two main parts: the first, as far as *Dixit Dominus*, Psalm cix. [cx.], is for the night office; the second, starting with *Dixit Dominus*, for the day office. S. Ambrose divided the first part into ten nocturns, *decuriae*, or *diguriae*, as the common folk call them. The first *diguria* consists of sixteen psalms, the second of fourteen, the seven following ones of ten each, the last of eight. These ten *diguriae*, in the Ambrosian Office, serve for a fortnight, five being used each week, for the first five week-days, throughout the course of the year. As for the Saturday and the Sunday,

---

¹ Hieron. *Pref. in Lib. Psalm.*: '*Psalterium Romae . . . emendaram, et iuxta LXX interpretes licet cursim magna illud ex parte correxeram.*'

[² While the Vulgate Old Testament is, generally speaking, a translation from the Hebrew, the Vulgate *Psalms* are very evidently not from the Hebrew, but the Septuagint. S. Jerome, however, in his second version, added some corrections from the Hebrew; see his preface to the Psalms.—A. B.]

in the Ambrosian rite they have their own special canticles. But at Rome the whole psalter is recited every week, ... and the first portion of the psalter, as far as *Dixit Dominus*, is divided into seven nocturns, the first, of eighteen psalms, being for Sunday, the other six, of twelve psalms each, being for the week-days, while some few psalms in this first portion of the psalter are reserved for use in the day hours.'[1]

The twelve psalms of the nocturn having been chanted, they passed on to the lessons. The psalmody, at Rome, was separated from the lessons by the Lord's Prayer and a *capitulum*,[2] such as '*Intercedente B. Principe Apostolorum Petro salvet et custodiat nos Dominus*.' Amalarius mentions only a versicle in this place. The versicle, the Lord's Prayer, and the *capitulum* at a later date maintained their places side by side. The lessons being now to be read in the pulpit (*analogium*), the clerk (or brother of the community) who is going to read, first asks of the officiant his blessing, saying '*Iube domne benedicere*,' to which the officiant replies by pronouncing a short benediction, such as those still used at this service, and the choir respond *Amen*. Then the reading begins, the lessons being taken from the text of the Holy Scriptures in order. The distribution of the Bible over the seasons of the Christian year was canonically regulated. Here is the formula given by Gerbert's anonymous liturgist: from the first of December to Epiphany, Isaiah, Jeremiah, Daniel; from Epiphany to the Ides of February (Feb. 13) Ezekiel, the Minor Prophets, Job; in the spring, until

[1] Radulph. *De Canon. Observant.* 10.
[2] [Now called *Absolutio*, and always having a benedictory character.—A. B.]

Holy Week, the Pentateuch, Joshua, Judges; from Easter to Pentecost, the Catholic Epistles, Acts, Revelation; then, for the summer, the four Books of the Kings, and Chronicles; from the beginning of autumn to December 1, the Sapiential Books, [1] Esther, Judith, Maccabees, Tobit.

For a long time the custom of reading the Holy Scriptures after the nocturnal psalmody was confined to Sundays and station-days; the ferial Nocturns did not include any lessons. It was only in the seventh century that they began to have them, from the time of S. Gregory, or of Pope Honorius (625-638): Theodemar, Abbot of Monte Cassino (777-797), gives this as the reason why S. Benedict does not prescribe any lessons for the Nocturns of 'private days' or ferias.[2] The reading went on for such a time as was convenient, and until the officiant signed to the reader to stop (*quousque praecipiat ut finiatur*). The reader always ended the lesson with the *Tu autem Domine miserere nostri*, and the choir replied with *Deo gratias*. After each of the three lessons of the Nocturns was sung a respond.

It would be a mistake to identify these responds used in the Roman Church with the primitive *psalmi responsorii*: of these we have found the analogue in the Invitatory Psalm, and nothing can be less like the invitatory than a respond. The respond is in reality a gradual. The lesson

[1] Proverbs, Ecclesiastes, Wisdom, Ecclesiasticus.
[2] Migne, *Patr. Lat.* tom. xcv. p. 1584: '. . . Necdum eo tempore in Romana ecclesia, sicut nunc leguntur, sacras Scripturas legi morem fuisse; sed post aliquot tempora hoc institutum esse, sive a B. Papa Gregorio, sive ut ab aliis affirmatur ab Honorio. Qua de re nostri maiores instituerunt ut hic . . . tres, cotidianis diebus, . . . lectiones in codice legantur, ne a S. Romana Ecclesia discrepare viderentur.'

of Scripture read at Mass was followed by a piece of music sung as a solo and then repeated by the congregation: this is what is called the Gradual. The gradual at Rome is the most ancient form of ecclesiastical chant in anything like elaborate notation.[1] It is composed of a text or *capitellum*, taken indifferently from the psalter or any other part of Holy Scripture, and thus at once distinguished from the *psalmus responsorius*, which is by definition and in fact a psalm from the psalter. Nevertheless, at Rome the word *responsorium* was so far widely applied that the gradual of the Mass, though not a *psalmus responsorius*, was called Respond, and Amalarius gives it no other title.[2] Later on, this use of the term was lost; people spoke of the *gradual* of the Mass, the *respond* of the Office, and their original identity ceased to be recognised.[3] It is possible that the respond, both in

[1] Duchesne, *Origines*, p. 107.

[2] *De Eccl. Off.* iii. 11. So also the *Ordo* of Montpellier: '*Lecta lectione . . . de die, sequitur Responsorium et Alleluia*' (fol. 89).

[3] [Though the gradual at Mass and the respond at Nocturns were once both called Responsorium, and though they both occupy a similar position, coming after a lection, it does not seem probable that they were developed from a common germ, but were from the first different in their structure. This difference appears, (1) as regards the *matter*. The gradual is *nearly always* taken from the Psalms, though there are some notable exceptions; and we find a few not taken from Holy Scripture at all—as, for instance, those at Dedication of a Church, the ordinary votive Mass of our Lady, the beautiful one in the votive Mass on behalf of women travailing with child, in the Sarum Missal, and, in the same book, two very curious metrical graduals in the votive Masses of S. Sebastian and S. Gabriel. The famous gradual *Ecce Sacerdos magnus* is rather a reminiscence of the words of Holy Scripture than an actual quotation from them. The verse of the gradual is nearly always taken from the same context as the text of the gradual itself. On the other hand, the respond is *rarely* from the Psalms, and very commonly not from Holy Scripture at all; while its verse is generally *not* from the same context as

the Mass and in the Office, was a creation of the Roman Church, and that it is in this sense that we are to understand the saying of S. Isidore of Seville (*d.* 636): '*Responsoria ab Italis longo ante tempore sunt reperta.*'[1] S. Benedict prescribes the singing of responds after the lessons, a fact which supports the *longo ante tempore* of S. Isidore. The same writer defines the respond, such as it was conceived of in the seventh century, thus: '*Uno canente chorus consonando respondet.*'[2] The respond the text of the respond. (2) The most striking feature of the respond is the 'resumption,' not from the beginning, but from some point in the course of the text; and this must be part of the original design, from the clever way in which the 'resumption' is made to fit on to the conclusion of the verse. No such feature occurs in the gradual. (3) Though the *Gloria Patri* was not probably a part of any respond originally, yet it must have been added pretty early, as the *Gloria Patri* had not yet got its second verse, *Sicut erat*, already extensively used in the sixth century, and introduced into Gaul in A.D. 544 (Second Council of Vaison, can. 5). But the *Gloria Patri* finds no place in the gradual. (4) As regards music: the responds have a music of their own, so have the graduals; and these are so distinct that no plain-chantist can possibly confuse them, or regard them as variant developments of a common germ. The introit, again, has a structure of its own, having been originally a psalm, with antiphon repeated after every verse. The psalm has then been cut down to a single verse, the antiphon being sung before the verse, after the verse, and after the *Gloria Patri*. In modern times the second of these three repetitions has been dropped. The *Gloria Patri* was probably not only not an original feature, but was added here much later than it was to the respond, as it not only has the *Sicut erat*, but the antiphon seems never to have been sung between *Gloria Patri* and *Sicut erat*, as would certainly have been the case had the addition taken place early (see pp. 94, 95). The introit has also its own style of music, simpler than those of the gradual and respond, and in fact nothing more than a festal form of that used in the psalmody of the Divine Office. Perhaps, after all, these Introit psalms are what are referred to in that famous passage about Pope Coelestine and his psalms before Mass; see chap. ii. p. 47.—A. B.]

[1] Isid. Hisp. *De Eccl. Off.* i. 9.   [2] *Ib.*

was in fact composed of three elements: the *responsorium* properly so called, the verse, and the doxology. In the eighth century each of the three responds of the nocturn had its *Gloria Patri*, a feature which Amalarius considers as an innovation made by Popes of recent date.[1] In fact, S. Benedict only indicated a doxology for the third respond. All three responds were executed as follows, which is the ancient method, and, as Amalarius tells us, the method authorised at Rome. First, the precentor sang the text of the respond, the *responsorium*, as a solo, and the choir repeated it all together; then the precentor sang the verse, and the choir once more repeated the whole *responsorium*; then the precentor sang the doxology, and the choir this time sang the latter part of the *responsorium* (*circa mediam partem intrant in responsorium et perducunt usque in finem*); finally, the precentor once more sang the entire *responsorium*, and the choir repeated it entire. The matter of the respond had relation to the part of Scripture which was in course of reading: there were responds from the prophets; there were responds taken from Genesis (among others the beautiful *responsoria de Ioseph*); there were *responsoria Regum, responsoria de Sapientia, de Iob, de Tobia, de Iudith, de Hester, de Maccabaeis*. The *responsoria de psalmis* went with the lessons from the New Testament. The collection of responds taken from one book of the Bible was called *Historia*,[2] and the whole body of such *historiæ* which we possess, text and notation, constitutes a literature, the special creation of Rome, the critical study of which has yet to be undertaken.

With the third respond, following the third lesson, the

[1] Amal. *De Ord. Antiph.* 1.   [2] *Ib.* 53 *sqq.*

nocturn ended. Twelve psalms, three lessons, three responds constituted the nocturn, as well dominical as ferial. But while this one nocturn was the whole of the *ferial* nocturnal office, on Sundays there were added six more psalms, six lessons, and responds, divided into two portions or nocturns of three each. In the first of these two portions, the three psalms had antiphons as at Vespers; in the second, the psalms were *alleluiaticised*: that is, their antiphons consisted of nothing more than an Alleluya. At each of these nocturns, as at the first, the psalmody ended with a versicle or *capitulum*, on which followed the lessons. But the lessons in these two supplementary nocturns of the Sunday office were not taken from Holy Scripture. They were readings from the Fathers: '*Tractatus SS. Hieronymi, Ambrosii, caeterorumque Patrum, prout ordo poscit, leguntur*,' says Gerbert's anonymous writer. This custom was, at Rome, certainly older than the time of S. Gregory, who mentions it expressly[1]; it must have been anterior to S. Benedict himself, since he prescribed it in his 'Rule.' It seems certain that among these authors the place of honour was given to the discourses of S. Leo, whose stately eloquence was peculiarly suitable to the solemnity of the offices on the principal feasts; thus these discourses have more especially come down to us in the Lectionaries. We possess, in fact, one Lectionary entirely composed of the sermons of S. Leo, which has served for the use of the basilica of S. Peter, and another which has belonged to the basilica of the Holy Apostles.[2]

[1] S. Greg. *Epistul.* xii. 24.
[2] See the preface of the Ballerini to the edition of S. Leo in Migne, *Patr. Lat.* tom. liv. p. 122, '*De MSS. Lectionariis certe*

A copy of the Holy Bible sufficed for the lessons of the first nocturn, but for those of the other two a whole library would not have been too much. Accordingly we find Pope Zachary (741–752) bestowing on the basilica of S. Peter all the manuscripts he possessed, to serve for use at the nocturnal office on Sundays and festivals: '*Hic in ecclesia Principis Apostolorum omnes codices domui suae proprios, qui in circulo anni leguntur ad matutinos, armariorum ope ordinavit.*'[1] But in this same eighth century, the century of liturgical codification, the task of publishing collections of homilies was undertaken. Hence those *homiliaria* and *sermonaria*, numerous enough in our libraries, as everyone knows: '*Omeliae sive tractatus BB. Ambrosii, Augustini, Hieronymi, Fulgentii, Leonis, Maximi, Gregorii, et aliorum catholicorum et venerabilium Patrum, legendae per totius anni circulum,*' is the title we read at the beginning of one of these, selected by hazard; it is MS. No. 29 of the Montpellier Library, of ninth century date. Some of these collections have the name of the compiler. Mention is made of a *homiliarium* compiled by a Roman priest named Agimundus (*circa* 730), in a manuscript of the eighth century.[2] The name of Alanus, abbot of Farfa in the second half of the eighth century (*d.* 770) is attached to a homiliary compiled by him, of which several manuscript copies exist, of the eighth and ninth centuries. Similar collections were made by Bede (*d.* 735), and also by Alcuin (*d.* 804). But the

Romanis.' The S. Peter's Lectionary is the MS. 107 and 105 in the archives of S. Peter's; that of the basilica of the Holy Apostles is the MS. 3835-6 (8th century) in the Vatican collection.

[1] *L. P.* (Duchesne), tom. i. p. 432; cf. tom. ii. pp. 132, 195.

[2] As to Agimundus, see Bäumer, *Geschichte*, p. 286; and as to Alanus, see Migne, *Patr. Lat.* tom. lxxxix. p. 1198.

name of Paul the Deacon, the most erudite and famous in his day of the monks of Monte Cassino, and one of the best-read men in Charlemagne's book factory, ensured the success of another of these homiliaries, published at the request of Charlemagne, and with a preface by him: 'considered in his time a masterpiece of sound critical judgment, and the source whence in great measure the present homiliary of the Roman Church has been derived.'[1]

The ninth lesson in the Sunday office was followed by its respond, just as the others. At Rome, even in the time of Amalarius, there was no thought of substituting for this ninth respond the *Te Deum*, or of adding the *Te Deum* after it. On the other hand, S. Benedict, in whose Rule the nocturnal Sunday office is so different, as regards the distribution of psalms and lessons, from that which we are describing as used at Rome in the eighth century, prescribes the singing of *Te Deum* after the respond of the last lesson. The Roman liturgy in the time of Amalarius reserved the *Te Deum* for the nocturnal office of the festivals of sainted Popes (*tantum in natalitiis pontificum*). That is to say this hymn, or, to use the more antique term, this *psalmus idioticus* in rhythmical prose, did not appertain, any more than, as we shall see, did the *Quicunque vult*, to the office of the season according to Roman tradition. In Gaul the *Te Deum* was believed to be the joint production of S. Ambrose and S. Augustine on the occasion of the baptism

---

[1] Dom Morin, *Revue Bénéd.* 1891, p. 270. The text of the homiliary of Paul the Deacon is to be found in Migne, *Patr. Lat.* tom. xcv. pp. 1198 *sqq.*, but this text is to be viewed with caution. See F. Wiegand, *Das Homiliarium Karls des Grossen* (Leipzig, 1897).

of the latter; but nobody any longer dreams of assigning to this hymn any such origin. Recent researches seem to establish the fact that it is the work of Nicetas, Bishop of Remesiana, and that it was composed about the year 400.[1]

There being no *Te Deum*, the Sunday nocturnal office at Rome ended with the ninth respond. Before beginning Lauds, they waited until the sun rose. The interval was longer or shorter according to the time of year: the clerks and monks made use of it as an opportunity for taking breath awhile: '*Nocturnis finitis, si lux non statim supervenerit, faciunt modicum intervallum, propter necessitates fratrum, et iterum ingrediuntur ad matutinis laudibus complendas*,' says Gerbert's anonymous author in his lay brother's Latin. At Rome, so much importance was attached to beginning Lauds as soon as ever the sun rose, that if it happened that, at that moment, the nocturns were not yet finished, they were to be cut short in order to begin Lauds at once.[2] Like Vespers, Lauds began with the versicle *Deus in adiutorium* and its response, followed by *Gloria Patri*; and the psalmody, as at Vespers, consisted of five psalms. But of these, some, as is still the case, were invariable, viz. the *Deus, Deus meus*, Ps. lxii. [lxiii.], and, united to it, as forming one psalm,[3] the *Deus misereatur*, Ps. lxvi. [lxvii.], and the last three psalms of the psalter, *Laudate Dominum de caelis, Cantate Domino*, and *Laudate Dominum in*

---

[1] The researches of Dom Morin, Hümpel, and Zahn are reviewed in the *Guardian* of March 10, 1897, p. 390. See also the Bishop of Salisbury's article on the *Te Deum* in the *Dictionary of Hymnology*, 1892, pp. 1119-1130.

[2] Amal. *De Ord. Antiph.* 4.   [3] *Ib.* 2.

sanctis, counted as one psalm. The other three were: on Sundays, the *Dominus regnavit*, Ps. xcii. [xciii.]—replaced on week days by *Miserere*, Ps. l. [li.]—one other psalm, and a canticle from the Old Testament.[1] The programme, therefore, of Lauds, as regards psalmody, is exactly the same now as it was in the eighth century. The psalms were furnished with antiphons like those at Vespers, and the psalmody was followed by a short lesson, a versicle and response, and then the *Benedictus* with its antiphon. The office concluded with *Kyrie eleison* and *Pater noster*. The nocturnal course was now finished, and the monks could take a little rest, before beginning the day's work.

For the day there was the diurnal course, *i.e.* the three hours of Terce, Sext and None. Each of these had the same programme: the *Deus in adiutorium* and its response, followed by *Gloria Patri*, and three psalms, or rather three sections of Ps. cxviii. [cxix.]. These comprised sixteen verses each, and were without antiphons. Then came a short lesson, a versicle and response, the *Kyrie eleison*, and *Pater noster*. It will be seen that the office for these three little day-hours was quite independent of the nocturnal course, and was as invariable as a rosary.

In speaking of these day-hours we have passed by the office of Prime, which, like Compline, belonged neither to the diurnal course nor to the nocturnal, and was an exercise purely conventual and not basilican. It was the prayer of the monks on rising, just as Compline was their prayer at bed-time. In fact, they did not come from the dormitory, where they had gone to rest awhile

[1] Amal. *De Eccl. Off.* iv. 10 and 12.

after Lauds, and go into S. Peter's to say Prime: it was sung in the place where they slept: '*ista prima ibi cantatur ubi dormiunt*,' says Gerbert's anonymous liturgist. And, as a confirmation of the day-hours also having been originally purely conventual, we may remark that, like them, Prime comprised three psalms, and that one of these consisted of the first sixteen verses of Ps. cxviii. [cxix]. Like them, Prime began with *Deus in adjutorium* and its response, and the *Gloria Patri*, and ended with a verse and response, the *Kyrie eleison* and the *Pater noster*: but there was no short lesson.[1] So far, Prime was very similar to the little day-hours; but what gave it its special character as an office originally private, just as is the case with Compline, was the fact of its being lengthened out by an exercise purely conventual, the Chapter, or *capitulum*, so called both by Amalarius and Gerbert's anonymous author, as well as by the monastic *Ordines* which are contemporary with both these two liturgists.[2] The Chapter was the meeting together of the whole community at the beginning of each day. It began with the recitation of the Apostles' Creed. Then the monks 'confessed their faults one to another' (S. James v. 16), each in his turn: '*Donent confessiones suas vicissim*,' says the monastic rubric.[3] The *Miserere* followed, serving as a profession of contrition for the past, and right intention for the future. Then came the

---

[1] Amal. *De Eccl. Off.* iv. 3.

[2] See the monastic *Ordo* printed by Migne, *Patr. Lat.* tom. lxvi. pp. 937-942. Of this *Ordo* MS. copies of the ninth century are extant.

[3] By the eleventh century the *Confiteor* has made its appearance both at Prime and Compline. See Joann. Abrin. *De Off. Eccl.* p. 30.

reading of the Martyrology, followed by the versicle and response '*Pretiosa in conspectu Domini : Mors sanctorum Eius,*' and the collect *Sancta Maria et omnes Sancti,* or some other of the same kind: all of them monastic observances, which Amalarius does not note as being in use at Rome in his time, but destined, nevertheless, to find their way in later. Besides, all this is of secondary importance just here : the *raison d'être* of the Chapter was neither the mutual confession nor the reading of the Martyrology: it took place thus at the beginning of the day, for the purpose of assigning to each member of the community his task, and invoking the blessing of God on the work undertaken by His servants. Therefore it is that we find at this point of the office the thrice repeated verse and response, *Deus in adiutorium* ... *Domine ad adjuvandum* ... with *Gloria Patri* after the third repetition, and the versicle *Respice in servos tuos,* with its response, and the lovely collect *Dirigere et sanctificare*: an observance constituting the essential feature of the Chapter, and given in identical terms by Amalarius and by the monastic *Ordines* of the seventh century.[1] Are we now at the end of the Chapter office ? Not quite, for Gerbert's anonymous author informs us that the basilican monks of Rome did not dismiss the Chapter without having read some short portion of the Rule of S. Benedict, that no one might have any excuse for pleading ignorance of that rule ; after the reading, the abbot dismissed the Chapter with his blessing : two purely monastic observances, which even in the time of Amalarius had already become part of the Roman liturgy, with this difference only, that the reading of the Rule of S. Benedict was

[1] Amal. *De Eccl. Off.* iv. 2.

replaced by a short lesson from Holy Scripture. Here again, everything is peculiar in this office of Prime, as we might expect in an exercise not canonical, but private and conventual.

Here we finish our description of the ordinary Office of the Season. Is there any need to remark once more, as we conclude it, how clearly there is to be distinguished in it the juxtaposition of different cycles of offices: the ancient ecclesiastical cycle of the night vigils—Vespers, Nocturns, Lauds; the supererogatory cycle of the day hours—Terce, Sext, None; the altogether monastic cycle of conventual exercises—Prime and Compline? But now, these three cycles, once so distinct, blended together and formed a single cycle, recognised as composing 'the canonical Office'; a single euchological poem, of which the festivals of the Christian year were the episodes.

II

The cycle of the festivals of the Christian seasons begins at Advent. The custom of observing with special solemnity the four Sundays before the great anniversary of Christmas, of Gallican origin, but ancient, had been introduced at Rome before the time of S. Gregory, though after that of S. Leo. These solemnities took the form of 'stations': on the first Sunday, the station was at S. Mary's the Greater; on the second, at Holy Cross in Jerusalem; on the third, the most solemn of all, the Sunday *Gaudete*, at S. Peter's. The fourth Sunday had no station until the twelfth century.[1] On these Sundays, the psalmody was that of the ordinary Sunday office:

---

[1] Tommasi, tom. iv. p. 30.

the first three lessons were from the Scripture then in course of reading (Isaiah); the next five were expositions taken from the Fathers; the ninth was a homily on the Gospel of the station Mass. The responds were what gave to the office its special character; so much is this the case that the whole office took its name from the opening words of the first respond: to designate the office of the first Sunday in Advent, the term used was 'the office *Aspiciens a longe*.' Amalarius has no other name for it.[1]

I much regret the fact that I am no musician, so that I am unable to appreciate the *chant* of these responds, and can only judge of them as we judge of the choruses in the Greek tragedies. But even thus viewed, how much beauty there is in these responds of the Proper of the Season, these ingenious and eloquent compositions, which, by the humble process of piecing together scattered texts from Holy Scripture, succeed in uttering a language so striking and dramatic that they seem to revive within the sanctuaries of Christian basilicas the tones of the tragic stage of ancient Greece! Take, for example, that admirable respond for Advent Sunday, the *Aspiciens a longe*, where, assigning to Isaiah a part which recalls a celebrated scene in the *Persae* of Aeschylus, the liturgy causes the precentor to address to the listening choir these enigmatic words:

> Aspiciens a longe, ecce video Dei potentiam venientem, et nebulam totam terram tegentem. Ite obviam ei et dicite:

---

[1] [Thus also were designated other turning-points of the Christian seasons: the Sunday after the octave of the Epiphany was known as 'Domine, ne in ira,' and the first Sunday after Trinity as 'Deus omnium,' from their responds.—A. B.]

'Nuntia nobis si tu es ipse qui regnaturus es in populo Israel.'[1]

And the whole choir, blending in one wave of song the deep voices of its monks and the clear notes of its boy readers, repeats, like a reverberating echo of the prophet's voice:

> Aspiciens a longe, ecce video Dei potentiam venientem, et nebulam totam terram tegentem.

PRECENTOR

℣. Quique terrigenae et filii hominum, simul in unum, dives et pauper,—

CHOIR

Ite obviam ei et dicite,—

PRECENTOR

℣. Qui regis Israel, intende: qui deducis velut ovem Joseph: qui sedes super Cherubim,—

CHOIR

Nuntia nobis si tu es ipse qui regnaturus es in populo Israel.[2]

But what need thus to scan the horizon in doubt? He Who is coming is known; He is the Blessed One, and no triumph can be fair enough to welcome His advent:

PRECENTOR

℣. Tollite portas, principes, vestras, et elevamini portae aeternales, et introibit—

---

[1] 'Beholding from afar, lo, I see the might of God approaching, and a cloud covering the whole earth. Go ye forth to meet Him, and say, "Tell us if Thou art He that is to be Ruler over the people of Israel."'

[2] 'All ye inhabiters of the world and children of men, rich and poor, one with another,—Go ye forth to meet Him, and say,—Hear, O Thou Shepherd of Israel, Thou that leadest Joseph like a sheep, Thou that sittest upon the cherubims,—Tell us,' &c.

CHOIR

Qui regnaturus es in populo Israel.[1]

PRECENTOR

Gloria Patri et Filio et Spiritui Sancto.

And then the whole of the opening text is repeated in chorus:

Aspiciens a longe, &c.

Amalarius comments on this respond of Advent Sunday with just admiration, for it is one of the most perfect models of this sort of composition which I know. And undoubtedly there are many other responds the inspiration of which is far from being so grand or so brilliant. Moreover, by the end of the eighth century it would seem that the taste for these chanted compositions began to be lost: people wished them shorter; they were pared down and grudgingly rendered. The respond *Aspiciens a longe* has three verses: but already at Rome, Amalarius tells us, only two of them were sung,[2] and it became the general rule to assign only one verse to a respond. Such as they are, however, they have lasted down to our own times, and, in spite of much opposition, they have kept their place even in the private recitation of the office. But our habit of saying over and over again the most commonplace of them indisposes us to recognise the beauty of these antique creations, some of which are in very truth unappreciated masterpieces.

The four Sundays of Advent, which, under the influence of Frankish monastic customs, were soon to be

---

[1] 'Lift up your heads, O ye gates, and be ye lift up, ye everlasting doors, and He shall come in,—Who is to be Ruler,' &c.

[2] Amal. *De Ord. Antiph.* 8.

regarded as so many stages in a penitential season, marked at Rome, on the contrary, in the eighth century, and even in the twelfth, the progress of a season of gladness, in which everything took its tone from the joyful expectation of the coming of the Redeemer; and the third, the Sunday *Gaudete*, with all the pomp of its 'station' at S. Peter's, was the culminating point of this joyous going up to Bethlehem. The six days before the 24th of December garnished their ferial psalms at Vespers and Lauds with antiphons which already reflected the sparkle of the Saviour's star: *Rorate caeli*; *Haurietis aquas in gaudio*; *Constantes estote, videbitis auxilium Domini*; *Consurge, induere fortitudinem*; *Elevare, consurge, Hierusalem!* While the antiphon to *Magnificat* at Vespers on these last days of expectation was, as early as the eighth century, taken from that series which we call 'the great O's': *O Sapientia*; *O Adonai*; *O Radix Iesse*; *O Clavis David*; *O Oriens*; *O Rex gentium*; *O virgo virginum*, with their lofty and primitive symbolism.[1] And so at last the 24th was reached, when the *Benedictus* at the ferial Lauds had for its antiphon that which is now transferred to the first Vespers of Christmas: '*Dum ortus fuerit sol, videbitis Regem regum procedentem a matre* [sic], *tanquam sponsus de thalamo suo.*' Yet but one more night, and the King of kings would come forth from His tabernacle.

The Station of Christmas was at S. Mary the Greater, no doubt ever since the reconstruction of the basilica in the fifth century under the invocation of the Virgin Mary, during the pontificate of Sixtus III. (432–440);

---

[1] Amal. *De Ord. Antiph.* 13.

and it derived still greater solemnity from the presence in the basilica of the famous relic which, since the seventh century, had gained for it the title of S. Mary's *ad Praesepe*. Christmas was a festival observed at Rome from very early times : it is mentioned as far back as 336 in the Philocalian Kalendar.[1] At Christmas we meet, for the first time, with an office which is neither dominical nor ferial: an office of three nocturns, comprising nine psalms and nine lessons. It appears to me to be merely a reduced form of the Sunday office, in which the first nocturn has three psalms with antiphons, instead of twelve sung *in directum*. At Christmas, indeed, all the the psalms, at Vespers, the three Nocturns, and Lauds, were sung with antiphons repeated after every verse, or at all events after every short group of verses :

> In die Natalis Domini, ad omnes antiphonas vigiliae chorus choro respondet, et sic omnes antiphonas cantamus *ante psalmos, et infra psalmum ubi inveniuntur, et in fine psalmorum, et post Gloria Patri et post Sicut erat*.[2]

The presence of the Pope added all the distinction of a stately ceremonial to that of the chant thus embellished. It was a glorious vigil, which both was and deserved to be the liturgical model of which all other festivals, except indeed Easter and Pentecost, were the copies.

Epiphany, more than the rest, was a copy of Christmas—was it not the Christmas of the Greeks? It was

[1] [Philocalus was a famous engraver of inscriptions, employed by Pope Damasus.—A. B.]

[2] Tommasi, tom. iv. p. 37: 'On the festival of the Lord's Birthday, in the case of all the antiphons, one choir replies to the other ; and thus each antiphon is sung at the beginning of its psalm, and in the course of the psalm at the points marked, and at the end of each psalm, and after *Gloria Patri*, and after *Sicut erat*.'

kept at Rome, as over the West generally, from the fourth century onwards. The station on this day was at S. Peter's, and the office was like that of Christmas, of nine psalms and nine lessons, with antiphons to all the psalms. These two offices of the 25th of December and the 6th of January ousted the ferial office of twelve psalms and three lessons for eight days following; thus was kept the 'Octave' both of Christmas and Epiphany.

On thus arriving at the ides of January (January 13), the date on which Easter would fall was announced; and very shortly the process of preparing, by a long season of penitential mourning, to keep the anniversary of the Saviour's resurrection, would be beginning. The Roman Lent, even in the fourth century, extended over six weeks; but the custom of having a station on every day of these six weeks, even as was the case on the three Sundays *in Quinquagesima*, *in Sexagesima*, and *in Septuagesima*, cannot with certainty be traced back further than about the seventh century.[1] As for Septuagesima, it was a Sunday of joy, a last look back upon Bethlehem, on which antiphons and responds still re-echoed the Alleluias of Christmas; and such was its observance at Rome even down to the time of Alexander II. (1061–1073).[2] But after Septuagesima the Church entered on her period of sadness: no more Alleluias. And very soon it was a time of fasting as well.[3] Then, starting with Passion

---

[1] Duchesne, *Origines*, pp. 234-236.   [2] *Microlog.* 47.

[3] *Ordo* of Montpellier, fol. 96: '*Graeci a Sexagesima de carne levant ieiunium; monachi vero et Romani devoti vel boni Christiani a Quinquagesima; rustici autem et reliquus vulgus a Quadragesima. Primum autem ieiunium quarta et sexta feria post Quinquagesimam, i.e. una ebdomada ante Quadragesimam, apud eos publice agitur.*'—
'The Greeks begin to fast from flesh-meat at Sexagesima; our monks

Sunday, came the time when there was not even a *Gloria Patri* to the responds. And more sombre still would the the office become. In the meantime the office of all these nine Sundays before Easter was the ordinary dominical one of eighteen psalms and nine lessons. In the same way the office for the stations (week-days) of Lent was the ferial one of twelve psalms and three lessons. It was the responds which gave to these offices their distinctive character; for besides the *responsoria de Abraham, de Ioseph*, &c., corresponding to the Scripture then in course of reading, which up to Holy Week was the Octateuch,[1] the Sundays and stations had a series of penitential responds—*Ecce nunc tempus acceptabile* . . ., *Emendemus in melius* . . ., *Paradisi portas* . . ., which have all kept their place in the Roman Breviary, but which, it must be confessed, are sensibly inferior to most of those of Advent. On the other hand, the responds of Passion-tide form a group of the highest order of merit. We have still in the Breviary nearly all of these admirable compositions, of which Amalarius says expressly that they are the work of the chief liturgists of the Roman Church: '*Compositi sunt a magistris S. Romanae ecclesiae*':[2]

> In proximo est tribulatio mea, Domine, et non est qui adiuvet, ut fodiant manus meas et pedes meos. Libera me de ore leonis, ut narrem nomen tuum fratribus meis.
>
> Deus, Deus meus, respice in me; quare me dereliquisti longe a salute mea?

---

and devout Roman people or earnest Christians at Quinquagesima; country folk and the rest of the common people at Quadragesima. However, the first fasts publicly observed by them are on the Wednesday and Friday after Quinquagesima, *i.e.* the week before Quadragesima [first Sunday in Lent].'

[1] Genesis to Ruth inclusive.
[2] Amal. *De Ord. Antiph.* 43.

> Libera me de ore leonis !
> In proximo est tribulatio mea, et non est qui adiuvet.[1]

Thus they expressed the heart-rending complaint of Christ in the garden of Gethsemane, forsaken and betrayed—'*compunctio traditionis Eius,*' to use the words of Amalarius.

Then in the background is the conspiracy of His enemies:

> Dixerunt impii, non recte cogitantes: 'Circumveniamus iustum, quoniam contrarius est operibus nostris. Promittit se scientiam Dei habere: Filium Dei se nominat: et gloriatur patrem se habere Deum. Videamus si sermones illius veri sint. Et si est verus Filius Dei, liberet illum de manibus nostris. Morte turpissima condemnemus eum !
> Haec cogitaverunt, et erraverunt; excaecavit enim illos malitia eorum, et nescierunt sacramenta Dei.
> Morte turpissima condemnemus eum ![2]

There we have the crowd still undecided, all their sarcasm, and their pitiless spirit; the terrible rumbling of the threats of a blinded people. Then in another

---

[1] 'Trouble is hard at hand, O Lord, and there is none to help me. They pierced my hands and my feet. Save me from the lion's mouth, that I may declare Thy Name unto my brethren.—My God, my God, look upon me! Why hast Thou forsaken me, and art so far from my health?—Save me from the lion's mouth.—Trouble is hard at hand,' &c. (Ps. xxi. [xxii.].)

[2] 'The ungodly said, reasoning with themselves, but not aright, "Let us lie in wait for the righteous, because he is clean contrary to our doings. He professeth to have the knowledge of God, and he calleth himself the Child of the Lord. He maketh his boast that God is his Father. Let us see if his words be true. If he be the Son of God, He will deliver him out of our hands. Let us condemn him with a shameful death."—Such things they did imagine, and were deceived, for their own wickedness hath blinded them; and as for the mysteries of God, they knew them not.—"Let us condemn him with a shameful death."' (Wisdom ii.)

ROMAN OFFICE IN THE TIME OF CHARLEMAGNE 123

respond, the cry of Christ, 'Hearest Thou not, O Heavenly Father?'—

> Adtende, Domine, ad me, et audi voces adversariorum meorum. Numquid redditur pro bono malum? Quia foderunt foveam animae meae.
> Homo pacis meae in quo sperabam, qui edebat panes meos, ampliavit adversum me supplantationem.
> Numquid redditur pro bono malum?
> Adtende, Domine, ad me, et audi voces adversariorum meorum.[1]

So we enter on the Holy Week. The office of the Monday, Tuesday, and Wednesday was simply the ordinary ferial one: twelve psalms, three lessons. But on coming to the *triduum*, the last three ferias of the Holy Week, the office assumes the amplitude which characterises the most solemn anniversaries.

The office of these three days is minutely described in the purest and most ancient *Ordines Romani*, such as that of Einsiedeln and that of S. Amand. It was undoubtedly a purely Roman creation. The office commenced at midnight, and, contrary to the general custom, neither *Deus in adiutorium* nor the Invitatory psalm were said, but the psalmody began at once, without any preliminaries. There were three nocturns, each having three psalms with antiphons. After the third psalm followed the versicle and response, and the reader stood up to begin the lessons; but he neither asked for a blessing on beginning them nor said the *Tu autem, Domine*, at their conclusion. The lessons of the first

---

[1] 'Give ear to me, O Lord, and hear Thou the voice of mine enemies. Shall evil be rendered for good? For they have digged a pit for my soul.—Yea, even mine own familiar friend whom I trusted, who did also eat of my bread, hath laid great wait for me.—Shall evil be rendered for good?—Give ear,' &c. (Ps. xl. [xli.].)

nocturn were from the Lamentations of Jeremiah on each of the three days; those of the second, from S. Augustine: those of the third, from the Epistles of S. Paul. Neither the psalms nor the responds had the *Gloria Patri.* After the Nocturns came Lauds, with antiphons to the psalms and *Benedictus*: but at the conclusion, no *Kyrie eleison* as usual, but simply the text *Christus factus est,* &c.—' Christ became obedient for us unto death, &c.' (Phil. ii. 8). Then the congregation retired in silence. On Maundy Thursday the night office was celebrated at S. John Lateran, the basilica being lit up as usual. But on Good Friday, when the office was at Holy Cross in Jerusalem, all the lights were extinguished one after another, so that at the end of *Benedictus* only one remained alight, which was then hid behind the altar (*reservetur absconsa usque in Sabbato sancto* [1]), in token that the Light of the world was extinguished, Christ being dead; and that darkness was upon the face of all the earth. The night office of Easter Eve was celebrated in the dark (*tantum una lampada accendatur propter legendum* [2]). Most eloquent was this symbolism! What are we to say of the Frankish observance which subsequently took its place, and of which our triangular stands of unbleached candles are the persistent survival? Amalarius was acquainted with this form of the observance, having seen it in use in France in his time; but having asked the Archdeacon Theodore at Rome if he was aware of its having ever been practised on Maundy Thursday at S. John Lateran, the Roman dignitary was

---

[1] 'Let it be kept hid until Holy Saturday.'
[2] 'Let one lamp only be lit, to read by.'

able, thank goodness, to assure him that he had never seen anything of the kind.[1]

Indeed, the Roman Church had not even any need of this dramatic symbolism to impress the minds of her faithful people. The whole mystery of the Passion of the Saviour was set forth in the responds of her office. All the compassion of the Victim, resigned and forgiving:

> Eram quasi agnus innocens; ductus sum ad immolandum, et nesciebam : consilium fecerunt inimici mei adversum me, dicentes: 'Venite, mittamus lignum in panem Eius, et conteramus Eum de terra viventium.'
>
> Omnes inimici mei adversum me cogitabant mala mihi; verbum iniquum mandaverunt adversum me.
>
> Venite, mittamus lignum, &c.
>
> Eram quasi agnus, &c.[2]

All the emotion of His mother, calling for help to the Apostles, who have fled:

> Vadis propitiatus ad immolandum pro omnibus! Non Tibi occurrit Petrus, qui dicebat mori Tecum? Reliquit Te Thomas, qui aiebat: 'Omnes cum Eo moriamur'? Et ne unus ex illis? Sed Tu solus duceris, qui castam me confortasti, filius et Deus meus!
>
> Promittentes Tecum in carcerem et in mortem ire, relicto Te fugerunt!
>
> Et ne unus ex illis . . .?
>
> Vadis propitiatus, &c.[3]

---

[1] Amal. *De Ord. Antiph.* 44.

[2] 'I was as a lamb without guilt; brought to the slaughter and knowing it not; mine enemies devised devices against me, saying: "Come, let us make Him taste of the tree, let us cut Him off from the land of the living."—All Mine enemies whisper together against Me; even against Me do they imagine this evil.—"Come, let us make Him taste of the tree,"' &c. (Jer. xi. 19; Ps. xl. [xli.].)

[3] 'Thou goest, our Propitiation, to be slain for all! And doth not Peter come to Thee, he who said he would die with Thee? Hath Thomas left Thee, he who said "Let us die with Him"?

All the horror of the conscience of mankind at the sight of such iniquity:

> Barrabas latro dimittitur et innocens Christus occiditur!
> Nam et Iudas armidoctor sceleris, qui per pacem didicit facere bellum, osculando tradidit Dominum Iesum Christum.
> Verax datur fallacibus, pium flagellat impius.
> Osculando tradidit, &c.
> Barrabas latro dimittitur, &c.[1]

The shuddering of Nature itself, and the witness of the very fabric which enshrined the Law of God:

> Tenebrae factae sunt, &c.
> Et velum templi scissum est, &c.

And after this storm of grief, and treachery, and blood, after this quaking of earth and heaven, the tumult dies away in the relief of tears:

> Recessit pastor noster, &c.
> Ecce quomodo moritur Iustus, &c.

What, not one of them all? But Thou art led away to death alone, Thou Who hast preserved me in chastity, O my Son and my God!—Though they promised that they would go with Thee into prison and to death, they have forsaken Thee and fled!—What, not one of them?—Thou goest, our Propitiation,' &c. See *Paléographie Musicale*, vol. v. pp. 6 *sqq.* (Solesmes, 1896), where the singular history of this respond is given. It was independently adapted for liturgical use by the Churches of Rome and Milan evidently from an acrostic Greek poem by the celebrated S. Romanus. The respond in the two uses has a different verse, as well as other variations. We may notice the readings *propitiator* and *conservasti* (for *confortasti*) as being found both in the Milan and in some Roman books.

[1] 'The robber Barabbas is set free, and Christ, the Innocent, is slain! For Judas, that very master of the arms of wickedness, who knew how by means of peace itself to make war, hath betrayed the Lord Jesus Christ with a kiss.—To deceivers is given over the True; unholy hands scourge the Holy One.—He hath betrayed the Lord Jesus Christ with a kiss!'

> Domine, post passionem Tuam, et post discipulorum fugam, Petrus plorabat, dicens: 'Latro Te confessus est, et ego Te negavi: mulieres Te praedicaverunt, et ego renui. Putas iam vocabis me discipulum Tuum? Aut iterum constitues me piscatorem mundi? Sed repoenitentem suscipe me, Domine, et miserere mei.'
> Ego dixi in excessu meo, omnis homo mendax.
> Putas iam vocabis me discipulum Tuum? ...
> Domine, post passionem Tuam, &c.[1]

Thus the night office of these three days was made, throughout, one great representation of the sorrowful mystery of the Passion, death and burial of the Saviour, and of the unutterable grief of penitent humanity. And it ended, in the early morning of Easter Eve, amid the darkness and weeping of Lauds: *Sedentes ad monumentum lamentabantur flentes Dominum.*[2]

During the rest of the daytime, on Easter Eve, no further ceremony called for the assembly of the faithful in the basilica.[3] But at about three o'clock in the afternoon the Paschal vigil would begin. There was no benediction of the new fire or of the Paschal candle, customs which came from France to Rome after the eighth

---

[1] 'O Lord, after Thy Passion, and the flight of Thy disciples, Peter lamented, saying, "The thief confessed Thee, and I denied Thee; women acknowledged Thee, and I rejected Thee. Thinkest Thou that Thou canst yet call me Thy disciple? Canst Thou once again send me forth a fisher of men? Yet raise Thou me up again, O Lord, and have mercy upon me, forasmuch as I repent.—I said in my haste 'All men are liars.'—Thinkest Thou that Thou canst yet call me Thy disciple? ..."'

[2] 'Sitting over against the sepulchre they wept, and lamented for their Lord.' (Antiphon to *Benedictus*.)

[3] [The late date at which the other hours were added to the public office of the *Triduum* is indicated by the fact that while Nocturns and Lauds have their solemn chant, all the rest, even Vespers, are without note.—A. B.]

century: but (and this was a matter of ancient usage at Rome) that long series of lessons and *responsoria*[1] which we still find in the liturgical office of Easter Eve, and which constitute the best representation we possess of the original observance of every vigil. Two subdeacons, carrying torches, placed themselves before the altar at the foot of the pontifical throne, and gave light to the reader. So the lessons began, without title or benediction: '*In principio creavit Deus caelum et terram*, &c.' Each lesson was read first in Greek, then in Latin, and was followed by *Oremus, Flectamus genua*, and the collect. After every three lessons came a *responsorium*, sung first in Greek, then in Latin. Altogether six lessons, each read twice over: '*Sex lectiones ab antiquis Romanis Graece et Latine legebantur*,' says Amalarius. What is this office but a nocturn shorn of its psalmody—in other words, a vigil on the pattern of those of the fourth century, but without psalms? To this vigil office was added the baptism of the catechumens, which was celebrated in the baptistery of the Lateran, while in the basilica the people and the *Schola Cantorum* sang the litanies, repeating each suffrage fifteen times; then, when at last they arrived at the *Agnus Dei* of this prolonged litany, the chief of the *Schola* said '*Accendite*,' and the whole basilica was with all speed illuminated to welcome the return in procession of the Pope and his attendants, bringing in the newly-baptised. And then the Mass, the first Mass of Easter,

[1] [These *responsoria* have no resemblance to the responds at ordinary Nocturns, nor are they like graduals at Mass. They are, in fact, as they are now entitled, *Tractus*, consisting simply of a series of verses, and set to a simple and striking melody (the same in all), the cheerful tones of which at once remind us that with this vigil Easter begins and the last wail of Passion-tide has died away.—A. B.]

began, with the triumphal chant of the *Gloria in excelsis* and the Alleluya. It must then have been long past midnight.

One might have thought that this liturgy of the Paschal night, being nothing else than the ancient vigil, would have taken the place of the ordinary canonical nocturn office. But nothing of the kind. As at Jerusalem in the time of S. Silvia, after the vigil the daily nocturnal office kept its place. 'Even in the night of the Resurrection,' says the *Ordo* of S. Amand, 'we rise after cockcrow, we go into the Church, and, after a prayer, the kiss of peace is given in silence.' Then begins the usual nocturnal office, the *Deus in adiutorium*, the invitatory psalm with its Alleluyas, three psalms with Alleluyas, the versicle and response,[1] three lessons with their responds. Then Lauds, with Alleluyas. This canonical nocturn office was, we see, one of but three psalms, three lessons, three responds. The reason for this brevity was that, beginning *post gallorum cantum*, and not *media nocte*, it would have been impossible to give it the amplitude of the office of Christmas, for instance, with its nine psalms, nine lessons, and nine responds. All through the octave of Easter they repeated this single nocturn of three psalms and three lessons, following the rule that the office of the octave must correspond with that of the feast. And this is how that Paschal office came to be introduced, the shortest of all, destined so often to be brought forward as a pattern by clerks devoid of zeal, ignorant, or pretending to be ignorant, that this office of three psalms was only short because it was an

[1] Here the *Ordo* of S. Amand inserts the prayer—'*Et orationem dat presbyter*'—no doubt the *Pater Noster*.

appendage to the long liturgical office of the Paschal vigil.[1]

The octave of Easter, or, as it was then called, the seven *dies baptismales*, had an exceptional office. We have seen that the *Ordines Romani*, which furnish us with such minute particulars as to the liturgy of the last three days of Holy Week, and as to that of Easter, not only do not mention the three hours of Terce, Sext, and None, but say nothing about Vespers either: no public Vespers were contemplated for Maundy Thursday or Good Friday, no Vespers of any kind for Easter Eve.[2] The *Ordines* are in this respect faithful to the ancient Roman use, which did not regard Vespers as a canonical office, but as being merely monastic and supererogatory. On the other hand, these same *Ordines* prescribe Vespers for each of the *dies baptismales*. It would be a matter for surprise if these Paschal Vespers proved to be similar to those we have already met with in the Common and Proper of the Season. But nothing of the kind is the case; they have nothing in common with the Vespers of the ordinary canonical Office beyond the name, which is a

---

[1] Amal. *De Eccl. Off.* i. 32.

[2] The *Ordines* which are purely Roman, such as those of Einsiedeln and S. Amand, make no allusion to any diurnal office during the *Triduum*. On the other hand, the *Ordo Romanus Primus* of Mabillon, which, in the case of the Paschal Liturgy, represents the Roman use as practised elsewhere than at Rome (Duchesne, *Origines*, p. 141), mentions the diurnal office: on Maundy Thursday, *Ipsa vero die omne diurnale officium insimul canunt*; on Good Friday, *Vesperam dicit unusquisque privatim*; but on Easter eve nothing (Mabillon, *Musaeum Italicum*, tom. ii. pp. 19 *sqq.*). The Antiphonary of S. Peter's, which testifies to the old Roman use as it still existed in the twelfth century, gives this rubric: '*Primam, tertiam, sextam et nonam usque ad Pascha secreto dicimus; similiter vesperum Parasceven*' (Tommasi, tom. iv. p. 90).

fresh proof that at Rome quite another exercise had originally been known as Vespers than the Benedictine and Gallican office so named. On the evening of Easter Day, for instance, when the station was at S. Peter's, the clergy came in for Vespers in procession, wearing vestments of silk, preceded by the cross and the incense, and took up their places in the presbytery round the high altar. The office began with *Kyrie eleison*; then the *Schola Cantorum* sang the *Dixit Dominus*, Ps. cix. [cx.], the *Confitebor*, Ps. cx. [cxi.], and the *Beatus vir*, Ps. cxi. [cxii.], three psalms with Alleluyas. Between the second and third of these psalms came a group of versicles and responses: *Dominus regnavit, decorem induit . . ., Parata sedes tua ex tunc . . ., Elevaverunt flumina, Domine . . .*,[1] all being allusions to the resurrection and triumph of Christ. After the psalmody there was a prolonged chant of Alleluya, executed by the *Schola*, '*cum melodias simul cum infantibus*,' says the *Ordo* of S. Amand. Lastly, the *Magnificat*, with its antiphon, and by way of conclusion a collect. Here is an extraordinary programme for Vespers! And this is not the whole. The procession, in fact, took up its march again, and the clergy, leaving the presbytery —that is to say, the apse of the basilica—went and ranged themselves in front of the 'triumphal arch' between the nave and the sanctuary, before the great cross which was suspended in the centre of the arch. There they sang a psalm with Alleluyas, the *Laudate pueri*, Ps. cxii. [cxiii.], the *Magnificat*, for the second time, with an antiphon, and, for the second time also, a collect. There still

[1] ['The Lord is King, and hath put on glorious apparel.' 'Ever since the world began hath Thy seat been prepared.' 'The floods are risen, O Lord,' &c. All are from Psalm xcii. (xciii.).—A. B.]

remained a third vesperal station. The procession now takes its way to the baptismal font, where was chanted a fifth psalm, the *In exitu Israel*, Ps. cxiii. [cxiv. and cxv.], with Alleluyas; then, for the third time, the *Magnificat* with an antiphon, and a collect. Such are the rubrics given by Amalarius.[1] The *Ordo* of S. Amand, which represents a liturgy even more ancient, directs a long verse in Greek to be sung at the font. On the whole, these Paschal Vespers are exceedingly different from those of the canonical Office: it is true they include five psalms, and these psalms are of those which the canonical Office reserves for Vespers; but these three stations, this thrice repeated *Magnificat*, these verses in Latin and Greek, are all features of a Roman liturgy which is sensibly more ancient, and which belongs to a time when our canonical Vespers were certainly unknown at Rome.

On Low Sunday (the Sunday *in albis depositis*), and thereafter, the exceptional office of Easter Day and the *dies baptismales* gave place to the ordinary office, both as regards Sundays and ferias; the rest of the Paschal season had nothing proper to itself beyond the antiphons and responds. The festival of the Ascension of our Lord was celebrated forty days after Easter; like Christmas and Epiphany, it was a feast of nine psalms and nine lessons, with proper antiphons and responds. But, fifty days after Easter, Pentecost brought back once more the office of three psalms and three lessons. For Pentecost —*Pascha Pentecosten*, as the Antiphonary of S. Peter's calls it—has, like Easter, its liturgical vigil of six lessons,

---

[1] Amal. *De Ord. Antiph.* 52. [See Wordsworth and Procter's *Sarum Breviary*, vol. i. cols. dcccxvij-dcccxxij, for the form of this beautiful service preserved in England down to the Reformation.—A.B.]

read twice over, in Greek and Latin, with their *responsoria* and the collects which accompany them; and this vigil, like that of Easter, was followed by the baptism of catechumens: '*In vigilia Pentecoste sicut in sabbato sancto ita agendum est,*' says the *Ordo* of S. Amand. The canonical Office, therefore, by analogy would also be similar to that of Easter, and this abbreviated office would be repeated throughout the octave. But it would seem that for some time they hesitated thus to assimilate the office of Pentecost to that of Easter: while the Antiphonary of S. Peter's attests that the office of Pentecost and its octave is of three psalms and three lessons, Amalarius, on the contrary, assigns to Whitsun Day itself an office of eighteen psalms and nine lessons, *i.e.* the ordinary Sunday office; and to the octave one of twelve psalms and three lessons, the ordinary ferial office.[1] This may be taken as one proof the more of the absolutely exceptional character of the Paschal office.

We have now come to the end of the cycle of the feasts of the Christian year (for the observance of the feast of the Holy Trinity is long posterior to the eighth century), and we see the canonical Roman Office range itself under four liturgical types:

(1) The ferial office of twelve psalms and three lessons;

(2) The Sunday office of eighteen psalms and nine lessons;

(3) The festal office of nine psalms and nine lessons;

(4) The Paschal office of three psalms and three lessons.

Moreover—and it will be of some service to anticipate

[1] Amal. *De Ord. Antiph.* 57.

here a question which will come under our notice by-and-by—these four liturgical types are again met with, formally set forth in a decree of Gregory VII. (1073–1085):

>   (1) Omnibus diebus . . . XII psalmos et.III lectiones recitamus;
>   (2) In Dominicis diebus XVIII psalmos . . . et IX lectiones celebramus;
>   (3) Si festivitas est . . . IX lectiones dicimus;
>   (4) In die Resurrectionis usque in Sabbatum in albis, et in die Pentecostes usque in Sabbatum eiusdem, III psalmos tantum ad nocturnos tresque lectiones antiquo more canimus et legimus.

I have reproduced the exact terms of the decree,[1] and I conclude from it that the Roman Office of the eighth century remained intact at Rome in the eleventh, and that those liturgists are mistaken who have looked upon this decree as a *reform* on the part of Gregory VII., making a fresh regulation as to the office, when in reality he was but confirming the custom of the eighth century. I further conclude—to confirm what I advanced before on the subject of the settlement of the canonical Roman Office during the seventh and eighth centuries—that these four liturgical types constitute a system, in regard to the office, which is sensibly different from that formulated by the '*Liber Diurnus*' at the beginning of the seventh century, which may be summed up thus:

>   (1) A Pascha ad aequinoctium III lectiones;
>   (2) Ab aequinoctio ad Pascha IV lectiones;
>   (3) Dominico tempore . . . IX lectiones.[2]

In other words, the settlement of the canonical Office of the Season in the form we have just described dates from the seventh and eighth centuries. To these two centuries, the golden age of the chanted liturgy of Rome,

---

[1] Friedberg, *Corpus Iur. Can.* tom. i. p. 1416.
[2] *Liber Diurnus*, iii. 7; quoted above, p. 51.

belongs the creation of that admirable office, whose exquisitely proportioned beauty we have so imperfectly analysed.

III

We have seen in the preceding chapter how, about the year 750, the office of the saints in the *Sanctorale*, which had up to that time been kept separate from the daily office of the basilicas within the city, and was in this respect faithful to its tradition as an office belonging to the cemeteries, at last acquired a place in the office of the basilicas. That place was at first a humble one, compared with the great daily office. Far from displacing that office, whether dominical or ferial, the office of the saints was an appendage to it : the office of the season having been said, the office of the saint was added, just as we might add now to the office of the day the office for the dead. Thus the office of the saints, admitted at so late a date into the liturgy of the great urban basilicas, was regarded as something supplementary and adventitious. But it speedily blended itself with the great daily office. In the time of Amalarius, the fusion was already accomplished.

From this time, two degrees came to be distinguished in the offices of saints. There were lesser and greater feasts—*minores et maiores festi*—such are the very terms used in the *Ordo* of the Vallicellan Library [1]; so Gerbert's anonymous author speaks of *sancti principales* by way of distinction from the saints who were not so considered ; which comes to the same thing.

[1] Tommasi, tom. iv. pp. 321-327, has published this curious *Ordo* rom the Vallicellan MS. D. 5, of the tenth or eleventh century. It will be found to furnish us with several important rubrics. But it is not an *Ordo* purely Roman ; it is an adaptation of the Roman

The lesser feasts corresponded to our simple feasts of to-day: the ferial office was scarcely modified for them. Thus, at Vespers, there was the ferial office; the versicle and response, and the antiphon to *Magnificat*, alone were of the saint. At the nocturn the psalms and responds were of the feria; the invitatory, the versicle and response, and the three lessons, were of the saint. At Lauds, as at Vespers, all was of the feria, except the versicle and response, and the antiphon to *Benedictus*, which were of the saint. Had it not been for the proper lessons for the saint ousting those from the Scripture then in course of reading, one might say that the 'lesser feast' was scarcely more than a memorial, and was no infringement on the ferial office.[1]

In principle the greater feasts were not to supersede the ferial office any more than the lesser ones; but this principle was not long maintained. From the second half of the eighth century we find that on these feasts the Vespers are no longer of the feria but of the saint: the five psalms are those of Sunday (*psalmi dominicales*), with antiphons proper to saints' days (*antiphonae de sanctis*). It is just the same at Lauds. But at the Nocturn, the ferial office was better able to maintain its ancient right of possession.

At first the saint's day had a supplementary nocturn, distinct from that of the feria; this nocturn was executed as a preliminary to the other, coming soon after Vespers. A second stage in the transformation consisted in making the ferial nocturn office optional; in its place might be

Ordo or *Capitulare* to the customs of some cathedral unknown. Possibly this editing was done at the extreme end of the eighth century.   [1] *Microlog.* 44.

said a nocturn *de sanctis*. Amalarius bears witness to this transitional state of things liturgical, saying:

> Sunt festivitates quarum officia celebrantur nocturnalia circa vespertinam horam, quae vulgo appellantur propria; et in posteriore parte noctis canitur alterum officium, sive de propria feria seu de communibus sanctis.[1]

Finally the ferial nocturn was ousted altogether, and lost even the precarious position which had remained to it: every vestige of the duality of the office, of the joint celebration of the offices of the feria and the saint's day, was effaced: there was on these greater feasts only one nocturnal office, and that office was altogether given up to the saint:

> In vigiliis omnium apostolorum, vel ceterorum principalium, ... ipsa nocte ad vigilias eorum passiones vel gesta leguntur; ... psalmi cum eorum passionibus vel gestis cum responsoriis et antiphonis de ipsis pertinentes canuntur; ... in novem leccionibus ... gesta ... leguntur. Et octabas eorum cum responsoria vel antiphonas ... sicut die prima festivitatis eorum celebrantur.

Such is the rubric given by Gerbert's anonymous writer.[2] The Carolingian liturgists recognised no other custom than this. Amalarius, however, writes: 'On the more solemn festivals of saints it is the custom of our mother the holy Roman Church to celebrate two offices

---

[1] Amal. *De Ord. Antiph.* 17: 'There are some feasts whose nocturn offices, commonly called their proper offices, are celebrated some time in the evening; later in the night there is sung a second office, which may be that of the feria or of the common of saints.'

[2] 'On the vigils of all the Apostles, and other principal saints, their passions or mighty deeds are read in the night office; and, along with their passions or mighty deeds, the psalms, responds, and antiphons proper to them are sung; their acts are read in nine lessons; and their octaves are kept with these responds and antiphons, as on the first day of their festival.'

during the night. This double office is called "the vigils." ... The first is celebrated at the beginning of the night; it does not include the invitatory, because the people generally are not invited to the vigil at this time [?], but only to the vigil at midnight. Then, indeed, when the people and clergy together are entering on the second vigil, the invitatory is sung.'[1] No doubt, these double vigils were not assigned to all the greater feasts without distinction; in the ninth century the festivals of SS. Peter and Paul, S. Andrew, S. Laurence, the Assumption, and the Nativity of S. John the Baptist were the only ones which were observed with this special kind of solemnity. But the solemnity endured, and was a survival of the ancient observance of such festivals. After the thirteenth century it vanished even at Rome itself, and nothing was left of it but the liturgical expression (inexplicable unless by reference to its true origin) 'a double office' *officium duplex*—or more precisely, *officium duplex maius*.[2]

What were the festivals of saints kept at Rome? One would like to have a Roman Kalendar of the second half of the eighth century; but we have none. The Antiphonary of St. Peter's, however, furnishes us with a purely Roman Kalendar of the office in its time, and this Kalendar of the twelfth century can easily be brought into the state in which it would have been three centuries earlier; it is sufficient for us to compare it with the list of festivals given in the Sacramentary called by the name

[1] Amal. *De Ord. Antiph.* 59 and 60.

[2] The use of the term 'semidouble" must have originated at a time when this primary sense of the word 'double' was already obsolete and forgotten. Durandus (*Rat.* vii. 1, 31) explains such terms as referring to the number of officiants employed in rendering certain portions of the chanted service.

-of S. Gregory, which represents the Roman *Sanctorale* of the time of Pope Adrian I. (772–795), and, as a further help, with the lists given in the *capitularia* of the Carolingian 'Evangeliaries,' such as that of Ada at Trèves, an admirable manuscript of the first years of the ninth century. Thus we eliminate from the Kalendar of the Antiphonary of S. Peter the feasts posterior to the opening of the ninth century, and construct a Kalendar of the Roman Office in the time of Charlemagne.[1]

The following table contains those feasts of the Antiphonary of S. Peter's which are also marked in the Gregorian Sacramentary and in the 'Comes' of Ada at Trèves. Those in brackets are given by the latter, but *not* by the Gregorian Sacramentary. At the end of each month we give those which are in the Kalendar of the Antiphonary, but are neither marked in the Sacramentary nor in the 'Comes' of Ada.

January

1. Octave of Nativity. [S. Martina.]
6. Epiphany.
13. Octave of Epiphany.
14. S. Felix, Priest.
16. S. Marcellus, Pope.
18. S. Prisca.
20. S. Fabian, Pope, and S. Sebastian.
21. S. Agnes.
22. [S. Vincent, and] S. Anastasia.
25. Conversion of S. Paul.
28. S. Agnes, for the second time.

[1] The Gregorian Sacramentary will be found in Migne, *Patr. Lat.* tom. lxxviii., or in Tommasi, tom. vi.; the 'Comes' of Ada in *Die Trierer Ada-Handschrift* (Leipzig, 1889), pp. 16–27.

Additional, in the Antiphonary only
2. S. Telesphorus.
15. S. Maurus.
17. S. Antony.
18. S. Aquilas.
19. SS. Maris and Martha.
23. S. Emerentiana.
29. SS. Papias and Maurus.
31. SS. Cyrus and John.

February

2. Purification of Mary.
5. S. Agatha.
11. S. Valentine, Priest.
22. S. Peter's Chair.
24. S. Matthias, apostle.

Additional, in the Antiphonary only
2. S. Simeon.
3. S. Blaise.
10. S. Scholastica.

March

12. S. Gregory, Pope.
25. Annunciation of Mary.

Additional, in the Antiphonary only
10. The Forty Martyrs.
21. S. Benedict.

April

14. SS. Tiburtius, Valerian and Maximus.
23. S. George.
25. S. Mark, Evangelist.
28. S. Vitalis, Martyr.

Additional, in the Antiphonary only
26. S. Cletus.

MAY

1. SS. Philip and Jacob, Apostles.
3. Invention of the Cross.
   SS. Alexander and companions.
6. S. John before the Latin Gate.
10. SS. Gordianus and Epimachus.
12. S. Pancras.   SS. Nereus and Achilles.
19. S. Pudentiana.
25. S. Urban, Pope.

Additional, in the Antiphonary only

5. Translation of S. Stephen.
8. S. Michael.
14. S. Boniface.
26. S. Eleutherius, Pope.
27. S. John, Pope.
31. S. Petronilla.

JUNE

1. S. Nicomede.
2. SS. Peter and Marcellinus.
9. SS. Primus and Felicianus.
12. SS. Basilides, Cyrinus, Nabor and Nazarius
17. SS. Marcus and Marcellianus.
19. SS. Gervase and Protase.
24. Nativity of S. John Baptist.
26. SS. John and Paul.
28. S. Leo, Pope.
29. SS. Peter and Paul.
30. Commemoration of S. Paul.

Additional, in the Antiphonary only

2. S. Erasmus.
11. S. Barnabas.
15. SS. Vitus and Modestus.

July

2. SS. Processus and Martinianus.
6. Octave of SS. Peter and Paul.
10. The Seven Brethren.
15. [S. Cyrus.]
21. [S. Praxedis.]
23. [S. Apollinaris.]
25. S. James, Apostle.
29. S. Felix, Pope. [SS. Simplicius, Faustinus and Beatrix.]
30. SS. Abdon and Sennen.

Additional, in the Antiphonary only

10. S. Rufinus.
12. SS. Nabor and Felix; S. Pius, Pope.
13. S. Anacletus.
17. S. Alexis.
18. S. Symphorosa.
22. S. Mary Magdalene.
24. S. Christina.
26. S. Pastor.
27. S. Pantaleo.
28. S. Nazarius; S. Victor, Pope.

August

1. S. Peter's Chains.
2. S. Stephen, Pope.
6. S. Sixtus, Pope; SS. Felicissimus and Agapitus.
8. S. Cyriac.
10. S. Laurence.
11. S. Tiburtius.
13. S. Hippolytus.
14. S. Eusebius.
15. Assumption of Mary.

18. S. Agapitus.
22. S. Timothy.
25. S. Bartholomew, Apostle.
28. S. Hermes; S. Augustine, Bishop.
29. Beheading of S. John Baptist; S. Sabina.
30. SS. Felix and Adauctus.

Additional, in the Antiphonary only

1. The Maccabees.
3. Invention of S. Stephen.
4. S. Justin.
7. S. Donatus.
9. S. Romanus.
12. SS. Euplius and Lucius.
24. S. Aura.
28. S. Balbina.
31. S. Paulinus.

September

8. Nativity of Mary; S. Adrian.
11. SS. Protus and Hyacinth.
14. Exaltation of Holy Cross; SS. Cornelius and Cyprian.
15. S. Nicomede.
16. S. Euphemia; SS. Lucy and Geminianus.
21. S. Matthew, Apostle.
27. SS. Cosmas and Damian.
29. S. Michael the Archangel.

Additional, in the Antiphonary only

1. S. Giles.
2. S. Antoninus.
9. S. Gorgonius.
22. S. Maurice.
23. S. Linus, Pope; S. Thecla.
25. S. Eustace.
30. S. Jerome.

October

7. S. Marcus, Pope.
14. S. Calixtus, Pope.
18. S. Luke, Evangelist.
25. [SS. Chrysanthus and Darius.]
28. SS. Simon and Jude, Apostles.

Additional, in the Antiphonary only

7. SS. Sergius and Bacchus.
9. SS. Denys, Rusticus, and Eleutherius.
26. S. Evaristus, Pope.
30. S. Germanus of Capua.
31. S. Quintin.

November

1. All Saints; S. Caesarius.
8. The Four Crowned Martyrs.
9. S. Theodore.
11. S. Martin, Bishop; S. Mennas.
22. S. Caecilia.
23. S. Clement, Pope; S. Felicitas.
24. S. Chrysogonus.
29. S. Saturninus.
30. S. Andrew.

Additional, in the Antiphonary only

10. S. Trypho.
12. S. Martin, Pope.
13. S. John Chrysostom.
25. S. Katherine.

December

13. S. Lucy.
21. S. Thomas, Apostle.

25. The Nativity; S. Anastasia.
26. S. Stephen.
27. S. John, Evangelist.
28. The Holy Innocents.
31. S. Sylvester, Pope.

Additional, in the Antiphonary only

2. S. Bibiana.
4. SS. Barbara and Juliana.
5. S. Sabas.
6. S. Nicolas.
7. SS. Ambrose and Sabinus.
11. S. Damasus, Pope.
13. S. Eustratus.
23. S. Gregory of Spoleto.
25. S. Eugenia.

Anyone who is familiar with the Roman topographers of the seventh and eighth centuries,[1] will at once have recognised in this Kalendar the names of many saints which are also the names of the most celebrated sanctuaries of the suburban cemeteries: on the Flaminian Way, the basilica of S. Valentine (February 11); on the Aurelian, that of S. Pancras (May 12); and at the second milestone, that of SS. Processus and Martinianus (July 2); at the third, that of S. Calixtus (October 14), in the cemetery of *Calepodius*: on the road to Porto, at the second milestone, the basilica of SS. Abdon and Sennen (July 30), *ad ursum pileatum*; at the third, that of S. Felix (July 29), in the cemetery *ad insalatos*; at the fifth, the crypt where reposed SS. Faustinus, Simplicius, and Viatrix (July 29), in the cemetery of *Generosa*: on the road to Ostia, in the cemetery of *Commodilla*, the crypt of SS. Adauctus and Felix (August 30); and at the seventh mile-stone, the

[1] See especially Urlichs, *Codex Romae Topographicus*, pp. 82-85.

basilica of SS. Cyriac, Largus, and Smaragdus (August 8) : on the Ardeatine Way, in the cemetery of *Domitilla*, the cemetery basilica of SS. Nereus and Achilles (May 12), and of S. Petronilla (May 31) ; not far off, the cemetery of SS. Marcus and Marcellianus (June 17): on the Appian Way, the subterranean crypt of S. Caecilia (November 22), in the cemetery of *Calixtus*, adjoining the pontifical crypt where reposed, along with other Popes of the third century, SS. Fabian (January 20), Stephen [I.] (August 2), and Sixtus [II.] (August 6) ; on the *area* of the same cemetery stood the basilica of S. Cornelius (September 14) ; and on the *area* of the cemetery of *Balbina*, the basilica of the Pope S. Marcus (October 7) ; on the *area* of the cemetery of *Praetextatus*, the basilica of SS. Tiburtius, Valerius, and Maximus (April 14), and underground, the crypt of the Pope S. Urban (May 25), and that of SS. Felicissimus and Agapitus (August 6); further on, *ad catacumbas*, stood the basilica of S. Sebastian (January 20) : on the Latin Way, the basilica of SS. Gordianus and Epimachus (May 10) : on the Labican, *ad duas lauros*, the crypt of SS. Peter and Marcellinus (June 2), and that of S. Tiburtius (August 11): on the Praenestine, at the very gates of Praeneste (Palestrina), the basilica of S. Agapitus (August 18): on the Tiburtine, the basilica of S. Laurence (August 10) and the crypt of S. Hippolytus (August 13): on the Nomentan, the basilica of S. Agnes (January 21) ; and at the seventh milestone, that of S. Alexander (May 3): on the *Via Salaria nova*, in the cemetery of *Basilla*, the crypt of S. Hermes (August 28), and that of SS. Protus and Hyacinth (September 11) ; in the cemetery of *Maximus*, the crypt of S. Felicitas (November 23), and in the cemetery *Jordanorum*, that of three of her sons; further on, the crypt of SS. Chrysanthus and Darius (October 25); in the cemetery of *Thrason*, the little church of S. Saturninus (November 29); and lastly, on the *area* of the cemetery of *Priscilla*, the basilica of S. Sylvester (December 31), and in the same cemetery, the crypt of Pope S. Marcellinus.[1] Add to this list of martyrs SS. John and Paul (June 26), buried within the walls of Rome, on the very site of their dwelling: on which spot was erected the *Titulus Pammachii*, on the Coelian. If one considers that all these cemetery basilicas, themselves enough to be the glory of twenty cities, were nothing in comparison of the 'Confession' of S. Paul on the Ostian Way and that of S. Peter at the Vatican, one will be in a better position for estimating the profound effect which must have been produced on the minds of pilgrims in the seventh and eighth centuries by the roll of saints belonging to the Eternal City, and for feeling with what truth we may apply to her the beautiful Liberian distich:

> Ecce tui testes uteri tibi praemia portant;
> Sub pedibusque iacet passio quaeque sua.[2]

Rome, however, did not consider herself sufficiently enriched by the glorious memories of the martyrs enshrined in her cemeteries; the churches within the city, whether presbyteral or diaconal, received the names of saints, and kept the feasts of these their patrons, and hence arose a second group of festivals of saints, connected with the basilicas of the city. The Kalendar of feasts kept

---

[1] [Not included in the Kalendar given above, but now commemorated on April 26. He died A.D. 304.—A. B.]

[2] De Rossi, *Inscript. Chr.* tom. ii. p. 71:

> 'Lo! gifts to thee Christ's martyrs, thine own offspring, bring;
> See, at thy feet each one with joy his passion lays.'

at Rome thus contains a catalogue of these city churches. Thus S. Martina (January 1) is the name of a church installed in the old *secretarium* of the Roman senate, in the Forum; S. Felix [of Nola] (January 14), of the ancient private chapel of the *Anicii*, on the Pincian; S. Prisca (January 18) is the name bestowed on the *Titulus Priscae*, on the Aventine; S. Anastasius [of Persia] (January 22), the name given to the church called *Tres Fontes, ad aquas Salvias*, on the Ostian Way; S. Agatha [of Catania] (February 5) is that given to a church in the Suburra, taken from the Arians by S. Gregory; S. George (April 23), that favourite saint of the Greek-speaking Churches of the East, gave his name to the diaconal church of the district called *Velabrum*—largely inhabited by Greeks—situated in the *Forum Boarium* (cattle-market); S. Vitalis (April 28), and, before him, SS. Gervase and Protase (June 19), to the *Titulus Vestinae*, on the Quirinal; S. Pudentiana (May 19), to what had been the *Titulus Pudentis*; S. Praxedis (July 21), to the *Titulus Praxedis*; S. Apollinaris [of Ravenna], to an oratory near the Piazza Navona; S. Eusebius (August 14), to the *Titulus Eusebii*; S. Sabina (August 29), an Umbrian martyr, to the *Titulus Sabinae*, on the Aventine; S. Adrian (September 1), to the ancient *Curia Hostilia*, the hall where the Roman senate used to meet, transformed into a church by Pope Honorius (625-638); S. Euphemia [of Chalcedon] (September 16), to an oratory near S. Pudentiana's; S. Lucy [of Syracuse] (December 13), to a diaconal church built by Pope Honorius on the Palatine; SS. Cosmas and Damian (September 27), the two unfee'd physicians so popular throughout the Greek-speaking East, to the diaconal church installed by Pope Felix IV. (526-530) in the *aula* anciently devoted to the keeping of the Roman archives; S. Caesarius [of Terracina] (November 1), to the oratory established, in the time of S. Gregory, in the Imperial Palace on the Palatine; the 'Four Crowned Martyrs' (November 8), to an old church, hitherto unnamed, on the Caelian; S. Theodore (November 9), to a diaconal church near the Forum; S. Clement (November 23), to the old *Titulus Clementis*; S. Chrysogonus [of Sirmium] (November 24), to the *Titulus Chrysogoni*, in the Trastevere; S. Anastasia [also of Sirmium] (December 25), to the *Titulus Anastasiae*, on the Palatine. In addition to these, there were others among the patrons of churches at Rome whose names were not marked in her Kalendar, or were only placed there at a later date than the eighth century: such as SS. Bibiana (December 2), Sabas (December 5), Nicolas (December 6), Balbina (August 28), Eustace (September 25), Sergius and Bacchus (October 7), Alexis (July 17), Boniface (May 14), Erasmus (June 2), and Vitus (June 15). And the connection of all such feasts as these with the Roman Kalendar, though based on perfectly intelligible grounds, is after all only accidental. There is a sensible difference between these secondary feasts of the *Sanctorale* and the ancient festivals of the saints of the Roman cemeteries.

The remaining festivals of the Roman Kalendar have not that local and monumental character in virtue of which such anniversaries become peculiarly and distinctively Roman. Of the festivals of the Virgin Mary, the only one which was really Roman had already been erased from the Kalendar. It was that which had been celebrated on the octave of Christmas, a day which, in the eighth century, was devoted to the commemoration of our Lord's Circumcision. At the beginning of the seventh century, on the contrary, in the time of Pope Boniface IV. (608-615), it was kept at the Pantheon, consecrated as a Christian church by that pontiff under the invocation of Blessed Mary and All Saints, and the beautiful respond,

> Gaude, Maria virgo, cunctas haereses sola interemisti, quae Gabrielis Archangeli dictis credidisti, dum virgo Deum et hominem genuisti, et post partum virgo inviolata permansisti'—

composed, as it is said, by a blind chanter in the time of Boniface IV. (608-615)—was sung for the first time at the Pantheon.[1] This station at the Pantheon on January 1 was the ancient feast-day of the Blessed Virgin at Rome. Her other festivals found a place in the Roman Kalendar at a later date: her Nativity (September 8), Annunciation (March 25), Purification (February 2), and Repose or Assumption (August 15), which were all four kept at S. Mary's the Greater, are all of Byzantine origin, and their importation into Rome cannot be traced further back than the time of Pope Sergius I. (687-701).[2] The festivals of the Apostles, at the head of which stands that of S. Andrew, the brother of S. Peter, and after that those of S. John, SS. Philip and Jacob, and S. Peter's Chains, were the anniversaries of the dedication of basilicas in the city, and at Rome dated back to the sixth century at the earliest.

We have demonstrated the existence of a principle which, until the middle of the eighth century, did not permit the keeping of the festival of a saint unless localised

---

[1] Tommasi, tom. iv. p. 212: 'Rejoice, O Virgin Mary; thou alone hast destroyed all heresies, thou who didst believe the word of Gabriel the Archangel, conceiving, whilst a virgin, Him who was both God and man, and after His birth remaining still a pure virgin.'

[2] L. P. (Duchesne), tom. i. p. 381.

in some particular basilica, in a cemetery or within the city. At a later date, when this principle has ceased to dominate the liturgy as to saints' days, and not until then, appear the feasts which have no such local reference. The grand traditions of the monastic orders cause the institution of festivals such as those of S. Benedict, S. Maur, S. Antony, S. Sabas, S. Scholastica; legendary literature leads to the creation of such feasts as those of S. Nicolas, S. Barbara, S. Katherine, S. Eustace, S. Maurice, S. Christina, S. Christopher, S. Alexis; admiration and gratitude suggest the commemoration of Christian writers, such as S. Justin Martyr, S. Paulinus, S. John Chrysostom, S. Jerome, S. Ambrose, and S. Augustine. The *Sanctorale* reaches its autumnal period.

Among all these feasts of the Roman Kalendar, one would like to be able to say which were 'greater,' and which 'lesser,' but I abandon such researches to those better qualified to undertake them. A small number of festivals had octaves.[1]

The office for saints' days, at least for the greater ones, was framed on the model of that for Christmas, Epiphany, and the Ascension; it was an office of nine psalms, nine lessons, and nine responds. Amalarius writes:

> Sicut per novenarium numerum qui celebratur in nativitate Domini, ... ita per eumdem numerum gratias agimus in festivitatibus sanctorum.

And elsewhere he says:

> [Natalitia sanctorum] recolimus per novenarium numerum.[2]

---

[1] Amal. *De Eccl. Off.* iv. 36.
[2] Amal. *De Ord. Antiph.* 15, *De Eccl. Off.* iv. 35: 'Just as the number nine is observed in celebrating our Lord's Nativity, so,

The nine lessons were taken from the Acts of the saint; so were the words of the antiphons, responds, versicles and responses. The nine psalms were not left undetermined: each class of festivals had its own set, whether Apostles, Martyrs, Confessors, or Virgins, under which four heads the office of the Common of Saints was classified. The present distribution of psalms in the Roman Breviary for such offices is the same as it was then. The office of the Common, besides its nine psalms, had antiphons, responds, versicles, and responses proper for each of the four classes of Apostles, Martyrs, Confessors, and Virgins.[1] We may remark that, for a good part of its antiphons and responses, the office of the Common is indebted to that of the Proper of Saints: as, for instance, the office of the Common of Apostles to that of the feast of S. Peter, and the office for the Common of Virgins to that of S. Agnes. In fact, the Proper offices served as models for those of the Common, which probably do not date from further back than the period when the *Sanctorale* was codified, whereas the Proper offices composed for local feasts ('*ad ipsum natalitium pertinentes*'[2]) represented severally the tradition of the various basilicas where these were celebrated. And this explains the fact of each of these Proper offices having its own distinctive character.

Thus, the office of SS. Peter and Paul belonged to the basilica of S. Peter. In this office there is nothing of a legendary character: the lessons were taken from the

observing that same number, we give thanks on the festivals of the saints.' 'The anniversaries of the saints, which we celebrate, observing the number nine.' [1] Tommasi, tom. iv. pp. 150–157.

[2] Tommasi (*Ordo Vallicell.*), tom. iv. p. 324.

Acts of the Apostles, and from the most classic Fathers, S. Jerome, S. Augustine, S. Leo.[1] The antiphons and responds were made up of texts of Scripture (*Si diligis me, Simon Petre*: *Domine, si Tu es, iube me venire*: *Tu es Petrus, et super hanc petram*: *Beatus es, Simon Petre,* &c.), or were at all events suggested by the words of Holy Scripture: *Tu es pastor ovium, princeps Apostolorum: tibi tradidit omnia regna mundi,* &c.[2] In the chastened taste displayed in the choice of such matter as this for liturgical use, we recognise the spirit of the same school to whom we owe the Responsoral of the office of the Season. There was only one respond in the office for June 29 which was not Biblical, and it is one which serves, as it were, for the hall-mark of the basilica for which the office was composed, the basilica of the Vatican. It is the respond '*Qui regni claves*' which appropriates to itself the words of the metrical inscription carved over the entrance to the basilica by Pope Simplicius (468–483):

> Qui regni claves et curam tradit ovilis,
> Qui caeli terraeque Petro commisit habenas,
> Ut reseret clausis, ut solvat vincla ligatis;
> Simplicio nunc Ipse dedit sacra iura tenere,
> Praesule quo cultus venerandae cresceret aulae.[3]

---

[1] Tommasi (*Ordo Vatican.*), tom. iv. pp. 319–20.

[2] 'If thou lovest me, Simon Peter, feed my sheep' (S. John xxi. 17). 'Lord, if it be Thou, bid me come unto Thee on the water' (S. Matt. xiv. 28). 'Thou art Peter, and on this rock' (S. Matt. xvi. 18). 'Blessed art thou, Simon' (S. Matt. xvi. 17). 'Thou art the shepherd of the sheep, the prince of the Apostles; to thy care He entrusted all the kingdoms of the world.'

[3] De Rossi, *Inscript. Chr.* tom. ii. p. 55: 'He Who bestows the keys of His kingdom, and the care of His fold, Who committed to Peter the reins of Heaven and earth, that he might open the prison

This same respond had for its verse a beautiful distich,

> Solve, iubente Deo, terrarum, Petre, catenas:
> Qui facis ut pateant caelestia regna beatis,

which in the seventh century appeared in the basilica of S. Peter, engraved '*in icona S. Petri.*'[1]

The office of SS. Peter and Paul was, like that of S. John Baptist, one of the few saints' day offices which conformed themselves faithfully to the severe tradition of the office of the Season. The other proper offices accommodated themselves to the taste for legends and legendary literature. The antiphons and responds of the office of S. Andrew were borrowed from those *Acta Andreae* which had been rigorously condemned in the Gelasian catalogue of apocryphal books; and so was sung, ever since the eighth century, the respond '*O bona Crux,*' which is, it is true, an admirable composition, which we can admire without recognising the Gnosticism which certain theologians of our own time have found in it:

> O bona Crux, quae decorem et pulchritudinem ex membris Domini suscepisti, accipe me ab hominibus et redde me Magistro meo, ut per te me recipiat Qui per te me redemit. Salve, Crux, quae in corpore Christi dedicata es, et ex membris Eius tanquam margaritis ornata.[2]

---

for the captives and loose the chains of those that are bound, has now granted to Simplicius to wield that sacred power, that under his rule reverence for His holy courts might yet more increase.'

[1] De Rossi, *ib.* p. 254: 'At God's command, O Peter, loose the chains of earth; thou by whose means the heavenly realms are opened to the blest.'

[2] 'Good Cross, which from the limbs of our Lord hast received glory and beauty, take me from among men and give me up to my Master, that through thee He may receive me, Who through thee hath redeemed me. Hail, O Cross, consecrated by bearing the Body of Christ, and adorned with His sacred limbs as with pearls.'

Thus the Acts of S. Laurence furnished the words of the antiphons and responds of his office ; and the same was the case with S. Caecilia, S. Sebastian, S. Agnes, SS. John and Paul, and many others.

The Virgin Mary was more fortunate in finding at S. Mary's the Greater almost as severe a school of liturgy as the Apostles did at S. Peter's. Apocryphal matter for the office of such feasts as those of the Blessed Virgin it would not have been hard to find: but the Roman composers chose rather to derive from nothing but the Holy Scripture their theme for the praises of Mary. We owe to them some of the most beautiful passages of the Responsoral:

> Vidi speciosam sicut columbam, ascendentem super rivos aquarum, cuius inaestimabilis odor erat magnus in vestimentis eius, et sicut dies verni circumdabant eam flores rosarum et lilia convallium.
>
> Quae est ista qui ascendit per desertum sicut virgula fumi ex aromatibus myrrhae et thuris?
>
> Et sicut dies verni, &c.[1]

And others less closely inspired by Scripture, but penetrated with a piety equally marked by tender affection and grasp of dogmatic truth:

> Pulchra facie sed pulchrior fide, beata es, Virgo Maria: respuens mundum laetaberis cum angelis. Intercede pro omnibus nobis.
>
> Sancta et immaculata virginitas, quibus te laudibus referam nescio.
>
> Intercede pro omnibus nobis.

---

[1] 'I beheld her, beautiful as a dove, rising above the waterbrooks, and her raiment was filled with perfume beyond all price. Even as the spring-time was she girdled with rosebuds and lilies of the valley.—Who is this that cometh up from the desert, like a wreath of sweet smoke arising from frankincense and myrrh?—Even as the spring-time,' &c.

Virgo Maria, semper laetare, quae meruisti Christum portare, caeli et terrae Conditorem, quia de tuo utero protulisti mundi Salvatorem.

O quam gloriose migrasti ad Christum, beata et venerabilis Virgo Maria, cui Abrahae sinus non sufficit, sed Caeli palatia patent.[1]

I will not enlarge further on the subject of the Roman *Sanctorale* of the end of the eighth century. What has just been said is sufficient to show that the saints' day offices—a late addition to the canonical Office of the basilicas—could only find room there by infringing on and mutilating that ancient office, and moreover that they sanctioned the introduction into the liturgy of elements characterised by a style of literature decidedly less pure. The *Sanctorale*, in fact, was the first portion of the liturgy to manifest the symptoms of approaching decadence, while at the same time its acceptance undermined the regular and consistent use of the office of the Season.

The Roman Office, such as we have now described, had reached a pitch of perfection destined not to be surpassed, nor even adhered to,[2] but undoubtedly

---

[1] 'Lovely for thy beauty, and yet more lovely for thy faith [S. Luke i. 45], blessed art thou, O Virgin Mary. Forsaking the world, thou shalt rejoice with the angels. Pray thou for us all.—O holy and spotless virginity, I know not with what praise worthily to extol thee! Pray thou for us all.

'O Virgin Mary, thou who wast counted worthy to bear the Christ, the Maker of Heaven and earth, rejoice for evermore, in that thou didst send forth from thy womb the Saviour of the world.

'O how gloriously didst thou depart to be with Christ, thou blessed Virgin Mary, worthy of all veneration, for whom the bosom of Abraham sufficeth not, but the palaces of Heaven itself are thrown open.'

[2] On the speedy decadence of the Roman Office in France see Helisachar, 'Epistul. ad Nedibrium Episc. Narbonen.' published by M. Bishop, *Neues Archiv* (1886), tom. xi. pp. 566-68; and Ioann. Diac. *Vita Greg.* ii. 7.

worthy of the extraordinary acceptance secured to it by the admiration of the Anglo-Saxon, Frankish and Germanic Churches. It was the work of many an unknown hand, a work shaped slowly and as it were unconsciously, but a remarkable work, in which there lived the very soul of Rome. For Rome had enshrined there the very best of her literature and her history: her Psalter, her Bible, her Fathers, her Martyrs. She had set on it the stamp of her straightforward and simple piety, more deeply characterised by faithful adherence to old historic utterances of divine truth than by subtilty of dogmatic expression. It was marked with her fine sense of the beautiful, so amply revealed in its broad, sober and harmonious compositions. It had all the charm of her language, clear, concise, direct, Biblical in its phraseology, with the true ring of S. Jerome about its sentences, and music in every cadence. Above all, she had endowed it with her chant, that Gregorian plain-chant, distorted by the later middle ages, scorned by the Renaissance, no longer even understood in the seventeenth century—under the yoke of whose tradition we still live—but which we only need to hear executed in its true notation and on its true principles by the monks of Solesmes or Beuron in order to recognise—and with the added charm of its delicate archaism—that elegance and expressiveness which thrilled of old the pilgrims to the shrine of S. Peter and which, while in its principles it inherited the art of the old classic world, had found in its Christian inspiration a new well-spring of beauty.

CHAPTER IV

THE *MODERNUM OFFICIUM* AND THE BREVIARIES OF THE *CURIA*

We read in a Bull of June 7, 1241, addressed by Pope Gregory IX. to the Franciscans :—' We give you authority to rest content with the observance of the *modern office*, which you have in your Breviaries, carefully corrected by us, and conformed to the use of the Church of Rome.'[1] These words may serve as a motto for the present chapter, whose whole object consists in investigating, first, What was this ' use ' of the Roman Church down to the thirteenth century ? secondly, What was this non-Roman Office which the Pope calls *modernum officium*? thirdly, What are we to understand by the expression *breviary* of this modern office ?

I

The Roman Office, such as we have seen it to be in the time of Charlemagne, held its ground at Rome itself, in

---

[1] Potthast, No. 11028 : ' *Vestrae itaque precibus devotionis inducti, ut observantia* moderni officii, *quod in* Breviariis *vestris exacta diligentia correctum a nobis ex statuto regulae vestrae, iuxta ecclesiae Romanae morem excepto psalterio celebrare debetis, sitis contenti perpetuo.* . . .'

the customs of the basilicas without any sensible modification throughout the tenth and eleventh centuries, and even down to the close of the twelfth. Of this proposition I proceed to furnish the entire proof.

There is extant an office book of the basilica of S. Peter, namely the Antiphonary published by Cardinal Tommasi. This most important monument of the liturgy of the Roman basilicas is of the twelfth century. And in the previous chapter we have sufficiently established the conformity of its text and its rubrics with the information given by Amalarius to warrant us in saying that here we have a first proof of the substantial identity, as regards text and rubrics, of the office of the twelfth with that of the eighth century. A celebrated letter of Abelard, of about the year 1140, testifies that the basilica of S. Peter was not alone in its maintenance of the ancient office, since he tells us that this was equally the case with the Lateran basilica : 'Ecclesia . . . Lateranensis, quae mater est omnium, antiquum officium tenet.' It is true, we hasten to add, that in this same passage Abelard tells us that the Lateran stood alone in this observance of the ancient office : Sola ecclesia Lateranensis. . . .' But this restriction of his cannot be upheld in the face of what we find in our Antiphonary of S. Peter's ; while we here have the fact recorded, that at the Lateran it was the *antiquum officium* that was observed at that date.[1] This, then, is our first proof.

A second one is furnished to us by the *Ordines Romani* of the twelfth century, which, describing the pontifical ceremonial, supply on several occasions a full account of the office at solemn Vespers, Nocturns and Lauds, just

[1] Abelard, *Epistul.* x.

as much as of the Mass itself. Now this description accords with an *Ordo* of the office substantially the same as that of the eighth century. As witnesses to this fact we may take two well-known *Ordines Romani* of the twelfth century.[1] One is that of Canon Benedict, a canon of the basilica of S. Peter: it is called *Liber Polypticus*, and was written shortly before 1143; it is the '*Ordo Romanus* XI.' of Mabillon. The other, Mabillon's '*Ordo Romanus* XII.,' was drawn up by Cencius, the same man who, as Chancellor of the Roman Church, edited in 1192 the '*Liber Censuum.*' On the whole, we have in these two *Ordines* the consuetudinary of the pontifical ceremonies under the Popes Coelestine II. (*d.* 1144), and Innocent III. (1198-1216). And the ceremonial as described in them is in accord with the ancient office described in the preceding chapter, and not with the modern one which we are now about to take in hand.

Keeping this carefully in mind, let us see what was, in the twelfth century, the ceremonial of the offices in which the Pope and the Curia took part.

The Pope and the Curia did not take part, as a body, in the *daily* public office at any basilica, but only in the solemn office on certain festivals, in certain particular churches. For these festivals the old name of 'stations' was retained; and two kinds of stations were distinguished; the diurnal, which included nothing more than the Mass of the station, and the nocturnal or greater

---

[1] Mabillon, *Mus. Ital.* tom. ii. pp. 118 *sqq*.

stations, which comprised the first Vespers on the evening before the feast day, the nocturnal office at midnight, and the solemn Mass in the morning. Of these nocturnal stations there were but few, which all belonged to the greatest festivals, viz. the Sunday *Gaudete* (third Sunday in Advent), Christmas, Epiphany, Ascension Day, Whitsun Day, the Nativity of S. John Baptist, and the feasts of SS. Peter and Paul, the Assumption, and S. Andrew. But on these vigils all the pomp of the pontifical ceremonial was displayed.

The Pope sets out from his palace of the Lateran, the *patriarchium*, robed in a white chasuble, having on his head the crowned tiara or *regnum*, and mounted on a horse with scarlet trappings. At the head of the procession walks a subdeacon, carrying the pontifical cross. Then come twelve clerks carrying banners, followed by the foreign bishops who happen to be in Rome at the time. Then the abbots of the monasteries of Rome, and the cardinals, whether priests or bishops. After these the *scriniarii* (papal secretaries) and the *advocati* (legal officials) the subdeacons of the diaconal districts and those of the basilicas, and the *Schola Cantorum*. Lastly, two and two, forming a single file on each side of the Pope, the cardinal deacons. The Prefect of Rome, robed in a rich mantle and wearing buskins, of which one was gilded and the other red, attended by the judges in their copes, closed the procession, which was marshalled by the archdeacon, with a staff in his hand. The *maiorentes* (knights of the Papal Court), wearing silk mantles, and bearing wands, kept order in the streets.[1]

---

[1] Cencius, 7; Benedict, 21.

Thus the Papal *cortège* advances towards the basilica where the station is to be celebrated. On its threshold stand the canons (who have by this time replaced the basilican monks of the ninth century) awaiting the arrival of the Pope. As soon as he has come to the entrance of the church, he descends from his horse, and lays aside the tiara. The canons present to him the holy water and incense. The pontiff puts incense into the censer, and sprinkles holy water on the multitude. Then they enter processionally into the basilica, and, after a short prayer, pass on into the *secretarium* (sacristy). There, when the clergy of all orders have put on their vestments, the Pope gives the kiss of peace to the two bishops who are to assist him during the office, then to the cardinals, the Prefect of Rome, and other lay dignitaries. The dean of the district subdeacons calls over the names of the various readers and chanters who are to take part in the execution of the office. Then the Pope rises, and taking his place in the procession between the two assistant bishops, he re-enters the basilica, wearing his mitre. The *cubicularii* (chamberlains), holding over his head a *mappula* or canopy, accompany him as far as the altar. He takes his seat on the central throne of the presbytery, and the office begins—the office of Vespers.[1]

When Vespers are over, the Pope does not return to the *patriarchium* of the Lateran—supposing the station to be S. Peter's. Among the buildings attached to that basilica there were apartments for the Pope, constructed by Gregory IV. (827–844), for the express purpose of providing a place for the Sovereign Pontiff to retire

---

[1] Benedict, 46, 47.

to and rest, in the intervals between these solemn offices:

> Fecit etiam ... pro quietem Pontificis, ubi post orationes matutinales vel missarum officia eius valeant membra soporari, hospicium parvum sed honeste constructum, et picturis decoravit eximiis.[1]

The other members of the Curia are lodged *in domo Aguliae*—'in the house by the Obelisk'—and the master of this hospice (*dominus hospitii*) is bound to provide for them 'beds with good sheets,' and to take care of their horses in his stables.[2]

At midnight the bell is tolled, and everyone gets up. The Pope and the Curia assemble in the *secretarium*, which at S. Peter's was a large chapel at the south-west corner of the atrium. There they all vest, and the procession is marshalled. A censer is handed to the Pope, and four torch-bearers take their places before him. Then the procession starts in silence, by the light of candles. Having passed through the porch of the basilica in procession, and entered the church, they come to the altar of S. Gregory, which the Pope censes. This is the first halting-place, in the side-aisle on the left. The second halt is made before the altar of SS. Simon and Jude, at the bottom of the nave: here is reserved the Blessed Sacrament, which the Pope censes. Then they pass on to the altar of S. Veronica, in the side-aisle on the right, where are enshrined the holy winding-sheet and lance of our Lord's Passion, which also the Pope censes; this is the third halting-place. Then, going up

---

[1] *L. P.* (Duchesne), tom. ii. p. 81.

[2] Benedict, 7; the obelisk is still called *la Guglia di San Pietro* in prints of the seventeenth century.

the nave, the procession arrives at the 'triumphal arch' at the entrance to the sanctuary, where they make their fourth halt, before the altar of S. Pastor, which the Pope censes. So, from altar to altar, they come at last to the Confession of S. Peter, and go down the steps which lead to it. The Pope censes the altar set up over the tomb of the Prince of the Apostles; then he takes his seat, the four processional lights being set down before him.

And now, before the Confession of S. Peter, begins the first vigil—that first vigil which we have already pointed out as being, in the eighth century, a survival of the original distinction between the office of saints' days and the ferial office,[1] the memory of which has been preserved in the Frankish liturgy in the term '*officium duplex.*' There is no invitatory psalm at this first vigil: the chief chanter, or *paraphonista* with the *Schola Cantorum*, begins the office absolutely with the antiphon of the first psalm of the first nocturn. There are three nocturns, each of three psalms and three lessons. The canons of the basilica chant the lessons, and at the end of each it is the archdeacon who says the *Tu autem, Domine*. The responds are sung by the *Schola Cantorum*. After the ninth lesson comes the *Te Deum*,[2] and the moment it is finished one of the district subdeacons brings a Sacramentary, and one of the two assistant bishops holds it open before the Pope, who recites the collect for the day. Then the archdeacon says *Benedicamus Domino*,

[1] See p. 138.

[2] The *Te Deum*, which in the time of Amalarius was confined to festivals of martyr Popes, was already sung at Rome in the eleventh century on all feasts of saints, as well as in the Sunday office of the season, except in Advent and from Septuagesima to Easter. See *Microlog.* 46.

and the Apostolic Father blesses the congregation. So ends the first vigil.[1]

Again the procession takes up its march; the Pontiff leaves the 'Confession,' goes up to the high altar of the basilica, and censes it. Then he sits down before the altar, with the cardinal deacons ranged on each side. The cardinal bishops and priests take their seats with the canons in the stalls of the choir or *presbyterium*. The four lights stand before the Pope, who himself intones the *Domine, labia mea aperies*. The *Schola Cantorum* begin the invitatory, followed by the three psalms of the first nocturn with their antiphons. The lessons and responds of this nocturn are executed by the canons of the basilica. In the second and third nocturns, the fourth lesson is read by one of the *scriniarii*, the fifth by the senior cardinal bishop, the sixth by the senior cardinal priest, the seventh by the senior cardinal deacon, the the eighth by the senior subdeacon, and the ninth by the Pope himself. Two lights stand on the pulpit. Each reader, in his turn, pronounces the *Iube, domne, benedicere*, and the Pope blesses him. The Pope also, when his turn comes, says *Iube, domne, benedicere*, but no one blesses him, 'unless it be the Holy Ghost,' and those present, after a short pause, respond *Amen*. After the ninth respond the *Te Deum* is sung by the *Schola*, who forthwith proceed with the psalms and antiphons of Lauds, the versicle and response, and the *Benedictus*, with its antiphon. After which, the assistant bishop holds the Sacramentary open before the Pope, who reads from it the collect, and the office concludes as before. Then, as Cencius says, ' *Dominus Papa intrat lectum* ' ('our lord

[1] Benedict, 8.

the Pope retires to rest '), as do all the Curia, and return in the morning to celebrate the solemn Mass.[1]

Such is the ceremonial of a *statio nocturnalis*, such as would be celebrated, for instance, on the feast of S. Peter. These long and solemn night vigils are not performed without plenty of light. Peter Mallius, who, like Benedict, was a canon of S. Peter's, tells us that on station days two hundred and fifty lamps are lit in the basilica. In addition to which, on certain festivals, as on that of S. Peter, and during the octave, the nets (*retia*) are lit up, including the great net (*rete magnum*), which illuminates the portico and the front of the church.[2] No doubt these were large chandeliers and *coronae* of lights. The Divine Office, with this brilliant and complicated ceremonial, and the attendance of so splendid a hierarchy, has certainly assumed the character of a pageant: but how grand a pageant! No wonder the people came together to it in crowds. They press round the procession as it passes along the streets, they spread themselves over the steps of the portico, and in the nave of the basilica. On the principal nocturnal vigils it must have been a regular swarm of Romans, men and women, and of foreigners. On certain festivals, the seneschal of the Apostolic Palace threw handfuls of coins on the dense ranks of the crowd, to disperse them, and so to open up an easier passage for the Pope and his attendants. The people remained to the end of the office, for they would not depart until they had received the benediction of the Pontiff: '*Dominus pontifex*,' we read, '*benedicit populum fatigatum*.' And

---

[1] Benedict, 14.
[2] Mabillon, *Mus. Ital.* tom. ii. p. 161; cf. De Rossi, *Inscr. Christ.* tom. ii. pp. 193 *sqq*.

in all this grandeur, and in all this pressing and thronging, they delighted: '... *ut omnis populus cum benedictione laetus recedat.*' [1]

But, to resume the thread of our argument, who can fail to see that this ceremonial of the twelfth century is in accord with, and belongs to, an office which is the same with that of the eighth: the same as regards the number of psalms, of lessons, of responds; the same with respect to the rubrics for beginning and conclusion of the office; the same, above all, in the absence of those elements which, as we shall see, are characteristic of the modern ultramontane office? It is a ceremonial which might well be of the time of Charlemagne. And we are entitled to infer from this the substantial identity of the basilican office in the time of the canons Benedict and Cencius with what it was in the time of Amalarius.

A grave objection has, however, been made to this identity. Liturgical writers—and their opinion on this point was embraced by Pope Pius V.—agree in attributing to Gregory VII. a reform of the Roman Office. Here is the account which Dom Guéranger gives of this supposed reform: 'The press of important business by which a Pope in the eleventh century was besieged, the infinitely numerous details of administration into which he had to enter, made it impossible to reconcile with duties so vast and so anxious a constant attendance at the long offices which had been in use during the preceding centuries,' and therefore Gregory VII. 'abridged the

[1] Cencius, 37; Benedict, 74, 76.

offices for the canonical hours of prayers, and simplified the liturgy, for the use of the Roman Curia.'[1]

But we shall not find that this theory deserves much consideration. Was it, then, only in the eleventh century that the Popes began to be besieged with a press of business, and had to enter into an infinite number of details of administration? Dom Guéranger would be the last man in the world to wish us to think so. It is, besides, quite certain that in the time of the immediate predecessors of Gregory VII. the Pope and the Curia, faithful to the obligation of reciting the Divine Office, without neglecting the other duties imposed on them by their station, acquitted themselves of that obligation by a private recitation of their office. S. Leo IX. (1048–1054) is praised, in his Life, for having every day fulfilled the obligation of reciting the entire 'Psalter,' as it was wont to be called, meaning thereby the diurnal and nocturnal office; for having recited it at the proper hours, including those of the night; for reciting it in his oratory in company with a single clerk; and for never omitting it.'[2] Here we see how a Pope of the eleventh century, besieged as much as any other by a press of important business, reconciled easily the duties of so busy a life, I do not say with daily attendance at the long offices of the basilicas (a thing which it had never been the custom for the Pope to undertake, even in the preceding centuries), but with the constant and punctual recitation of the Divine Office in private.[3]

---

[1] Guéranger, *Instit. Liturg.* tom. i. p. 281.
[2] Migne, *Patr. Lat.* tom. cxliii. pp. 501–2.
[3] The 'Ordo Romanus X.' in Mabillon, *Mus. Ital.* tom. ii. pp. 97 *sqq.*, a document of the end of the tenth century, describes the

In the second place, it is peculiarly improbable that S. Gregory VII., of all men, should be the one to interfere with the old Roman *Ordo* of the Office. At the very moment when this same Pope is employed in introducing into Spain nothing more nor less than this ancient Roman Office; at the moment when he is congratulating the kings of Aragon and Castile on the zeal shown by them in establishing in their realms the Office according to the Roman order ('*Romani ordinis officium*'), and that, too, after the ancient use ('*ex antiquo more*'),[1] are we to think of him as himself abridging and simplifying the Roman liturgy?

But, to pass on from these preliminary considerations, the point is to ascertain precisely what this reform of Gregory VII. was: here Dom Guéranger cites as his witness the *Micrologus*, which, so he assures us, 'gives us to understand that it is upon the Office as authorised by Gregory VII. that its comments are founded.'[2]

---

ceremonies in which the Pope took part on the last three days of Holy Week. The following are some of its rubrics: 'Antequam dominus Papa exeat de camera, dicit tertiam. . . . Intrat ecclesiam S. Thomae et dicit cum capellanis suis nonam. . . . Dominus Papa cum clero intrat secretarium, et abstracta planeta cum pallio, sedeat in sede sua, et lotis pedibus ministri calcient eum quotidiana calciamenta; veniens ad faldistorium dicit nonam; et post paullulum reindutus planeta et pallio, praeeunte eum cruce et evangelio ad altare procedant. . . .'—'Before the Pope leaves his room he says Terce. . . . He goes into the Church of S. Thomas and says None with his chaplains. . . . The Pope goes into the sacristy with the clergy, and, having taken off his chasuble and pall, let him sit down in his seat, while the attendants wash his feet and put on them such shoes as he useth to wear ordinarily. Then, coming to the faldstool, he says None; and after a little while, having put on again his chasuble and pall, and the cross and gospel-book being borne before him, let them proceed to the Altar.'

[1] Jaffé, 4840, 4841.   [2] Guéranger, *loc. cit.*

The *Micrologus* is a most valuable liturgical commentary on the Roman *Ordo*, both of the Mass and the Divine Office. It was long attributed to Ivo of Chartres; but it now seems to be clearly proved to be the work not of a Frenchman but a German, Bernold of Constance (*d.* 1100), monk of the abbey of S. Blasian.[1] Now the question is, on what text did Bernold found his comments? I find him citing various manuscript Antiphonaries: '*omnes authentici antiphonarii . . ., antiqui antiphonarii.*' I find him settling points in accordance with Roman use: '*iuxta Romanam consuetudinem . . ., iuxta traditionem S. Romanae ecclesiae . . ., Romano more.*' And he certainly calls both the Sacramentary and Antiphonary to which he refers *Gregorian*. In one place he uses the expression *officium Gregorianum*. But all this *Gregorian* literature of his has relation to S. Gregory the Great: '*S. Gregorius Papa,*' he says, '*B. Gregorius Papa . . ., S. Gregorius Papa primus.*' Whenever he means Gregory VII., Bernold mentions him in such a way as to distinguish him quite clearly from Gregory I.: '*Gregorius Papa septimus . . ., Gregorius huius nominis Papa septimus . . ., Reverendae memoriae Gregorius Papa*'; and he never gives him the title of *Saint*. So Bernold, when treating of the *Ordo* of the canonical Office, attributes the arrangement of it which he describes, not to Gregory VII., but to S. Gregory I. Thus we find him saying: '*Sciendum est quod S. Gregorius ita ecclesiastica officia ordinavit.*'[2] And he attributes to his contemporary, Gregory VII., nothing more than the two decrees given

---

[1] *Revue Bénédictine*, 1891, pp. 385 *sqq.*; cf. *Neues Archiv*, 1893, tom. x iii. pp. 429–446.

[2] *Microlog.* 61 and 50.

below, as to which anyone can see how far they affect the general character of the Roman canonical Office :

> *First Decree.*—Gregorius huius nominis papa septimus, Apostolicae sedi praesidens, constituit ut SS. omnium Romanorum pontificum et martyrum festivitates solemniter ubique cum pleno officio celebrentur. . . .[1]
>
> *Second Decree.*—Gregorius papa in Apostolica sede constitutus . . . promulgavit : ' A die,' inquit, ' Resurrectionis usque in Sabbatum in Albis, et a die Pentecostes usque in Sabbatum eiusdem hebdomadae, tres psalmos ad nocturnas, tresque lectiones antiquo more cantamus et legimus. Omnibus aliis diebus per totum annum, si festivitas est, novem psalmos et novem lectiones et responsoria dicimus ; aliis autem diebus duodecim psalmos et tres lectiones recitamus ; in diebus Dominicis octodecim psalmos, excepto die Paschae et die Pentecostes, et novem lectiones dicimus. Hoc etiam usquequaque iuxta Romanum ordinem ita fieri statuimus, ut supra notavimus. In octava Paschae historiam *Dignus es Domine* et Apocalypsin iuxta ordinem incipimus.'[2]

By the first of these decrees Gregory VII. merely extends to all Christendom the obligation of celebrating the feasts of sainted Popes, whether martyrs or confessors ; here, therefore, the *Roman* Office is not in question.

As for the second, it tells us that Gregory VII. decreed that on Easter Day and the six weekdays in its octave, as also Whitsun Day and its six weekdays, the nocturnal office is to have only three psalms, three lessons, and three responds ; but that, all the rest of the year, this office is to have, on festivals, nine psalms, nine lessons, and nine responds, on ordinary weekdays twelve psalms, three lessons and three responds, and on Sundays eighteen psalms, nine lessons and nine responds. But is not this *Ordo* for the nocturnal offices exactly that which we

[1] *Microlog.* 43.　　　[2] *Ib.* 54.

have seen in full vigour at Rome in the time of Amalarius at the beginning of the ninth century? And does not Gregory VII. himself, while enacting these rules, tell us that he is thereby making no innovation? '*Antiquo more cantamus et legimus*,' he writes—'such is the ancient Roman custom, and we make no change therein.' He even insists on this point: 'We ordain that it be none otherwise done, but that the *Ordo Romanus* be adhered to, which has not ceased to be the canon of our customs, and which is for us, as we love to repeat, the *antiquus mos*.' Are these expressions those of a reforming and innovating Pope? Are they not rather such as would be used by one who condemned any attempt to modify the ancient use?

As a matter of fact, the text of these decrees as cited by Bernold is only an imperfect one, while we find them given in full by Gratian.[1] And in this full text we find that in the time of Gregory VII. some clergy were tempted by the brevity of the nocturnal office of the octaves of Easter and Pentecost. Only three psalms and three lessons! And so they were introducing the custom of abbreviating after this pattern the daily ferial office, and the office of saints' days as well.[2]

---

[1] Friedberg, tom. i. p. 1416.

[2] This attempt at shortening the ancient Roman office was, even at Rome itself, not confined to the ferial office. The office for saints' days was also shortened in conformity with that of Easter week. S. Peter Damian (*d.* 1072), speaking of the liturgy as it was immediately before the pontificate of Gregory VII., relates in one of his *Opuscula* a vision vouchsafed to a certain clerk of the basilica of S. Peter, who one night saw the Prince of the Apostles officiate in his own basilica: 'B. Petrus Apostolus ad ecclesiam suam venit, cui protinus omnium successorum suorum, pontificum scilicet Romanorum, chorus infulatus ac festivus occurrit: ipse quoque B.

Et novem lectiones dicimus [celebramus *Grat.*]. Illi autem qui in diebus cottidianis tres tantummodo psalmos et tres lectiones celebrare volunt, non ex regula SS. patrum, sed ex fastidio comprobantur hoc facere.[1]

In other words, Gregory VII. makes no account of the reasons which some of the clergy might have for retrenching the length of the office or simplifying its arrangement.

Petrus, cum eatenus videretur indutus Hebraicis vestibus, sicut in picturis ubique conspicitur, tunc et Phrygium suscepit in capite et sicut ceteri sacerdotalibus infulis est indutus in corpore. Tunc responsorium illud quod dicitur *Tu es Pastor ovium* melodiis atque mellifluis coeperunt intonare clamoribus, sicque illum usque ad sacerdotalis chori consistorium deduxerunt. Quo perveniens ipse Apostolorum Princeps nocturnum est exorsus officium, dicens *Domine, labia mea aperies*; deinde *tres psalmos totidemque lectiones ac responsoria quae in Apostolorum natalitiis recensentur* canonico more persolvit. Omnibus itaque per ordinem decursis, matutinis quoque laudibus consequenter expletis, eiusdem ecclesiae tintinnabulum sonuit et continuo presbyter qui haec videbat evigilans somnium terminavit.' (*Opusc.* xxxiv. p. ii, no. 4.) 'Blessed Peter the Apostle came to his church, and forthwith the company of all his successors in the Roman pontificate met him, robed in festal vestments. Then S. Peter himself also, who had previously appeared in Hebrew attire, as he is always represented in pictures, put the tiara on his head and assumed priestly robes like the rest. Then all, with resounding tones of surpassing sweetness, began to chant the respond, "Thou art the shepherd of the sheep," and so conducted their chief to the throne of the presbytery. And having arrived there, the Prince of the Apostles himself began the nocturnal office, saying, "O Lord, open Thou," &c.; and so in due order followed *the three psalms, three lessons, and three responds, which are wont to be said on the feasts of Apostles*. And when all had been duly gone through, and Lauds also in their turn were finished, the church bell sounded, and immediately the priest who witnessed these things awoke, and his vision was at an end.'

[1] 'Also we say nine lessons. But those who on weekdays are not willing to recite more than three psalms and three lessons are convicted of acting thus, not in accordance with the rule of the holy Fathers, but out of their aversion to divine things.'

In all this he only sees a sign of laxity, and he refuses to deal with it either by tolerating the custom which had begun to be introduced or himself inaugurating a regular reform, as the circumstances might have seemed to suggest. And he concludes :

> Nos autem et ordinem Romanum investigantes et antiquum morem nostrae ecclesiae, imitantes patres, statuimus fieri sicut superius praenotavimus.[1]

The full text, therefore, as given by Gratian is even stronger than that of Bernold. Gregory VII., as regards the Divine Office, holds fast to the *Ordo Romanus*, the old use of the Roman Church; he is determined to remain faithful to the ancient Fathers. That is how much he is disposed to innovate.

In saying this, do we mean that in the eleventh century there were not introduced into some churches at Rome new or strange customs, and that even the '*Romani palatii basilica*' as Abelard calls the chapel of the pontifical palace of the Lateran, had not bowed down to the spirit of innovation ? That is the question which is about to come before us. In the meantime, we may say that neither Bernold of Constance in the *Micrologus*, nor Gregory VII. himself in his decrees, says anything of any reform of the traditional office made at Rome, by the Popes, in the course of the eleventh century. On the contrary, they bear witness to the tenacity with which, at Rome itself, the old *Ordo Romanus* of the office was maintained, that *Ordo* which we have seen established there from the end of the eighth century, and which we

---

[1] 'We, therefore, examining into the Roman *Ordo* and the ancient use of our Church, faithfully copying the Fathers, decree that all shall be so done as we have signified above.'

have found still in full use in the latter part of the twelfth, both in the daily service of the Lateran and S. Peter's, and in the pontifical ceremonial.

II

We saw that the expression, *modernum officium* was employed by Gregory IX. in the thirteenth century; a century earlier we meet with an equivalent expression in the letter of Abelard already quoted, where we find him distinguishing between the *antiquum officium*—the term by which he very justly describes the office used in his time at the Lateran—and another use, observed both by clerks and monks, a use which is already of long standing and which is still in vogue : '*consuetudo tam clericorum quam monachorum, longe ante habita et nunc quoque permanens.*' For anyone who is familiar with the terminology of canon law, these expressions of Abelard's amount to saying that there is an ancient canon of the office, and that there is also a use which has been introduced since the promulgation of that canon, which is already of long standing, which is general, and which is in full vigour. Yet let us not suppose that this more modern use possessed anything like the unity of the *antiquum officium* : Abelard tells us immediately after that the greatest diversity existed, even among the customs used by clerks, not to speak of those of the monks : '*In Divinis officiis. . . . . diversas et innumeras Ecclesiae consuetudines inter ipsos etiam clericos.*'[1] Here then we have a definition of the Modern Office in the twelfth century as compared with the ancient Roman Office.

[1] Abelard, *Epist.* x.

Let us try and make out the general characteristics of this office—modern, and not Roman.

We possess a little liturgical treatise of the twelfth century which is for this Modern Office what the writings of Amalarius and Bernold are for the ancient and purely Roman Office. It is the *Rationale* of John Beleth. As to the author, we cannot tell whether he was of Normandy, Poitou, Paris, or Amiens. The very dates of his life are open to doubt, and we only know two things for certain about him: first, that he wrote his book at Paris, '*apud nostram Lutetiam*,' as he says; and secondly, that he was, as again he himself tells us, a contemporary of the Blessed Elizabeth of Schönau, who died in 1165.[1] The *Rationale* must, in fact, have been written between 1161 and 1165. It is a book full of learning, and written in a graceful style. It describes and comments on the Divine Office as used at Paris towards the middle of the twelfth century. This gives the author occasion to inform us that the clergy of his time were far from being as faithfully observant of that office as duty would demand. No doubt they did not go so far as to imitate those prelates and clergy of the ninth century, spoken of in the *Benedictio Dei*,[2] who sat up at night drinking until cock-crow, and then got through the nocturnal office, God only knows how, before going to bed, while the diurnal office they despatched while they were dressing. Nor were they guilty of the fault against which S. Peter Damian cautions the clergy of the eleventh

---

[1] *Hist. Litt. de la France*, tom. xiv. pp. 218–222. The actual text of the *Rationale*, as printed from the sixteenth century onward, must be viewed with caution.

[2] [See *Magna Bibliotheca Veterum Patrum*, vol. xv. pp. 1029 *sqq.* (Cologne, 1618–22): '*Commentariolus . . . a monacho, ut videtur, Ratisbonensi*' (Catal. Bodl.).—A. B.]

century, who were tempted to recite the entire office for the day at one time, in the morning, so as to be free to go about their secular business.[1] But the absence of zeal shown by John Beleth's contemporaries was no less grievous to him as a Churchman. 'Alas,' he writes, 'the very purpose and object of the Divine Service is now so completely lost sight of that scholars rise earlier than the ministers of the Church, and the sparrows begin to sing before the priests, so chilled in the heart of men is the love of God.' And in another passage: 'How many among us are found to rise joyfully with the sun to say the Divine Service? In this respect we of to-day are like Penelope's suitors, "*nati in medios dormire dies.*" And why do I speak of the *nocturnal* office? How many are there who conscientiously recite in due course the hours of the *day*? Few indeed, and very few, if the real truth be told!'[2]

The Modern Office, then—and this is the very first characteristic of it which we recognise—had to accommodate itself to this spirit of laziness on the part of the clergy, by abbreviation. Long since the antiphons had got to be only said before and after each psalm, instead of being repeated after every verse; long since the responds were reduced to having but one verse each, and one *Gloria Patri* to every three. That was a reform dating from the very introduction into France of the Roman Office. As for the double offices on saints' days, still retained by the Roman Church in the twelfth century, they had never gained a footing in the general use of the Frankish churches.[3] All this was a mere nothing: far more

[1] Pet. Dam. *Opusc.* xxxiv. 5.   [2] John Beleth, *Rationale*, 20.
[3] Amal. *De Ord. Antiph.* 60.

sweeping reforms had been attempted. In the eleventh century, as we have already seen, they wanted to cut down the nocturnal office of the season and of saints' days to three psalms and three lessons, as was the rule for the octaves of Easter and Pentecost. But such a practice was too manifestly contrary to all tradition to succeed: we have seen in what terms it was condemned by Gregory VII. But if they could not interfere with the Psalter, they might with the lectionary. The nocturnal office, beginning at cock-crow and ending at sunrise, varied in length with the season; and since the number both of psalms and lessons was fixed, and the length of the psalms unchangeable, it was only in the length of the lessons that any variation was possible. In this matter, then, the liturgy, in the very nature of things, allowed a certain latitude, of which the abbreviators took full advantage; their attention was principally directed to the lectionary. If we compare the homiliaries of the ninth century (as, for instance, that of Paul the Deacon), with those of the eleventh and twelfth, we shall see the great difference in the length of the lessons for the same festival which has come about in the lapse of two hundred years. One of the things aimed at in the reforms made by the Abbey of Cluny in the eleventh century was to re-establish the long lessons which by this time had fallen into desuetude—for instance, to make only six lessons include the whole of the Epistle to the Romans, or to read through Genesis in choir in one week. The lesson, in fact, was to be long enough to allow of one of the brethren to go round and see that nobody in the church was asleep; during the reading of one lesson he was to have time to make the round of the whole choir, and the side aisles as well.

But this use of Cluny was looked upon as singular and exaggerated: '*Audio lectiones vestras in hieme et in privatis noctibus multum esse prolixas.*'[1] The contrary custom, on the other hand, was general, and John Beleth gives it the authority of an established rule, saying that it is necessary to abridge even the narratives of the passions of martyrs.[2]

The lectionary underwent also an alteration of another kind, in regard to the material of the sermons or homilies from the Fathers which were read. In the eighth century, the Roman Church allowed the writings of no authors to be read in the nocturnal office but such as may be called the classics of the Catholic Church—'*Catholici et venerabiles patres.*' The Modern Office, on the contrary, admitted readings which were more varied, but of less authority. The writings of Origen, genuine or spurious, found their way in by the ninth century, and seem to have been much in favour. Cassian, the pseudo-Eusebius of Emesa, and Clement of Alexandria, were admitted to the honour of being read in the liturgy—in smaller quantity, it is true. More modern authors followed them. Bede abounds, and we find also Alcuin, Rabanus Maurus, Paschasius Radbert, Ambrose Ansbert, Odo of Cluny, Peter Damian, and even such recent writers as S. Bernard and Yvo of Chartres.

It was natural that the old Roman Office, introduced into France with its own Proper of the Season and of Saints, should in course of time admit new local festivals. Amalarius recognises the fact that such must needs be the case, as do liturgists generally, whether regulars or

---

[1] 'I hear that your lessons in winter and on ferias are enormously long.' Udalric, *Consuetudines,* i. 1.

[2] Ioann. Beleth, *Rationale,* 62.

seculars.[1] Thus such festivals of local saints make their appearance as those of SS. Maurice, Remigius, Boniface, Medard, &c. But other festivals were introduced of more general interest, such as the Conception of Mary (a festival of English origin, the first notice of which is found in the second quarter of the eleventh century, in connection with the Benedictine Abbey of Canterbury), and the festival of the Trinity, first established at Liège under Bishop Stephen (903-920), and, singular to relate, long disapproved by the Holy See. The following significant saying is attributed to Pope Alexander II. (1061-1073): on being asked if there ought to be a festival of the Holy Trinity, he replied that he saw no greater reason for it than for having a festival of the Unity.[2] Then there is the feast of the Transfiguration of our Lord, first found existing in Spain in the ninth century, its observance being afterwards adopted and propagated by the Abbey of Cluny, an abbot of which, Peter the Venerable (*d.* 1157), is said to have been the compiler of the office for this festival.

There is a third characteristic of this Modern Office, and that the most important. John Beleth, faithful as he is to Roman use, is obliged, in deference to the customs of Churches outside Italy, to allow the introduction of metrical hymns into the canonical Office of the secular clergy. He does it with a bad grace. 'At Vespers,' says he, 'when the five psalms [3] have been sung, a short lesson,

---

[1] Amal. *De Ord. Antiph.* 28.

[2] *Microlog.* 60; Ioann. Beleth, *Rationale*, 62.

[3] We may note here a difference, as to the Vesper psalms for festivals, between the Modern Office and the old Roman, as represented by the Antiphonary of S. Peter's. The former employed five psalms beginning with *Lauda* or *Laudate*, Pss. cxii. [cxiii.], cxvi.

the *capitulum*, is said, without *Iube Domne* and without *Tu autem*; and after the *capitulum* comes a respond.' (This is a Roman custom, mentioned in the *Micrologus*, and by Amalarius.[1]) 'Or, instead of the respond, a hymn is sung. After that comes the versicle and response, and the *Magnificat* preceded by its antiphon. But as a general rule, the *Magnificat*, which is the hymn of the Blessed Virgin Mary, is reckoned as the hymn, and no other than that is sung (*Magnificat loco hymni ponitur, ut praeterea nullus alius canatur*).'[2] Thus John Beleth, about 1165, bears witness that metrical hymns have found their way into the secular canonical Office, though he flatters himself that this feature, borrowed from the monastic liturgy, has not acquired the authority of an indispensable rule. John Beleth is ultra-conservative. Abelard, who belongs to the opposite party, in his letter to S. Bernard, about 1140, gives us clearly to understand that in the secular office of the countries north of the Alps, hymns held a much more important position than that which John Beleth would wish to assign to them, and that the entire monastic hymnal has been received into the office used by clerks: '*Ecclesia pro diversitate feriarum vel festivitatum diversis utitur*

[cxvii.], cxlv.–cxlvii. [cxlvi-cxlvii.]. The latter made use of the Sunday psalms, merely changing the last one, as in the present Roman Breviary.

[1] [In the Sarum Breviary the *capitulum* at Vespers retained its respond down to the Reformation, and in Flanders in the fifteenth century Thomas à Kempis alludes to it in a queer little story (*Serm. ad Nov.* pt. iii. serm. 8, exempl.' 2): '*Expectavit . . . horam vespertinam, de S. Agnete solemniter in choro decantandam. Cumque cantor responsorium* Pulchra facie *altius incepisset, et conventus chori . . . residuum prosequeretur*,' &c.—A. B.]

[2] Ioann. Beleth, *Rationale*, 52.

hymnis.[1] And in the term 'the Church,' he means to include the churches of the secular clergy—'*omnibus ecclesiis*,' as he says expressly—as well as conventual churches. It is even possible that in the eleventh century metrical hymns had been introduced into the office as it was actually recited in some churches at Rome, but no rigorous proof of this has yet been given.

How was the hymnal of the Church formed, and under what influence did it find its way into the Modern Office? This is the question which now lies before us.

S. Hilary of Poitiers wrote metrical hymns, and was the first to write them—'*hymnorum carmine floruit primus*'—if we may believe Isidore of Seville; but if we are to judge of his hymns by the three which survive, and which M. Gamurrini has only lately discovered, such learned but awkward compositions, written in an involved and obscure style, were not likely to be popular. Certainly they did not become so, and there is no evidence that their author wrote them for such a purpose. S. Ambrose, on the contrary, wrote popular hymns, which were not the mere verses of a scholar, like the trochaics and asclepiads of S. Hilary. Ambrose wrote good straightforward iambic dimeters—that is to say, he wrote in the metre most akin to prose. He wrote hymns full of instruction in dogma, marked at the same time by sober elegance and perfect clearness of expression. The hymns of S. Ambrose were sung all over Milan, and soon spread themselves throughout Italy and Gaul, as Faustus of Riez tells us. The title of *Ambrosian* was thenceforth given to all hymns in stanzas composed of iambic dimeters,

[1] Abelard, *Epistul.* x.

which were produced on all sides on this Christian model, the creation of S. Ambrose. The amount of authentic work in the way of hymns by this saint which has come down to us is but small; yet we must not any longer limit it to four hymns only:[1] the number of Ambrosian hymns now established as authentic may be extended to fourteen; and four others which are probably so raise the total of our collection of hymns written by S. Ambrose to eighteen. In the sixth century, the hymns in iambic dimeters, whether really written by Ambrose or only supposed to be his, formed a sort of authorised hymnal which demanded the honour of being employed liturgically in the Divine Office.

But when we search for documentary evidence of the introduction of hymns into the office, we must exercise some caution, owing to the use that for a long time was made of the word *hymnus*. In the fourth century this word was synonymous with *psalm*, and what we call a hymn was designated *carmen*. A passage often quoted from S. Jerome[2] expresses this use of the word, and one from the *Variae* of Cassiodorus[3] shows that even at that period (507-511), the word *hymnus* had not yet replaced *carmen* as designating what we call a hymn, but was still used as meaning 'psalm' in the language of Rome, and the same is the case in the language of Gregory of Tours. And this is why Canon 30 of the Council of Agde in 506, in which the word *hymnus* is used without any precise explanation of its meaning, seems to me to be speaking of

---

[1] See Dreves, *Aur. Ambros. der Vater des Kirchengesanges*, 1893.

[2] [*Comm. in Ephes.* v. 19. He applies the title *hymnus* to a particular class of psalm.—A. B.]

[3] Ed. Mommsen, p. 71.

psalms and not of hymns, and I cannot agree with M. Chevalier [1] that the said Council of Agde 'rendered the use of hymns obligatory at Mattins and Vespers,' since it is not possible to affirm that hymns, properly so called, are in question in the canon alluded to.

The Rule of S. Aurelian, Bishop of Arles (546-551), on the contrary, does show that, at least in some of the monasteries of Arles, the introduction of Ambrosian hymns into the office was then an accomplished fact. We possess the text of the *ordo psallendi* set forth under his auspices, and this text not only mentions 'a hymn' (*hymnus*) at the nocturnal vigils, at Lauds, at Prime, at Terce, at Sext, at None, and at Vespers, but also gives the first words of ten of these hymns, to which he adds the *Te Deum* for Lauds on Saturday, the *Gloria in excelsis* for Lauds on Sunday, and '*ad secundos nocturnos*' of the ferial office a hymn entitled *Magna et mirabilia*.[2] But be it observed, first, that these metrical hymns are introduced into an office which is not one for clerks, but for monks, and, secondly, that this hymnal or germ of a hymnal is composed of pieces unknown to the hymnal of the Benedictines. Moreover, Aurelian, Bishop of Arles, does not seem to have been the first author of this introduction of hymns into the monastic office: one of his predecessors in the see of Arles, S. Caesarius (*b.* 470, *d.* 542), also put forth a Rule for monks in which their *ordo psallendi* is described; and this *ordo* already includes hymns, six of them being specified by their first words,

---

[1] *Poésie Liturgique* (Tournai, 1894), p. x.

[2] I believe that this hymn may be identified with the little prose composition published by Tommasi, tom. ii. p. 404, *Magna et mirabilia opera tua sunt, Domine.*

and four out of these six are among the ten enumerated by Aurelian. It would not be easy to deny that Aurelian is following Caesarius in this matter. Caesarius himself in turn is following the customs in use at Lerins:

> Ordinem etiam quomodo psallere debeatis, ex maxima parte secundum regulam monasterii Lyrinensis in hoc libello iudicavimus inserendum,

says the text of the Rule of S. Caesarius.[1] We may, then, assert that the introduction of Ambrosian hymns into the Divine Office was a monastic custom already received at Lerins and at Arles in the first half of the sixth century. Exactly at the same epoch, S. Benedict, when putting forth the *Ordo* of the office for his monks, assigns a place in it for the ' hymni Ambrosiani.'

The custom of singing hymns in the office gradually spread itself in Gaul round Arles and Lerins, but the progress was slow. A Council held in 567 shows us this custom seeking to gain a footing in the province of Tours, and the bishops offering no opposition : ' *Licet hymnos Ambrosianos habeamus in canone* . . . :' and not only the hymns of S. Ambrose, but others also ' *qui digni sunt forma cantari.*' These the bishops accept : ' *volumus libenter amplecti eos praeterea,*' provided only that the names of their authors are known. We cannot say that the bishops of the province of Tours show any great zeal for the propagation of the hymnal. And the Council of Braga, in 563, proscribes it without mercy : ' . . . *extra psalmos . . . nihil poetice compositum in ecclesia psallatur.*'

In the seventh century we remark that, if the use of the hymnal is spreading, it has not conquered all resist-

[1] *Poésie Liturgique*, p. xi.

ance. Canon 13 of the fourth Council of Toledo, in 633, threatens with excommunication those who dare to reject hymns, telling us at the same time that there are some who disapprove of hymns, even those of S. Hilary and S. Ambrose, on the ground that they are compositions foreign to the Holy Scriptures and the Apostolic tradition. The Council does not admit that hymns are to be rejected, any more than the collects and the *Gloria in excelsis*, and it concludes : '*Hymnos in laudem Dei compositos nullus vestrum ulterius improbet, sed pari modo Gallia Hispaniaque celebret.*'[1] One might believe, on the faith of this council, that Gaul and Spain are at one in decreeing the introduction of the hymnal into the office, and that those who refused to conform to this custom are few and of little account, but such a conclusion can only be accepted with considerable reservations. The *Cursus Gallicanus* (that is to say, the Gallican liturgy) in most churches did not really include the hymnal. We quoted just now Canon 23 of the Council of Tours in 567, which concedes permission to sing hymns by known authors ; but it is worthy of remark that Canon 18 of the same Council, which gives the order of the office for the basilica of S. Martin and the churches of Tours, does not mention hymns, but only antiphons and psalms. Nor is there any notice of metrical hymns in the *De cursu stellarum* of Gregory of Tours, which includes a curious *ordo psallendi*. Here *hymnus* is still synonymous with 'psalm.' Nor is there any question of metrical hymns in the works of S. German of Paris (*b.* 496, *d.* 576). At Vienne and at Lyons we know for certain that they were repudiated. Would it be too rash a generalisation to say that in the land of the Franks the office of the secular clergy

[1] *Poésie Liturgique*, p. xv.

THE MODERN OFFICE AND THE BREVIARIES 187

remained closed against the introduction of hymns, while in the south of Gaul and in Spain they were accepted, in imitation of the monastic uses?

This state of things was not modified by the introduction into France of the Roman Office in the time of Charlemagne. Leidrad, Archbishop of Lyons (798–814), writing to Charlemagne, reports to that prince that he has restored the Divine Office: '*in Lugdunensi ecclesia est ordo psallendi instauratus*': that he has done so in conformity with the liturgy of the Imperial palace, *i.e.* the Roman liturgy, '*secundum ritum sacri palatii*': and that he has instituted schools for chanters: '*habeo scholas cantorum ex quibus plerique ita sunt eruditi ut alios etiam erudire possint.*'[1] But did the office thus restored by Leidrad include metrical hymns? Not so. Agobard,[2] in fact, when he reproaches Amalarius for having dared to alter the text of the Roman Office received in France, goes so far as to reprove him even for having introduced antiphons and responds the words of which were not taken from Holy Scripture:

> Sed et reverenda concilia Patrum decernunt nequaquam plebeios psalmos in ecclesia decantandos, et nihil poetice compositum in Divinis laudibus usurpandum.[3]

On this point Agobard appeals to the ordinances of the Council of Laodicea and that of Braga; and in his book '*De Correctione Antiphonarii*' he returns to the same point with fresh insistence: he could hardly have attacked with such vehemence the introduction into the office of non-Biblical prose if the office of his own Church had included metrical hymns. And, independently of this, we know that

---

[1] Migne, *Patr. Lat.* tom. xcix. p. 871.
[2] [Archbishop of Lyons, died A.D. 840.—A.B.]
[3] Agob. *De Divina Psalmod.* 104, col. 327.

the office of Amalarius did not include such hymns, being in this respect in agreement with the traditional use alike of Lyons, the Imperial chapel, and the Roman Church.

In fact, when the hymnal did find its way into the office of the Frankish Churches, it did so *en bloc*, just as it was then in use in the monasteries of the order of S. Benedict.

This hymnal of the Benedictines was originally composed of hymns, metrical or rhythmical, which were styled Ambrosian: that was the kernel of the hymnal, a kernel formed in the sixth century. The Carolingian renaissance adorned it with pieces selected from Prudentius, Sedulius, and Venantius Fortunatus, and enriched it with the compositions of poet monks like Paul the Deacon and Rabanus Maurus. This anthology, compiled by monks, remained the property of the monks.

At the end of the eighth century and the beginning of the ninth, under the triumphant influence of the Roman Church, which was opposed to the admission of the hymnal into its liturgy, it seemed as if metrical hymns were going to be altogether proscribed and banished from ecclesiastical use. A number even of monasteries among the Franks, in their zeal for perfect agreement with the Roman liturgy, renounced them.[1] There was a moment, at the end of the eighth century, when hymns might almost be looked on as generally abandoned by clerks, and even by monks, with the exception of some abbeys, like Monte Cassino and Fulda, where they still sang them and still composed them, as Paul the Deacon and Rabanus Maurus testify. But this state of things lasted but for a

[1] Columban, *Reg. Coenob.* No. 7; Lup. Ferrar. *Epistul.* ciii.; Paul. Diac. *Epistul.* i.

moment. That influence of Rome in the direction of promoting uniformity in liturgical matters beyond the Alps soon came to an end. Already, in the first half of the ninth century, a monk of Fulda, Walafrid Strabo, who died abbot of Reichenau in 849, tells us that many Churches north of the Alps had taken up the hymnal: '*quamvis in quibusdam ecclesiis hymni metrici non cantentur*,' he writes.[1] Soon after this—that is to say, dating from the pontificate of John VIII. (872-882)—there begins for the Holy See a melancholy period of eclipse, servitude, and impotence. Latin Christendom is in travail of a new order of things; the Carolingian empire has disappeared; the feudal system, and the crumbling away of all centralisation which accompanied it, naturally produced a condition of anarchy as regards ecclesiastical customs, which was aggravated and consecrated by the rivalry between different Churches. But at the very moment when the star of Rome was eclipsed, and the Italian, German and Frankish Churches involved themselves in the feudal system, the presage and the means of their worst period of debasement, there appeared the new power which was destined to repair all this ruin, and this power was that of the Benedictine abbey of Cluny (A.D. 910). The influence of Cluny on the reform of the Church in the tenth and eleventh centuries was capital and decisive, and in its wide extent did not fail to include the liturgy. We shall have many proofs to give of this, but one proof at all events is the general adoption of the hymnal, and that hymnal in all respects identical with that of the Benedictines.

---

[1] Walaf. Strab. *De Rebus Eccl.* 25.

The modification of the Kalendar, the abbreviation of the lectionary, and the adoption of the monastic hymnal, are the three most salient characteristics of this non-Roman Modern Office. It remains for us to note some other details which were features of this office, and for which it secured general adoption—viz. the Creed *Quicunque vult*, the suffrages which we call *Commemorationes*,[1] the Little Office of our Lady, and the Office for the Dead.

The question of the origin of the *Quicunque vult* is one of those which have been most constantly debated for the last two hundred years without arriving at any clear conclusion. On the one hand, it is indisputably not the work of S. Athanasius; it is also certain that it is of Latin, or, to speak more precisely, of Gallican origin. But on the other hand, the date at which it was put forth is a matter on which people find it very hard to agree. Some critics of our own time have seen in it a work of the time of Charlemagne or Charles the Bald; others, a work of the sixth century; some date it back as far as the fifth. Harnack recognises two distinct portions in it: the first devoted to the doctrine of the Trinity, the second occupied entirely with the Incarnation. He thinks the first part, which, according to him, is the outcome of the theology of S. Augustine and of Vincent of Lerins, must have been a profession of faith in use among the clerks and monks of Southern Gaul, who came in contact with the Arian Visigoths of Spain: which

---

[1] [Otherwise called *Memoriae*, Memories, or Memorials, and comprising an antiphon, versicle, response, and collect; appended to Lauds and Vespers, and sometimes to the Little Hours of the day.— A. B.]

would carry us back to the fifth century and the first half of the sixth. The clerks learnt it by heart, just as they learnt the Psalter. The most ancient mention we find of the *Quicunque vult* is in a decree of a Council at Autun about the year 670 :

> Si quis presbyter, diaconus, subdiaconus, vel clericus symbolum quod inspirante S. Spiritu Apostoli tradiderunt, et fidem S. Athanasii praesulis, irreprehensibiliter non recensuerit, ab episcopo condemnetur.[1]

As for the purely Christologic portion of the *Quicunque vult*, Harnack considers that its origin is involved in obscurity. It cannot, however, but be 'anterior to the ninth century,'[2] and, we may add, probably older than the eighth.

This old Gallican Creed, which we find in the most ancient Psalters of that Church, written at the end of the psalms and canticles, was not received into the liturgy at Rome. Neither Amalarius nor the *Micrologus* mentions it. A Creed was indeed recited in the Roman office at Prime, but it was the Apostles' Creed—'*credulitas nostra quam SS. Apostoli constituerunt*'—as Amalarius says.[3]

In the Frankish Churches, on the contrary, the *Quicunque vult* was very popular. Hincmar, in 852, enjoins his clergy at Rheims to know it by heart and to be prepared to expound it like a catechism,[4] though he does not give us to understand that this '*sermo Athanasii de fide, cuius initium est Quicunque vult*,' as he calls it, has any place in the Divine Office. Hayto, Bishop of Basle (*d.* 836), on the contrary, imposes on his clergy

---

[1] Mansi, tom. xi. p. 125.
[2] Harnack, *Dogmengeschichte* (Fribourg, 1894), tom. ii.³ p. 296.
[3] Amal. *De Eccl. Off.* iv. 2.   [4] Hincmar, *Capitular.* 2.

the obligation, not only of knowing it by heart, but of reciting it every Sunday at Prime: '*Fides S. Athanasii . . . omni die Dominico ad horam primam recitetur.*'[1] In the eleventh century there was no part of the Church north of the Alps where the *Quicunque vult* was not recited at Prime, at least every Sunday; and in most churches not only on Sundays, but at Prime every day. John of Avranches, Archbishop of Rouen (*d.* 1079), and more especially Ulric of Cluny (*d.* 1087) do not leave us in any doubt as to this custom. The latter writes:

> Textus fidei, a S. Athanasio conscriptus, cuius nonnullae ecclesiae nec meminerint nisi in sola Dominica, nullo die obmittatur—

thus showing us how, here again, the use of Cluny becomes that of the majority of Churches outside Italy.[2]

Passing on to the common memorials or suffrages, we note that Amalarius never prescribes, either at Lauds or Vespers, any memorial of the Blessed Virgin or of any Saint. Nor is there any trace of such in the pontifical ceremonial described by the Roman Canon Benedict at the beginning of the twelfth century. But, on the other hand, both the Antiphonary of S. Peter's (twelfth century) and Canon Benedict prescribe a memorial *of the Cross*, to be made both at Lauds and Vespers in Paschal-tide:

> In omnibus laudibus et vespertinis horis, fit commemoratio Passionis Christi et Resurrectionis, antiphona *Crucem Sanctam* et *Noli flere* cum versibus et orationibus suis.[3]

John of Avranches bears witness that this memorial of the Cross was also prescribed on the other side of the

---

[1] Migne, *Patr. Lat.* tom. cxv. p. 11.
[2] Udalric, *Consuetud.* i. 2; cf. Jo. Abrin. *De Off. Eccl.* p. 5.
[3] Bened. 55; cf. Tommasi, tom. iv. p. 100.

Alps for the whole of Paschal-tide.¹ But while at Rome the memorial of the Cross stood alone at that season, at Rouen there are added the memorials of the Blessed Virgin and of All Saints. At Rome, according to the Antiphonary of S. Peter's, these two latter memorials, with the addition of one of SS. Peter and Paul, were said at the end of Lauds and Vespers every day in the year, except from Passion Sunday to Whitsun Day, and in the season of Christmas.² These common memorials of the Blessed Virgin and the Saints at the end of Lauds and Vespers were in general use in the churches north of the Alps, both monastic and secular. Ulric of Cluny prescribes them under the title of *suffragia sanctorum*.³ John of Avranches enumerates a dozen of them: the Virgin Mary, All Saints, the Holy Angels, S. John Baptist, S. Peter, S. John Evangelist, the Apostles, S. Stephen, the Martyrs, S. Martin, the Confessors, the Virgins. But he notes that none of these memorials are to be used during Lent. It appears that the use of common memorials is originally a custom of the monastic churches beyond the Alps, not imported into Rome until the eleventh century. The first Roman mention of it is in the *Micrologus*.

In the third place we come to the Little Office of our Lady.

Here again we have monastic influence triumphing over secular custom. The most ancient mention of this daily office of the Blessed Virgin is of the eleventh century, and comes from the Italian abbey of Fons

---

[1] Jo. Abrin. *op. cit.* p. 29.
[2] Tommasi tom. iv. pp. 22, 27, 30, 52, 100.
[3] Udalric, *Consuetud.* i. 2.

Avellanus, founded in 1019 by Ludolf, Bishop of Eugubium, as a Benedictine community, the brethren being, however, as much hermits as monks. The institution of this office is generally attributed (following Cardinal Baronius[1]) to S. Peter Damian, who, before being made Cardinal and Bishop of Ostia, belonged to Fons Avellanus; but this attribution is not clearly established. What is certain is that S. Peter Damian is the first to speak of this office. Writing to the monks of S. Barnabas at Gamugno, a monastery of the same congregation as Fons Avellanus, he relates that the rule of daily reciting the Office of our Lady had been established in the Monastery of S. Vincent, near to Petra Pertusa:

> Statutum erat atque iam per triennium fere servatum, ut cum horis canonicis quotidie B. Mariae semper Virginis officia dicerentur.

Then, at the instigation of a bad monk, it was given up on the pretext that its recitation constituted an additional obligation, which was both novel and burdensome. But scarcely had they given it up when temptations, storms, robbers, and all the worst calamities imaginable poured down on the convent.[2] This happened about 1056. Elsewhere, in his *opusculum* on the canonical hours, S. Peter Damian recommends the recitation of the Office of the Blessed Virgin as an additional exercise, very well calculated to ensure the final perseverance of the clergy, and to give them consolation in their last moments. And he takes this opportunity of relating the story of a poor clerk, who had

---

[1] Baronius, *Annales*, tom. xvii. p. 119.
[2] Petr. Damian. *Epistul.* viii. 32.

sinned long and grievously in his life, and who, at his last hour, not knowing to what good work he could point, was only able to remind the Virgin Mary, 'Gate of Heaven, and Window of Paradise,' with what faithfulness he had recited her office every day : ' Seven times a day I have set forth thy praises, and, unworthy sinner as I am, I have never, in the Divine Service of the canonical hours, defrauded thee of the homage which is thy due.' It is what S. Peter Damian calls ' *quotidiana canonicis horis officia in Mariae laudibus frequentare.*[1] And he assures us that the mercy of God was gained for that sinful clerk through the intercession of the Virgin whom he had so devoutly served. In another passage again— this time in the Life of S. Peter Damian by his disciple the monk John—we have a whole chapter devoted to telling us with what zeal the holy cardinal laboured for the salvation of souls, by his devotion to the Cross and to the Blessed Virgin, and how he applied himself especially to the promotion, among the cold and lax secular clergy of his time, of the custom of reciting daily that Office of our Lady which the monks of the congregation of Fons Avellanus were wont to recite: ' *Omnium horarum officia, in honore almae Dei Genitricis in pluribus ecclesiis [instituit].*'[2]

Dom Mittarelli published, in 1756, the text of 'The Office of the Blessed Virgin Mary after the use of the monks of the monastery of the Holy Cross at Fons Avellanus,' from a MS. of about the twelfth century.[3] The office comprises Vespers, the Nocturn with its invitatory, Lauds, Prime, Terce, Sext, None and Com-

[1] Petr. Damian. *Opusc.* x. 10.
[2] Migne, *Patr. Lat.* tom. cxliv. p. 132. [3] *Ib.* tom. cli. pp. 970-4.

pline. There is but one nocturn of three lessons, each of only a few lines in length. Here we have the Office of our Lady as practised in Italy in the time of S. Peter Damian. But at Rome itself such an office was, long after this time, still unknown; the Antiphonary of S. Peter's has no trace of it, and the first mention we find of it at Rome goes no further back than the pontificate of Innocent III. (1198–1216).[1]

Fourthly, and last, we come to the Office of the Dead.

The Penitentials of Theodore of Canterbury (*d.* 690), and Egbert of York (*d.* 766), which are both based on Roman use in the seventh century, bear witness that at that period there was no vigil of the dead at Rome. 'According to the Church of Rome,' so we read in them, 'the custom is to carry the dead to the church, to anoint his breast with chrism, and to say Mass for him; then to carry him to the grave with chanting (*cum cantatione portare ad sepulturam*), and when he has been laid in the tomb to say a prayer over him. Mass is said for him on the day of burial itself, on the third, ninth, and thirtieth day after, and on the anniversary if it is desired.'[2] That is all, and there is no question of a vigil of any kind. This is in the seventh century.

To find the Office of the Dead established we must come down to the eighth century and to the time of Amalarius. Then only alongside of the *ordo sepulturae* do we find a real canonical Office for the Dead, *officium pro mortuis*.[3] The Antiphonary of S. Peter's and the

---

[1] Radulph. *De Canon. Observ.* 20.
[2] Theod. *Paenit.* 5; Egbert, *Paenit.* i. 36.
[3] Amal. *De Ord. Antiph.* 65, 79.

Ordines Romani[1] give us both its text and its rubrics. The body of the departed has been brought in the evening to the basilica, say of S. Peter. They have traversed, amid the tolling of bells, the fore-court of the church, and they have stopped at the threshold of that one of its five doors which is called 'Gate of Judgment' (*porta iudicii*), because it is the door of the dead; there they have chanted the psalm *Miserere*, with two antiphons:

> Qui cognoscis omnium occulta, a delicto meo munda me. Tempus mihi concede ut repaenitens clamem, 'Peccavi Tibi.'
> Induc eum, Domine, in montem haereditatis Tuae, et in sanctuarium quod praeparaverunt manus Tuae, Domine.[2]

The door has been opened, the body has been brought into the 'sanctuary,' and the office begins. It is a vigil, in the full and true sense of the term, and, like every such vigil, includes Vespers, three Nocturns, and Lauds. Here we have the genuine office of the Roman clergy, clear of all monastic influence. The Vespers have their five psalms with antiphons, the versicle and response, the *Magnificat* with its antiphon, the *Kyrie eleison*, and the Lord's Prayer. No hymn, no short lesson: it is entirely the Roman Office in its purest state. The three nocturns begin without the invitatory psalm: there is no place for *Venite exultemus* in a funeral vigil. Each nocturn includes three psalms with antiphons, and three lessons from the book of Job, each lesson being followed by a

---

[1] Mabillon, *Mus. Ital.* tom. ii. pp. 155 sqq. (*Ordo X*).
[2] Tommasi, tom. iv. p. 163. 'Thou who knowest the secrets of all hearts, cleanse Thou me from my sin. Grant me time to cry in penitence "Against Thee have I sinned." '—'Bring him in, O Lord, to the mountain of Thine inheritance, even to the sanctuary which Thine hands have prepared, O Lord.'

respond, also taken from the same book. The ninth respond is *Ne recorderis peccata mea*: our admirable *Libera me, Domine*, does not belong to the Roman Office of the time of Charlemagne. The Nocturns are followed by Lauds: five psalms with antiphons, the versicle and response, the *Benedictus* with its antiphon, the *Kyrie eleison*, and the Lord's Prayer. The vigil of the dead is ended: in the morning Mass will be sung before the body, and followed by the *diaconia*, or *absolutio* as it was afterwards called. Then comes the burial.

This pathetic office for the vigil of the dead, having been created at Rome at the beginning of the eighth century at latest, was received at the same time as the rest of the canonical Roman Office by the Frankish Churches, before the end of the same century. No essential modification was introduced; beyond the Alps it remained what the Roman liturgy had made it, and, what is most noticeable, in all ages without hymns. But instead of being, as it was at Rome, only an accompaniment of solemn obsequies, the prelude to the '*sacrificium pro dormitione*,' or Mass at the burial, it was considered as the necessary complement of every solemn Mass for the dead, whether on the day of burial, the anniversary, or at other times. From this the vigil of the dead got in time to be celebrated daily, both in monasteries, and by the chapters of the secular clergy, and even in parish churches. '*Agenda mortuorum per totum annum celebratur*,' writes John of Avranches.[1] At Cluny the Vespers of the dead were said after Vespers of the day, and Lauds of the dead after Lauds. As for the Nocturns

---

[1] Jo. Abrin. *De Off. Eccl.* p. 71.

of the dead, they were recited every night after supper, in choir:

> Post coenam cum psalmo L. [Miserere] in ecclesiam reditur . . .; agitur officium vel quod a nostratibus vigilia vulgo appellatur . . .; ipsum quoque officium nunquam agitur modo, nisi cum novem lectionibus et responsoriis, et collectis quae ipsum officium sequuntur.[1]

It is, as we see, the entire nocturnal office, with its nine psalms, nine lessons, and nine responds. The writings of S. Peter Damian furnish us with proof that this daily Office of the Dead was, in the eleventh century, practised in Italy just as it was in France, and that certain clergy, who found it too heavy a burden to recite both the canonical Office of the day and the Office of the Dead, even confined themselves to the latter, as being shorter and simpler. He relates the story of 'a certain brother' who was accustomed to say neither the Office of the Season nor of saints' days, but only the Office of the Dead. Well, he died, and as soon as he appeared before the tribunal of God, the devils made accusation against him with vehemence, that, neglecting the rule of the ecclesiastical state, he had refused to render to God His due, in the matter of the Divine Service. But the Virgin Mary and along with the Blessed Queen of the world, all the choirs of saints intervened, to save the soul of this friend of the dead.[2] So at least the story was told to S. Peter Damian by a tender-hearted visionary, his friend

---

[1] Udalric, *Consuetud.* i. 3.

[2] Petr. Damian. *Opusc.* xxxiv. pt. 2. No. 5. Similarly, in the thirteenth century, as Salimbenus tells us: '*Item iste Patriarcha [Antiochenus] parvae litteraturae fuit, sed recompensabat hunc defectum in aliis bonis quae faciebat: nam largus eleemosynarius fuit, et cotidie cum IX lectionibus officium defunctorum dicebat*' (Salimb. ad annum 1247).—'This patriarch of Antioch was illiterate, but he

the Bishop of Cumae, not that either of them had any intention of encouraging the daily recitation of the Office of the Dead to the prejudice of the canonical hours, '*eclesiasticae institutionis regulam.*'

Here is another legend of the same period. A pilgrim of Aquitaine, returning from Jerusalem, lost his way one day, and found himself close to a barren and desolate little islet, inhabited by a hermit. This holy man extended hospitality to the wandering pilgrim, and asked him, since he belonged to Aquitaine, if he knew a monastery called Cluny, and its abbot, Odilo. The pilgrim replied that he did. 'Listen, then,' said the hermit; 'in this place we are quite close to the regions where the souls of sinners undergo the temporal penalty of sins committed on earth; and from where we are we can hear them lamenting that the faithful, and, in particular the monks of Cluny, are so niggardly as to offering up prayers for the mitigation of their sufferings and their release from them. In God's name, good pilgrim, if you ever get back to your country, seek out the abbot of Cluny, and beseech him, from me, to redouble—both he and his congregation—their prayers, vigils, and almsgivings, for the deliverance of these souls in pain, and so increase the joy of heaven and the grief of the devil.' On hearing this from the pilgrim, S. Odilo (*d.* 1049) ordained that, in all the monasteries of his congregation, the morrow of the feast of All Saints should be devoted to the commemoration of all the faithful departed [1]—one more liturgical

made up for this defect by the good he did in other ways: for he was a liberal almsgiver, and every day said the Office of the Dead, with all nine lessons.'

[1] Jotsald, *Vita Odil.* ii. 13; Udalric, *Consuetud.* i. 42.

creation of the abbey of Cluny, propagated thence throughout the West, and finally received at Rome: one more proof, the last we shall give, of the preponderating influence of Cluny on the formation of the '*Modernum Officium.*'

It remains for us to see how it was that this 'Modern Office,' which we have shown to be nothing but a transformation of the Roman Office of the time of Charlemagne effected by the Churches north of the Alps, was finally introduced at Rome itself.

III

We have reached the period of that liturgical evolution which took place at Rome in the thirteenth century, and which was destined to give birth to the Breviary of the Roman *Curia*. In other words, what we have now to relate is the manner in which there was formed a *breviary* of that Modern Office which we have just described, and how this breviary was adopted by the Popes, by the *Curia*, and eventually even by the churches of Rome.

The daily recitation of the Divine Office implied that the clergy—who by this time were *individually* bound to this recitation—had in their possession the text of that Office; and this text constituted an immense mass of writing. The psalmody properly so called required a Psalter and an Antiphonary; the responds, a Responsoral or *liber responsalis*; the lessons, a Bible, or '*Bibliotheca*,' as it was often called, also an Homiliary or *Sermologus*, and a *Passionarium* or book of the passions of the saints; to these books we may add a *Collectarium* or book of collects, a Hymnal, and a Martyrology. Some of these numerous books might themselves extend over several volumes.[1] It was well if monasteries and chapters had no difficulty in procuring and keeping up such a voluminous and costly collection. But how about the poorer religious houses, the country parish churches, the poor clergy? There was clearly a pressing necessity, now that the recitation of the Divine Office had become a duty incumbent on all the clergy, to make it easier to each of them. Hence proceeded a series of attempts at codification, which at last resulted in the production of a breviary of the entire office.

When we run over the ancient catalogues of monastic or chapter libraries of the tenth, eleventh, and twelfth centuries, we are struck by the appearance—in the eleventh century—of a new class of books.[2] The *libri responsales*, such as we should meet with at Rome in the eighth century, have disappeared: but we meet with frequent mention of *libri nocturnales* or *libri matutinales*. These collections we find generally to be in three volumes, and most of them without note (*absque cantu*). They contain the lessons, both of the season and for saints' days, for the whole year, and each lesson is accompanied by its respond. To these are sometimes added the psalms and antiphons of the Nocturns. Finally, united to all these, we find, not only the *collectarium*, but everything pertaining to the nocturnal office (Mattins and Lauds), and even in addition to these, the Little Hours of the day, and Vespers. Thus we have liturgical collections answering to the following description :

---

[1] Ioann. Beleth. *Rationale*, 60.
[2] G. Becker, *Catalogi Bibliothec. Antiq.* (Bonn, 1885).

> Libri nòcturnales absque cantu, primus ab Adventu Domini usque ad Pascha, secundus a Pascha usque ad Adventum Domini, tertius de Sanctis per anni circulum; cum psalterio et ymnario officiali—

or more briefly:

> Ordo cantandi et legendi per circulum anni, in tribus voluminibus.

These liturgical collections are still to be found in goodly number among the MSS. preserved in our libraries: they are generally of the eleventh and twelfth centuries, some even of the thirteenth. The modern catalogues, whose compilers have not always been sufficiently well up in the distinctions to be observed in liturgical bibliography, describe them indifferently as Lectionaries, Antiphonaries, or even as Breviaries: but no one of these descriptions exactly suits them.

We needly hardly say that these collections were very voluminous, since they gave the entire text of the canonical Office. They were emphatically *choir* books: for saying the office out of choir something different was needed, and they succeeded in producing for this purpose a little book, capable of being suspended to a clerk's girdle by a ring. From the *liber nocturnalis pleniter scriptus*[1] they eliminated the psalter: the clergy knew all the 150 psalms by heart. There remained the Office of the Season and of Saints' days: it was thought sufficient to write down merely the first words of each antiphon, verse, or respond, as constant use was sure to have taught a clerk the whole passage. As for the lessons, they abridged them so far as to give but a few lines of

---

[1] Becker, p. 252.

each. So we have, alongside of the ponderous *libri nocturnales* for the choir, little books, which are not a mere compression of the former, but abridgments, '*epitomata sive breviaria*,' as a catalogue of the end of the eleventh century calls them.[1] And thus, at this period, name and thing together, appears the Breviary of the Divine Office.

In reality, however, the word was already 300 years old. Alcuin (*d.* 804) had been the author of an abridgment of the Divine Office, which he dedicated to the Emperor Charlemagne, and of which a copy is extant, written specially for Charles the Bald. But this book has hardly anything in common with the office of the clergy, and what is more, was not written for their use. Alcuin himself in his preface takes care to point out that clerks and monks have their own canonical hours, and that what he has been asked to do is to put forth a shorter office for the laity living in the world :

> Rogastis ut scriberemus vobis breviarium commatico sermone qualiter homo laicus, qui adhuc in activa vita consistit, per dinumeratas horas has Deo supplicari debeat.

Alcuin assigns to each day of the week a number of psalms ; these psalms are grouped together according to their connection with a mystical subject which is different for each day: on Monday, thankfulness to God; on Tuesday, contrition; on Friday, the Passion of our Saviour, and so forth. Each psalm is followed by a collect. Each day has also a Litany of the Saints, these litanies being so arranged as to comprise between them in the six days the principal saints in the whole martyro-

[1] Becker, p. 174.

logy. There are no lessons from Holy Scripture, still less from the Fathers or from the Lives of the Saints. At the end of the psalmody there are some beautiful prayers or *elevationes,* taken from S. Augustine, S. Ambrose, S. Cyprian, S. Gregory the Great, Bede, &c., and also some metrical hymns, such as the *Pange lingua gloriosi praelium certaminis,* or the *Christe caelestis medicina Patris.* The Breviary, then, of Alcuin was not an abridgment of the Roman or of the Gallican Office of the eighth century; it was merely a book of prayers for the laity, pious, learned, and diversified, made to suit a liturgical fancy on the part of his prince. But this experiment of Alcuin's, though it remained isolated and provoked no imitation, brought into liturgical use a certain word, the word Breviary.[1]

In the language of Alcuin—that is, in the ninth century—this word still retains its most general meaning, and therefore generally requires for its determination the addition of a second word. They used the phrase *Breviarium psalterii* to designate the little psalter, or collection of selected verses from the psalms, compiled by S. Prudentius, Bishop of Troyes (*d.* 861). At the same period the inventory of the books of the monastery of S. Gall is called *Breviarium librorum,* just as in the next century that of the books of the abbey of Lorsch is called *Breviarium codicum.* Even in the eleventh century the word has not assumed the peculiar and exclusively liturgical acceptation which it was eventually to retain, since we find the expression *Breviarium* or *Adbreviatio computi* as the designation of an exposition of the 'com-

[1] Migne, *Patr. Lat.*, tom. ci. pp. 1383-1416.

potus': and '*Breviarium id est de computo*' as the title of a MS. of the cathedral of Puy in the eleventh century.[1] But after the end of this century the use of the word Breviary is exclusively liturgical.

This new word, at the time when it came into liturgical use, in the eleventh and twelfth centuries, denoted a thing which was newer still, and of which the ultimate results were no doubt at first quite unforeseen. The office as contained in these *epitomata sive breviaria* was, at least as regards the lessons, considerably shorter than that found in the *libri nocturnales*:[2] and these *epitomata sive breviaria* were not meant for the use of clergy taking part in the Divine Service in choir, but for reciting the office out of choir, in their own rooms, or when travelling. Among the books in the possession of the cathedral of Durham in the twelfth century is one called a Breviary, which fully bears out this, for it is described as a little travelling Breviary (*breviarium parvum itinerarium*).[3] In the thirteenth century (1227) a Council at Treves authorises the clergy to make use of breviaries of the office when travelling:

> Breviaria in quibus possint horas suas legere, quando sunt in itinere.[4]

Thus, by way of toleration, was introduced the use of an office differing from that said in choir, contained in books styled *breviaria itineraria* or *breviaria portatilia*.[5]

---

[1] [The whole body of rules for finding the movable feasts was called *Computus* or *Compotus*.—A. B.]

[2] '*Nocturnale breve totius anni*,' we read in a Cassinensian catalogue (Becker, p. 240).

[3] Becker, p. 244.   [4] Roskovány, tom. v. p. 58.

[5] Martene, *Thesaurus Nov. Anecd.* tom. iv. p. 1757.

What happened next was that the use of such books spread rapidly, and that this shortened office ousted from the choir that which was ancient and traditional.

The influence of the pontifical *Curia* on this movement of transformation was great and decisive. The Pope and the clergy of the *Curia* recited the daily office in private. Moreover, the movements from place to place of the Pope and his train were continual. The Pope's chapel, therefore, could not be tied down to the canonical Office as said in choir. A liturgist of the latter part of the fourteenth century, very learned, and greatly in love with Roman customs, Raoul de Rivo, who was provost of Tongres in the diocese of Liège, and died in 1403, instructs us as to the peculiar use of the pontifical chapel. 'Formerly,' he writes, 'when the Roman Pontiffs were residing at the Lateran, the Roman Office was observed in their chapel; but less completely than in the collegiate churches of the city of Rome. The clerks of the Papal chapel, whether of their own accord or by order of the Pontiff, always abridged the Roman Office, and often modified it in other ways, to suit the convenience of the Pope and the cardinals.'[1] Thus, even before the Popes had left Rome for Avignon, the *Curia* had an office different from that of the churches of the city of Rome, both as regards its length and its rubrics. Raoul de Rivo goes on to settle the date at which this use of the Roman *Curia* originated. Not only, he tells us, is it anterior to the time of Clement V. (1305-1314), but it goes back at least as far as Innocent III. (1198-1216); for, he adds, 'I have seen at

[1] Radulph. *De Canon. Observ.* p. 22. We cite the treatise of Raoul de Rivo from the *Maxima Bibliotheca Patrum* (Lyons, 1677) tom. xxvi. pp. 289-320.

Rome an *ordinarium* of this palatine office which was compiled in the time of Innocent III.' This testimony is very important, Raoul being an accurate liturgist, who had consulted and examined, at Rome itself, the office books of several churches—'*Romae plura ex diversis ecclesiis et libris scriptitavi*'—and the testimony is definite:

> Clerici capellares . . . officium Romanum semper breviabant, et saepe alterabant, prout Domino Papae et Cardinalibus congruebat observandum, et huius officii *Ordinarium* vidi Romae a tempore Innocentii III. recollectum.

Moreover, there are several things which confirm this testimony: we find, in fact, traces of rubrics, and those, too, of importance, which bear the name of Innocent III. and which appear to belong to a general reorganisation of the office. Thus the introduction of the daily office of the Virgin and of the departed into the canonical Office is attributed to Innocent III.; so are the rubrics concerning the recitation of the penitential and gradual psalms in Lent.[1] This seems to give us a right to affirm that Innocent III. made rules for the recitation of the office by the *Curia*, and to indulge a hope that some day a MS. copy may be found of this first edition of the pontifical breviary.

We may even define within narrower limits the time when this new *ordinarium* of the office was established. We have a bull of Innocent III., dated May 25, 1205: Baldwin, who had been made Emperor of Constantinople on May 9, 1204, wrote to the Pope, asking him for 'Missals, Breviaries, and other books, containing the

[1] Radulph. pp. 20-22.

THE MODERN OFFICE AND THE BREVIARIES 209

ecclesiastical Office according to the use of the Holy Roman Church':

> Postulavit missalia, breviaria, caeterosque libros, in quibus officium ecclesiasticum secundum instituta S. Romanae ecclesiae continetur.

And the Pope makes inquiry among the bishops of France, in order that they may be good enough to procure for the Emperor the books which he asks for: '*ut Orientalis Ecclesia in Divinis laudibus ab Occidentali non dissonet.*'[1] If there had been at Rome, in 1205, a Roman *ordinarium* of recent promulgation, would Innocent III. have had recourse to the bishops of France in order to furnish Baldwin with office books *secundum instituta S. Romanae Ecclesiae*? Hence we may conjecture that the *ordinarium* of Innocent III. is posterior to 1205. Would it not even be posterior to 1210? We shall see that such a conjecture is not without foundation.

It would have been quite conceivable that the *ordinarium* of Innocent III. would remain peculiar to the Papal chapel, and not travel outside the Lateran palace; on the contrary, however, it was, as a matter of fact, propagated with astonishing rapidity in Latin Christendom. This propagation was not, at first at all events, the work of the Popes, but of the sons of S. Francis. Raoul de Rivo himself tells us that the shortened office of the Palatine clergy was adopted by the Friars Minor:

> Huius officii Ordinarium vidi Romae a tempore Innocentii III. recollectum, . . . et illud officium breviatum secuti sunt Fratres Minores.

The first companions of S. Francis, not being clerks,

[1] Potthast, No. 2512.

were not bound to the recitation of any office.¹ Thomas of Celano relates that, when S. Francis was at Rivo Torto,

> Deprecati sunt eum fratres tempore illo ut doceret eos orare, quoniam, in simplicitate spiritus ambulantes, adhuc ecclesiasticum officium ignorabant.

And S. Francis, for their only prayer, taught them to say the *Pater Noster*, and the antiphon, '*Adoramus Te, Christe, et benedicimus Tibi, quia per S. Crucem Tuam redemisti mundum.*'²

S. Bonaventure tells us the same, saying that these primitive Friars Minor

> Vacabant ibidem [*at Rivo Torto*] Divinis precibus incessanter, mentaliter potius quam vocaliter, studio intendentes orationis devotae, pro eo quod nondum ecclesiasticos libros habebant, in quibus possent horas canonicas decantare: loco tamen illorum librum Crucis Christi continuatis aspectibus diebus ac noctibus revolvebant.³

At a later time, when the Order was open to clergy and laity without distinction, the obligation to recite the Divine Office followed into its ranks the clerks who joined it. So it is specified by the Franciscan Rule of

---

¹ See the author's 'Origine de l'Obligation personelle des Clercs à la Récitation de l'Office Canonique' (*Canoniste Contemporain*, 1894), pp. 9-15.

² Thom. de Celano, *Vita Prima S. Franc.* 45 (Bolland. Octobr. ii. 696): 'We adore Thee, O Christ, and we bless Thee, because by Thy holy Cross Thou hast redeemed the world.'

³ S. Bonav. *Vita S. Franc.* 41 (Bolland. Octobr. ii. 751): 'There they remained occupied incessantly in prayer to God, more with the mind than with the mouth, giving themselves up to the exercise of devout supplication, for they had not yet any ecclesiastical books from which they might sing the canonical hours: but instead of these they pored upon the book of Christ's Cross keeping their eyes ever on It, day and night.'

1210, which enjoins on the clergy of the Order the singing of the office *secundum consuetudinem clericorum*: simply that—no mention of the office according to the use of the *Curia* or of the Roman Church. But on the other hand the Rule of 1223 enjoins on the clergy of the Order the singing of the office according to the *ordinarium* of the Holy Roman Church, and commands them to provide themselves for that purpose with Breviaries of the said office. Whence one may conclude that between 1210 and 1223 the Friars Minor had adopted the Breviary of the Roman Office. Now see how Salimbenus, in the second half of the thirteenth century, expresses himself on this point:

> A.D. MCCXV. Innocentius papa III. apud Lateranum sollemne concilium celebravit.
>
> Hic ... officium ecclesiasticum in ... [?] correxit et ordinavit; et de suo addidit et de alieno dempsit.[1] Sed non adhuc est bene ordinatum secundum appetitum multorum, nec etiam secundum rei veritatem, quia multa sunt superflua, quae magis taedium quam devotionem faciunt tam audientibus quam dicentibus. Ut prima Dominicalis, quando sacerdotes debent dicere missas suas, et populus eas expectat, nec est qui celebret, occupatus in prima. Item dicere XVIII psalmos in Dominicali et nocturnali officio ante *Te Deum laudamus*, et ita aestivo tempore, quando pulices molestant et noctes sunt breves et calor intensus, ut yemali, nonnisi taedium provocat. Sunt adhuc multa in ecclesiastico officio quae possent mutari in melius, et dignum esset, quia plena sunt ruditatibus, quamvis non cognoscantur ab omnibus.[2]

---

[1] There is no mention of this fact in the chronicle of Martin of Poland, any more than in the Pontifical Registers; and nothing about it in the Canons of the Lateran council.

[2] F. Salimbenus, *Chronica* (ed. Parma, 1857), p. 3: 'A.D. 1215. Pope Innocent III. held a solemn council at the Lateran. He corrected the ecclesiastical Office and set it in order, and added somewhat of that which rightly pertained to it, and removed other matter which belonged not to it. But not yet is it well set in order,

Here we are told that the *ordinarium* or breviary of Innocent III. was published in 1215; that it was actually a new edition of the office: '*correxit, ordinavit, addidit, dempsit*'; that this edition, when Salimbenus wrote, was in everyone's hands just as the Pope had made it, and that superior persons like Salimbenus made no scruple of reproaching it with its prolixity and barbarisms—'*plena sunt ruditatibus.*'

In 1223, at all events, we find breviaries of the Divine Office according to the use of the Holy Roman Church, books which do not seem to have been in existence in 1210 any more than in 1205, and these new books are adopted by the Franciscan family:

> Et illud officium breviatum secuti sunt Fratres Minores; inde est quod breviarium eorum et libros officii intitulant ' secundum consuetudinem Romanae Curiae.' [1]

But this breviary of the Roman *Curia* was not adopted by them just as it was in the time of Innocent III. The Friars corrected it for their own use, and the modifications introduced by them constituted really a second

according to what many would wish, nor indeed really and truly; for many superfluous things remain, which are a greater cause of weariness than of devotion, both to those who hear the Office and to those who say it. Such is the long Sunday Prime, when the priests ought to be saying their Masses, and the people are waiting for them, and lo! there is none to celebrate—he is busy, forsooth, saying his Prime. So, to say xviii psalms in the Sunday Nocturn Office or ever you come to *Te Deum*—and that just as much in the summer (when the fleas are so troublesome and the nights are short and the heat intense) as in the winter—is nought but a weariness. There are many other things in the ecclesiastical Office which might well be changed for the better—and should be, of right; for they are full of barbarisms, though all men perceive it not.'

[1] Radulph. *De Canon. Observ.* pr. 22.

edition of the breviary of the *Curia*, an edition which we have seen authorised by Gregory IX. in 1241, and which was mainly the work of the General of the Order, Aymo.

> Breviarium a F. Aymone sanctae recordationis, praedecessore meo, pio correctum studio, et per sedem apostolicam confirmatum, et approbatum postea per capitulum generale.¹

Thus writes John of Parma in 1249 in a circular letter, wherein he enjoins on all the Friars Minor the use of the breviary of Aymo, authorised by Gregory IX., without changing anything, in the chant, in the text, in the hymns, in the antiphons, in the responds, or in the lessons:

> Praeter id solum . . . nihil omnino in cantu vel littera, in hymnis seu responsoriis vel antiphonis aut lectionibus, vel aliis quibuslibet B. Virginis antiphonis . . . quae post completorium diversis cantantur temporibus, in choro cantari vel legi, nisi forte alicubi compellant librorum nostrorum defectus.²

So here we have a sort of second edition of the breviary of the Roman *Curia*, an edition for the use of the Franciscans, for which, in a few years, they are to gain a universal popularity, and which, before long, the *Curia* itself will adopt for its own use.

This adoption by the *Curia* of the breviary of the Friars Minor took place between the pontificate of Gregory IX. (1227-1241) and that of Nicolas III. (1277-1280), but no trace of it is found in the Pontifical Registers. Raoul de Rivo simply tells us that Nicolas III. 'caused all the antiphonaries and other books of the ancient office to be suppressed in all the churches of

---

[1] Wadding, tom. iii. p. 209; Potthast, No. 11028.

[2] Wadding, *loc. cit.*; cf. the bull of Innocent IV., Nov. 14, 1245 (Potthast, No. 11962).

Rome, ordering that henceforth they should make use of the books and breviaries of the Minorites, whose Rule he at the same time confirmed.' 'And this,' adds Raoul, 'is why all the books at Rome now are new and Franciscan.' Thus the grand old Roman Office, the office of the time of Charlemagne and of Adrian I., was suppressed by Nicolas III. in those of the Roman basilicas which had hitherto remained faithful to it, and for this ancient office there was substituted that breviary or epitome of the modernised office, which the Minorites had observed since the time of Gregory IX.

> Nicolaus papa III., natione Romanus, de genere Ursinorum, qui coepit anno 1277, et palatium apud S. Petrum construxit, fecit in ecclesiis Urbis amoveri . . . libros officii antiquos, . . . et mandavit ut de caetero ecclesiae Urbis uterentur . . . breviariis Fratrum Minorum, quorum Regulam etiam confirmavit. Unde hodie in Roma omnes libri sunt novi et Franciscani.[1]

The Palatine breviary of Innocent III. had become the breviary of the Minorites; under Nicolas III. the breviary of the Minorites became the breviary of the Roman Church, and henceforth there was to be no other Roman Office but according to this new form. In 1337, the Holy See being established at Avignon, a decree of Benedict XII. (which recalls to our mind that which Raoul de Rivo attributes to Nicolas III.) suppressed the old books which were used by the clergy and in the churches of Avignon, in order to impose on them the breviary of the *Curia*:

> Ordinamus et statuimus quod amodo universi et singuli clerici ac personae ecclesiasticae praedictae civitatis et dioecesis a consuetis officiis liberi et immunes existant, et pristinis veterum codicum rudimentis omissis . . . officium Divinum, diurnum

---

[1] Radulph. pr. 22.

pariter et nocturnum, dicere valeant iuxta ordinem, morem, vel statutum quo Ecclesia utitur et Curia Romana supradicta. . . . Statuimus ut in universis et singulis ecclesiis eiusdem civitatis et dioecesis, quarum libri ex antiquitatis incommodo renovationis vel reparationis remedio indigent, illi ad quos pertinent emant seu fieri faciant libros convenientes et aptos, qui dictae Ecclesiae et Curiae Romanae usui congruant opportuno.[1]

Anyone who wishes to know what these books 'conformed to the use of the *Curia* and the Roman Church' were, has only to cast his eye over the ancient catalogues of the library of the Popes at Avignon: he will not find any longer the books which used to serve for the Divine Service, *libri responsales, libri nocturnales,* &c., but crowds of books entitled *Breviarium ad usum Romanum, Breviarium de Camera, Breviarium pro Camera.*[2] The liturgical revolution which substituted the Breviary of the Roman *Curia* for the old *Ordo psallendi* of S. Peter's was an accomplished fact.

And what had the Roman liturgy of the Divine Office gained by this change? This is the question we have now to discuss.[3]

The Breviary of the Roman *Curia* is divided into five parts: the Kalendar, the Psalter, the *Temporale*, the

[1] Martene, *Thesaurus Nov. Anecd.* tom. iv. p. 558.

[2] F. Ehrle, *Historia bibliothecae Romanorum Pontificum* (Rome, 1890), tom. i, pp. 200, 214, 404, 507, &c.

[3] See the *Rationale* of Durandus, a work composed about 1286 by William Duranti, chaplain of the Roman *Curia*, and considered to be the commentary of highest authority on the Office of the thirteenth century. We quote it from the Lyons edition of 1574. Our observations on the Breviary are founded on the following MS. copies: Paris Library, Nos. 756, 760, 1044-1050, 1058, 1064, 1260, 1262, 1280-1283, 1288-1290, 1314, 9423, 10481, 13227, 13236, 13244, 17993; Arsenal Library, Nos. 101, 596, 597, 601; Mazarin Library, Nos. 351, 365, 366.

Proper of Saints, and the Common of Saints. To these five essential parts we may add the Rubrics.

The Psalter is placed either at the head of the volume, immediately after the Kalendar, or in the middle, between the *Temporale* and the *Sanctorale*. Generally speaking, the Psalter has no title, though sometimes one is given, such as '*Incipit psalmista cum invitatoriis et ymnis,*' or '*Incipit psalterium ordinatum.*' The leading characteristic of this Psalter is that it is arranged in a different order to that in which the 150 psalms stand in the Bible: the psalms are in the order in which they serve for the Sunday and ferial offices, and they are interspersed with the hymns, invitatories, antiphons, versicles and responses, and *capitula* (each in their respective places) of these offices, both of Mattins, Lauds, Vespers, and the Little Hours of the day; the hymns of the Proper of the Season and of the Common of Saints are placed at the beginning or end of the psalter. In a word, what we now call the Common of the Season, ' the psalter arranged for the week with the ordinary of the office of the season,' is an existing feature of these Franciscan Roman breviaries of the thirteenth century. The version of the Psalter used by the Minorites is that called the Gallican: at Rome, at least in the basilicas, the version called the Roman held its ground in liturgical use up to the end of the fifteenth century.[1] At beginning each hour of the office the cleric says the Lord's Prayer,

---

[1] Tommasi (tom. ii. Preface) cites a Psalter written in 1480 for the chapter of S. Mary's the Greater: the text is that of the Roman psalter, '*secundum consuetudinem clericorum Romanae urbis eiusque districtus.*' The 'Gallican' was S. Jerome's second version. See p. 100.

not an early custom, for it does not even go back to the eleventh century: John of Avranches (*De Off. Eccl.* p. 30) has no acquaintance with it. To the Lord's Prayer the custom grew up of adding the *Ave Maria*.¹ The *Pater Noster*, in a low voice, was also said after the versicle and response which follows the psalmody of every nocturn.² At the Little Hours there was an antiphon and a prayer.³ At the end of each of the hours, after the *Benedicamus Domino*, came the memorials (*suffragia sanctorum*); ⁴ but after Compline, every day, an antiphon in honour of the Blessed Virgin, varying with the season; John of Parma, in the letter already quoted (A.D. 1249), enumerates, as the four adopted by the Minorites, the *Regina caeli*, the *Alma Redemptoris Mater*, the *Ave Regina*, and the *Salve Regina*.⁵ Amalarius would probably have considered the

¹ Durand. *Rationale*, v. 2, 6: '*Laudabili consuetudine inductum est ut sacerdos ante canonicarum horarum initia, et in fine Dominicae orationis* [sic], *et ante horas B. M. V. et in fine,* "*Ave Maria*" *voce submissa praemittat. Quidam etiam in fine horarum dicunt* '*Dominus det nobis suam pacem.*"' Mr. Baylay thinks that Durandus may be alluding to the strange custom that grew up of putting in the *Ave* at the end of *Pater noster* almost whenever it was said: for instance, after the versicle and response of a nocturn they said silently, '*Pater noster*,' then '*Ave*,' and then, aloud, '*Et ne nos inducas*,' &c. In some cases this was done even when *Pater noster* was said after *Kyrie eleison*—*e.g.* in Mattins of the Dead.
² *Ib.* v. 3, 14.   ³ *Ib.* v. 5, 3, and 2, 55.   ⁴ *Ib.* v. 2, 63.
⁵ Wadding, *Annales Min.* tom. iii. p. 208. The *Regina caeli* is an antiphon for Vespers at Easter, found as early as the twelfth century in the Antiphonary of S. Peter's (Tommasi, tom. iv. p. 100). The *Salve Regina*, made popular in the twelfth century by S. Bernard, is the work of a monk of Reichenau, Hermann Contractus. The *Alma Redemptoris Mater* has been wrongly attributed to the same author. The *Ave Regina* is closely related to the *Salve*, but its exact origin is unknown. See W. Brambach, *Die verloren geglaubte Historia de S. Afra und das Salve Regina des Hermannus Contractus* (Karlsruhe, 1892), pp. 13, 14.

psalmody greatly weakened by all these additions of *Pater noster*, memorials and hymns. The liturgy had gained nothing but the antiphons addressed to the Virgin, which are four exquisite compositions, though in a style enfeebled by sentimentality.

The *Temporale* is the principal part of the Breviary, which gives to the whole book its distinctive name:

> In Nomine Domini incipit ordo Breviarii secundum consuetudinem Curiae Romanae.
> In Nomine Domini nostri Ihesu Christi incipit Breviarium Fratrum Minorum secundum, &c.
> In Nomine sanctissimae et individuae Trinitatis, Patris et Filii et Spiritus Sancti. Amen. Incipit ordo Breviarii secundum, &c.

Note that it is only to the *Temporale* that the term Breviary is applied, and that, whether the book is for the Friars Minor or not, it is always 'according to the use of the Roman *Curia*.'

The *Temporale* contains the Proper office of the Season from the first Sunday in Advent to the last Sunday after Pentecost: *capitula*, antiphons, versicles, responds, collects, all still identical, with few exceptions, with what they were in the eighth century. The lessons from Holy Scripture are allotted according to the traditional order, which the Modern Office has not forsaken; but these lessons from Scripture are what they are now in our present Breviary, each extending over a very few lines, and often not more remarkable for their consecutiveness than for their extent. The lessons taken from the sermons and homilies of the Fathers are of no greater length: we find passages from SS. Leo, Gregory, Ambrose, Augustine, John Chrysostom, Jerome, alongside of others from

Origen, and from spurious works attributed to Augustine, Ambrose, and Leo; but no author is included later than S. Gregory. An important novelty characterises the *Temporale* in the introduction of the festivals of the Holy Trinity and of *Corpus Christi*. The office of the Holy Trinity, '*Gloria Tibi, Trinitas aequalis*,' was certainly absent from the breviary of Innocent III. and that of Gregory IX. and even at the beginning of the fourteenth century we find MS. breviaries which are without it. '*Romani nunquam de Trinitate celebrant festum*,' says Durandus in 1286.[1] The office of *Corpus Christi—Sacerdos in aeternum*—the work of S. Thomas Aquinas, is wanting in some breviaries of the beginning of the fourteenth century. The festival was first observed at Liège in 1246; promoted by Urban IV. in 1264, in consequence of the miracle of Bolsena; became neglected towards the end of the thirteenth century, but was re-established in full dignity by Clement V. in 1312.[2] With the exception of these two observances, the *Temporale*, though reduced and altered as regards its lectionary, is the *Temporale* of the ancient Roman Office.

The *Sanctorale* never mentions in its title the Roman *Curia*:

Incipiunt festivitates sanctorum per totum anni circulum

is its invariable heading, both in MSS. and in printed

---

[1] *Rationale*, vi. 114, 7. There are two offices extant of the Holy Trinity: one of the end of the fourteenth century (?) (*Sedenti super solium*), which is detestable; the other (*Gloria Tibi*), which is found in the present Breviary, is, if we may believe Durandus (vi. 114, 6), the work of Stephen of Liège—that is to say, dating back to the tenth century.

[2] Baronius, *Annales*, tom. xxii. p. 140, and tom. xxiii. p. 550.

breviaries. Nor does the Common of Saints mention the *Curia*; the heading is simply

or
    Incipit commune Sanctorum

    Incipit commune Sanctorum per totum anni circulum.

It comprises the office of Apostles, Evangelists, of One and Many Martyrs, of Confessors, Bishops and otherwise, of Virgins, Martyrs and not Martyrs, and of holy women other than virgins, with the addition of the office of the Virgin Mary, and of the Dedication of a Church: the latter sometimes appears at the end of the Proper of Saints, while the Office of the Dead is always found after the Common of Saints. The office of the Saints, common or proper, includes nine lessons: the festivals of three lessons have gone out, and the saints who are only commemorated do not exceed a half-dozen in number. Of these nine lessons, the first six are taken from the history of the saint; the other three generally from a homily on the Gospel of the Mass. These homilies or sermons are taken from the writings of SS. Jerome, Gregory, Ambrose and Augustine, and from Origen, genuine or spurious. But the apocryphal Acts of Apostles, the fabulous legends of saints, the notices of ancient Popes from the *Liber pontificalis*, interpolated with forged decretals, the whole blended with much excellent matter, make up a lectionary as alluring as it is dangerous. I have found on the margin of late copies of the breviary annotations such as these: *Neutiquam* . . ., *Fabula* . . ., *Apocrypha* . . ., *Falsa narratio* . . ., *Fabula anilis* . . ., *Officium stolidum et ridiculum* . . .; these critical notes are by clerks of the Renaissance. But, long before the Renaissance, Raoul de Rivo reproached the breviary of the Minorites with having admitted apocryphal writings condemned in the list drawn up by Pope Gelasius, and Acts such as those of S. George, S. Barbara, and S. Katherine, 'apocryphal and contemptible writings, full of incredible tales': not to speak of a number of passions of saints inserted in particular local editions of the breviary, accepted without any discernment, which cannot safely be read in the office.[1] The lectionary of the *Sanctorale*, in fact, tells us of a degree of literary taste and judgment which puts Aymo—if it is he who is responsible for the selection of these pieces of history—far below Paul the Deacon. In old times the lessons were taken from books of legends and homilies edited by various compilers, from which the choir of each church could choose; it was only the lessons from Holy Scripture that were fixed by the liturgy; but now the breviary, by enjoining the use of certain hagiographic and homiletic passages, without liberty of choice, put into circulation works that were far from being all of equal value, and in this matter the loss is greater than the gain.

The Kalendar—that of the thirteenth century, to wit—is richer than it was in the eighth, but it differs very little from that given by the Antiphonary of St. Peter's in the twelfth; we may say that the tradition of Rome still imposed its rule, and that at first, at all events, faithful adherence was yielded to it. Some names which were in the Antiphonary of S. Peter's have been eliminated from the Kalendar of the Roman *Curia*—about eighteen altogether.[2]

[1] Radulph. pr. 12.
[2] SS. Telesphorus, Aquilas, Papias, Simeon, Euplus and Lucius, Aura, Balbina, Thecla, Eustace, Germain of Capua, Quintin, Juliana, Savin, Eustratus, Gregory of Spoleto, Eugenia, and, wonderful to relate, S. John Chrysostom.

Others have been added: such as SS. Basil, Paul the Hermit, Ignatius, Gilbert of Sempringham, Bernard, Justina, Remigius, Hilarion, Leonard, Vitalis and Agricola, Brice, Peter of Alexandria, Lucy, Thomas of Canterbury, and a group of early Popes, SS. Hyginus, Marcellinus, Felix, Sylverius, Zephyrinus, Pontianus, and Miltiades. The net increase is barely ten festivals. And it would be a mistake to suppose the Kalendar of the Roman *Curia* suffered any great increase from the thirteenth to the fifteenth century. In the course of the thirteenth century it received the feast of the Conception of the Virgin;[1] those of the Minorite Saints, SS. Francis (canonised 1228), Clare (1255), Antony of Padua (1232), and Elizabeth of Hungary (1235); so also those of the Black Friars, SS. Dominic (1234) and Peter Martyr (1253). The fourteenth century contributed the festival of the Stigmata of S. Francis (1304), and those of SS. Thomas Aquinas (1323), Louis, Bishop of Toulouse (1317), Louis, King of France (1297), also the feast of S. Mary of the Snows. At the end of the fifteenth century, in the printed Breviaries, we note indeed a more numerous accession of feasts, the Transfiguration of our Lord (1457), the Presentation of the Virgin (1464), the Visitation (1475),[2] SS. Bridget (1419), Nicolas of Tolentino (1447), Bernardine (1450), Vincent Ferrier (1455), also SS. Joseph, Anne, Juliana, Patrick, and Anselm; S. John Chrysostom returns, and

---

[1] The breviaries of the fifteenth century give an Office for the Conception, *Sicut lilium inter spinas*, the work of Leonard of Nogarola, protonotary to Sixtus IV., published by that pontiff in 1477. There is another, *Conceptio gloriosae Virginis*, attributed to the Council of Basle.

[2] The Office for the Visitation would also be the work of Leonard of Nogarola (Fabricius, *Biblioth. Lat. Med. Aev.* tom. v. p. 134).

there are, it may be, a few more, but the upshot is that the number of festivals admitted by the Popes into the breviary of the *Curia* is a limited one—very limited, if we compare with it the number of feasts which the breviaries not strictly of the *Curia* admitted into their Kalendars.[1]

But if the feasts of the *Sanctorale*, in the office of the Roman *Curia*, have not increased immoderately in number, they have at all events gained as to the degree of solemnity with which they are to be observed. All the feasts of the Virgin are greater doubles, equal to Christmas or Easter; so are those of S. Peter, S. John Baptist, and All Saints.[2] The festivals of Apostles, Evangelists, and Doctors,[3] of S. Laurence, S. Michael, the Commemoration of All Souls, the dedication of the basilicas of S. Peter, S. Paul, and S. John Lateran, the two festivals of the Holy Cross, the Octave-days of S.

---

[1] It is important carefully to distinguish the Kalendar of the Roman *Curia* from those which are not of the *Curia*. The latter are much more rich in festivals, not only in such as are connected with the locality or the religious Order for which each book may have been written, but in some which might claim an interest for Christendom at large: such as the festivals of the Wisdom of our Lord, of the Finding of the Child Jesus (in the temple), of Moses, Zacharias, Simeon, Agabus, Silas, Longinus (the centurion of the Crucifixion), of the Apparition of S. Mark, the Sisters of the Blessed Virgin, the Conversion of S. Augustine, *Saint* (instead of 'the Venerable') Bede, S. Christopher, the Eleven Thousand Virgins, S. Margaret, S. Mary the Egyptian, S. Apollonia.

[2] Christmas, the Circumcision, Epiphany, Easter, Ascension Day, Whitsun Day, Trinity Sunday, Corpus Christi, and for each church its patronal festival and the anniversary of its dedication, are greater doubles.

[3] That is, the *four* Latin doctors, SS. Ambrose, Jerome, Augustine, Gregory. Their festivals were raised to the dignity of lesser doubles by Boniface VIII. in 1298.

Peter, the Assumption, and the Nativity of our Lady, are lesser doubles. The ordinary Sundays are no more than greater semi-doubles, as are also the festivals of the Holy Innocents, the Apparition of S. Michael, S. Mary Magdalene, and S. Martin. All the other feasts of the Kalendar are festivals of nine lessons. We may reckon that the number of festivals of nine lessons and of superior rank amounted to nearly 150 by the end of the thirteenth century, and on all these 150 feast-days (some with Octaves) the Office of the Season was thrust aside.

Through all these elements thus massed together in a 'portable breviary' the clergy had to steer their way: and it was not easy, for there were no tables, no numbering of pages, no references, to help them to join together the dispersed portions of their daily office. The codification of the breviary remained until the sixteenth century in this imperfect state. They met the difficulty, as well as they could, by means of rubrics; but these, of various dates and workmanship, interlaced one another, and repeated one another, without succeeding in enunciating anything like a clear set of general rules.

Then, further, the daily office was burdened with the Little Office of our Lady, which was to be said every day, except on greater doubles, the last three days of Holy Week, the Octave of Easter, and the feasts of our Lady. It was still further burdened with the Office for the Dead, which was obligatory on all days on which the canonical Office had but three lessons. Still further, on all days when the ferial office was used, it was burdened with the recitation of the Penitential psalms and the Gradual psalms. It is true that in the fourteenth century there were not wanting those who felt how onerous were all these additions to the canonical Office; Raoul de Rivo reproaches the Minorites with being exceedingly lax about their obligation to recite daily the Office of our Lady; he also reproaches them with having multiplied saints' days of nine lessons in order to get out of the obligation to recite the Penitential and Gradual psalms and the Office for the Dead, 'to whom they are thereby the cause of perpetual injury.'[1]

To sum up, how far we have got from the broad and harmonious simplicity of the Roman Office of the eighth century! The antiphonary and the responsoral, the *ordo psallendi* and *ordo legendi* of old, are preserved, and the hymnal is added; but the lectionary is become scanty and corrupt. And if we owe a just debt of gratitude to those who gave us the antiphons of the Blessed Virgin, what are we to say, on the other hand, of the additional daily offices?

It is difficult not to see in these additions, these numerous and burdensome services of adventitious prayer, a grave wrong done to the canonical Office itself. The grand and simple lines of the edifice remain, but a huge number of parasitical little chapels block up the nave and aisles. The feasts of the *Sanctorale* have been so multiplied as to make the Office of the Season practically a thing condemned to desuetude. The Councils of the fifteenth century vie with one another in deploring the coldness with which the clergy perform their duty of

[1] Radulph. pr. 15, 21, 22.

reciting the canonical Office, even in choir.[1] They do not, as its seems, sufficiently recognise the fact that this coldness, this scandalous negligence, proceeds in part from the deterioration of the Office itself, from those '*religiosae prolationes*' which have disfigured it, those '*preces perlongae per omnes horas*' for which the devotion of a saint would scarce suffice. 'The Divine Office,' writes Martin of Senging to the Council of Basle in 1435, ' is recited in disorderly fashion, in haste, without devotion, and with a perverse intention, viz. an itching desire to get to the end of it: the clergy come to prefer to the canonical Office the superfluous additions which are tacked on to it.'[2] No doubt the remedy for all this would partly consist in the reformation of the clergy, but to be perfect it would have to include the reformation of the Office as well, the clearing away of encumbrances, the restoration of an earlier and purer state of things: but neither Martin of Senging nor the Council of Basle had any thought of this second part of the task of reformation. Raoul of Tongres alone seems to have got hold of the just view of the case, when, writing to his canons at Windesheim, he denounced the deterioration of the canonical Office, both in its text and in its rubrics. He accuses the Minorites of having been the authors, and their Breviary the instrument, of this deterioration. They called their Breviary, he says, 'The Breviary according to the use of the Roman *Curia*,' without concerning them-

---

[1] Roskovány, tom. v. pp. 108 *sqq*. [In my own neighbourhood the fifteenth century Visitations of Southwell Minster reveal a deplorable state of things in regard to this matter.—A. B.]

[2] Martin of Senging, 'Tuitiones,' ap. Pez, *Bibliotheca Ascetica* (Ratisb. 1725), tom. viii. p. 545.

selves about what was the use of the Roman *Church*. And he adds: 'The Roman Church was once celebrated and glorious, living waters sprang out from under her feet, whence, as from a fountain, were derived all ecclesiastical rules.' He appeals from the liturgy of the Minorites to that of Amalarius and the *Micrologus*.[1] The provost of Tongres was right, but no one listened to him.

With this liturgical deterioration we come to the end of the middle ages. Printing receives the Roman Breviary from the hands of the Roman *Curia*:

> In nomine Sanctissimae et Individuae Trinitatis, Patris et Filii et Spiritus Sancti. Amen. Incipit ordo Breviarii secundum consuetudinem Romanae Curiae.
>
> Breviarium ad usum Romanae Curiae, ob Dei gloriam et honorem, animarumque salutem, ac totius ecclesiae militantis utilitatem.

Such are the titles we read at the head of early printed Roman Breviaries.[2] We have reached the end of the fifteenth century, and the Breviary of the Roman *Curia* has now existed for about three hundred years.

[1] Radulph. pr. 22.

[2] In L. Hain's *Repertorium Bibliographicum* (Stuttgart, 1826) will be found a descriptive list of Roman Breviaries printed before 1500. The dates are: Turin 1474, Venice 1474, Lyons, 1476, Naples 1477, Rome 1477, Venice 1477, Venice 1478, Venice *iterum* 1478, Venice 1479, Rome 1479, Venice *iterum* 1479, Nonantola 1480, Venice 1481, Venice *iterum* 1481, *sine loco* 1482, Venice 1482, Venice *iterum* 1482, Venice *tertio* 1482, Nuremberg 1486, Venice 1486, Venice 1489, Venice 1490, Venice *iterum* 1490, Venice 1491, *sine loco* 1492, Pavia 1494, Venice 1494, Venice *iterum* 1494, Venice 1496, Brescia 1497, Venice 1497, Venice *iterum* 1497, Venice *tertio* 1497, Turin 1499, Venice 1499. (Hain, Nos. 3887-3927.)

Will the wishes of Raoul of Tongres be realised, and a return be made to the liturgy of the eighth century? Or for these changed times will some new sort of euchology be produced? Or is this book of the thirteenth century destined to endure?

CHAPTER V

THE BREVIARY OF THE COUNCIL OF TRENT [1]

I

HUMANISM, the *cultus* of Pagan literature, received from Nicolas V. the freedom of the city of Rome, and established its rule there under Pius II., that truly Virgilian Pope. And if it aroused in the austere Paul II. nothing but fear and distrust, and was viewed with some indifference by Sixtus IV., Innocent VIII. and Alexander VI., while from Julius II. it received no more than an indulgent toleration, it recovered under Leo X., at all events, the very height of Pontifical favour.[2] Erasmus, who visited Rome in 1509, treasured all his life the recollection of what had so greatly enchanted his erudite and refined intelligence :
' *Quam mellitas eruditorum hominum confabulationes, quot*

---

[1] As types of the Roman Breviary of the sixteenth century anterior to that of S. Pius V. we have consulted the following: *Breviarium secundum consuetudinem Romanae Curiae, cum aliis quamplurimis de novo superadditis* (Venice, 1503), and *Breviarium Romanum de Camera, optime castigatum et ita ordinatum ut omnia suis in locis sint posita* (Venice, 1550).

[2] The dates of the Popes here mentioned are: Nicolas V. 1447-1455, Pius II. 1458-1464, Paul II. 1464-1471, Sixtus IV. 1471-1484, Innocent VIII. 1484-1492, Alexander VI. 1492-1503, Julius II. 1503-1513, Leo X. 1513-1521, Clement VII. 1523-1534.

mundi lumina !' he exclaims when thinking of it, and he loves to recall the high esteem he saw conferred upon 'good studies,' in that 'peaceable home of the Muses, the common fatherland of all men of letters.' Leo X., who had as secretaries Bembo and Sadoleto, 'desired that whatever was to be heard or read should be expressed in really pure Latin, full of spirit and elegance.' Bembo's one ideal was to write in the style of what another Cardinal, Adrian of Corneto, called 'the immortal and almost divine age of Cicero.' This revival of the Latin language extended itself to poetry and oratory. Sannazar, 'the Christian Virgil,' beloved of Leo X. and Clement VII., makes the shepherds of Bethlehem sing, round the manger of the Saviour, the Fourth Eclogue. One Good Friday, preaching before the Pope, the most famous orator of the Roman Court considered that he could not better praise the Sacrifice of Calvary than by relating the self-devotion of Decius and the sacrifice of Iphigenia.[1] In the eyes of these superfine scholars, in love with Ciceronianism and mythology, what sort of figure would be made by our old chief chanters of S. Peter's, Catalenus, Maurianus and Virbonus? In the opinion of such men as Inghirami, Sadoleto, or Bembo—that Bembo who persuaded his friend Longueil to read nothing but Cicero for five whole years—what would be the flavour of the Latinity of our antiphons, our responds, the lessons of the Breviary, and all that liturgical literature, the work of schoolmen and friars?

---

[1] P. de Nolhac, *Erasme en Italie*, 1888, p. 76; J. Burckhardt, *La Civilisation en Italie au Temps de la Renaissance*, tom. i. pp. 277, 311-17 (French edition); cf. J. Janssen, *L'Allemagne et la Réforme*, tom. ii. p. 26, and, still more, p. 65 (French edition).

To this morbidly refined literary taste the Roman *Curia* was tempted to accommodate its breviary. The initiative of this design belongs to Leo X., the execution of it to a Neapolitan, a fellow-countryman of Sannazar, by name Zacharias Ferreri, Bishop of Guardia Alfiera, the printing to a Roman bookseller, and the approbation of it to Clement VII. A start was made by issuing a sample of a new hymnal. It is only a sample, but it was intended to prepare the way for the publication of 'an ecclesiastical breviary made much shorter and more convenient, and purged of all mistakes' (*breviarium ecclesiasticum longe brevius et facilius redditum, et ab omni errore purgatum*). For such seem to have been the terms of the commission given by Leo X. to Ferreri.

In fact, if we wish to know in what spirit he was prepared to abridge, simplify and expurgate the traditional liturgy, it is sufficient to cast our eyes over the hymnal of Ferreri, the first stone of the projected edifice. It received the Papal approval on November 30, 1523, and was published on February 1, 1525. The title reads: '*Hymni novi ecclesiastici iuxta veram metri et latinitatis normam . . . sanctum et necessarium opus.*' The approbation of Clement VII. follows, couched in fine Ciceronian phrases:

> Etsi a teneris annis nobis semper cordi vehementer fuerit bonarum disciplinarum, sacrae praecipue doctrinae, exercitia, et in eis se cum optimo virtutum odore versantes omni studio fovere, &c. ;

and granting by his Apostolic authority leave to read and employ these new hymns, even in Divine Service (*etiam in Divinis*). Then comes Ferreri's preface, in which he anticipates the charge which some might bring against him, of having dared, in opposition to the judgment of S. Augustine and S. Gregory, to submit the words of the sacred oracles to the rules of Donatus, and the interpretation of holy writings to the authority of Quintilian: but what? he cries: if it is indeed possible to introduce genuine Latinity and the classical style into Divine worship, is it not contrary to all reason to prefer to it the barbarisms of a style devoid of taste (*barbariem et insulsam orationem amplectamur*)? For his part, he is content to justify himself by the esteem of Leo X., to whom he submitted each one of his hymns as fast as he composed them, and who read and approved them all (*singulos quidem hymnos prout a me quotidie prodibant perlegit et probavit*). Here, then, we are definitely assured that this liturgical experiment is really a thing devised by Leo X., Clement VII., and the *Curia*, who do not fail to intimate to us that its execution surpasses their expectation: the work is not merely 'holy and necessary,' it is 'Divine'; and Ferreri has gained thereby, not immortality, but eternal glory (*aeternitatem proculdubio consecuturum*).

The hymns of Ferreri have been judged with more severity than justice. I have before my eyes his pretty little book, printed in italic and roman type of rare elegance. Most assuredly, I am far from loving this laboured poetry, redolent of classical reminiscences and clever tricks of versification: as when he sings of the Holy Innocents in sapphics:

> Hos velut flores veniens pruina
> Coxit, et gratum superis odorem
> Reddere effecit, meritoque summis
>   Condidit astris;

or the Virgin Mary in iambics:

> Ave, superna ianua!
> Ave, beata semita!
> Salus periclitantibus,
> Et Ursa navigantibus!

or S. Peter in choriambics:

> Tu, Petre, et reseras caelica limina
> Et claudis, sapiens arbiter omnium;
> Dum terris animas solvis et alligas,
>   Firmatur super aethera.[1]

One can better relish the rude Christian originals of which these verses are imitations, correct, clever and insipid. But did not Urban VIII., a century later, take up the same task of metrical correction, and has he not disfigured, in the attempt to improve them, the old hymns which we still read in our Breviary in the form they assumed under his correcting hand? And if there is in the poetry of Ferreri too much about Phoebus, Olympus,

---

[1] [With, I fear, inexcusable rashness, I give the following versions of these stanzas:

> 'These were the flow'rs that fell before the north wind;
> Yet did its blast but summon forth their fragrance
> Dear to the skies, and called them to the glory
>   Stored in the heavens.'

> 'Hail, Mary! hail, thou door of Heav'n
> And pathway to our home afar!
> In danger bringing safety near,
> Upon earth's sea a guiding star.'

> 'Thou, Peter, openest wisely the Heav'nly door;
> Thou also closest, of all things the arbiter;
> Binding or loosing the soul here on earth below,
>   Thy word stands firm for aye above.'—A. B.]

Styx, Quirites, Penates, and *astra aetherea*; if there are Lenten stanzas such as this:

> Bacchus abscedat, Venus ingemiscat,
> Nec iocis ultra locus est, nec escis,
> Nec maritali thalamo, nec ulli
>   Ebrietati;[1]

and hymns for S. Francis of Assisi with such verses as:

> Ibat in sylvas tacitosque saltus
> Solus, ut caelum satius liceret
> Visere, et mundas agitare dulci
>   Pectore curas,

we must at all events grant that he has the virtues of his defects, that faultless purity of language, and that elegance of workmanship which justly delighted his contemporaries, and an ingenuity sufficiently happy in its expression to be capable of stirring our hearts still. As in the hymn for S. Gregory:

> Roma quae tantum decus edidisti,
> Quid triumphales meditaris arcus?
> Cogita magnum peperisse mundo
>   Gregorium te!

---

[1] [Preposterous as this stanza is, it is perhaps hardly fair to represent it as follows; the comic associations of the *Needy Knife-grinder* are too strong for the English reader:

> 'Hence with thee, Bacchus! Venus, fall a-weeping!
> Here's no more place for laughter or for feasting;
> Nor for the joys of marriage, nor for any
>   Drunkenness either.'

The hymn for S. Francis is not so unpleasing:

> 'Far in the greenwood's shadow and its silence
> Lonely he walked, while Heav'n itself grew nearer;
> Pure were the thoughts that in his gentle bosom
>   Rose and were cherished.'—A. B.]

or the ingenious and spirited hymn for the Common of Apostles:

> Gaudete, mundi principes,
> Quorum fide et constantia
> Et supplici innocentia
> Sunt victa regum culmina.[1]

These two hymns are worth the greater part of ancient and modern hymns put together.

What was deplorable in this experiment of Ferreri's was the whole state of mind which produced it, the ignorance of all liturgical tradition, and aversion to the study of it. And it is melancholy to see churchmen so enslaved to their Ciceronianism that Ferreri could write in the preface to his hymnal the following passage, which no one has remarked on, and which is his inexorable condemnation:

> Qui bona latinitate praediti sunt sacerdotes, dum barbaris vocibus Deum laudare coguntur, in risum provocati sacra saepenumero contemnunt.[2]

What humanists, and what priests!

What the humanist breviary would have been like it is impossible to imagine. The terrible blow which fell on the Eternal City in 1527, that frightful sack of Rome

---

[1] [' Rome, who hast gained so great a height of glory,
  Why on triumphal arches dost thou ponder?
  This may suffice—that thou hast shown the dark world
    Gregory's splendour!'

' True princes of the world, rejoice!
  Patience and faith in lofty tones,
  And innocence with pleading voice,
  Have triumphed o'er earth's proudest thrones.'—A. B.]

[2] ' Priests who are accustomed to good Latinity, when they are compelled to praise God in such barbarous language, are moved to laughter, and frequently led to despise sacred rites altogether.'

by the Spanish and German army of Charles V., forbids us to follow up the inquiry, or to pass judgment on the frivolity of that band of wits and scholars. Their brilliant and volatile society was dispersed, never to reassemble. Graver thoughts and forebodings succeeded, aroused by the echoes of the formidable voice of Luther. Sadoleto, from his retirement in France, wrote these melancholy words, marked by deep Christian feeling: 'If our misfortunes have disarmed the fierce anger of Heaven, if these terrible chastisements only make us return to the path of right conduct and the observance of wise laws, our situation, it may be, will be less cruel. ... Let us seek in God the true glory of sacerdotal dignity.'[1] It was indeed to the esteem and defence of these wise laws that it was necessary to return. And yet a new act of unfaithfulness to them was about to be committed.

When Ferreri died, Clement VII. did not give up the idea of presenting to the Church that 'ecclesiastical breviary, short, convenient, and purged from all errors,' which he had hoped to obtain from the Bishop of Guardia.[2] He cast his eyes, for the execution of this project, on a grave and devout man, whose nationality, which was Spanish, and his religious profession, that of the Franciscans, seemed to have preserved from the contagion of humanism. Francis Quignonez, of the family of the Counts of Luna, entered the Order of

[1] Quoted by Burckhardt, *op. cit.* tom. i. p. 156.
[2] F. Arevalo, *De Hymnodia Hispanica* (Rome, 1785), pp. 385 *sqq*. *Historia uberior de Fatis Breviarii Quignoniani*, reprinted by Ros kovány, tom. xi. pp. 3–47.

S. Francis when young, and in 1522 the chapter of the Order made him its General. Immediately after this he was sent by Charles V. to Rome, to treat with Clement VII. on certain delicate affairs, in which he acted to the entire satisfaction, we are told, both of the Pope and the Emperor. In 1529 he received the Cardinal's hat and the title of Holy Cross in Jerusalem. He was a man of cultured mind and austere gravity, a precursor of the coming interior reform of the Church. He understood that Clement VII. had desired him to 'arrange the canonical hours, bringing them back as far as possible to their ancient form, to remove from the office prolixities and difficult details: it was to be faithful to the institution of the ancient Fathers, and the clergy were to have no longer any reason for revolting against the duty of reciting the canonical prayers.' So he expresses himself in the preface to his breviary. We see that the idea of the Roman *Curia* has been perceptibly modified: it is no longer a question of praying according to the rules of good Latinity, but in accordance with the institution of the ancient Fathers—not to flatter the Ciceronianism of the clergy, but to give them an office against which they should have nothing to object. Humanism has made way for reformation.

But what a singular novelty, and no less dangerous than singular, to speak of reforms to be carried out by a return to antiquity, while what antiquity is meant is not expressed! Was not this just such a way of speaking as had been employed by the German Protestant reformers? And this echo of their protestations, met with at Rome, is one indication among many of the fact that at a particular moment in its history this Roman

Curia, itself so fiercely attacked by these violent theorists, was, after all, the medium in the whole of Catholicity the most attentive to their grievances, the most ready to listen to them, and to respond to their reproaches in a spirit of fairness.[1] But it is also allowable to see in the liturgical experiment made by Cardinal Quignonez an *individual* approach on his part towards the spirit of the German reformers. It is this which gives its special interest to his work: this also which constitutes its secret and fatal vice.

Cardinal Quignonez began his work in 1529. It has been proved that he had several assistants: Diego Neyla, a canon of Salamanca, a canonist and Hellenist; another learned Spaniard, Gaspar de Castro; and perhaps a third, better known than the others, Genesius de Sepulveda.[2] At the death of Clement VII., September 25, 1534, the constitution of the new breviary was not yet agreed upon: that point was not reached until 1535, under Paul III.

And even then the new breviary appeared at first in the form of a project submitted to public judgment. Quignonez says himself, and we may fully believe him, that he had no other intention than 'to open a public discussion with a view to collecting several opinions on the subject.' This first form of the breviary of Quignonez has now become exceedingly scarce, although from February 1535 to July 1536 there appeared no less

---

[1] '*Nos certe in omnibus quae per nos, Deo interveniente, fieri poterunt, neque amore, neque studio, neque liberalitate deerimus*' (Clement VII. to Cardinal Campeggio, quoted by Janssen, *op. cit.* tom. ii. p. 347). 'As for ourselves, in all that by God's help can be done, we shall not be wanting in goodwill, or zeal, or liberality.'

[2] Roskovány, tom. xi. pp. 23-25.

than six editions of it, at Rome, Paris, Venice, and Antwerp; but recently the University of Cambridge has had the happy thought of reprinting it.[1] The criticisms for which Quignonez had asked did not fail to make their appearance: the Sorbonne in particular signalised itself by issuing a censure which set forth the grounds on which it was made, July 27, 1535.[2] 'Wherefore,' writes Quignonez, in his preface to the revised form of his work, 'having duly weighed the advice which has been addressed to us, whether in word or in writing, we have added, changed, revised, still retaining the general form of our breviary.' And so the breviary in a revised form, and now with its text definitively settled, was at last published. The title of my copy runs thus:

> Breviarium Romanum a Paulo Tertio recens promulgatum, ex sacra potissimum Scriptura et probatis Sanctorum historiis constans. Ab authore denuo recognitum, et antiphonis, homeliis, precibus, sanctorum commemorationibus et aliis id genus additamentis multifariam locupletatum, variisque modis immutatum, ut in prefatione luculentius explicatur.[3]

Cardinal Quignonez sets forth in the preface of his breviary the principles by which he has been guided. The clergy, he says, are called by their office not only to pray but to teach, and it is proper that they should instruct themselves by the daily reading of the Holy Scriptures and ecclesiastical history. The Divine Office was so fashioned by the ancient Fathers as to provide perfectly for this double need. But what has come to

---

[1] *Breviarium Romanum a Fr. Card. Quignonio editum et recognitum, iuxta editionem Venetiis A.D. 1535 impressum*, ed. J. W. Legg, Cambridge, 1888.

[2] Roskovány, tom. viii. pp. 32–41.

[3] Paris, 1538, chez Yolande Bonhomme.

pass by men's negligence? The books of Holy Scripture are hardly read in the office at all, their place in it is reduced to almost nothing, and they are replaced by matter which cannot be compared to them for utility or importance. Of the psalms of David, intended to be sung completely through every week, only a few are ever used, which few are continually said over and over again all the year. The histories of saints in use are of no authority and written in barbarous style. The order of the office is so complicated that as much time has to be spent in finding the office as in reciting it.

To remedy, therefore, these defects, there have been suppressed in the new office versicles, *capitula*, and responds: there is nothing left in the breviary but (1) psalms, (2) antiphons, and (3) lessons. Such of the hymns have been retained as appeared to have most authority and impressiveness. The psalms have been distributed in such a way that the entire psalter is recited every week, but each canonical hour has but three psalms, the length of some being compensated by the shortness of others, so that all the offices are of the same length. On every day in the year the lessons are three in number, the first from the Old Testament, the second from the New, the third is either the legend of the saint, if it happens to be a saint's day, or a homily on the Gospel for the day, if it has a proper Mass, or, on ordinary days, a lesson from the Epistles or from the Acts of the Apostles.

Such were the objects proposed to himself by Cardinal Quignonez in his revised breviary, and such the method he adopted to secure them.

There is something to say, no doubt, for these objects,

but is there enough to justify such a thorough upsetting of the whole order of the breviary? Was it not possible to make reforms as to the points complained of, the scanty amount of lessons from Scripture, the incomplete recitation of the psalter, the undesirable character of many of the saints' day lessons, and the complicated character of the office, while allowing its main structure to stand?

After all, was not this traditional office conceived on a certain plan, a plan harmonious in itself? And had not the details of this ancient edifice their own beauty of form, to which historical associations had added interest? But Quignonez sweeps all away, and proceeds to build up a new edifice on a new plan.

In his first edition he suppressed antiphons altogether; but in his second, to meet the general protest made against this, he was obliged to re-establish a few. But responds are suppressed without mercy, and therewith disappears at one stroke all that beautiful literature of the responsoral, the most original portion of the Roman Office! The Roman distribution of the psalms disappears equally; the psalms are rearranged on a new plan, in an order which is no doubt practical, easy, attractive, but unknown to the ancient Church. No more expositions or sermons from the sainted Fathers—thus traversing the custom of the Church for the past thousand years: a patristic homily is just allowed by way of third lesson on festivals of the Season, and even this is a concession made in the second edition. No more distinction of rite between festivals: every day is to have the same degree of solemnity. The only distinctions by which a saint's day is marked are in the invitatory, the hymn, the third lesson, and the collect. To make up for this we have the Holy Scripture: that is, 'the most useful and important books of the Old Testament, and the whole of the New,' with the exception of the Apocalypse, of which only the first few chapters are to be read. And thus the Divine Office becomes principally a reading of the Bible, and in a subsidiary degree a study of ecclesiastical history. It was a very moderate utterance on the part of the Sorbonne when it said of Quignonez: 'The author of the new breviary has preferred his private judgment to the decrees of the ancient Fathers, and to the common and time-honoured customs of the Church.'

Can it be said that Cardinal Quignonez has at least shown more sense in the matter of expunging from the lessons of the *Sanctorale* whatever was calculated to excite 'contempt or ridicule,' desiring that nothing should appear there but what was 'distinguished by refinement of style and gravity of matter, founded on ecclesiastical history and the writings of grave and trustworthy authors'? The saints' day lessons of Quignonez have an elegant sobriety, and are in good Latin; their 'refinement of style' is irreproachable. But the sources from which they are drawn are far from being equally pure. Eusebius is a grave and trustworthy author, no doubt, but how about Platina's Lives of the Popes, and Mombrizo's Lives of the Saints? What an acute and cautious spirit of criticism would have been needed to deal successfully with this matter! The sagacity of Quignonez did not extend so far as to make him suspect that the apocryphal Acts of the Apostles, and the apocryphal Gospels were fabulous; and it never occurred to him that certain lessons in the old breviary, such as those on the festival of S. Mary of the Snows, needed to be replaced by others. These few examples will suffice to show that, even in the one direction in which it was legitimate, the work of revision undertaken by Quignonez was one for which he was not sufficiently equipped.

It is only fair to say, in defence of Cardinal Quignonez, that his breviary was, after all, only intended by him as tentative, that it was made to be used solely for private recitation of the office, and not for its performance in choir; that the Holy See granted the right of using it only to such clergy as should individually ask permission to do so, and that the intention of the Church was, by means of this abridged and simplified office, to recall to the duty of reciting the canonical hours the large numbers of clergy who had abandoned it. The Blessed Canisius, with this object, propagated in Germany the use of the breviary of Quignonez.[1] But it is also fair to relate that what was at first a privilege granted to individuals soon became a widely extended custom, in Italy, in France, in Germany and in Spain. The author of the Life of S. Francis Xavier calls the breviary of the Cardinal of the Holy Cross 'the breviary

[1] Canisius to S. Ignatius Loyola, December 28, 1560, quoted by Schober, p. 15: '*Complures ecclesiastici homines nihil recitarunt de horis canonicis. Eos pensum hoc nobiscum persolvere curavimus, ut recitandi morem addiscerent; et quia breviarii novi Romani usus maxime placebat, impetravimus illis quod petebant a legato pontificio. Itaque pergunt quotidie in recitandis horis canonicis.*'— 'Many ecclesiastics never recited the canonical hours at all. We induced them to fulfil this task along with us, so that they might learn the method of saying them; and since they preferred to use the new Roman Breviary, we got leave for them from the papal legate to do so. And so they persevere in reciting daily the canonical hours.'

of busy people,'[1] and on this score no doubt it was that the Jesuits adopted it as soon as it was published;[2] but from 'busy people' it passed into the hands of canons, who are people of leisure, or generally supposed to be so, at all events; and in Spain it was introduced into the choirs of several cathedrals: thus from private recitation it passed into solemn and public celebration. It was under these circumstances that the people of Saragossa, unable to recognise the office of *Tenebrae* one Maundy Thursday, and no doubt thinking that the Chapter had turned Huguenots, made an uproar in the cathedral itself, and went near to making an *auto da fé* of the canons and their new breviary.[3] Thus these good folk defended in their own fashion the just rights of liturgical tradition.

All this was too much for the breviary of Quignonez.

In a memorandum dated 'Trent, August 1, 1551,' and addressed to Cardinal Marcello Crescenzi, the legate of the Holy See at the Council, John de Arze, a Spanish theologian, submitted to the Fathers of this Council certain reasons which should move the Church to repudiate the breviary of Quignonez. This memorandum, which for a long time remained in manuscript, has been printed and published in our own time.[4] Father Arevalo, who had read the MS., praises its conclusions, but considers that

[1] Roskovány, tom. xi. p. 13: '*Breviarium in occupatorum hominum levamen editum.*'

[2] P. Michel, *Histoire de S. Ignace de Loyola* (Tournai, 1893), tom. ii. p. 331.

[3] Roskovány, tom. v. pp. 656-7.

[4] '*De novo breviario tollendo consultatio* . . . D. Ioann. de Arze presbyter Pallantinus professione theologus, apud Roskovány, tom. v. pp. 635-720. The MS. is in the Vatican, Lat. 5302.

it contains more declamation than strong reasoning; we cannot agree with this opinion. To our mind, John de Arze has shown a just and penetrating judgment in estimating both the tendencies and the results of the work of Cardinal Quignonez. He was perfectly right when, while recognising the fact that 'many legends of the old breviaries required reformation,' he deplored the rejection of so many on too slight grounds, the retention of others which were scarcely, if at all, better established, the attaching of too much faith to the *dicta* of such a historian as Platina, '*sciolus interdum et amator novitatis.*' He was right when, while expressing a warm desire to see the ferial office more frequently celebrated, out of love to the psalter and the Holy Scripture, and the Sunday office made obligatory every Sunday, in order to preserve fidelity to the institution of the ancient breviary (*et ita constabit ratio veteris breviarii*), he demanded that the Kalendar of the festivals of the Saints should be secure from interference, that these festivals should have their proper office, and that these offices should be able to be transferred, as had been the custom. He was right in undertaking the defence of the responds, versicles, and *capitula*, and in saying that, if these details are proper to an office which is sung in choir, and are only fully intelligible when this is borne in mind, one cannot, for all that, allow two offices, one for the choir and the other for private recitation, without introducing into any canonical Office an inevitable confusion. He was right in saying that the office was made to be sung, being in its essence an address to God, and not a matter of study, and that it was mixing two distinct forms of religious exercise, and confounding two distinct aims, to try and transform the recitation of the office into a Bible-reading: even putting aside the consideration that, if the mere instruction of the clergy were our object, it would be better to give them some easy portions of the Bible to read and reflect on, passages which had a direct tendency to edification and the formation of Christian character, than to throw open the Holy Scriptures promiscuously to the misunderstanding and the levity of persons who might be ill prepared to profit by it, or devoid of a right intention to do so. He was still more emphatically right when he entered his protest on behalf of the rights of the traditional *ordo psallendi* of the Church, the Roman Church particularly: on behalf of the traditional distribution of the psalms among the various canonical hours, the traditional allotment of the lessons from different parts of Holy Scripture to different seasons of the Christian year, the traditional number of nocturns—in fact, on behalf of the whole of that liturgical order, based as it was on deep and mystical reasons, and constituting a conspicuous monument (*haud obscura vestigia*) of the most venerable antiquity.

These were judicious criticisms; and if there were others less well founded, or which prove nothing by trying to prove too much; if it is true that some considerations of John de Arze are pushed too far in the direction of declamatory vehemence, there are on the other hand some pages of his memorandum which are characterised by a simple and lively eloquence. 'What!' he cries; 'is it when our people see the clergy, and the highest dignitaries of the Church, so anxious to increase the income of their benefices, that we are to regard it as a happy moment for shortening that Divine Service for for which those revenues are the remuneration? Worse still, is it in this iron age, an age in love with the most dangerous novelties, when the ecclesiastical chant is mocked at, the canonical hours proscribed, the ceremonies of the Church despised, and her laws treated as mere human inventions, and that, too, all over the world, in Germany, in Switzerland, in England; when even among ourselves, who adhere to the old faith, we see disgust for the usages of the Church freely expressed, a growing contempt for holy things, a more and more widespread audacity in judging, each man for himself, of dogmas and canons: is this the time to give up our liturgical traditions and seem tacitly to allow that our adversaries are right, when our first duty is to stand firm, and the more the state of ruin manifests itself among them, the more on our part to exert ourselves to uphold the tottering edifice (*et quo plura apud eos cadunt, plura a nobis sunt substituenda*)?'

And observe that there was some boldness shown by John de Arze in expressing himself in such an outspoken manner. He defends himself, in the first lines of his memorandum, against the imputation of wishing to condemn anything which has proceeded from the Holy See, or has once received its approval, and deprecates the idea of bringing any charge against so august a throne:

> Id profiteri libet nos ... nec quidpiam damnare quod a Sede Apostolica sit profectum aut eius auctoritate aliquando comprobatum, ... nec tantam sedem, quod absit, in ius vocamus.

And yet with what vigour he attacks the breviary which *has* 'proceeded from the Holy See, and has once received its approval'! This Spanish theologian, thoroughgoing like all his countrymen, clothes his indictment in terms which, for all the deprecatory tone assumed by him, strike the heaviest and most direct blows. He conjures the Fathers of the Council to be on their guard against that innovating spirit which despises antiquity and takes up with novelties, some of them positively erroneous, all of them worthy of being suspected —the spirit which was so applauded in that century, and which, not content with giving birth in Germany to new rites, new chants, new hymns, new sacraments, new canons, new breviaries, was now endeavouring to gain credit among the orthodox themselves, and to bring to its full development among them also the mystery of iniquity: *Caveant pastores !*

It amounted to a denunciation of the affinities, unrealised but only too real, which subsisted between the work of Cardinal Quignonez and the spirit of the Reformation.[1]

The revised breviary of Cardinal Quignonez had been published at Rome in 1536; twenty-two years later it was proscribed there. By a rescript dated August 8, 1558, Pope Paul IV., without condemning its temporary use, decreed that there was no longer any reason for allowing it to be reprinted.[2] There still remained the task of providing for the reform of the old breviary. After the attempts of Clement VII. and Paul III., the work was still to do; would Paul IV. have better success?

[1] Several writers have pointed out the influence exercised by the breviary of Quignonez on Cranmer and on the constitution of the Book of Common Prayer. See *Edward VI. and the Book of Common Prayer*, F. A. Gasquet and Edm. Bishop (London, 1890), pp. 29 *sqq.*

[2] Roskovány, tom. xi. p. 26.

He undertook this reform with the clearness of ideas which was natural in a man who had long ago deeply studied the subject. His historian, Caracciolo, tells us that he had never been willing to use the breviary of Quignonez, which he considered 'unsuitable for its purpose, and contrary to the ancient form.'[1] Nor was his judgment less severe on the unreformed Roman breviary. In fact, at a time when he was simply Peter Caraffa, being then Bishop of Chieti (*Teate*), he joined with S. Cajetan of Thiene in forming a congregation of Clerks Regular— the first in order of time of all such institutions, and the prototype of that of S. Ignatius Loyola—known as the congregation of the Theatines; and one of the most novel of the points comprised in the Rule which he gave them was that, for the use of these Theatines, a reform of the old Roman breviary was to be undertaken. In 1533, in a letter addressed to the *datarius*[2] Giberto, Caraffa expressed the disgust he felt for the recitation of this breviary; he complains of the barbarism of its style, and of having to read in it so many passages from authors of doubtful authority, such as Origen, and so many legends unworthy of credit.[3] In 1529 (January 21), Pope Clement VII. had addressed a brief to Caraffa for the purpose of congratulating the Theatines on having, for the honour of the worship of God and our holy religion, conceived the design of bringing the Divine Office, as used in the Holy Roman Church, into a form which appeared to them more suitable for its purpose, and better calculated to

---

[1] Roskovány, tom. xi. p. 26.
[2] [The chief officer of the Roman Chancery.—A. B.]
[3] Quoted by Silos, *Historia Clericorum Regularium* (Rome, 1650), p. 95.

secure the edification and the devotion alike of those who officiated and of those who assisted at it.[1] Even at this time, Caraffa's ideas did not stop short of procuring the adoption by the Roman *Curia* of the Theatine reform of the breviary. The Theatines, in fact, not only asked permission of Pope Clement VII. to recite the breviary as corrected by themselves, but when they should have made practical trial of it, they wished to present it to the Holy See, that it might be examined and a resolution come to as to whether it would not be well to bring it into public use in churches generally. . And the Pope, in the brief above quoted, gives them some hope that what they wished might be granted.

But at this very moment (1529), Cardinal Quignonez on his part had set to work, nor is there any room for doubting that he would never have undertaken the reform of the breviary without the approbation of Clement VII. And this circumstance causes Caracciolo, not without some appearance of reason, to accuse the Pope of changeableness and inconstancy : 'This Pontiff,' he writes with some bitterness, ' had no one to guide him to the choice of such things as were good, and the reforms which were really advantageous for the Church of God ; and all the plans he formed were either never put into execution or were abandoned after the very first trial, as Florebello also says, who was his secretary.'[2] Such was certainly not the character of Paul IV., who, ascending the pontifical throne in 1555, carried thither the same views on Catholic reform which he had held ever since 1524, and set before himself as his object what had been

---

[1] Silos, *l.c.* [2] Roskovány, tom. ix. p. 10.

with Clement VII. no more than a passing wish, the approbation for the whole Church of that Theatine breviary which had been waiting twenty-five years for its authorisation.

In the first place, however, the Pope wished to revise it once more. We really know very little about the details of this reform of the breviary projected by Paul IV. Father Silos himself knew no more of them than such as were mentioned by the Theatine Isachino, the Pope's chamberlain, in a letter dated 1561, and found by Silos in the archives of the convent of S. Sylvester at Rome.[1] By this it appears that Paul IV. suppressed all lessons from Origen and other authors not approved as being thoroughly orthodox; he wished to have only such passages from the holy Fathers as were irreproachable both as to doctrine and as to style; and at Nocturns, only such blessings as were distinguished by devout gravity, instead of some 'silly and absurd' ones which were in use; he removed those narratives of martyrdoms which were without authority, so as to admit none that were not of certain and unquestionable authenticity; he suppressed the uncouth hymns (*hymnos absonos*) which had been assigned to the festivals of the Transfiguration and the Holy Trinity; he shortened the Sunday Prime office, which he considered inordinately long. If we may judge by these few particulars, we may say that Paul IV. understood better than Clement VII. and Paul III. the true conditions of a good reform of the breviary, which he, equally with them, felt to be needed: viz. that such a reform ought to be a return, not to an ideal antiquity such

[1] Silos, p. 98.

as Quignonez dreamed of, but to the ancient tradition which was represented by the existing liturgy; that there was no need of change in the traditional arrangement of the Divine Office as it stood in the old breviary of the Roman *Curia*: all that was necessary was to purge that breviary from historical errors, from literary defects, and from wearisome prolixities, which discouraged the clergy from using it with devotion. Pius V., in fact, afterwards well expressed the essence of the idea of Paul IV. when he wrote:

> Totam rationem dicendi ac psallendi horas canonicas ad pristinum morem et institutum redigendum suscepit.[1]

Thus, at last, liturgical tradition (*pristinus mos*) found the highest authority of all able to comprehend and willing to protect it. A fortunate reaction took place in favour of the old Roman breviary, and the Council of Trent found the question brought before it in the excellent terms in which it was stated by Paul IV.

It was inevitable that the Council of Trent should deal with the question of the breviary: it was one of those points on which more synods than one can number had demanded a reform, during the last twenty-five years. Thus, in 1522, the Synod of Sens requested the Ordinaries to inspect the breviaries, and especially the legends of the saints, so as to suppress whatever they should find there which was 'superfluous,' or unbecoming the dignity of the Church. Similarly the Synod of Cologne in 1536.[2]

---

[1] See the bull *Quod a nobis*.
[2] Roskovány, tom. v. pp. 211, 222.

At Augsburg, in 1548, the 'scheme of ecclesiastical reform,' adopted by Charles V., expressed itself somewhat to this effect: 'The tradition as to the method of chanting and praying, which goes back to the holy Fathers, and has been handed down to us by S. Gregory and other rulers of the Church, is not to be called in question. But it cannot be denied that, in the lapse of time, many things have crept into it which are silly, apocryphal, and by no means accordant with a pure worship. Wherefore it is fitting that the bishops, each in his own diocese, should apply themselves to the correction of the breviaries, bringing back the rites to their pure and ancient form; so that not only the current fashion observed in the prayers may be reformed, but that nothing may be allowed to be recited in them but what is holy, authentic, and worthy of a place in the Divine Office. It will be the part of the bishops to see if anything can be set forth concerning the histories of the saints of which the churches of Germany may make use temporarily in the lessons of Nocturns, until a General Council has pronounced upon the question; the bishops will also have to see if there is any means of suppressing the wearisome repetitions of the same prayers and psalms on the same day, as well as the commemorations,[1] and the memorials of the saints, and everything else which hinders priests from saying the ferial office of the Season, and causes them to prefer the office of the Saints, which is shorter, but less profitable; finally, they must see if there is any means of suppressing

[1] [I take these to be the commemorations of saints or mysteries assigned to certain days of the week, if vacant, which were the ruin of the ferial office. See Wordsworth and Procter's edition of the Sarum Breviary, Fascic. III. Append. II. § vi.—A. B.]

certain additions to the canonical Office, which do not belong to the essence of that Office.'[1] This programme of the German bishops is somewhat confused and vague: how much clearer and more practical were the views of Paul IV.! We are therefore not surprised to find that his programme was preferred without hesitation by the Council of Trent.

The Council only attacked the question of the breviary in 1562—that is to say, in the year before that in which its labours ended.[2] The demand for a reform of the canonical Office was made simultaneously by the Cardinal of Lorraine in the name of the king and bishops of France, and by the Emperor Ferdinand I. The latter, taking up and stating in more precise terms the scheme drawn up at Augsburg in 1548, demanded that the breviaries should be corrected, that nothing should be allowed to remain in them which was not from Holy Scripture; and that, on the other hand, to remedy the lukewarmness with which the clergy regarded the recitation of their office, it should be notably abridged: for, said he, 'far better is it to recite five psalms with calmness and spiritual joy, than to say the entire psalter through with a heart filled with gloom and ill at ease.'[3] The Germans, in fact, did not seem satisfied with the experiment which had already been made with the breviary of Quignonez of this Protestant and chimerical scheme of reform: we here find them taking up on their own account the very notion which had been entertained

---

[1] Roskovány, tom. v. p. 224.

[2] See Schmid, 'Studien über die Reform des Römischen Breviers unter Pius V.,' in the *Theologische Quartalschrift* of Tübingen, 1884.

[3] Roskovány, tom. v. p. 226; Schmid, p. 621.

by the Cardinal of Holy Cross. The French contented themselves with vague expressions: they demanded from the Council the restoration of rites to a purer form, and the suppression of superstitions.[1] The Spaniards, showing themselves better acquainted with the state of the question than either the Germans or the French, made their request to the Pope, expressing to him their grief at the harm done by the breviary of Cardinal Quignonez, and demanding the correction of the old Roman breviary according to the plan of Paul IV.: '*repurgatis paucis, quae iudicio eiusdem pontificis per ignorantiam et temeritatem multis saeculis irrepserant.*' To this end, they asked the Pope to charge the Cardinal Archbishop of Trani, Bernardino Scotti, and with him, Father Isachino, and the prelate Sirleto, to inform the Council of the state of the work commenced by Paul IV.[2]

The ideas of the Spaniards prevailed at the Council. Their request was forwarded to Trent by the Secretary of State to Pope Pius IV., the sainted Cardinal Charles Borromeo, in November 1562, in terms which allowed it to be clearly seen that the mind of the Spanish prelates was also that of the Roman *Curia*. Eight months later, June 24, 1563, the legates informed the Sovereign Pontiff that the correction of the breviary had been delegated to a Conciliary Commission, that of the Index. The commission was composed of Leonardo Marini, Bishop of Lanciano, Muzio Calinio, Archbishop of Zara, and Egidio

---

[1] Grancolas, *Comment. Hist.* p. 10: '*Que le service Divin soit pur, toutes les superstitions retranchées, les prières et les cérémonies corrigées.*'

[2] Schmid, pp. 623-25. The letter of Isachino already quoted probably relates to this inquiry; see p. 251.

Foscarari, Bishop of Modena; to whom was added Thomas Godwell, the deprived Bishop of S. Asaph, a Theatine of English race, a friend of Cardinal Pole and S. Charles Borromeo.[1] In the same letter, the legates begged the Pope to be good enough to place in the hands of the Commission the MSS. containing the corrections made by Paul IV., which were in the possession of the Cardinal Archbishop of Trani, who was also a Theatine.[2] By July 22 all these were in the hands of the Commission.[3] But by this time it was too late for the Council itself to come to a decision on the changes proposed by Paul IV.

On December 4, 1563, the Council of Trent came to an end, without the Commission having settled anything about the breviary, except that its reformation should be remitted to the care of the Holy See itself, to be pursued and brought to completion. When, at the last sitting of the Council, the Archbishop of Catania read out the decrees which awaited its approval and ratification, among which was the decree concerning the bréviary, although a prelate remarked on the fact that these decrees had never been submitted to the various Commissions for discussion, and had not been actually deliberated by them, the Council adopted the resolution which remitted the reform of the breviary to the care of the Pope.[4] One can hardly imagine a conciliary assembly discussing the infinite details of the constitution of the

---

[1] Schmid, p. 626.   [2] *Ib.* p. 269; Silos, p. 447.
[3] Schmid, p. 625.
[4] Theiner, *Acta Authentica Conc. Trid.* (Agram, 1874), tom. ii. p. 506; cf. Grancolas, *op. cit.* p. 11, for the objections made by the Bishop of Lerida, Ant. Agostino.

THE BREVIARY OF THE COUNCIL OF TRENT 257

text of the Divine Office, as it might do the wording of a canon: but, it being granted that the idea of Pius IV. was in accord with that of Paul IV., to remit the affair to the care of the Pope was simply to approve the programme of reform proposed by these two Pontiffs, a programme which the Conciliary Commission had made their own, and which the Council, by continuing the delegation of the matter to the bishops who were members of that Commission, made in their turn their own. One may say, then, that the Council of Trent adopted the views of Paul IV., and that the old Roman breviary, so harshly viewed by the French and Germans, so disowned even at Rome in the hey-day of success of the Quignonez breviary, came out victorious and consecrated from this trial, so important and so decisive. And in addition to this, the upshot of the course taken by affairs on this occasion was that the committee which had to achieve the reform of the Office was a Roman committee, and the reformed breviary, in becoming the breviary authorised by the Council of Trent, did not cease to be, even in its title, the Roman breviary.

II

Scarcely had the Council come to an end, when Pope Pius IV. summoned to Rome the three bishops appointed by it for the correction of the breviary: Marini, Calinio and Foscarari. One would like to know something more about the labours of this Committee than merely the conclusions they arrived at; and perhaps some day more will be known, if it should turn out that the MSS. recording their proceedings are in existence

s

somewhere or other; but at present they are not to be found. The names even of the members whom Pius IV. added on his own account to the three delegates from the Council are imperfectly known; the Cardinal Archbishop of Trani, Scotti, seems to have been made the chairman of the Committee, at all events for a time; there was the modest, learned, and industrious William Sirleto, one of the most learned men of the Roman *Curia* at that time, and subsequently a Cardinal, of whom it was afterwards said that he was '*il principal istitutore et essecutore di questo bel ordine de' uffici*': Curtius de' Franchi, Canon of S. Peter's; Vincent Masso, a Theatine renowned for his knowledge of ecclesiastical history; an elegant Latinist, Giulio Poggiano; and, lastly, perhaps Antonio Caraffa, afterwards a Cardinal.[1] For our information as to the aims and the methods of this Congregation of the Breviary we have only the book itself in the shape in which it left their hands, and two other documents: the bull of Pope Pius V. which serves as Preface to the Breviary, and a letter in Italian, supposed to have been written by Leonardo Marini, one of the members.[2]

Pius V. tells us that, after the disappointing experiment tried by Cardinal Quignonez, many Ordinaries attempted on their own account to reform the breviary for the use of their own clergy, an undesirable custom (*prava consuetudo*), from which the worst confusion had proceeded; to remedy which, Pope Paul IV. of happy memory had abrogated the permission granted for the use of the breviary of Quignonez, and undertaken the task of

---

[1] Schmid, pp. 628–631. See the author's *La Vaticane de Paul III. à Paul V.* pp. 25 and 65.

[2] Roskovány, tom. v. pp. 576–583; Schmid, p. 459.

bringing the office back to its ancient form (*ad pristinum morem*); but Paul IV. having died without bringing this work to its completion, the Council of Trent expressed its desire to see the breviary reformed in accordance with the idea of that Pontiff (*ex ipsius Pauli Papae ratione restituere cogitarunt*); and the Council in its turn delegated the care of this reform to a Committee, which eventually completed, under the pontificate of Pius V., the work of which the initiative belonged to Paul IV. And the Pope adds: 'Having ascertained that in the accomplishment of its work the Congregation has not departed from the form of the ancient breviaries of the most notable churches at Rome, and our library of the Vatican; and while eliminating whatever was of foreign origin or uncertain authority, they have not omitted anything which is of the essence of the ancient Divine Office, we have given our approval to their work.' In other words, the Roman Congregation of the Breviary had as the object before them, in accordance with the idea of Paul IV., the restoration of the liturgical tradition, which they were to carry out by studying the Office in its ancient manuscript forms, and by removing from it all that was foreign to those forms or for the insertion of which there was no sufficient justification (*remotis iis quae aliena et incerta essent, de propria summa veteris officii Divini nihil omittere*).[1] Such at least was the notion of Pius V.

Leonardo Marini enters into detail as to the application of this leading idea expressed by the Pope. The Congregation, he says, 'convinced that the ancient form of prayer was good, and that it had become disliked simply through the fact of other offices having been

[1] See the bull *Quod a nobis*.

superadded to it, aimed at restoring the ancient order, and reducing to just proportions the additions with which it had been burdened.'

Starting from this principle, they maintained the traditional division of the offices into those of nine lessons and those of three. But, in order to give the psalter greater scope, they enjoined for the office of simple feasts the twelve psalms of the ferial nocturn, in accordance with the ancient rubric. And in order to give more scope for the reading of Holy Scripture as well, they ordained that one lesson out of three, and three out of nine, should at all times be taken from the book of the Bible then in course of reading. They felt (and the point is excellently expressed by Marini) that the ferial office is the fundamental one; it was most unbecoming that that office should be the one least often said, especially in Lent, when the canons of the Church ordained, on the contrary, that it should be the only one used; they were sensible that the recitation of the psalter, which ought to be performed in its entirety every week, was so cut up in practice, that the psalms of the Common of Saints, and none other, came over and over, to the weariness of those who said the office; and that the reading of Holy Scripture could not be diminished as it was, without the ignorance of the clergy being increased in the same degree.[1] The Sunday office, with its eighteen psalms, was no longer to be ousted by semidoubles; while in Advent and Lent it was even to have the preference over doubles. Thus did the Congregation aim at restoring the ancient order.

The Gradual and Penitential psalms, which had

[1] Roskovány, tom. v. p. 578.

become obligatory on all ferias in Advent and Lent, were no longer then to be recited, except the Gradual psalms on Wednesdays, and the Penitential psalms on Fridays. The Office for the Dead, which had been made obligatory on every day which was kept as a feria or as a simple feast, was henceforth only to be recited every Monday in Advent and Lent, and at other times on the first vacant day of each month. The Little Office of our Lady, which was obligatory on every day when the office was of the feria, of a simple, or of a semi-double, was now only to be recited on Saturdays (*quovis sabbato non impedito*), excluding Ember Saturdays, vigils, and the whole of Lent. The Nocturns of the Sunday office, however long they might be, were not to be touched, but the Sunday Prime was relieved of the burden of Ps. xxi. to xxv. [xxii.–xxvi.]. which used to precede the *Beati immaculati*,[1] but which it was now decided to distribute over the Prime of the ferias during the week. Thus did the Congregation endeavour 'to reduce to just proportions the additions' with which the ancient order of the office had been burdened.[2]

From these declarations on the part of Marini we can see what kind of spirit animated the Congregation. It is impossible to say whether their action fell short of what Paul IV. had proposed to himself or went beyond it: more probably the latter. But what is most worthy of notice is the extent to which the imprudences committed by Quignonez made them on their part circumspect, and even timid, possessed, perhaps excessively, with the idea of abolishing nothing: '*Nihil quod in usu erat c*

---

[1] The first thirty-two verses of Ps. cxviii. [cxix.].
[2] Roskovány, tom. v. pp. 579-581.

medio sublatum, sed temperatum,' as Marini says. Pius V. shows himself more decided, when, by his sovereign authority he rendered optional the recitation on certain days of the Office of the Virgin, the Office of the Dead, and the Penitential and Gradual psalms, an obligation religiously maintained by the Congregation, and to this day enjoined by the rubrics of the Breviary.[1] Here were, indeed, foreign elements (*aliena*), as to the removal of which no hesitation need have been shown.

The Congregation manifested the same scrupulous tenderness as to the elimination of such elements of the old breviary as were of uncertain authority (*incerta*). The reproach has been made, writes Marini, that some of the legends of saints in the old breviary were apocryphal, unedifying, or written in a bad style. The Congregation has decided to retain the more authentic, putting them into a better literary form, thus securing both the edification and the pleasure of readers. They feel that many of the Lives of Saints in the old breviary are excellent, being taken from authors venerable for their antiquity, or from the *Acta sincera* of the Martyrs, and to these preference ought to be given, while carefully revising them from the point of view of historical accuracy as well as correctness of literary style. This task was entrusted at first to Foscarari, afterwards to Poggiano, and these two had all the legends of the *Sanctorale* to revise.[2] Here again the indications furnished by Marini tend to confirm our impression that the Congregation viewed the Reform of the Breviary merely as a correction, and that correction

---

[1] See the bull *Quod a nobis.*
[2] Roskovány, tom. v. p. 582; cf. *Julii Pogiani Epistolae et Orationes* (Rome, 1756), tom. ii. pp. xl–lii.

as one to be confined to what was strictly indispensable. Marini says as much, in conclusion, in a sentence which leaves no doubt about the matter: *Perstitit inconcussa deputatorum convictio nil mutandum esse in ipsis Ecclesiae libris.'*

The Roman Breviary, corrected according to these views, appeared in 1568, hardly five years after the close of the Council of Trent. It would even seem that its correction was finished by 1566, from a letter written by Cardinal Borromeo to Sirleto.[1] At this rate the reform must have occupied barely three years in its execution. The bull *Quod a nobis*, publishing the new Breviary, is dated July 1, 1568. The book itself was printed at Rome, and the printer, Paul Manutius, received the privilege to do so on November 11 in that year. The office according to the new Breviary might thus come into use at the beginning of the year 1569. The title runs as follows:

> Breviarium Romanum, ex decreto Sacrosancti Concilii Tridentini restitutum, Pii V. Pont. Max. iussu editum. Romae, MDLXVIII. Cum privilegio Pii V. Pontificis Maximi, in aedibus Populi Romani, apud Paulum Manutium.

The bull *Quod a nobis* pronounced the absolute abolition of the breviary of Quignonez, as well as of all breviaries precedent to the new one now published, with the exception of such as could claim Pontifical approval, or a prescription of two hundred years duration: along with a prohibition to change the new Breviary in whole or in part, to add to it or take from it anything whatsoever.

[1] Borromeo to Sirleto, September 4, 1566 (Schmid, p. 654).

Bearing in mind the scrupulously conservative spirit with which the liturgists of Pius V. were animated, we must not expect to find in the breviary of 1568 anything but the traditional breviary of the Roman *Curia*, as it had been printed ever since 1474—amended, however, and rendered in all respects both more handy to use and more polished in style. Quignonez had pronounced the old rubrics obscure and involved; at the head of the new breviary was placed the excellent exposition of the general rubrics of the office which is still to be found there, and which was partly borrowed from the *Directorium Divini Officii* published by L. Ciconiolano in 1540, with the approbation of Paul III.[1] Quignonez had deplored the inroads made on the office of the Season by the *Sanctorale*; the Kalendar of fixed feasts was now lightened by the removal of several festivals— those of SS. Joachim, Francis de Paula, Bernardin, Antony of Padua, Anne, Louis de Toulouse, Elizabeth of Hungary, and the Presentation of our Lady. Several more were reduced to have a memorial only—SS. Euphemia, Thecla, Ursula, Saturninus. The total number of semidoubles was brought down to 30; of doubles of all classes, 57; of memorials, 33. Thus the offices of the Common of Saints now took only about a hundred days from the office of the Season.

The text both of the psalter and of the lessons from Holy Scripture was that of the Vulgate. It has often been asserted that this was an innovation of this date; but in reality it had been introduced at a period which cannot be stated with precision, but certainly anterior to the sixteenth century.[2] The distribution of Holy Scrip-

[1] Schmid, p. 637.   [2] Schober, p. 41.

THE BREVIARY OF THE COUNCIL OF TRENT 265

ture for the lessons of the first nocturn was made conformably to the decree commonly called that of Gregory VII.[1]—in reality, as regards its main outlines, it agrees with the distribution the use of which in the eighth century we have already verified.[2] Every day had its lesson from Scripture, and these were chosen, with few exceptions, from the plainest and simplest pages of the Bible.

The Antiphonary and Responsoral remained intact: that is to say, in accordance, with the exception of a few details, with what they had been in the eighth century.

The Lectionary for the second nocturn of fixed feasts underwent notable changes. New lessons were given for the festivals of SS. Hilary, Paul the Hermit, John Chrysostom, Ignatius of Antioch, Matthias, Joseph, Soter and Caius, Cletus and Marcellinus, Athanasius, Gregory Nazianzen, and Basil; the Visitation, the Octave of S. Peter, S. Mary Magdalene, S. Peter's Chains, the Invention of S. Stephen, S. Dominic, S. Mary of the Snows, the Transfiguration, S. Laurence, the whole Octave of the Assumption, S. Bartholomew, S. Augustine of Hippo, the Beheading of S. John Baptist, the Octave of the Nativity of our Lady, SS. Matthew, Jerome, Francis of Assisi, Simon and Jude, Martin, and Damasus. A dozen or so additional homilies for the third Nocturn were introduced, or the old replaced by new: on the

---

[1] See chap. iv. pp. 170-173.
[2] It comprises Isaiah for Advent; Genesis in spring; Acts, Apocalypse, and the non-Pauline Epistles in Paschal-tide; the Kings in summer; Sapiential books in August; Job, Tobit, Judith, and Esther in September; Maccabees in October; Ezekiel, Daniel, and the Minor Prophets in November: the Pauline Epistles in the Christmas season. See ch. iii. pp. 102, 103.

feasts of SS. Agnes, Vincent and Anastasius, Ignatius, Agatha, Martha, Matthew, Bernard, Augustine, Jerome, Nicolas, Lucy, &c. But it is here we come on the weak point in the reform of Pius V. His liturgists had no hesitation in suppressing the lessons given in the breviary of 1550 for the festival of S. Margaret, as also those for SS. Thecla, Eustace, and Ursula: but this was not suppressing enough. And as for new lessons, if we judge by those for S. Bartholomew, the Invention of S. Stephen, and S. Mary of the Snows, they admitted more than they ought. And how many more lessons there were which, either in their origin or in the form they had been made to assume, remained undoubtedly worthy of censure! No one can question the fairness and openness of mind with which these liturgists approached their task; but it may be doubted whether the time was ripe for such an enterprise, and their critical ability seems not to have been equal to the strain put upon it. We cannot blame Bellarmine and Baronius on the one hand, and Benedict XIV. on the other, for reproaching them on this score.

And yet, on the whole, a great progress was effected. This respectful and timid treatment of the Breviary of the *Curia* was the best restoration of the ancient Roman Office which was possible at the time. It preserved the traditional *ordo psallendi* of the Roman Church; it preserved the Antiphonary and Responsoral of the time of Charlemagne; it restored the *ordo canonis decantandi* of the eighth century; it suppressed the additional offices introduced into the liturgy in the post-Carolingian period; it reduced the Kalendar of fixed feasts to juster proportions, and restored to its due place of honour the office of the Season. If it did not venture to suppress the hymnal, it is because at that time no one had any idea of doing such a thing, and, indeed, no one has thought of doing so since. And if in the matter of correcting the lectionary its literary and historical criticism was somewhat at fault, that was in great measure inevitable, owing to the then state of critical scholarship.

Catholic Christendom did full justice to the wise and sincere work of Pius V. All Italy, the whole of Spain, including Portugal, through the influence of Philip II., and France, rather more tardily, dating from 1580,[1] and then owing to the efforts of the Jesuits, received with esteem the new Roman Breviary. 'If in the ninth century,' writes the Sorbonnist Grancolas, 'the Roman Breviary deserved such universal praise as to be preferred to those of all other Churches, it shone with even greater lustre after Pope Pius V. brought it out afresh; and it may be said that, since that time, particular Churches have adopted it universally, at all events to this extent, that those who have not received it under the title of the Roman Breviary have incorporated it almost entire in their own, adapting it to their own rite.'[2]

We may even say, with Dom Guéranger, that the success of the Breviary of Pius V. was excessive. The Holy See contemplated the continued use of liturgies with a prescription of two centuries and upwards. Thus, by a rescript of September 10, 1587, it accorded to the Church of Aquileia the privilege of continuing to celebrate the Divine Office according to its

---

[1] A fine edition of the Breviary of Pius V. was, nevertheless, published at Paris by Kerver, 1574.

[2] Cf. Guéranger, tom. i. pp. 450 *sqq.*; Roskovány, tom. ii. pp. 236-262; Bäumer, *Geschichte*, pp. 457-467.

ancient patriarchal rite.¹ It would have been a good thing if Churches which might have availed themselves of the exception made by the bull *Quod a nobis*, had preserved their own traditional *ordo*. When the Chapter of the Cathedral of Paris, in 1583, refused to its Bishop, Peter de Gondy, the reception of the Breviary of Pius V.—'*maxime quod recepta dudum tam illustris Ecclesiae consuetudo non facile suum immutari officium pateretur*'²—it was in accordance with the conservative views expressed by the Holy See. 'We are far from blaming the Chapter,' writes Dom Guéranger. 'It was only right that the Romano-French liturgy, which several religious Orders had adopted, and which had made its way into the Churches of Jerusalem, Rhodes, and Sicily, should stand as one of the glories of our nation. Already abolished in the greater part of the French cathedrals by the introduction of Roman books, by Paris, at all events, it ought not to be allowed to perish. Rome itself had prepared the way for this preservation by the provisions of her bull; if, then, this beautiful and poetic form of Catholic worship now no longer exists, it is not from the Holy See that we are to demand the reason, but from those Parisians who, *a hundred years later*, thought fit to overthrow the venerable and noble edifice which their forefathers had defended with so much affection.'³

---

¹ Guéranger, tom. i. p. 430.

² *Breviarium insignis Ecclesiae Parisiensis restitutum ac emendatum R. in Christo Patris D. Petri de Gondy Parisiensis Episcopi authoritate, ac eiusdem Ecclesiae Capituli consensu editum* (Paris, 1584; preface by De Gondy).

³ Guéranger, tom. i. p. 452. But Dom Guéranger is wrong in falling foul of the Parisians of the seventeenth century. It was Peter de Gondy who, in 1584, caused the Parisian service-books to

III

In promising—in the bull *Quod a nobis*—that the Breviary 'should never at any time be changed either in whole or in part, and that no one should add to it or take away from it anything whatever,' Pope Pius V. engaged himself to something which his successors were not disposed to observe.

His immediate successor, Pope Gregory XIII. (1572-1585), did not consider himself bound by the terms of the bull *Quod a nobis*. Pius V. had not instituted any office in commemoration of the victory of Lepanto (1571), contenting himself with inserting in the Roman Martyrology under October 7 the mention of our Lady of Victory. Gregory XIII. was not satisfied with this, and by a decree dated April 1, 1573, he instituted the feast of the Rosary, fixed it for the first Sunday in October of each year, and assigned to it the rank of greater double. It is true that this festival was not extended to the Church at large—that was not the case until October 3, 1716, under Clement XI. But, all the same, Gregory XIII. felt no scruple as to interfering with the Breviary of 1568. We see this plainer when, in 1584, he re-established, as a double, the festival of S. Anne, which Pius V. had removed from the Breviary, and introduced a memorial of S. Joachim, all mention of whom had been suppressed by his predecessor.[1]

After him, again, Sixtus V. (1585-1590) laid his hands

be corrected, and 'introduced into them nearly the whole of the Breviary of S. Pius V' (Guéranger, *loc. cit.*).

[1] Schober, p. 49.

on the work of Pius V. He re-established in 1585, as a double, the feast of the Presentation of the Virgin, which had been abolished by Pius V. In the same way he re-established the festivals of SS. Francis de Paula and Nicolas de Tolentino. The next year (1586) he re-established the festivals of SS. Januarius and his companions, Peter Martyr, and Antony of Padua, all suppressed by Pius V. In 1588 he bestowed on S. Bonaventure the title of Doctor of the Church, and raised his festival from a semidouble to a double.[1] He had thoughts, indeed, of doing far more, and of perfecting, if not of recasting throughout, the correction of the Breviary carried out under Pius V. Dom Bäumer has been the first writer to bring forward proofs of the fact that Sixtus V. requested his nuncios in the various Catholic Courts to use all necessary diligence in order to collect '*quelli avvertimenti, osservationi et fatiche che sin hora si ritrovassero haverci fatte alcune persone pie, dotte et accurate*'—'any admonitions, observations, and works which up to the present time may be found to have been made by any pious, learned, and accurate persons'—because the Pope had the intention '*restituire alla loro purità il Breviario et il Missale Romano*'—of restoring to their purity the Roman Breviary and Missal.[2]

This project of Sixtus V. did not lead to any result during his pontificate, but Dom Bäumer has also discovered traces of a Commission to whom Gregory XIV.

---

[1] Schober, p. 50.

[2] Bäumer, *Geschichte*, p. 486. Letters to Cardinal Gesualdo, July and August, 1588.

(1590–1591) entrusted the execution of the revision projected by his predecessor, recorded in certain '*Acta Congregationis pro purgando breviario sub Gregorio XIV.*'[1] Cardinal Gesualdo was the president of this Commission, whose programme is stated thus:

> Ut in lectionibus sanctorum et aliis quibusque rebus ea solum mutentur quae nullo pacto sustineri possunt. At quae satis bene digesta noscuntur, non ulterius laborandum ut ampliora et perfectiora reddantur; cum importunae novitates, hoc praesertim tempore, nihil expedire . . . videantur.[2]

The Commission met several times in May and June 1591; the text of a few timid corrections proposed by them for the lessons of the *Sanctorale* is given, and it must be confessed that these reveal a most elementary and insufficient perception of the principles of historical criticism! We gather also that the Commission was entrusted with the task of correcting the hymnal, for there are '*diversae annotationes et correctiones hymnorum a multis allatae.*'[3]

The pontificate of Sixtus V. gave the Catholic Church an edition of the Vulgate of S. Jerome (1589). In the bull '*Aeternus Ille,*' which serves as a preface to this Sixtine edition of the Vulgate, the Sovereign Pontiff gave the printers a permission or rather, a command, which was not without grave effects—viz. the command to

---

[1] Bäumer, *Geschichte*, pp. 488–492. From the Vatican MSS., Lat. 6097.

[2] 'In the legends of saints and all other passages let those things only be altered which are in no way tolerable. As for such as are fairly well expressed, let no labour be bestowed on making them fuller or more perfect; for constant changes, especially at the present time, seem altogether inexpedient.'

[3] Baümer, *loc. cit.*

correct, in accordance with this edition, in missals, breviaries, psalters, rituals, pontificals, ceremonials, and other ecclesiastical books, all the passages taken from Holy Scripure (*iuxta hunc nostrum textum ad verbum et ad literam corrigantur*). Well, we know what sort of criticism the Sixtine text of the Vulgate aroused, and how it became necessary at once to undertake its revision; hence there appears a fresh edition of the Vulgate in 1592. What disturbances in the text of the Roman Office does all this imply! We have got to about the year 1600; the Breviary of 1568 has already been thirty years in use. What book would not be found to betray some flaws under such an ordeal as it had to face? Textual criticism, the knowledge of history, literary taste, were all of them more developed and more exacting than they had been when the revision was made. The Congregation of 1568, coming after Cardinal Quignonez, had worked at a time of reaction, when circumspection was peculiarly necessary; a fresh body of revisers might venture on bolder courses without being rash. What Cardinal Sirleto in the time of Pius V. could not do might well lie within the power of Cardinal Bellarmine in the time of Clement VIII.[1]

It was not, however, to Bellarmine that reference was most especially made. The chief part in the Clementine revision of the Breviary belonged to Cardinal Baronius.

The initiative in the matter of revision was taken by the Holy See. From Rome messages were sent, asking the advice, not of the Ordinaries of Churches, but of the

---

[1] A. Bergel, 'Die Emendation des Römischen Breviers unter Papst Clemens VIII.,' in the *Zeitschrift für Katholische Theologie* (Innsbruck, 1884).

most learned members of the various learned theological bodies of Europe; and the *Adnotationes Criticae* thus addressed to the Pope by the theologians of Poland, Savoy, Spain, Germany, Naples, Venice, the Sorbonne, the Dean of the theological faculty at Salamanca, and so forth, not omitting Ciacconio and Bellarmine, have been preserved among the papers of Baronius in the library of the Vallicellan at Rome.[1]

In fact, all these replies were consigned to Cardinal Baronius for him to pass judgment upon them and report his conclusions to the Pope; and we possess the text of his Report.

'I have examined,' he says, 'all the criticisms which have come in from various countries, or which have been sent to me by learned persons at Rome itself. In accordance with these I have ruled out, all through the Breviary, whatever seemed indefensible, thus applying myself first, for greater despatch in the work of correction, to suppress, rather than to add anything fresh. As it is but just that my work should be submitted to the censorship of others, the best course would be for your Holiness to appoint one of the Cardinals of the Congregation of Rites, joining with him two or three learned and erudite consultors, who would take the trouble to review it carefully. A decision could thus be arrived at in a few days as to this matter. I have everywhere indicated my reasons for correcting or leaving uncorrected this or that passage of the Breviary; and, moreover, I would attend myself, so as to be ready to give any necessary explanations, should any point seem obscure or ambiguous. As soon as the corrections had been reviewed by these

[1] Bergel, pp. 293-94, gives a list of them.

censors, they might be submitted—at least, as regarded the more important modifications—to the Congregation of Rites, and lastly your Holiness might take cognisance of them, and decide on the whole work as might seem good to yourself. As regards the best plan for applying the corrections, it has been suggested that a small volume might be printed, containing the new offices approved by Sixtus V., and the *correctorium* of the whole Breviary. As far as the new offices are concerned, some of which (those for the Conception, Visitation, and Presentation of our Lady) have not yet been printed, there might be some good in this; but as regards the *correctorium*, I altogether disapprove of it. To publish the *correctorium* would amount to exposing to all the world, including the enemies of the Church, the numerous and grave errors which we have hitherto tolerated in the Breviary: this would be a scandal, and a slight upon the authors of our Breviary besides, not to mention how irksome it would be to many persons to make all these corrections in their books. It will be much better to print a Breviary, corrected and purged from errors, not obliging any persons to discard those they are using and to buy the new one forthwith, but only as they have occasion to do so. Thus the religious and the poor priests will not be put to inconvenience; and at the same time, while few people would notice these new corrections of all the errors which really have crept into the Breviary, in a few years there would be none but corrected Breviaries in circulation. If it is decided thus to print a corrected Breviary, a thing which all well-instructed persons keenly desire and eagerly (*avide*) await, your Holiness might explain, in a bull prefixed to it, the reasons for this new edition . . ., especially that its object is to put an end to the temerity of some who, on their own authority, have inserted in the Breviary false or uncertain matter (as is evidently the case with the lessons for S. Alexis and others), and that advantage has been taken of this opportunity to correct some other defects due to the carelessness of printers or of others.'[1]

The views here expressed by Cardinal Baronius would, on more grounds than one, be severely criticised. Let us gather from them one fact at all events: it was he who prepared the correction of the Breviary.

The special committee whose advice he asked for was forthwith nominated by Clement VIII. The names of its members are as follows: John Baptist Bandino, Canon of S. Peter's; Michael Ghisleri, a Theatine; Bartholomew Gavanto, a Barnabite; Louis de Torres, Archbishop of Monreale; Cardinal Antoniano, Cardinal Bellarmine, and Cardinal Baronius as President.[2] It met for the first time on September 10, 1592.

The committee, in the very first place, was agreed that in the text of the Breviary as few changes as possible were to be made: '*data est opera ut quam minima mutatio fieret.*' Cardinal Antoniano had proposed to correct the false quantities which occur in the hymns: but the committee, while recognising the fact that the hymns are full of errors of prosody (*scatent erroribus syllabarum*), did not consent to alter anything beyond those errors which seemed to be due to careless copying, or which could be corrected by the mere changing of a single letter or a single syllable, 'particularly in the hymns of

[1] Bergel, pp. 295-97.
[2] Gavanto, *in front.* '*Thesaur. Sac. Rituum.*'

Prudentius and Ambrose, whom we may not suppose to have composed them incorrectly.'[1] As to the Lectionary, the Antiphonary, and the Responsoral, they aimed at 'changing nothing but that which could not be retained without scandal (*ut ea sola mutaremus quae sine offensione tolerari non poterant*).'[2] They removed some homilies and sermons from the Lectionary and replaced them by others: thus, on August 15, they took away an apocryphal sermon attributed to S. Athanasius, to make way for one by S. John Damascene; on November 1 they restored the name of Bede to the sermon in the second nocturn, which the Breviary of Pius V. had attributed to S. Augustine. They removed from the legends of the *Sanctorale* a small number of assertions which were judged historically untenable: as, in the legend of S. Martin, the relation, borrowed from Gregory of Tours, of S. Ambrose coming in a vision to be present at the death of S. Martin;[3] and the assertion that SS. Gordian and Epimachus were

---

[1] Bergel, p. 297. Two new hymns were added: the *Fortem virili pectore*, written by Cardinal Antoniano for the Common of non-Virgins, and the *Pater superni luminis*, by Cardinal Bellarmine for the festival of S. Mary Magdalene. See his autobiography: '*Scripsit multa carmina. . . . Superest . . . hymnus de S. Maria Magdalena qui positus est in breviario, qui hymnus compositus fuit Tusculi, et a Clemente VIII. antepositus hymno quem de ea re scripsit Cardinalis Antonianus, et uterque nostrum quasi ex tempore scripsit, et ioco magis quam ut in breviario poni deberet*' (J. B. Couderc, *Le Vén. Card. Bellarmin*, Paris, 1893, tom. i. p. 25). 'He wrote many verses. There remains the hymn for S. Mary Magdalene's day in the Breviary, written at Frascati, and preferred by Clement VIII. to the hymn on the same subject written by Cardinal Antoniano. And both of us wrote *impromptu*, and more for amusement than with any idea of what we wrote being put in the Breviary.'

[2] Bergel, *ib*.   [3] *Ib*. p. 340.

condemned at Rome by the Emperor Julian,[1] &c. But most of the errors corrected were those of simple chronology: such as the date of the death of S. Ambrose or of S. Hilary, or of the martyrdom of SS. Gervase and Protase, Faustina and Jovita, &c.

Some corrections proposed by Baronius, however opportune, were not adopted. He considered disputable the fact related in the legend of the Dedication of S. John Lateran: '*Et imago Salvatoris in pariete depicta populo Romano apparuit.*'[2] But it was allowed to stand. He asked that in the legend of the apparition of S. Michael on Mount Garganus, the mention of the consecration of an oratory at Rome, '*in summo circo*,' should be modified so as clearly to indicate the oratory of S. Michael '*in summo circulo molis Adrianae*'—that is, on the terrace of the Castle of S. Angelo; but the old wording was retained, obscure as it is. The grave errors which Baronius pointed out in certain legends, particularly in that of S. Alexis, were not even examined by the committee, and the much controverted legend of that Saint has been left intact. On the other hand, some of the corrections which *were* adopted were open to dispute. For example, Baronius made the Breviary say that the bones of S. Andrew were translated to Constantinople in the reign of Constantius: the Breviary of Pius V. said 'Constantine,' a reading judiciously replaced by Urban VIII. The Breviary of Pius V. had styled S. Hippolytus priest; Baronius gives him the erroneous title of Bishop of Porto. The legend of S. James the Greater in the Breviary of Pius V. said, without

[1] Bergel, p. 317.
[2] 'There appeared to the people of Rome the image of the Saviour depicted on the wall.'

enlarging on the fact, that the Apostle 'traversed Spain and preached the Gospel there, afterwards returning to Jerusalem:' Bellarmine wished this assertion to be removed from the Breviary, as not resting on any testimony worthy of credence, but Baronius, so far from complying with this, had the following passage inserted:

> Mox Hispaniam adiisse, et ibi aliquos ad fidem convertisse, Ecclesiarum illius provinciae traditio est; ex quorum numero septem postea episcopi a B. Petro ordinati in Hispaniam primi directi sunt.[1]

And Urban VIII. was afterwards bound to suppress in this passage the words about *Ecclesiarum illius provinciae traditio,* giving way to the urgent protestations of the clergy of Spain, who held that S. James's coming into their country was something better than a Spanish tradition! In the Breviary of Pius V., the identity of Denis (Dionysius the Areopagite), Bishop of Athens, and Denis, Bishop of Paris, was assumed. Bellarmine wished them to be distinguished from each other, making the latter a bishop of the time of Decius, as he is regarded by Gregory of Tours and Sulpicius Severus: but Baronius insisted on the retention of the account given in the Breviary of Pius V. Baronius corrected the legends of the early Popes; but only to the extent of giving greater precision to the dates of their respective pontificates, still so uncertain.

And how many details '*quae sine offensione tolerari non poterant*' were nevertheless retained! Bellarmine denied

---

[1] 'It is the tradition of the Churches of Spain that S. James went into that province, and there converted some to the faith; of whom seven were afterwards ordained by S. Peter, and sent into Spain as the first bishops of that country.'

the authenticity of the False Decretals, and everybody knows how these are worked into the legends of ancient Popes in the Breviary; yet Baronius refused all correction on this point. Again, Baronius himself recognised the apocryphal character of certain Acts of Apostles, such as the 'Acts of S. Thomas'; yet he appeals to their authority, '*licet adnumerentur inter apocrypha*,' as he says. He admitted the corrupt character of some Acts of Martyrs : '*Acta S. Donati depravata esse nulla dubitatio est*,' he says; and speaking of S. Katherine : '*Multa eius historia habet quae veritati repugnant.*' Yet he did not think that anything further was necessary in their case beyond emendations.

In the end, the *correctorium* drawn up by Baronius as adopted by this Clementine Congregation, amounted to no more than some unimportant modifications,[1] very small even in comparison with the premises set forth by Baronius in his programme. But, such as it was, it established a point of great importance, implicitly recognised by Clement VIII. by his not reproducing, in his bull prefixed to the new edition of the Breviary, the strictly prohibitive terms of the Bull *Quod a nobis* of S. Pius V.: that is to say, that the text of the Roman Breviary is something capable of amendment. And if such is the case, it must be because it contains in its time-honoured and unchanging structure certain elements which are merely temporary and provisional, the true character of which the progress of time has revealed or has still to reveal.

Another matter in which Clement VIII. revised the work of Pius V. was the introduction of new festivals

[1] Bäumer, *Geschichte*, pp. 495-97.

into the Roman Breviary, or the re-establishment of some which had formerly had a place there: such as SS. Romuald (February 7), Stanislas (May 7), Lucius, Pope (March 4), Katherine of Sienna (April 29), John Gualbert (July 12), and Eusebius (December 15). Besides this he raised again the rank of some feasts which had been lowered by Pius V.: the feast of the Invention of the Cross became a double of the second class: the festivals of the Transfiguration, the Exaltation of Holy Cross, S. Mary of the Snows, the Visitation, Presentation, and Conception of our Lady, the Apparition of S. Michael, S. Peter's Chair, both at Rome and at Antioch, S. Peter's Chains, the Conversion of S. Paul, S. John before the Latin Gate, and S. Barnabas, were raised to the rank of greater doubles; some simple feasts were raised to semidoubles—SS. Timothy, Polycarp, Nereus and Achilles, and Gregory the Wonder-worker.[1] In 1568 the object in view was to reduce the *Sanctorale*, so as to restore to the office of the Season its due predominance in use and in dignity; in 1602,[2] the tendency was to give the *Sanctorale* the preponderance. And the example thus set by Clement VIII. was destined to be followed more and more by all his successors, with the exception of Benedict XIV. If I may be allowed to state my own view on so delicate a question, I believe the theory of Pius V. and Benedict XIV. to be preferable.

---

[1] Schober, p. 47.

[2] *Breviarium Romanum ex decreto Sacrosancti Concilii Tridentini restitutum, Pii V. Pont. Max. iussu editum, et Clementis VIII. auctoritate recognitum* (Rome, 1602).

Since the beginning of the sixteenth century, under Leo X., Clement VII., Paul IV., Pius V., and Clement VIII., we have now seen five reforms of the old Breviary of the Roman *Curia*. We have to add a sixth, that of Urban VIII.

This also, like the others, was provoked by the complaints of several pious and learned persons, who represented that the Roman Breviary still contained faulty elements:

> Piorum doctorumque virorum iudicia et vota, conquerentium in eo contineri non pauca quae, sive a nitore institutionis excidissent, sive inchoata potius quam perfecta forent ab aliis, certe a nobis supremam manum imponi desiderarent.[1]

It was made a reproach to the Roman Breviary that the sermons and homilies of the holy Fathers were not from a good text; they ought to be collated with 'printed editions and ancient MSS.' The punctuation of the psalter was defective: it ought to be conformed to that of the Vulgate, and, for convenience in chanting, the end of the mediation in each verse should be marked with an asterisk. But the subject of keenest complaint was that the hymns sinned against the laws of metre and prosody: if a more correct reading could be found in MSS., it should be restored; the lines should be made correct in their scansion, and the Latin in its grammar, wherever it was possible; if otherwise, the lines should be re-written altogether.[2]

Urban VIII. appointed a Congregation to carry out this reform. It was presided over by Cardinal Louis Gaëtani, and composed of nine consultors, several of whom were famous: Father Terence Alciati, a Jesuit;

---

[1] See the bull *Divinam psalmodiam*.   [2] *Ib.*

who prepared the History of the Council of Trent published after his death by Cardinal Pallavicini; Father Hilarion Rancato, the Curator of the Sessorian Library at Rome; Father Luke Wadding, a Minorite, and the historian of his Order; Father Bartholomew Gavanto, a Barnabite, the best liturgist of his time.[1] The other five were: Tegrimi, the secretary of the Congregation of Rites: Sacchi, the pontifical Sacrist: Riccardi, the Master of the Sacred Palace; Vulponi, an Oratorian; and Lanni, a prelate of the *Signatura*.[2] The especial work of the Congregation seems to have been the careful correction of the *letter* of the Breviary, rather than any amendment of the matter contained in it. Speaking of the legends of the saints, Gavanto tells us that, having been reformed under Clement VIII. by Cardinals Bellarmine and Baronius with a severe exactness which spared nothing that was doubtful, the text of these could hardly be rendered more historically correct; the revisers therefore determined on making the fewest possible changes. They retained even controverted facts, provided that, having the support of some one grave author, they might be deemed to possess some probability:

> Quae controversa erant, alicuius tamen gravis auctoris testimonio suffulta, dum aliquam haberent probabilitatem, retenta sunt eo modo quo erant, cum falsitatis argui non possint, quamvis fortasse, altera sententia sit a pluribus recepta.[3]

In fact, on the confession of Gavanto all through his commentary on the Breviary, the Congregation of

---

[1] We find him on the committee who advised Cardinal Baronius on the occasion of the previous revision.

[2] [A department of the Roman Chancery.—A. B.]

[3] Gavanto, *Thesaur. Sacr. Rit.* tom. ii. p. 75.

THE BREVIARY OF THE COUNCIL OF TRENT

Urban VIII. has left hardly any trace of new corrections made on the text as settled by Clement VIII.[1]

Moreover, it was not to this Congregation of liturgists that Urban VIII. entrusted the revision which he had most at heart, but to four Jesuits, Fathers Strada, Galluzzi, Sarbiewski, and Petrucci, who, under the personal direction of the Pope—himself a poet—were the workmen who carried out the chief feature of this reform, viz. the correction of the hymnal.[2] Urban VIII., like all the Barberini of the seventeenth century, was a man of refined literary taste; his Court, like that of Richelieu, was almost an Academy. He put his name to a whole volume of little Latin poems. Two of his hymns were eventually inserted in the Breviary, those for S. Martina:

> Martinæ celebri plaudite nomini,
> Cives Romulei, plaudite gloriæ,
> Insignem meritis dicite virginem,
> Christi dicite martyrem;[3]

---

[1] Bäumer, *Geschichte*, pp. 503-7. He has examined the original papers of this Congregation, preserved in the Vatican Library and in that of the Barberini.

[2] The *Civiltà Cattolica* of Jan. 10, 1896, p. 209, notices a letter from Father Strada to the Pope, published by Venturi (*Gli inni della Chiesa*, Florence, 1880, pp. ix-xii), from which it appears that Urban VIII. himself corrected some of the hymns of the Breviary, and submitted his corrections to Father Strada. But one cannot conclude from this letter that the correction of the hymns generally was made by the Pope himself, or that the Jesuit Fathers were not the persons actually responsible for the way in which this deplorable enterprise was carried out.

[3] 'Applaud Martina's ever glorious name,
    Ye citizens of Rome, her praises sing;
  The merits of the virgin saint proclaim,
    Christ's martyr hail her, faithful to her King.'

and that for S. Elizabeth of Portugal:

> Opes decusque regium reliqueras,
> Elizabeth, Dei dicata numini:
> Recepta nunc bearis inter Angelos;
> Libens ab hostium tuere nos dolis.[1]

Urban VIII. thought to give satisfaction to the predilections of his own time by undertaking the correction of the prosody, if prosody it can be called, of the ecclesiastical hymns. Singular demand, made by the taste of that particular epoch! In the same way the Barberini and others of that period restored antique statues, attaching to them new limbs which disfigure them more than all the mutilations which the hand of time had inflicted! That these Jesuits outran their commission, and, under the pretext of restoring the language of the hymns in accordance with the rules of metre and good grammar, 'deformed the works of Christian antiquity, is now an established fact,' writes the Abbé Chevalier, and he gives as examples two hymns as thus restored by the Jesuits. We print in italics the few words of the original retained by them in their revision.

---

[1] 'Thou royal state, Elizabeth, to God
　　In heart devoted, gladly didst resign;
　Now in thy bliss, mid angel choirs above,
　　Our foes' assaults ward off with prayer benign.'

[2] The text of the Roman hymnal of Urban VIII. will be found in Daniel, *Thesaurus Hymnologicus* (Halle, 1841). With regard to the ancient text of the hymns, see Chevalier, *Poésie liturgique*, pp. xlviii–liii. The two versions may be conveniently compared in *Hymni de Tempore et de Sanctis* (Solesmes, 1885).

1. Hymn at Vespers of Advent

Original Text	*Revised Text*
Conditor alme siderum,	Creator *alme siderum,*
Aeterna lux credentium,	*Aeterna lux credentium,*
Christe, Redemptor omnium,	Jesu, *Redemptor omnium,*
Exaudi preces supplicum.	Intende votis *supplicum.*
Qui, condolens interitu	*Qui,* daemonis ne fraudibus
Mortis perire saeculum,	Periret orbis, impetu
Salvasti mundum languidum,	Amoris actus, languidi
Donans reis remedium.	Mundi medela factus es.
Vergente mundi vespere,	Commune qui mundi nefas
Uti sponsus de thalamo,	Ut expiares ad crucem,
Egressus honestissima	E virginis sacrario
Virginis matris clausula.	Intacta prodis Victima.
Cuius forti potentiae	*Cuius* potestas gloriae,
Genu curvantur omnia,	Nomenque cum primum sonat,
Caelestia, terrestria,	Et coelites et inferi
Nutu fatentur subdita.	Tremente curvantur genu.
Te deprecamur, Hagie,	*Te deprecamur,* ultimae
Venturae Iudex saeculi,	Magnum diei Iudicem,
Conserva nos in tempore,	Armis supernae gratiae
Hostis a telo perfidi.[1]	Defende nos ab hostibus.

2. Hymn at Lauds in Paschal-tide

Original Text	*Revised Text*
Aurora lucis rutilat,	*Aurora* coelum purpurat,
Caelum laudibus intonat,	Aether resultat laudibus,
Mundus exultans iubilat,	*Mundus* triumphans *iubilat,*
Tremens infernus ululat.	Horrens avernus infremit.

---

[1] [Translation in *Hymns Ancient and Modern*, 45; and a better one in *Hymnal Noted*, 28. Translation of revised text in the *Office Hymn-book*, 729.—A. B.]

Cum Rex ille fortissimus,	Rex ille dum *fortissimus*
Mortis confractis viribus,	De mortis inferno specu
Pede conculcans Tartara,	Patrum senatum liberum
Solvit a poena miseros.	Educit ad vitae iubar.
Ille, qui clausus lapide	Cuius sepulcrum plurimo
Custoditur sub milite,	Custode signabat lapis,
Triumphans pompa nobili,	Victor triumphat, et suo
Victor surgit de funere.	Mortem sepulchro funerat.
Solutis iam gemitibus	Sat funeri, sat lacrymis,
Et inferni doloribus,	Sat est datum *doloribus*,
Quia surrexit Dominus,	Surrexit extinctor necis,
Resplendens clamat angelus.[1]	Clamat coruscans *angelus*.

'I do not mean to say,' writes M. Chevalier in his review of the work carried out by command of Urban VIII., 'that all the hymns in the old hymnal have undergone such cruel treatment as these two, but to all of them we may apply the Saturnian line '

Rogo te, mi viator, noli mi nocere!

The revisers set out altogether on false principles, through ignorance of the rules of rhythmic poetry, a kind of poetry utterly misunderstood in the time of Urban VIII., when people ventured to affirm that the hymns of S. Thomas Aquinas were composed " *Etrusco rhythmo.*" The Abbé Pimont, from another point of view, has shown with equal force of argument and moderation of language, how much Christian feeling and true piety have lost by these changes.[2] Altogether they altered 952 syllables; that is the total given in the preface to the

---

[1] [Translation, *Hymns Ancient and Modern*, 126; *Hymnal Noted*, 58. Translation of revised text, *Office Hymn-book*, 751.—A. B.]

[2] Pimont, *Les Hymnes du Bréviaire Romain* (Paris, 1874-84).

editio princeps of the new Hymnal, which appeared separately as an experiment in 1629,[1] and was actually introduced into the Breviary in 1632: 952 syllables in less than 1800 lines. It may be said that this revision did not commend itself to the Christian world: even at Rome, the basilica of S. Peter has always rejected it; none of the religious Orders who have preserved their ancient rites have adopted it; in France, I know of no Breviary but that of Auxerre (1670) which introduced it in its entirety. The best canonists—Bouix, for instance—while maintaining, what nobody can deny, the obligation to make use of it in reciting the Breviary, allow us to understand that it is possible that the Church, through her chief ruler, may one day cancel the decree of Urban VIII. and return to the pristine form of her hymns.'[2]

The recension made by Urban VIII. was promulgated by a bull ('*Divinam psalmodiam*') on Janury 25, 1631, and in the following year the Breviary was issued from the Vatican press.[3]

The revision of Urban VIII. closes the series of reforms in the text of the Roman Breviary made by the Holy See. In some sort, one may say that the Breviary of Urban VIII., in accordance with the wish which he expressed in his bull *Divinam psalmodiam*, has become the Vulgate of the Breviary. As a matter of fact, the

[1] *Hymni Breviarii Romani, Ss. D. N. Urbani VIII. iussu, et S. R. C. approbatione emendati et editi* (Rome, 1629).

[2] U. Chevalier, *Université Catholique*, 1891, tom. viii. pp. 122-25.

[3] *Breviarium Romanum ex decreto Sacrosancti Concilii Tridentini restitutum, Pii V. Pont. Max. iussu editum, et Clementis VIII. primum, nunc denuo Urbani VIII. PP. auctoritate recognitum* (Rome, 1632).

Popes who have succeeded him, except in the matter of introducing new offices, have not since touched its text; and when the Congregation of Rites, in 1884, published a standard edition of the Roman Breviary, embodying the various modifications of the rubrics, and containing the text of all the new offices introduced since 1632, it was in a position to declare that its object was the representation of the pure text of the Breviary of Urban VIII.

But was this Vulgate of the Breviary as free from faults as one would have wished? If in 1602, and again in 1632, matter for correction was found, did those two revisions exhaust the sum of desirable amendments? Were not more important sacrifices needed than those to which the criticism of Sirleto, timid in its attitude and premature as regards the acquisition of the necessary apparatus; the criticism of Baronius, too much concentrated on chronology and the debating of controverted facts of history; the criticism of the time of Urban VIII., with its merely literary and formal character, had each in their turn consented? Did not the introduction, since 1568, of new offices in such considerable number run counter to the main object aimed at by Pius V.? In other words, was not a new and more stringent revision desirable? It was the question which the Gallican Church already looked upon as ripe for treatment, and which the Holy See itself was in due course of time to take in hand.

CHAPTER VI.

THE PROJECTS OF BENEDICT XIV

Dom Guéranger, in the second volume of his '*Institutions Liturgiques*,' has written the history and investigated the character of the Gallican reforms of the Roman Breviary, and it would be difficult indeed to do either with greater erudition or more spirit. And our readers will have sufficiently perceived, from the beginning of our book down to the point we have arrived at, the direction in which our personal preferences run, to feel sure that we consider that history as abundantly supporting our judgment, and the charges brought by him as being legitimately and completely substantiated. But it will not be without use, following Dom Guéranger as concisely as possible, to relate these Gallican attempts to substitute for the Roman Breviary of Pius V., Clement VIII., and Urban VIII., something which called itself a better reformed Breviary. For in these attempts we find on the one hand criticisms, and on the other hand fantastic notions, which between them are qualified to show us in what respects the work of Pius V. and his successors was incomplete, and at the same time in what respects it was excellent.

We have already seen how the Roman Breviary of Pius V. was received in France, and notably at Paris. In 1643 the Archbishop of Paris, John Francis de Gondy, had the Parisian Breviary of 1584 revised, in order to render it as fully conformed as possible to the Roman Breviary; and one may say that until the accession of Louis XIV. the Roman Breviary was looked upon in France, if not as obligatory, at all events as the model of the canonical Office. It is only when the reign of Louis XIV. is well on its way that, concurrently with the disputes about the *regale*,[1] the first projects of liturgical reform make their appearance, projects in which one cannot help seeing the intention of withdrawing the Gallican Church from the Roman obedience and asserting her independence, but in which at the same time it would be wrong not to recognise the existence of just scruples, which the progress of sound criticism and accurate theology could not fail to create in the minds of the clergy. What Baronius and Bellarmine had been at Rome in 1600, learned men such as Thomassin, Mabillon, and many others, were to the clergy of France about the year 1682.[2]

The work of revising the Romano-Parisian Breviary had been begun at Paris since 1670, under the influence of the two ideas just alluded to. It was begun by command of Archbishop Hardouin de Péréfixe, and completed by Archbishop Francis de Harlay in 1680.[3] De Harlay and his assistant theologians proposed to themselves in this work the removal from the Breviary of

[1] The right claimed by the king of France in regard to the revenues of vacant sees.

[2] See on this point chapter ii. ('On the Influence of Contemporary Erudition on Bossuet') of M. Rébelliau's book, *Bossuet historien du Protestantisme* (Paris, 1892), 2nd ed. pp. 95-120.

[3] *Breviarium Parisiense Ill. et Rev. in Christo Patris DD. Francisci de Harlay, Dei et S. Sedis Apostolicae gratia Parisiensis Archiepiscopi, . . . et venerabilis eiusdem Ecclesiae Capituli consensu editum* (Paris, 1680).

'whatever was superfluous, or unsuitable to the dignity of the Church, and the expulsion of whatever superstitious matter had been introduced, so as to leave in it nothing but what was accordant with the majesty of Holy Church and the teaching of Christian antiquity . . . ; the taking away of some homilies falsely attributed to the Fathers, of erroneous or uncertain particulars in the legends of the saints: in a word, of everything not thoroughly in accordance with true piety.'[1] De Harlay here repeated almost the exact words of the bull *Quod a nobis*, of Pius V., but he gave them a particular tone of meaning, which is well expressed in these words of Tillemont: 'Everything should be banished from the Divine Office which is not based on some authority, either absolutely certain or at all events sufficiently firmly grounded, so that it may be read with respect, and with a piety informed by right reason, and which cannot give any room for heretics to mock at our devotions.'[2] In this Breviary of Archbishop de Harlay the text of a great number of responds and antiphons was changed, our reformers desiring that none of these should be taken from anything else than Holy Scripture. More than forty legends of saints were removed as being of insufficient authority, and replaced by passages from the homilies of the Holy Fathers. Others were retouched: S. Denis (*i.e.* Dionysius the Areopagite) was no longer said to be the first Bishop of Paris; S. Mary Magdalene was not called the sister of Martha; S. Lazarus was not asserted to have been a bishop; the relation of the Assumption of Mary by S. John

---

[1] Guéranger, tom. ii. p. 37.

[2] Tillemont, *Mémoires pour servir à l'histoire ecclésiastique*, tom. v. p. 188.

Damascene was cut out. It may certainly be said that the Parisian liturgists were without canonical authority thus to recast the text of a Breviary published and privileged by the Holy See. They were also without that special preparation which would have led them to study the liturgy in its original sources instead of treating it on *a priori* principles. But they had on their side a solid historical knowledge, and a judicious sense of the duties and liberties of true criticism. And if anybody had impugned as too sweeping the maxim quoted above from Tillemont, they might have replied: 'A much more considerable service is rendered to the cause of truth and the Church by entirely silencing particulars which are not altogether certain, than by allowing those which are false to appear among the true: for the result is that the smallest falsehood which a reader detects in a passage makes him doubt the very truest things, and he is no longer disposed to feel certain of anything, having once been deceived by some lie.' These are not the words of Tillemont, still less of Launoy, but of Cardinal Baronius.[1]

What compromised the reform of De Harlay was the idea that grew up that a further step might yet be taken, and the programme of Pius V. abandoned in favour of that of Quignonez.

This return to the liturgical Utopia of the sixteenth century was provoked by a series of publications which appeared one after another, at the beginning of the eighteenth century, simultaneously with that ecclesiastical *Fronde* which followed the publication of the Bull *Unigenitus*. We may mention the '*Traité de la Messe et de l'office divin*' (1713), by Grancolas, and his '*Com-*

[1] Baronius, *Annal.* tom. iii. p. 445.

mentaire historique sur le Bréviaire Romain'; and in 1720, Foinard's book, entitled '*Projet d'un nouveau Bréviaire, dans lequel l'office divin, sans en changer la forme ordinaire, serait particulièrement composé de l'Ecriture Sainte, instructif, édifiant, dans un ordre naturel, sans renvois, sans répétitions et tres court : avec des observations sur les anciens et les nouveaux bréviaires.*' All that Foinard did was to take up an idea put forward by Grancolas in his '*Traité*,' and developed by him in his '*Commentaire.*' Grancolas and Foinard agreed in proposing: (1) to give the Sunday office such privilege that it would no longer give way to anything but a feast of our Lord; (2) to give such privilege to the season of Lent that the ferial office in that season should not give way to any feast whatever, not even to the Annunciation, which would itself be superseded by it; (3) to abridge the ferial office : ' for, as soon as the ferial office becomes no longer than that of festivals, everyone will prefer it, since it is more varied and more moving to the soul than the office of the saints '; (4) to arrange festivals in five classes: a superior class for the feasts of our Lord, into which no festival of the Virgin or of the saints is to be admitted; a second class for *Corpus Christi*, the Assumption, S. John Baptist, SS. Peter and Paul, and the patronal festival of a church; a class of doubles for Apostles, of semidoubles for doctors, and of simples for martyrs, the confessors only claiming a memorial, except that their full office is to be celebrated in their own dioceses if they were bishops, in the churches of their own Order if they were religious, and in the localities where they won their saintly renown in the case of all other saints; (5) to admit into the lessons of the *Sanctorale* none but well-approved histories. Like De Harlay, Grancolas and Foinard wished to have only such legends as were indisputably authentic, in which matter they were quite right; but going further than the Archbishop, they turned the *Sanctorale* topsy-turvy under pretext of restoring the office of the Season to its proper place. And their indiscretion was destined even to be surpassed.

An Archbishop of Paris, M. Charles de Vintimille,[1] was found willing to carry out the project of Grancolas and Foinard, and go a step further than they had proposed. He entrusted the drawing up of the new Paris Breviary to Father Vigier, an Oratorian, suspected of Jansenism, and, as his assistants, two Masters of the College of Beauvais, Francis Mésenguy and Charles Coffin, both of them among those who appealed against the Bull *Unigenitus*. The Breviary of Archbishop de Vintimille was published in 1736, and remained in use down to our own times.[2]

The new Breviary gave to the Sunday service the prerogative of excluding the observance of all kinds of feasts, with the exception of 'those to which the Church has assigned the highest degree of solemnity.' A prerogative of the same sort was accorded to Lent: 'it being thought right to restore the ancient custom of the Church, which did not consider that the joyous solemnity of feasts accorded well with fasting and the salutary

---

[1] We may mention here, along with him, the Archbishop of Rouen, Louis de la Vergne de Tressan (1728), the Bishop of Orleans, Nicolas Joseph de Paris (1731), and the Archbishop of Lyons, Charles F. de Chateauneuf Rochebonne (1738).

[2] *Breviarium Parisiense Ill. et Rev. in Christo Patris DD. Caroli-Gaspar-Gulielmi de Vintimille e comitibus Massiliae Du Luc, Parisiensis Archiepiscopi . . . auctoritate, ac Venerabilis eiusdem Ecclesiae Capituli consensu editum* (Paris, 1736).

sadness of penitence,' no feasts might then be observed, 'except those on which abstinence from servile work was commanded.' In the third place, the psalms of the feria were to be recited on all festivals except those of the Blessed Virgin and of Martyrs. Fourthly—and this was one of the most notable innovations—the psalter was distributed anew, on the plan of assigning proper psalms to each day of the week, and even to each canonical hour of each day of the week, dividing such as were too long:[1] with the result that the entire psalter would almost always be recited in the course of each week.

The office of the Season being thus replaced in its due dignity, the next point was the lightening of the Kalendar. In the first place a whole series of festivals were suppressed altogether: S. Peter's Chair at Antioch; the Octave Days of S. Stephen, S. John Evangelist, the Holy Innocents, S. John Baptist, SS. Peter and Paul, the Conception of our Lady; the festivals of SS. Vitalis, Domitilla, Alexis, Margaret, Praxedis, Calixtus, Felicitas, &c. Some other saints' days were reduced to having a memorial only: SS. George, Martin the Pope, Sylvester, &c.

The hymnal, by way of concession to the taste of the time, was not suppressed, but was re-written and developed. Most of this work was done by Santeuil and Coffin, in a style which surpassed even the literary prettiness of the Jesuits of Urban VIII., and with a flavour about their poetic inspiration which suggested reminiscences of the *Augustinus*.[2]

[1] [For instance, Psalm lxxvii. (lxxviii.) is reckoned as *six* psalms and occupies two nocturns of Wednesday; Psalms ciii.-cvi. (civ.-cvii.) are each reckoned as three psalms, &c.—A. B.]

[2] [The famous work of Janssen, condemned by Urban VIII. in 1642.—A. B.]

The lectionary, so far as the legends of the saints are concerned, was, in the judgment of Dom Guéranger, which is often rather too severe, 'marked with the seal of the new criticism.'[1] The words of the antiphons and responds were entirely taken from Holy Scripture, in more than one place wilfully applied in a Jansenist and 'appellant'[2] sense. To show the 'Gallicanism' of the whole work, a single example may suffice: on the feast of S. Peter's Chair at Rome, the Invitatory, *Tu es pastor ovium, princeps Apostolorum,*' was replaced by '*Caput corporis Ecclesiae Dominum : venite adoremus.*'

We do not mean to imply that, because the predilections thus betrayed by the new Breviary are annoying, the reforms made by it produced no good effect. Ecclesiastics with whom we are acquainted, accustomed in their younger days to recite the Breviary of De Vintimille, have preserved an affection for it which the recitation of the Roman Breviary has not succeeded in effacing. One of them, a grave and wise old man, said to me: 'Your judgment on our French liturgies is severe: no doubt they were "*passus extra viam,*" and without the sanction of supreme authority; but how admirable was much that was contained in them! I recited the Paris Breviary for many years, and I confess, at the risk of scandalising you somewhat, that, greatly as I appreciate and love the Roman Breviary, I have never succeeded in altogether transferring my affection to it. When I recite the "*Te*

---

[1] Guéranger, tom. ii. p. 282.

[2] *Ib.* p. 267. ['Appellant,' *i.e.* against the bull *Unigenitus*, in which (1713) Clement XI. condemned the writings of Quesnel. Let me add one word of praise for the marvellous knowledge of Scripture and the exquisitely ingenious combination of texts which give to these Gallican Responsorals an inexhaustible charm.—A. B.]

lucis ante terminum" at Compline, I cannot help thinking of the "*O quando lucescet tuus*" : the "*Rerum Deus tenax vigor*" at None suggests some regret for the "*O Christe, dum fixus Cruci.*" Pardon my rashness. . . .' Well, we can hardly call it rashness, being well able to enter into the literary sympathies which are here expressed: but such sympathies must not be allowed to over-ride the just rights of the ancient liturgical tradition.

The Breviary of De Vintimille provoked vehement protests on the part of the Jesuits and others, which may be found in detail in Guéranger. What is less generally known is that the Holy See at first joined in these protests. Clement XII. 'demanded that Monsieur the Archbishop should give orders for the calling in of this Breviary, that certain antiphons and responds should be altered, and the hymns of the "appellant" Father Coffin removed.'[1] The Archbishop would consent to nothing of the sort. When the first edition was sold out, and the issue of a new one was being talked of, the nuncio expressed to Cardinal Fleury a desire that this new edition 'should be corrected in accordance with the remarks that had been sent from Rome.' Nevertheless, Benedict XIV., who had succeeded to the Papacy in 1740, instructed the nuncio ' not to insist on the issue of the mandate for calling in the Breviary, as he did not wish that this demand should prejudice its correction, by too greatly discouraging the Archbishop.' But he caused to be handed to M. Vigier 'both the

---

[1] Benedict XIV. to Tencin, Jan. 18, 1743 (*Corr. de Rome*, t. 791, f. 26). I have had placed at my disposal the unpublished correspondence of Benedict XIV. with Cardinal Tencin, preserved in the Archives of the Minister for Foreign Affairs at Paris, marked *Corr. de Rome*, t. 789 *sqq*.

document containing the corrections which Clement XII. had demanded, and that in which were indicated all the points requiring correction, even those of least importance,' without telling him that these contained the utterance of the Holy See, ' simply giving him the documents as the work of a zealous person, which might contribute something of value to a good new edition of the Paris Breviary.'[1] This was at the beginning of 1743. But the forbearance of the Sovereign Pontiff produced no effect, and the second edition of the Breviary of De Vintimille came out unchanged.[2]

The reason why the Holy See did not insist on obtaining from Archbishop De Vintimille the calling in of his Breviary was that Benedict XIV., taking quite a different view of matters from that of his predecessor Clement XII., was thinking of undertaking in his turn a reform of the Roman Breviary. Cardinal Fleury, as early as February 14, 1741, had welcomed this idea, as being likely to bring about a peaceful solution of ' the affair of the Breviary of the Archbishop of Paris ' ; and Cardinal Tencin, who was then *chargé d'affaires* at Rome, encouraged Fleury and the Pope in this undertaking to the utmost of his power. On July 21, 1741, he wrote to Fleury: 'The Pope has appointed a Congregation of prelates and religious to take in hand the reformation of

[1] *Ibid.* On this correspondence see the author's notice in the *Revue du Clergé Français* (1895), tom. ii. pp. 97-113, and the *Inventaire sommaire des Lettres inédites de Benoît XIV au Cardinal de Tencin* (Paris, 1894).

[2] On the curious negotiations concerning the correction of the Breviary of De Vintimille see the author's memoir entitled *Contribution à l'Histoire du Bréviaire: le Bréviaire Parisien de 1736 et le Pape Clement XII.; d'après une Correspondance diplomatique inédite* (Paris, 1896).

the Roman Breviary.' And on August 25: 'The Pope has adopted excellent principles in regard to the reformation of the Roman Breviary: for instance, as to not admitting any doubtful legend.' It is true he adds immediately after this: 'But will his project be carried out? I should not like to say. He has no idea either of resisting or of being on his guard against those who surround him.'[1]

Thus the reform attempted in France in 1680 and 1736, of which only I propose here to speak,[2] provoked at Rome the undertaking of a new and more thorough revision of the Roman Breviary. We have now to see how that revision was conducted, and why it never reached completion.

II

The papers containing the proceedings of this Congregation appointed by Benedict XIV. for the reformation of the Roman Breviary long remained forgotten and unpublished. Roskovány was the first to call attention to them; he found them in 1856 in the Corsini library at Rome, where they had been preserved since the time of Benedict XIV. They constitute a voluminous file of papers bearing the title:

> Acta et scripta autographa in sacra congregatione particulari a Benedicto XIV. deputata pro reformatione breviarii Romani a. 1741, in tres tomos distributa et appendicem.[3]

---

[1] Benedict XIV. to Fleury, March 4, 1741 (*Corr. de Rome*, t. 787, f. 8); Tencin to Fleury, July 21, 1741 (*ib.* t. 785, f. 229); the same to the same, August 21, 1741 (*ib.* f. 331).

[2] On the reforms attempted in Germany and in various bodies of religious see Dom Bäumer, pp. 538-562.

[3] Biblioth. Corsini, MSS. Nos. 361-363.

The publication of these papers in their entirety is much to be desired, as they would in themselves form an excellent treatise on the Breviary. Roskovány has only published the historical record of the labours of the said Congregation, edited and prefixed to the file of papers by the secretary Valenti: of the rest of the collection he gives nothing but certain chosen portions.[1] A French author, Chaillot, has since published some other important passages from the same papers.[2]

We will now analyse this history of the Acts of the Congregation of Benedict XIV., merely adding a few notes.

The memoir of Valenti[3] is dedicated to Cardinal Nereo Corsini. The author says in his dedication that he felt sure that posterity would be grateful to him for having edited the history of the propositions, discussions, and resolutions handled by the Pontifical Congregation of the Breviary, of which he was the secretary: and that no library seemed to him so honourable a place for the reception of his manuscript as that of Cardinal Corsini.[4]

A short preface follows this dedication, in which Valenti, quoting Thomassin, reminds the reader that the Divine Office, in its essential elements, the hours of prayer, the psalmody, and the reading of the Scriptures, goes back to the very beginning of the Church. But while this is true of such elements as the singing of psalms, the reading of passages from Holy Scripture, and,

[1] Roskovány, tom. v.
[2] *Analecta Iuris Pontificii*, tom. xxiv. (1885).
[3] Luigi Valenti Gonzaga was a nephew of Cardinal Silvio Valenti Gonzaga, Secretary of State to Benedict XIV. He was himself made a Cardinal in 1759.
[4] Roskovány, p. 532; *Analecta*, p. 506.

in some degree, of the use of those prayers which we call Collects, the same cannot be said of a number of other elements which find a place in the Divine Office. Not to speak of the diversity which exists between the Offices of the Greeks and Latins, it is very evident that the reading of the Acts of the Saints and the sermons of the Fathers cannot be traced back to the Church of the earliest times, any more than the custom of preferring to honour God through His Saints, whereas in those times the custom was to honour God directly, as is still done in the Sunday and ferial offices. These differences should not cause us any surprise, for it is right that the Church, like the Bride in the Psalms, should be '*circumamicta varietatibus.*'[1] But it is important that order should reign amidst all this diversity; the liturgy ought not to be handed over to people to deal with as they think fit, so that in the same province or the same diocese there should not be uniformity in the office, or that the office should stamp with its authority unauthentic sermons of the Fathers, or fables under the name of Acts of Saints. Unity and dignity in the Divine Office have been the points aimed at by the ancient Councils, and most of all by Roman Pontiffs such as Innocent I., Gregory VII., and in later times Pius V., Clement VIII. and Urban VIII. These latter have bestowed infinite care and solicitude on the restoration of the Divine Office to agreement with ancient custom, ordaining that no feature of the ancient office should be abandoned, but that what had been suppressed should be restored, and what had been corrupted should be reformed. Pope Benedict XIV., now gloriously reigning, has the same zeal for the worship of

[1] Ps. xliv. [xlv.], verse 14, Vulgate.

God as his predecessors; and, moved by the complaints which several persons of consideration have addressed to him, who expressed themselves as grieved to see the Roman Breviary in more than one respect depraved from its ancient purity, and fallen from its pristine glory, being also himself more sensible of these blots than anyone else could be, and more desirous to see them removed, he resolved, from the very beginning of his pontificate, to undertake the correction and reformation of the Breviary, entrusting to certain persons renowned for their knowledge of ecclesiastical antiquities the task of fulfilling this his desire. 'Often,' continues Valenti, 'did Benedict XIV. condescend to converse with me on this subject, and to ask me what I thought about this important project. Finally he resolved to select several learned prelates and theologians, who, being associated into a Congregation, might consult together on this matter.' The prelates were: Philip Mary Monti, the secretary of the Propaganda; Nicolas Antonelli, secretary of the Sacred College; and Dominic Giorgi, one of the Pope's chaplains. The theologians were: Thomas Sergio, consultor of the Inquisition: Francis Baldini, of the Order of the Somaschi,[1] and consultor of the Congregation of Rites; Antony Andrew Galli, Canon Regular of S. John Lateran; and Antony Mary Azzoguidi, of the Conventual Minorites.[2]

---

[1] [Founded by S. Jerome Aemilian about 1533 at Somasco, between Milan and Bergamo, as Clerks Regular. They were afterwards united to the Theatines.—A.B.]

[2] Monti (*d.* 1754), a prelate of the Academy, had just published his *Elogia Cardinalium Pietate, Doctrina et Rebus pro Ecclesia gestis illustrium* (1741). Antonelli (*d.* 1767) was a heavy man; to him we owe a conscientious *editio princeps* of the Greek commentary on the Psalms (1746) which he believed to be by S. Athanasius

The Pope desired Valenti to act as secretary to the Congregation.[1] The members, Valenti assures us, were fully agreed in principle as to the necessity for a reform of the Roman Breviary. The first point to be settled, therefore, was the nature of that reform. Pope Benedict XIV. had received two memoranda on the subject of the Breviary, one in French, the other in Italian. The French author expressed his regret at finding in the text of the Breviary more than one historical assertion which had escaped the vigilance of former correctors, but whose erroneous character had now been exposed by the progress of critical learning; as regards the distribution of the psalter, there were some psalms which were incessantly repeated, and others which were never recited at all, while the longest of all the psalms were heaped together in the office for Sundays and festivals; among the antiphons there were too many which presented no meaning to the mind of the reader, or which had no coherence with the office in which they occurred; too many new feasts had been made doubles, while many festivals of ancient and notable saints were only semidoubles or simples; the frequency of double feasts hindered the use of the Sunday office, which was devoted to honouring the mysteries of the life of our

and which has been reprinted by Migne; in 1756 he published a *Vetus Missale Romanum Praefationibus et Notis illustratum*. Giorgi (d. 1747), a learned man of the school of Muratori, was publishing his great work, *De Liturgia Romani Pontificis in Solemni Celebratione Missarum* (1731-1744). Baldini (d. 1767) was an antiquary who published in 1743 an esteemed edition of Vaillant's *Numismata Imperatorum Romanorum*. Azzoguidi (d. 1770) interested himself in the unpublished works of S. Antony of Padua, whose Life he wrote.

[1] Roskovány, pp. 533-87; *Analecta*, pp. 507-8.

Lord. Hence it was, according to the judgment of this French author, that so many Ordinaries had abandoned the use of the Roman Breviary, and adopted breviaries of their own, to the injury and confusion of the liturgy. The time had come to give the Roman Breviary a new form, by means of which these defects should be remedied, and these dangers averted.

On the other hand, the Italian memorandum did not demand a recasting, but merely an expurgation of the Roman Breviary. For this Breviary, it was urged, contained, in the first place, certain elements which were essential, and which therefore could not be modified without annihilating the Roman rite itself, such as the number, order, and arrangement of the canonical hours of prayer, the nocturns, psalms, antiphons, lessons, and collects. These were essential elements and were not to be touched. But, in the second place, the Kalendar, the words of the antiphons and responds, the matter of the lessons, were all of them elements which both were capable of and demanded correction.[1]

Benedict XIV. placed both these memoranda in the hands of the Congregation, which met for the first time on July 14, 1741, at the house of Valenti, and from the first it was manifest that the members were hardly more in agreement with each other than were the two memoranda. The one party wished to begin with discussing the distribution of the psalms: they praised the plan of distribution which had lately been adopted in some of

[1] The text of both these memoranda has been preserved for us by Valenti. They form the second and third of the illustrative documents attached to his memoir, *Monumentum II.* and *Monumentum III.* Neither has ever been published.

[2] Roskovány, p. 538; *Analecta*, p. 509.

the churches of France, and also the custom of the same churches to recite the ferial psalms in the office of saints' days, with the exception of a few festivals of saints, by which means the entire psalter was recited every week. While others, whose opinion eventually prevailed, urged that the Roman Church had always been tenacious of her own traditions, and that it was right that such should be the case; that it was wise to mistrust novelties; that the Roman distribution of the psalms was of venerable antiquity, and should not be lightly abandoned; that the question before them was not the recasting, but simply the correction of the Roman Breviary; and that, reserving the psalter for future discussion, their best plan was to begin with the Kalendar. This proposition was unanimously agreed to.[1]

Since, then, it was recognised that their task was simply one of correction, the great point was to ascertain what was the leading idea of the reform of the Breviary made under Pius V., and act in accordance with it. Valenti laid before the Congregation a document which he had found[2] and which expressed in a lucid manner what the idea of Pius V. had been. In the sixteenth century the ferial office had attached to it the recitation of the Little Office of our Lady, and the Office of the Dead: and in addition to these, in Lent the Penitential and Gradual psalms, accompanied by litanies; and further, at every canonical hour, and at every season, the *preces feriales*. To escape from the overwhelming prolixity of such a ferial office as this, people were led to give simple

[1] Roskovány, p. 540; *Analecta*, p. 510.
[2] We have already mentioned this document; see p. 258. Valenti has preserved the original (?) Italian text of it, *Monumentum V.*

x

feasts the character of semidoubles and doubles: that is to say, to assign to them an office of nine lessons, and the right of being transferred to vacant days if there was occasion for it, since an office of nine lessons was not saddled with any additional office beyond that of our Lady. The result was, that the ferial office ceased to be recited in Lent, in contravention of the letter of the ancient canon law; that hardly any lessons from Holy Scripture were read, in despite of the ordinances of Pope Gelasius; that there was no longer any weekly recitation of the psalter, but merely the daily repetition of the same psalms of the Common of Saints, in defiance of the authority of S. Gregory the Great, who ruled that no clerk should be promoted to the episcopate, unless he knew the whole psalter by heart. For this reason Pius V. suppressed this wrongful privilege of simple feasts, reducing them to a memorial in the case of their concurring with a feast of superior rank, but relieving them from the recitation of the Penitential and Gradual psalms, and of the Office of the Dead, as also from the *preces feriales*, except in Advent and Lent, and finally ordaining that they should have at least two lessons out of three from Holy Scripture with the psalms of the ferial nocturn. Next, comparing the Breviary in its present state with that of Pius V., they found that the number of doubles and semidoubles had been, since 1568, increased from 138 to 228, so that, there being also 36 moveable feasts of the highest rank, scarcely 90 days were left free for the Sunday and ferial office; and even these 90 days were for the most part appropriated by feasts allowed to particular Churches, dioceses, and religious Orders! Thus the situation in 1741 had got back to what it was in 1568, when the Roman Pontiffs first undertook the reform of the Breviary, and the fault was entirely the Kalendar's. It was therefore necessary, whatever special devotion the consultors individually might have for the saints, to erase a great number of names from the Kalendar, and to reduce several more festivals to the rank of simple feasts, since these only among festivals did not hinder the weekly recitation of the psalter.[1]

On August 11, 1741, the Congregation, having agreed in principle as to this reduction, assayed the application of it to the feasts of our Lord. Of course, Christmas, Epiphany, Easter, and Pentecost were excepted. There was some discussion as to whether it would be well to restore to the feast of the Circumcision of our Lord its old title of *Octava Domini*, given it by the Gregorian Sacramentary; but the question was passed by. The feast of the Transfiguration was of very late date, being unknown to the Gregorian Sacramentary: but it had been received among Greeks and Latins alike, and it was agreed to retain it. The same conclusion was come to in regard to the festival of the Holy Trinity, on the condition that the antiphons and responds of its office should be carefully revised. The festival of *Corpus Christi* was retained without discussion; but those of the Invention and Exaltation of the Holy Cross gave rise to lively debates: some wished to remove the Invention from the Kalendar altogether, others to unite the Invention and Exaltation in one festival on September 14, others again to maintain both as they were. At one time it seemed as if the festival on May 3 would be condemned to disappear;

[1] Roskovány, p. 542; *Analecta*, p. 519.

but finally it was resolved to make no change. The feast of the Holy Name of Jesus, however, found no favour with the Congregation;[1] it was modern, and its suppression was agreed on.[2]

The discussion of the above points was concluded by November 21, 1741, on which date the consideration of the feasts of the Blessed Virgin was begun. Of these, the Purification, Annunciation, Assumption and Nativity of our Lady were ancient and universally observed festivals, which were beyond discussion. The Congregation did, it is true, debate whether it would be well to substitute for the word *Assumption* the more ancient title of *Pausatio*, or *Dormitio*, or *Transitus*, in order that the Church might not appear, by the use in her solemn liturgy of the word 'Assumption,' to elevate into an article of faith the pious opinion of the entrance into Heaven of the body as well as the soul of the Virgin; but the title 'Assumption' was unanimously retained. Were octaves to be assigned to the Assumption and Nativity of our Lady? The question was answered in the affirmative, reserving the question of what degree of dignity was to be given to these octaves. The feasts of the Visitation and Conception of our Lady were unanimously retained: but those of the consultors who did not agree to the doctrine of the *Immaculate* Conception wished to do away with the octave of the latter festival; while those who feared that such a suppression would

---

[1] The feast of the Holy Name of Jesus was granted to the Minorites in 1530, and fixed for January 14. In 1721 Innocent XIII. extended its observance to the entire Church, and fixed it for the second Sunday after Epiphany. [But in England it had been observed since 1457 on August 7 as a greater double.—A. B.]

[2] Roskovány, p. 545; *Analecta*, p. 519.

prejudice the acceptance of the doctrine demanded that it should be maintained : and the Congregation being pretty equally divided on the point, it was decided to remit it to the Pope for his decision. The feast of the Presentation of our Lady had been eliminated by Pius V., and re-established by Sixtus V.: the Congregation, feeling the difficulty there is in determining exactly what mystery of Redemption is honoured by the observance of this festival, decided on adopting the course taken by Pius V. But they subsequently reversed this decision. On the other hand, the festivals of the Holy Name of Mary, the Rosary, our Lady of Mercy, our Lady of Mount Carmel, the Seven Dolours, the *Desponsatio* (Betrothal), the Patronage of our Lady, the Translation of the Holy House of Loretto, and the *Expectatio Partus* (our Lady's expectation of the Holy Birth), found but lukewarm defenders in the Congregation.[1] It was a pity that these festivals should interfere with the due recitation of the Sunday office : the feast of the Holy Name of Jesus being suppressed, that of the Holy Name of Mary could scarcely be maintained; the Rosary stood or fell with the last-named festival, both having the same *raison d'être*, viz. to thank God for victories gained over the Turks. The festivals of our Lady of Mercy and of

[1] The Holy Name of Mary had been granted *aliquibus locis* in 1513, and fixed for September 17. In 1693 Innocent XI. extended it to the entire Church, and fixed it for the Sunday in the Octave of the Nativity of our Lady. The festival of the Rosary, instituted by Gregory XIII. in memory of the victory of Lepanto (1571), was extended to the entire Church by Clement XI. in 1716. Our Lady of Mercy, and of Mount Carmel, the Seven Dolours, the Patronage of our Lady, the Translation of the House of Loretto, the *Desponsatio*, the *Expectatio*, all dated from Benedict XIII. (1725-27).

Mount Carmel had relation only to two religious Orders,[1] and not to the entire Church; the festival of the Seven Dolours had the special disadvantage of ousting the ferial office on the Friday in Passion Week. As for the Patronage of our Lady, the *Desponsatio*, and the *Translatio Domus Lauretanae*, without impugning the grave motives with which these festivals had been instituted, the Congregation felt that, since Christian antiquity had not seen any necessity for establishing them, they were within their right in deciding not to retain them. The feast of the *Expectatio Partus* found no defender.[2]

On March 9, 1742, discussion took place on the festivals of the Holy Angels. The feast of S. Michael on September 29 was unanimously retained. But that of the Apparition of S. Michael on Mount Garganus (May 8) was suppressed with equal unanimity, as one in which only the diocese of Siponto had any concern. The feast of the Guardian Angels (October 2) was modern, dating only from Paul V. (1605-1621);[3] and did it not seem a superfluous addition to that of S. Michael? It was nevertheless retained.

After the Angels the festivals of the Saints were discussed. The feast of the Maccabees was too ancient to be disturbed. But such was not the case with those of SS. Joachim, Anne, and Joseph. But universal devotion had adopted these three festivals with too great piety to allow of their being suppressed; it was therefore

[1] [The Order of our Lady of Mercy, founded 1218, for the Redemption of Captives, and the Carmelites.—A.B.]

[2] Roskovány, p. 418; *Analecta*, p. 515.

[3] [He instituted it as optional, 'to be celebrated *ad libitum* on the first day after Michaelmas not occupied by an office of nine lessons.' Urban VIII. left it optional in 1638.—A. B.]

resolved to unite the memory of SS. Joachim and Anne in one great festival; but, again, this resolution had to be abandoned soon after, and things were left as they were. The Nativity and Beheading of S. John Baptist were beyond debate: so was also the feast of the Holy Innocents, but it was thought it might be well to do away with the octave of the last. The festivals of SS. Peter and Paul, of the other Apostles, including S. Barnabas, and of the Evangelists, were passed without discussion: the only difficulty raised was about the exceptional octave assigned to the feast of S. John Evangelist. The festivals of S. Mary Magdalene and of S. Martha were to be retained, but the latter was to be reduced to the rank of a simple feast.[1]

On March 17, 1742, the discussion of the same subject was resumed. No difficulty was made over maintaining the feasts of the Conversion of S. Paul, S. John before the Latin Gate, and S. Peter's Chains. The question was raised of uniting in one festival the two feasts of S. Peter's Chair; but the agreement come to was to keep them distinct. On the other hand, there seemed no further reason to retain the Commemoration of S. Paul on the day after the festival of SS. Peter and Paul, since it was no longer the custom for the Pope to go and pontificate on that day, as he used to do of yore, at the basilica of S. Paul's Without the Walls; accordingly this festival was only to be retained for churches under the invocation of S. Paul; in all others the office on that day would be of the Octave of SS. Peter and Paul. The three anniversaries in honour of the dedication of Roman basilicas were to be maintained, viz. the Lateran (November 9),

[1] Roskovány, p. 511; *Analecta*, p. 518.

S. Peter's and S. Paul's (November 18), and S. Mary's the Greater (August 5) : the last, however, was no longer to bear the title 'S. Mary of the Snows,' but as in the ancient Kalendars, simply '*Dedicatio S. Mariae.*' When the consideration of the general body of saints' days was reached, difficulties began to multiply.[1]

The Congregation met on April 20 and on May 1 to discuss which saints were to be retained in the Kalendar, but it was found impossible to pass any resolution until a Kalendar should be drawn up by Azzoguidi containing the festivals which at the preceding meetings of the Congregation it had been decided to maintain. The work did not get on: Giorgi had gone to Castel Gandolfo to rest awhile; Galli to Bologna, to attend the general chapter of his Order; it was impossible to get a meeting together. Benedict XIV. nevertheless urged matters on, and Valenti redoubled his efforts. In union with Azzoguidi, he agreed to draw up a sketch of a Kalendar to be submitted to the Congregation, which should show the festivals already accepted, and those which had the best chance of being so eventually. As soon as this sketch of a Kalendar was drawn up, Valenti went to show it to Giorgi, for as he said, there was good hope that, if Giorgi approved it, all the other consultors would follow suit. But in the meanwhile Monti, who was president of the Congregation, and at whose house they were now holding their meetings, had had 'general rules' drawn up by 'a learned man,' in accordance with which it would be proper to judge which saints were to have offices assigned to them, and what rank the office of each ought to have. What were these rules? Valenti does

[1] Roskovány, p. 553; *Analecta,* p. 519.

not tell us: we only know one thing, viz. that Valenti, Azzoguidi, Baldini, and Galli were unanimous in rejecting them.¹ But how was Monti likely to take this opposition?²

At last the Congregation met, on July 15, 1742. Valenti had succeeded in arranging that Monti should say no more about his general rules, and Azzoguidi should put aside his Kalendar, and he himself proposed to retain only those festivals of which the Jesuit Guyet said that they were celebrated throughout the Church.³ Father

---

¹ Roskovány, p. 555; *Analecta*, p. 520.

² In the *Briefe Benedicts XIV. an den Canon. Fr. Peggi in Bologna*, published by M. Kraus (Fribourg, 1884), I find an interesting passage in which Monti is mentioned. The Pope writes: '*Gli eruditi in materie ecclesiastiche sono di tre specie. Alcuni hanno una buona guardaroba, lettura continua, ed ottima memoria delle cose lette: e questi non solo sono buoni per la conversazione; ma nelle occorrenze possono somministrare buone notizie. Ma se non passano più oltre, riescono in atto pratico il più delle volte non solo inutili, ma perniciosi. E nel numero di questi (sia detto in confidenza) si debbon riporre i due Cardinali Passionei e Monti.*'— 'Men learned in matters ecclesiastical are of three kinds: some have a good stock of knowledge, are always reading, and have an excellent memory for what they have read; and these are not only good for conversation, but on occasion may furnish some useful information. But if they stop there, they generally prove in practical matters not only useless but even mischievous. Among these (be it said in confidence) must be reckoned Cardinals Passionei and Monti' (p. 27). What follows, in praise of Muratori, would be well worth quoting as a charming example of the good feeling and sagacity of Benedict XIV.; but we have confined ourselves to that which concerned Monti, and which explains the way in which a good, practical man of business like Valenti may well have been hampered and embarrassed by the pernicious erudition of his president. '*Monti est un homme qui a beaucoup lu, mais sans aucune méthode,*' wrote, in 1743, the Abbé de Canillac, Superior of Saint-Louis-des-Français (*Corr. de Rome*, t. 792, f. 242).

³ C. Guyet, *Heortologia, sive de Festis propriis Locorum et Ecclesiarum* (Venice, 1729).

Guyet's statement on this point was read, and the Congregation found no fault with it, but considered that it would be better for them to devote their next few sittings to discussing the case of each saint themselves. They agreed on the following principles: (1) to retain all the saints whose names occur in the Canon of the Mass; (2) all those whose feasts are mentioned in the ancient Sacramentaries and Kalendars of the Roman Church; (3) all the saints of whom we possess the *Acta sincera*, or a eulogium pronounced on them by one of the Fathers, provided their *cultus* in the Church is ancient; (4) to retain only those sainted Popes of whom the *cultus* is ancient; (5) to retain the Doctors of the Church; (6) to retain the saints who are founders of religious Orders; (7) to retain some saint representing each nation of Christendom; (8) to eliminate all the saints not included in one of the above seven categories, unless universal devotion throughout the Church or some special (*urgentissima*) reason should induce them to determine otherwise.[1]

It would be a long and tiresome business to enumerate one by one the applications made by the Congregation of these principles to particular cases. It will suffice to record the testimony given by Valenti to the zeal with which Azzoguidi and the other consultors applied themselves to the collation of ancient Sacramentaries and Kalendars, so as to form an opinion regulated by these authorities, to submitting the points raised to general discussion, and to obtaining a unanimous agreement as to each resolution of the Congregation. August and

[1] Extract from the preface to the *Calendarium Reformatum*, ap. Roskovány, p. 586.

September were spent on this work; in October nothing but the summing up of results remained to be done, and this task was entrusted, not to Azzoguidi, whose health at this time was overtaxed, but to Galli, who gave up to it his autumn vacation.[1]

Valenti has preserved for us the expurgated Kalendar of the Congregation of the Breviary. The number of expulsions decreed by it was considerable. Besides the feasts of the Holy Name of Jesus, the Holy Name of Mary, *Desponsatio B. Mariae*, the *Expectatio Partus*, the Seven Dolours, the Patronage of the Virgin, Our Lady of Mercy, the Rosary, the *Translatio Domus Lauretanae*, the Commemoration of S. Paul, and the Apparition of S. Michael, the Congregation had erased from the Kalendar the names of the Popes Telesphorus, Hyginus, Anicetus, Soter, Marcellinus, Eleutherus, Sylverius, John, Leo II., Pius, Anacletus, Zephyrinus, Evaristus, Pontianus, and Gregory VII.;[1] of SS. Canute, Raymund of Pennafort, Casimir, Vincent Ferrier, Ubaldus, Antoninus,

---

[1] Roskovány, p. 558; *Analecta*, p. 523.

[2] The suppression of the festival of Gregory VII. was very significant. It had been granted to the Benedictine Order, and the patriarchal basilicas of Rome by Clement XI. in 1719, and extended to the entire Church by Benedict XIII. in 1729. The historical lesson contained a passage mentioning the resistance offered by the Pope to the Emperor Henry IV., the same which still appears there—'*Contra Henrici Imperatoris impios conatus*,' &c. The Parliaments of France saw in this an impeachment of the liberties of the Gallican Church and the King's majesty. Cardinal Fleury annulled their decrees, but they had the support of certain bishops— Caylus of Auxerre, Colbert of Montpellier, Coislin of Metz. Benedict XIII. (July 31, 1729) had to condemn the episcopal Charges of these bishops and the edicts of the Parliaments. The Parliament of Paris (February 23, 1730) condemned the condemnation pronounced by the Pope! There was a similar disturbance in the kingdom of Naples,

Bernardin, Felix de Cantalice, John de Sahagun, Louis Gonzaga, Liborius, Raymund Nonnatus, Laurence Giustiniani, Wenceslas, Francis Borgia, Andrew d'Avellino, John of the Cross; also of SS. Sabas, Peter Chrysologus, Peter of Alexandria, Eusebius of Vercellae, Hilarion, Venantius, Boniface, Erasmus, Alexis, Christopher, Pantaleon, Romanus, Cassian, Hyacinth, Januarius, Eustace, Placidus, Denis, Rusticus and Eleutherius, Vitalis and Agricola, Trypho, Respicius and Nympha, Diego, Hippolytus and Symphorian, Giles, the Twelve Holy Brothers, Modestus and Crescentia, Nabor and Felix, Faustinus and Jovita, Cyprian and Justina; also of the female saints Emerentiana, Martina, Dorothea, Scholastica, Petronilla, Rufina and Secunda, Symphorosa, Margaret, Christina, Hedwiga, Ursula, Katherine, Bibiana, Barbara, Margaret of Cortona, Mary Magdalene de' Pazzi, Juliana de' Falconeri, Rose of Viterbo, Gertrude, and Elizabeth of Hungary; to which are to be added the Invention of the body of S. Stephen, and the Impression of the Stigmata of S. Francis.[1]

By December 7, 1742, the Congregation had at last drawn up its Kalendar of feasts to be maintained. But it was as yet nothing more than a catalogue, and several questions required settling before it could take the form of a real liturgical Kalendar. In the first place, the consultors, in accordance with the leading idea of their entire work of reformation, desired to give privilege to

and another in Austria. The Congregation of Benedict XIV. thought to evade all these difficulties by suppressing the festival of Gregory VII.

[1] *Catalogus Festorum seu Officiorum quae visa sunt omittenda* (Roskovány, pp. 612-14).

the ferias of Lent, and as far as possible, of Advent: such was the rule of the ancient liturgy, as witnessed by the tenth Council of Toledo, which forbade the celebration of the festivals of the saints during the *dies quadragesimales*, and the Council of Laodicea, which forbade the keeping of *natalitia* during Lent.[1]

The Congregation resolved to restore this discipline: all festivals falling in Lent were to be omitted or transferred, according to their rank, with the exception of the Annunciation, S. Peter's Chair at Antioch, and S. Joseph, and leaving out of consideration simple feasts, which did not interfere with the ferial office. Secondly, it being agreed that the distinction of festivals into six classes, authorised by Clement VIII. and Urban VIII., should be maintained, and that no change should be made in the scheme of concurrence printed at the end of the rubrics prefixed to the Roman Breviary, it remained to settle the rank of each of the festivals retained in the reformed Kalendar. To this were devoted the meetings held in the early months of 1743.[2] The rank of greater double of the first class was conceded to ten feasts: Christmas, Epiphany, Easter, Ascension, Pentecost, *Corpus Christi*, Nativity of S. John Baptist, SS. Peter and Paul, Assumption, and All Saints; together with, in the case of each church, the anniversary of its dedication and the feast of its Patron. Twenty-seven feasts were to be greater doubles of the second class: the Circumcision, Trinity Sunday, Candlemas, Annunciation, Nativity and Conception

---

[1] [Even in 1619 the Milan Kalendar marked no festivals whatever between February 11 and April 11, except the Annunciation.—A. B.]

[2] Roskovány, p. 563; *Analecta*, p. 525.

of Our Lady, S. Stephen, Holy Innocents, S. Joseph, Invention and Exaltation of Holy Cross, the *natale* of each of the Apostles and Evangelists, S. Laurence, and S. Michael. Twelve more feasts were to be greater doubles of inferior rank to the above: viz. the Transfiguration, Dedication days of the Lateran, Liberian and Vatican basilicas, the Visitation and Presentation of our Lady, S. Peter's Chair at Rome and at Antioch, S. Peter's Chains, the Conversion of S. Paul, S. John before the Latin Gate, and S. Barnabas. The rank of lesser double was given to twenty-three feasts, and that of semidouble to thirty-four. The number of simple feasts amounted to sixty-three. The saints of whom only a memorial was to be made were twenty-nine in number.[1]

Thus was completed the new Kalendar agreed on by the Congregation. Should they go on at once to study the text of the office, and revise the homilies, legends, hymns, and responds of the offices they retained? It appeared wiser to submit to Benedict XIV. the work already done, for this constituted the base on which all the rest of their reform must be built, and they would be labouring in vain if the Sovereign Pontiff did not approve, or even, it might be, disapproved, their method and their first resolutions. By the unanimous advice, therefore, of all the consultors, Valenti laid the new Kalendar before Benedict XIV.[2]

The Pope, Valenti assures us, received it with great kindness, and said he would examine it: in fact, he kept

---

[1] Roskovány, pp. 592-612.

[2] Roskovány, p. 562; *Analecta*, p. 525. The Kalendar, and an exposition of the principles on which it was framed, are given by Roskovány, pp. 583-614.

it with him several months, which is not surprising when we consider how much he was occupied with the many other cares laid upon him by his Apostolic charge, and his natural desire to weigh most thoughtfully a matter so likely to cause difficulty as the reduction of the *Sanctorale*. In reality, it would seem that the projected Kalendar of the Congregation somewhat surprised the Pope. Here is a curious letter in which Benedict XIV. expresses his private opinion on the matter. It is dated June 7, 1743, and addressed to Cardinal de Tencin:

'We have received your Eminence's letter of May 20, in which you mention the project of a new Roman Breviary. We have remarked with most sensible pleasure the hopes which your Eminence suggests to us, that if we put forth such a new Breviary, it might be received in France, at all events in the dioceses in which the Roman Breviary is at present in use. The following is the general plan which we have proposed to follow in the composition of this Breviary. Criticism having become so exacting, and the facts which our good forefathers regarded as undoubted being now called in question, we see no other way of defending ourselves against such criticism than by compiling a Breviary in which everything should be drawn from Holy Scripture, which, as your Eminence is aware, contains plenty of matter on the subject of the mysteries celebrated in the feasts of the Church, as well as about the holy Apostles and the Blessed Virgin. Whatever the Scriptures themselves might not furnish would be supplied from the universally accepted writings of the earliest Fathers. As to the other saints which now have a place in the Breviary, a simple memorial of them would be deemed sufficient. All that can be said on the other side is, that this innovation derogates from the *cultus* which these saints have hitherto received; and true it is that the cutting out of their legends will make some people cry out, who consider the things related in them so certain that they would be ready to go to the stake in support of their truth. But such criticism as this appears to us of far less importance than that in which it is made a reproach to us that we have things read in the name of the Church which are apocryphal or of doubtful veracity. And then, too, with whatever care and ability the new Breviary was drawn up, it is inevitable that some such criticism as that alluded to above would be made.'[1]

Meanwhile, a person, whose name Valenti does not tell us, put forth the opinion that it would be better to keep all the festivals of the *Sanctorale* of the Roman Breviary, but to reduce them all to the rank of simple feasts, so as not to interfere with the ferial office. Valenti hastened to lay this opinion before the Pope, who wished to know why the consultors had not adopted it. The consultors replied in writing that it had seemed to them necessary to eliminate certain festivals of saints, and that with regard to this project itself, it clashed with the immemorial custom of the Church, and involved a thousand difficulties.[2]

All this time Benedict XIV. was being pressed to make his decision. Now it was Cardinal de Tencin; now it was the Pope's Nuncio at Paris, Crescenzi, who had been summoned to Rome to receive the Cardinal's hat; now it was Valenti himself, who assiduously recalled

---

[1] *Corr. de Rome*, t. 792, f. 21.

[2] Roskovány, p. 562; *Analecta*, p. 525. Their consultation is printed in Roskovány, pp. 614-19.

to the mind of his Holiness the interests of the work which had been begun, and which Benedict XIV. alone could bring to a successful issue. At last the Pope yielded, and nominated a Congregation of Cardinals to examine the Kalendar presented by the consultors: these consisted of their Eminences Cardinals Gentili, Valenti, Monti, Tamburini and Besozzi. The Abbé Valenti was to be the secretary of this Congregation also.[1]

They met at the Quirinal, March 2, 1744. The Cardinals made no objection to the plan of the Kalendar, but rather signified their approbation. Nevertheless, their decision was delayed by preliminary considerations. Monti, who had been made Cardinal in September 1743, having been one of the consultors of the Congregation which had prepared the Kalendar, had naturally great weight with his colleagues on the Congregation of Cardinals. He proposed to consult Cardinal de Tencin, and to await his advice. It was well known that he was keenly in favour of a reform. He was at this time a Minister of State at Versailles. He was a prelate of great influence and activity, and there was reason to hope that if they could make sure of his approval and assistance, the reformed Roman Breviary would be received in France, and if so, would also be received with all willingness by the other nations who were obedient to the Holy See. But other Cardinals remarked that the reform which had been undertaken was not sufficiently advanced to be communicated to outsiders, and Cardinal Tamburini, assenting to this observation, added that it would be better to settle without delay what distribution of the psalter they meant to adopt. Was not that, in fact, the

[1] Roskovány, p. 553; *Analecta*, p. 526.

most essential point of the projected reform? Was the entire psalter to be recited every week? How many psalms were to be recited each day? Were the week-day psalms to serve for saints' days? Were there to be some saints' days which would have psalms of their own? Such points as these were what the consultors ought to study forthwith. The advice of Tamburini prevailed. Since, in the meantime, the Congregation of consultors had lost two of its members (Monti having been made a Cardinal, and Azzoguidi having long been absent from Rome), Benedict XIV. nominated two new consultors, Orlandi, the Procurator-General of the Celestines, and Father Giuli, of the Company of Jesus, then Professor of Canon Law, and afterwards Examiner of Bishops.[1] These appointments were made on March 8, 1744,[2] and about the same time Benedict XIV. wrote to Cardinal de Tencin as follows (March 5, 1744):

'A Congregation has been held on the subject of the projected new Roman Breviary, before certain Cardinals; more than twenty meetings of the consultors by themselves having been held previously. Your Eminence will not be surprised to hear that they discoursed at large, and that the result was small; but we intend, as soon as ever we can, to begin having these Congregations held in our presence, and, more than that, we mean to discuss the

---

[1] [Benedict XIV. had established in 1740 a special Congregation of five Cardinals, who were to make themselves acquainted with the names of such ecclesiastics in every diocese as might be deemed eligible for selection as bishops, and to investigate their fitness, so that when vacancies occurred they might be prepared to suggest names of suitable persons to the Consistory. They would also employ official examiners.—A. B.]

[2] Roskovány, p. 564; *Analecta*, p. 527.

subject with Monseigneur the Archbishop of Bourges [the ambassador from the King of France], when he arrives, and all the more because he is likely enough to bring with him some clever Doctor of the Sorbonne.'[1]

The consultors met on March 19, to consider the question of the distribution of the psalter. Several churches in France had, within the last few years, adopted a new method of distribution, not even in entire agreement with one another, and this innovation had its partisans in Italy. On all sides, when the report spread that the Congregation was discussing this question, various projects for a distribution of the sort we have alluded to were sent in to Valenti, all of them claiming to make the recitation of the psalter easier and better ordered. The consultors, however, were unanimous in adhering to their former decision on July 14, 1741, and in affirming once more that the Roman distribution of the psalter was ancient and must not be abandoned. To give moie weight to their opinion, which rested on the testimony of Amalarius and Gregory VII., they had recourse to the manuscript treasures of the Roman libraries: Antonelli searched the archives of the Lateran; Giorgi, the library of the Vatican; Orlandi, that of the Vallicellan; Giuli, those of the *Collegio Romano* and the Sacred Penitentiary, and so forth. By April 29 these researches were completed, and amply confirmed the opinion of the Congregation; and Galli, summing them up in a treatise, supported the conclusion that none of the schemes of distribution now introduced in France or proposed elsewhere were worthy of being preferred to the ancient Roman

[1] *Corr. de Rome*, t. 796, f. 21.

distribution.¹ On June 17, this dissertation was read to the consultors and unanimously approved by them. At the same sitting they decided that lesser doubles falling on a Sunday should be transferred; but on the question whether semidoubles, under similar circumstances, should be transferred, or reduced to a memorial only, the votes were equally divided.²

There was need of despatch. The report spread, no one knows how—so Valenti assures us—that Benedict XIV. cared very little about the correction of the Breviary, that indeed, he rather disliked it, and allowed the consultors to occupy themselves with it, not so much with the wish to see it brought to completion, as not to oppose those persons who demanded it. Nothing could have less foundation than this report, or have been more contrary to the Pope's real mind,³ and he charged Valenti to tell the consultors that, far from feeling unfavourably towards their work, he was interested in it and supported it, and that the day would come when the Congregation should meet in his presence. Soon afterwards, in fact, he appointed an additional consultor, Nicolas Lercari, who had just come back from France, and had been made Secretary of the Propaganda; and after reading their last report, he invited the joint Congregation of Cardinals and consultors to hold a meeting in his presence, on September 29, 1744.

Benedict XIV., with the erudition and grace which

---

¹ This dissertation of Father Galli. *De non immutando veteri Psalmodiae Ritu*, has been inserted by Valenti among his authorities as *Monumentum XXII*. It has not been printed.

² Roskovány, p. 565; *Analecta*, p. 528.

³ Roskovány, p. 566; *Analecta*, p. 529.

characterised his eloquence, spoke of the necessity for a reform, and the method that ought to be adopted in the matter. That necessity, he saw, proceeded from the same causes which had of old swayed the minds of the Fathers of the Council of Trent : viz. the confusion that had come about in the recitation of the psalter, the presence of false or doubtful stories in the legends of the saints, the want of purity and elegance in the language used in addressing worship to the Almighty. As regards the method to be pursued, he, with the Cardinals, agreed in the resolution of the consultors not to interfere with the traditional distribution of the psalms ; for his own part, he desired that the Vulgate text should be left unaltered in the psalter ; he approved of the retention of the various ranks of feasts, doubles of the first class, doubles of the second class, &c. He made no objection to the eight rules which the consultors had formulated as to the reform of the Kalendar, but he would add a ninth. Some saints in the Kalendar had in fact been canonised, before the time of Alexander III. (1159–1181), by the *consensus* of the universal Church ; others, since the time of that Pope, by the decree of the Roman Pontiff, with the solemn ceremony which is called canonisation ; others again, in these latter times, without that solemn ceremony, by the mere prescription, issued by the Pope to the Catholic world, of a Mass and an office in their honour. It was not right to confound these three classes of saints, but what was proper for each of them should be carefully determined. In conclusion, he encouraged the consultors to bestow henceforth all their energies on the examination, correction, improvement, and even the replacing by fresh matter, of the several parts of the Breviary ; to share the labour between them, but to discuss each point in common, and finally to lay before him all their resolutions. Valenti set down in writing the discourse of the Sovereign Pontiff, and on October 2, the report of it, after having been laid before the Pope and approved by him, was distributed to the Cardinals and consultors.[1]

After the autumn vacation the Congregation of consultors again took up the work. Meetings were held on November 27 and December 30, to discuss the office of the Season. Lercari and Giorgi made a study of the homilies, lessons, and *capitula*; Sergio, Baldini, Giuli, and Valenti, of the antiphons, responds, hymns, versicles and responses. The examination of the lectionary resulted in only a small number of remarks; that of the antiphons, responds, &c., suggested merely a few doubts; and even the resolutions taken upon them were not maintained. The office of the Season was, in short, outside the sphere of discussion. One consultor proposed to substitute for the short lesson at Prime the reading of some canon of a Council: an innovation borrowed from the Breviary of De Vintimille. But within twenty-four hours Benedict XIV., to whom this was notified by Valenti, informed the Congregation that in his idea the question before them was the reform, and not the recasting, of the Breviary.[2]

On January 16, 1745, they undertook the Proper of Saints: on July 2 they were still at it. Valenti sets forth the plan on which the consultors shared the work between them, with what conscientious care they applied themselves to it, and what anxiety all felt to arrive at a

---

[1] Roskovány, p. 567–68; *Analecta*, p. 529.
[2] Roskovány, p. 569; *Analecta*, p. 530.

common understanding on every point. He impresses on us the respect which they entertained for antiquity, and gives us an example. One of the consultors, after calling the attention of the Congregation to the fact that the office for the Conversion of S. Paul had antiphons and responds which, though good enough, and taken from Holy Scripture, had no direct reference to the festival, undertook to compile a set, equally Scriptural, and bearing on the Conversion of the Apostle. The work was well done, but the Congregation did not accept it. As Valenti well expresses it, '*retenta est antiquitas et reprobata novitas : hoc est, nihil placuit immutari.*'[1] But in spite of all this circumspection and respect for antiquity, corrections multiplied. Then, all at once, the work came to a standstill.

Who would have believed, says Valenti, that consultors who were men of experience, and had had proved to them over and over again the firm intention of the Sovereign Pontiff, would have allowed themselves to be affected by the report, which was now for the second time spread by a certain cabal, that Benedict XIV. did not really wish for a reform of the Breviary? Alas, the falsest rumours have often an appearance of truth which suffices to deceive the keenest eyes and the most sagacious minds! This report was spread, not only away from Rome, but in Rome itself; it was believed, not only among people of no account, but by men eminent for their high position, their virtues, and their experience. The silence of the Pope was made the most of. The consultors got discouraged, and from July 9, 1745, to June 22, 1746, they could not be got together, until at

[1] Roskovány, p. 571; *Analecta*, p. 532.

last Benedict XIV. expressed to Valenti his astonishment at seeing their work so much delayed, and asked what it was that stopped them. Valenti, who, it seems, had shared in this feeling of discouragement, ingenuously avowed to the Pope what was the matter. The Pope assured him that the consultors had allowed themselves to be deceived with false rumours, exhorted him with all kindness to have the interrupted work resumed, and gave him an autograph letter, dated June 20, 1746, to read to his colleagues with the view of stirring them up to go on with and finish their task.[1] He was even willing to see them individually in order to confirm them in this determination, assuring them of the great desire he had to see the reform completed, and how much that desire was increased by the letters he received from France, especially from Cardinal de Tencin, and by the hope these gave him of seeing the reform undertaken at Rome fully accepted in that country.[2]

Accordingly, the meetings of the Congregation were resumed on June 22, 1746, and up to August 12 they met

[1] This note of Benedict XIV. figures among Valenti's authorities as *Monumentum XXXII*. We give here the text of it, never before printed: '*Dalla Seg^{ria} di Stato, 20 Giugno 1746. Avendo N^{ro} Sig^{re} una giusta premura, che si solleciti lo studio e l' affare spettante alla riforma del breviario Romano, si contenterà Mons. Promot^{re} della Fede di rappresentarla alla Congre^{ne} deputata, acciò abbia maggior stimolo di terminare questa opera.—Monsig^r Valenti, Promotore della Fede.*' 'From the office of the Secretary of State, June 20, 1746. His Holiness earnestly desiring that the study and the work undertaken with a view to the reform of the Roman Breviary may be hastened, Monsignor the Promoter of the Faith will be good enough to press this upon the Congregation charged with the task, so as to stir them up to finish the work.—Monsignor Valenti, Promoter of the Faith.'

[2] Roskovány, p. 572; *Analecta*, p. 532.

every week at the house of Valenti. At that date they had finished the revision of the Proper of Saints for the first six months of the year. On September 10 Valenti was able to present to the Pope the result of these labours of the Congregation : it was both a description and a justification of the corrections they proposed, entitled '*Specimen Breviarii reformati: pars hyemalis et pars verna.*'[1] The Pope was full of joy, and begged Valenti to complete so good a work, by causing the Congregation to study the offices for the other six months. For this they waited until after the autumn vacation, but from December 2, 1746 to March 10, 1747 they met every week. On the latter date the work was completed by the presentation of their Report on the offices for the Common of Saints, by Lercari, Antonelli, and Giorgi. The work of the Congregation had continued for not less than six years, but at last it was finished. Valenti edited the second part of his '*Specimen Breviarii reformati,*'[2] and sent it in to the Pope. Benedict XIV. now had in his hands the project of reform both as regarded the Kalendar and the office : he wished to have the opportunity of looking it over himself and discussing it, and anyone might well trust the sagacity of his mind and the extent of his erudition.[3]

Valenti concluded his Report with these words : ' We now await with confidence the decision of the Sovereign Pontiff.' It was about Easter, 1747.

We have now given a summary of the history, as

[1] Summarised by Roskovány; published entire in the *Analecta* pp. 633 *sqq.*
[2] *Analecta*, pp. 899 *sqq.*
[3] Roskovány, p. 575; *Analecta*, p. 635.

related by Valenti, of the labours of the Congregation appointed for the reform of the Breviary. We have already enumerated, always following Valenti, the various suppressions and reductions in rank agreed on in regard to festivals. It remains for us, in order to give a complete idea of the work, to indicate, as briefly as possible, the corrections proposed by the Congregation in the actual text of the offices they retained.

The corrections introduced in the Proper of the Season were few in number, and only affected the lectionary. The passage from S. Gregory, in the third nocturn of the first Sunday in Advent, in which he sees in the calamities of his own time the signs that heralded the end of the world, was replaced by another piece of the same homily, in which the saint simply expresses the joy which the faithful ought to feel at the approach of that end, regarded as the blessed coming of Christ. The curtailed and unpleasing portion from S. Jerome on Isaiah, which serves for the lessons in the second nocturn of the second Sunday, was replaced by a very beautiful passage of S. Fulgentius, full of theological instruction. On Christmas Eve S. Jerome's homily, disfigured by its rude plainness of diction, gave way to a delicately expressed exposition from S. John Chrysostom of the same text, 'When as his mother Mary was espoused to Joseph' (S. Matthew i. 18). The homily for the day after Ash Wednesday, taken from S. Augustine, and difficult of comprehension, was replaced by another homily of the same author on a simpler subject, and in a clearer style.

For the homily on Ember Wednesday in Lent, taken from S. Ambrose, was substituted a passage from S. John Chrysostom, plainer and more appropriate. On Ember Friday, for S. Augustine's development of the number 40 was substituted another passage from the same Father, more on our level. On the Friday after Mid-Lent Sunday instead of the homily of S. Augustine on Lazarus, a passage from S. Fulgentius was proposed, containing these beautiful and striking words :

> '... Iesus lacrimas fudit.... Plorabat, sed non utique plorabat ut Iudaei putabant, quia Lazarum satis amabat; sed ideo plorabat, quia iterum eum ad huius vitae miserias revocabat,' &c.[1]

On Wednesday in Passion Week, a better selection was made from S. Augustine's homily, making it begin at *Hiems erat*, and suppressing the useless passage about *Encaenia* which now serves as the first lesson. On the following day, suppressing the passage from S. Gregory, in which 'the woman which was a sinner' (S. Luke, vii. 37) is identified both with Mary of Bethany and Mary Magdalene, another passage from the same homily was substituted, in which Mary is not mentioned. On Thursday in Easter Week the same identity of Mary Magdalene with the sinful woman occurs in a homily of S. Gregory's; this was replaced by one of S. Augustine's. On Tuesday in the octave of the Ascension a sermon of S. Maximus, in which our Lord is compared to the eagle, was suppressed in favour of one by S. Bernard, without

---

[1] *Analecta*, pp. 634-42, and p. 890.—'Jesus wept.... Yet surely He grieved, not, as the Jews thought, because He loved Lazarus so dearly, but because He was to recall him to the miseries of the present life.'

the reason for the correction being quite apparent. Lastly, on the twelfth Sunday after Pentecost, instead of the homily from Bede, too vague and general in its expressions, one from S. Ambrose was given, on the parable of the Good Samaritan, the Gospel for the day. These are the amendments made by the Congregation in the lectionary of the Proper of the Season. The Proper of Saints underwent graver modifications.

Let us take first the Antiphonary and Responsoral.

The antiphons and responds for S. Andrew's Day, being borrowed from the Apocryphal Acts of that Apostle, were for that reason suppressed. The antiphons were replaced by new ones, taken from the New Testament: the responds were to be those of the Common of Apostles. The office of S. Thomas the Apostle was enriched with proper antiphons, instead of having only those of the Common, as in the Breviary at present, which proper antiphons were taken from the Gospel of S. John. The first antiphon at Lauds on S. John the Evangelist's Day was replaced by a new one, more in agreement, it was said, with the words of the Gospel. On Holy Innocents' Day, instead of the antiphons of the Common of Martyrs, new proper antiphons were given, from Isaiah and the Apocalypse. Instead of the antiphon of the Common of Sovereign Pontiffs, at *Magnificat* in the second Vespers of the Office of S. Peter's Chair at Rome, the antiphon of the first Vespers, *Tu es pastor ovium*, was repeated. No change was made in the antiphons and responds of Candlemas, except that the passage *Senex puerum portabat*, used for the antiphon to *Magnificat* at the first Vespers and eighth respond at Mattins, being taken from a spurious discourse attributed to S. Augustine, was replaced by a new antiphon and another respond,[1] both taken from the Gospel. The Annunciation lost the third and eighth responds at Mattins, the Congregation disliking the words *Efficieris gravida*, and *Cunctas haereses sola interemisti*. The proper antiphons and responds in the offices for SS. Lucy, Agnes, Agatha, Laurence, Caecilia, and Clement, were suppressed: they were taken from the Acts of these saints, documents the authority of which was not recognised by the Congregation. The antiphons and responds of the Common were substituted.

Next, the lectionary of the Proper of Saints.

S. Andrew was now to have for the lessons of the second nocturn, a portion of a sermon by S. Peter Chrysologus, a eulogium of the Apostle without any historical allusion, instead of the legend as at present, which is taken from the pretended letter of the priests of Achaia: this letter, in fact, 'is held for false and fictitious by modern critics, as Tillemont has proved to conviction; and even were it nothing more than doubtful and controverted, it would be wiser to remove it, and put in its place what cannot be impugned.'[2]

The following sets of lessons were also suppressed: (1) Those in the second nocturn of S. Thomas. Replaced by a sermon of S. John Chrysostom's on the incredulity of the Apostle. The legend given in the Roman Breviary

---

[1] This new respond, beginning *Nunc dimittis*, was in reality taken from the Antiphonary of S. Peter's published by Tommasi, tom. iv. p. 64.

[2] '*Cum vero acta illa supposititia et falsa a recentioribus criticis habeantur, ut pene ad evidentiam demonstrat Tillemontius, dubia certe quam maxime et in controversia posita sint, consultius visum est omittere, et quae inconcussae fidei sunt subrogare*' (*Analecta*, p. 643).

'is neither certain in itself, nor confirmed by other authorities, while it is controverted by critics.'[1] (2) Those in the second nocturn of S. Barnabas '*innituntur actis spuriis.*'[2] Replaced by a sermon of S. John Chrysostom's, a simple commentary on the canonical Acts. (3) Those in the third nocturn of S. Joachim, being a passage from S. John Damascene, setting forth the genealogy of Joachim and Anne; for 'that which Damascenus relates is drawn from Apocryphal writings, according to the common opinion of learned men.'[3] (4) Those in the second nocturn of S. Peter's Chains; for what they relate, viz. the story of the chains, 'is contested by almost all critics.'[4] The Congregation quote Tillemont and Baillet. Replaced by a sermon of S. John Chrysostom's (lessons v. and vi.), and a careful exposition of the claim to authenticity of the chains preserved in the basilica of S. Peter's ad Vincula on the Esquiline (lesson iv.). (5) Those in the second nocturn of the feast of S. Mary of the Snows. Replaced by a sermon of S. Bernard's which has nothing to do with the legend of the Liberian basilica.[5] (6) Those

---

[1] '*Quae illic narrantur . . . certa et explorata non sunt, pluresque patiuntur difficultates apud historiae ecclesiasticae tractatores*' (*Analecta*, p. 647).

[2] This is saying a great deal too much, since their foundation is mainly the canonical 'Acts of the Holy Apostles.'

[3] '*Cum nonnisi ex apocryphis desumpta existiment communiter eruditi*' (*Analecta*, p. 909).

[4] '*Quae in breviariis extant historiam exhibent quae criticis pene omnibus non probatur*' (*Analecta*, p. 913).

[5] On the Liberian legend the Congregation expresses itself as follows: '*Lectiones secundi nocturni, quae hac die usque modo recitatae sunt, immutandas sane esse existimatur. De ea solemnitate, quae hac die celebratur, eiusque institutionis causa, habentur, ait Baronius in Martyrologio Romano, vetera monumenta et MSS. Huiusmodi autem monumenta et MSS. nec unquam vidimus nec

in the second nocturn of S. Bartholomew; because nothing can be affirmed as certain about this Apostle, beyond what we are told in the Gospel. Not to speak of other critics, see Tillemont.[1] Replaced by a sermon of Bede's on the Twelve Apostles. (7) The fourth and fifth lessons for S. Matthew, because of the uncertainty of the things therein related about the Apostle.[2] Replaced by passages from S. John Chrysostom and S. Epiphanius.

On all the following festivals, the historical lessons were suppressed and superseded by those of the Common:[3] S. Nicolas, *Suspectae admodum fidei*; S. Lucy, *Certae et exploratae fidei non sunt*; SS. Marius, Martha, and Audifax, *Plura illis obicit Tillemontius quae difficillimum est complanare*; S. Peter Nolasco, *Eius gesta quae ibi narrantur, nunquam in examen adducta sunt;*

fortasse unquam videbimus. Mirandum profecto est, ait Baillet, non adhuc tanti miraculi et tam mirabilis historiae auctorem innotuisse; insuper quod tam novum tamque stupendum prodigium spatio annorum fere mille et amplius profundo sepultum silentio iacuerit, nec usquam inveniri potuerit, praeterquam in breviario et in Catalogo Petri de Natalibus lib. 7, cap. 21 ' (*Analecta*, p. 915). ' It is thought that the lessons hitherto read on this day in the second nocturn should certainly be changed. Baronius, in the *Roman Martyrology*, says that ancient records and MSS. exist on the subject of the solemn festival observed on this day and the cause of its institution. But any such records and MSS. we have never seen, and in all probability are never likely to see. Marvellous indeed is it, says Baillet, that the authority for so great a miracle and so wonderful a story should never yet have been produced; still more that so strange and stupendous a prodigy should have lain buried in silence for about a thousand years or more, and that it should be impossible to find a trace of it anywhere except in the Breviary and in the Catalogue of Peter de Natalibus, book 7, chapter 21.'

[1] *Analecta*, p. 920.
[2] *Ib.* p. 926.
[3] *Ib.* pp. 644 *sqq.*, 892 *sqq.*

S. Agatha, *Acta [eius] a recentioribus inter apocrypha accensentur*; S. Blaise, *Quae in eius vita narrantur inepta sunt et male consuta, ex Tillemontio*; SS. Tiburtius, Valerian and Maximus, *Desumpt. ex actis S. Caeciliae, expungend.*; S. Caius, Pope, *Nullius vel dubiae fidei*; S. Cletus, Pope, *Incerta*; SS. Alexander, Eventius and Theodulus, *Nihil certo . . ., mendosa*; S. Juvenal, *Acta erroribus plena pronuntiat Tillemontius*; SS. Gordian and Epimachus, *Incerta, multis difficultatibus sive controversiis subiecta*; S. Urban, *Monumenta falsa vel fidei admodum dubiae*; SS. Basilides, Cyrinus, Nabor, and Nazarius, *Acta apocrypha*; SS. Vitus and Modestus, *Acta spuria et falsa in pluribus*; SS. Processus and Martinian, *Acta non esse authentica probat Tillemontius*; S. Praxedis, *Acta parum sincera videntur . . . Tillemontio*; S. Pudentiana, SS. Abdon and Sennen, *Acta corrupta . . . fabulosa*; SS. Cyriac, Largus and Smaragdus, *Acta depravata*; S. Hippolytus, *Ex actis S. Laurentii . . ., actis corruptis*; S. Timothy,[1] *De quo maximae et spinis undique circumseptae lites apud criticos sunt*; S. Adrian, S. Gorgonius, SS. Protus and Hyacinth, *Acta apocrypha esse contendunt Tillemontius et Baillettus*; SS. Nicomede, Nereus and Achilles, *Fidei valde dubiae*; S. Calixtus, *Incerta sunt quae in ea lectione narrantur*; S. Mennas, *Plurimis scatent difficultatibus*.

New proper lessons replaced the suppressed historical lessons of the following: SS. Damasus, Sylvester, Hilary, Felix of Nola, Paul the Hermit, Marcellus, Antony, Fabian, John Chrysostom, Pius V., Peter Celestine, Felix the Pope, Peter and Marcellinus, Primus and Felician, Margaret of Scotland, Marcus and Marcellianus, Gervase and Protase, Paulinus of Nola, Elizabeth of

---

[1] A martyr, commemorated on August 22.

Portugal,[1] John Gualbert, Apollinaris,[2] Nazarius and Celsus, Popes Victor and Innocent, Martha, Pope Stephen, Pope Sixtus, Tiburtius, Susanna, Perpetua and Felicitas, Clara, Philip Beniti, Stephen of Hungary, the Forty Martyrs, the Exaltation of Holy Cross, SS. Nereus and Achilles, Cornelius, Cyprian, Januarius, Maurice, Remigius, the Dedication of S. John Lateran, SS. Gregory the Wonder-worker, John de Matha, Caecilia, Clement, Chrysogonus, and Polycarp.

Besides these legends, a certain number of apocryphal homilies and sermons were suppressed in the Proper of Saints. Thus the pretended sermon of S. Augustine, in the second nocturn of the Holy Innocents, was replaced by one of S. Bernard's, 'in order that all uncertain or

[1] The proper antiphons and responds for this festival were also suppressed, and it was proposed to lower it to the rank of a simple feast.

[2] The legend of S. Apollinaris was replaced by a panegyric sermon by S. Peter Chrysologus, without historical reference, and the correction was justified as follows: '*De S. Apollinare nihil asserere certius possumus quam quod legimus in hoc sermone S. Petri Chrysologi. Ab hoc dissentiunt Acta, quae S. Apollinarem in ipso martyrii actu obiisse narrant. Sed Acta ista, tametsi antiqua, inter sincera tamen non retulit Ruinartius, et interpolata esse fatetur Joannes Pinius. Addit Tillemontius multa in illis contineri quae ipsis detrahant auctoritatem. Hinc sermonem istum legendum exhibent breviaria Lugdunense et Parisiense*' (*Analecta*, p. 909). 'About S. Apollinaris we can assert nothing more certain than what we read in this sermon of S. Peter Chrysologus. There is a discrepancy between this and his Acts, which represent S. Apollinaris as having died in the very act of martyrdom. But these Acts of S. Apollinaris, although ancient, were not reckoned by Ruinart among the *Acta sincera*, and John Pinius acknowledges them to have had interpolations inserted in them. Tillemont adds that they contain many things which should deprive them of authority. For these reasons the Lyons and Paris breviaries give this sermon to be read in their stead.'

suspected things may be banished from our Breviary.'[1] Again, for the pretended sermon of the same S. Augustine in the second nocturn of Candlemas was substituted a sermon of S. Bernard's. For another apocryphal sermon of S. Augustine, in the second nocturn of the office of S. Peter's Chair at Rome, was substituted a fragment of S. Cyprian's *De Unitate Ecclesiae*. An apocryphal sermon of S. John Chrysostom,[2] in the second nocturn of the Visitation, was replaced by a sermon of S. Bernard's, and a homily really by S. John Chrysostom, in the third nocturn of the office of S. John Gualbert, took the place of the three lessons now in the Breviary, and attributed to S. Jerome, though only the first is by him, the two others being taken from an apocryphal sermon of S. Augustine.[3]

[1] *Analecta*, p. 649.
[2] *Ib.* p. 904: '*Illi substituendus sermo S. Bernardi, etsi isto utantur etiam in eodem festo breviaria Lugdunense et Parisiense.*' 'A sermon of S. Bernard's should be substituted for it, although the Lyons and Paris breviaries retain it on this festival.'
[3] *Analecta*, p. 907. This part of the revision of the consultors of Benedict XIV. is very incomplete. Dom Morin has gone into the subject recently, and notices a total number of fifty apocryphal sermons and homilies in the present Roman Breviary. It is true the greater part of this apocryphal literature is of recent introduction. Dom Morin writes: 'In most of the offices recently added to the Breviary, it seems to me that as much care has not been taken [as formerly] to select nothing but authentic passages to serve for sermons or homilies. Thus, for example, in spite of all the recastings to which it has been subjected at short intervals of time, the office of the Immaculate Conception, of such importance from a dogmatic point of view, gives as the second lesson of the second nocturn a passage from the notorious *Cogitis me*, which claims the name of S. Jerome, the authenticity of which was already called in question by the more acute-minded in the ninth century, and which all critics without exception since Baronius have rejected as manifestly apocryphal' ('Les Leçons apocryphes du Bréviaire Romain,' in the *Revue Bénédictine*, 1891, pp. 270–280; *cf.* Bäumer, pp. 623–630.)

The Common of Saints underwent only two corrections, of no great importance : in the Common of Evangelists, a different passage from S. Gregory was substituted for that now there ; and in the Common of many Martyrs, *secundo loco*, a homily of S. Gregory took the place of the homily from S. Ambrose. The Congregation considered these two portions of homilies as better fitted to the text of the Gospel, and more edifying.[1]

III

It will not be requisite to discuss one by one the various corrections proposed by the Congregation of Benedict XIV. ; nor indeed could that be done without unduly extending the limits of this work. But it is necessary to form a judgment on the general character of this projected reform of the Breviary, and to relate how it was that it was not carried out.

In the first place, we notice the respect shown by the Congregation for the ancient elements of the Roman Breviary : I mean, the traditional distribution of the psalter among the various canonical hours, and the office of the Season. They propose no correction on these points. So far from doing so, they show a remarkable determination to defend these vital and essential features of the ancient Roman Office. At their first meeting in July 1741, they declare the Roman distribution of the psalms to be a matter outside the sphere of discussion. When, in March 1744, Cardinal Tamburini gains over the other members of the Congregation of Cardinals, and demands that the distribution of the psalter should be

[1] *Analecta*, p. 933.

discussed before the revision of the Kalendar, the consultors refuse: they repulse the various schemes of distribution sent in to them, by a final resolution not to admit them, and in September 1744, they have the satisfaction of seeing Benedict XIV. confirm their decision. The very constitution of the ancient Roman Office is to their mind beyond discussion. Here we have a broad line of distinction between the work of the liturgists of Benedict XIV. and that of the Gallicans. The latter wished for, and carried out, a complete recasting of the whole Breviary; the former are unanimous in their determination to attempt nothing more than a correction on the same lines as those which commended themselves to the mind of Clement VIII. If, on one day in December 1744, they are tempted to make something more than a correction in the office of the Season, Valenti and the Pope are ready to remind them at once that it is a thing which they themselves have abjured: '*propterea quod breviarii reformatio sibi esset in votis, non innovatio*,' says the Sovereign Pontiff.[1]

In fact, beyond five or six unimportant modifications in the lectionary, the office of the Season comes forth intact from the revision of the Roman liturgists. The structure and the text of this, which is the real ancient Roman Office, are beyond and above correction, and these Romans have the advantage over the Gallicans, in being from the first convinced of this, and remaining firm in upholding it.

In the second place—and on this point they deserve our highest praise—their method of work did not run counter to that of the Council of Trent and Pius V., but was in

[1] *Analecta*, p. 580.

conformity with the spirit of the Council and the Pope to whom we owe the reformed Breviary. It was because the distribution of the psalter had been maintained and the office of the Season stamped with his authority by Pius V., that they held to them so firmly. And if, on the contrary, they undertook with so much boldness the reform of the Kalendar and the *Sanctorale*, it is because they were convinced, and that, too, on the word of the liturgists of Pius V., that it was the mind of the Pope and the Council to reduce the status of the *Sanctorale* and raise that of the *Temporale*, to promote the more frequent use of the Sunday and ferial offices, as compared with the office of saints' days. The *a priori* liturgical method, which is the vice of all the Gallican reforms of the Breviary, is conspicuously absent in the work of our Roman liturgists: De Vintimille carried out the projects of Grancolas, Foinard, and Vigier; Benedict XIV. is possessed with the idea of taking up the work of Pius V. and the Council of Trent—of restoring it where it had been corrupted, and perfecting it where it had remained incomplete.

As regards restoration, our liturgists had to lighten the Kalendar of the fixed feasts, which since 1568, had so largely increased in number and in rank: some they had to suppress, others to reduce to a lower status. Here their difficulties begin. Without doubt, it is reasonable to believe that the Church institutes certain feasts, or augments their solemnity, for reasons which lose their weight in the lapse of time: for instance, who could deny that the amount of devotion to the sanctuary of S. Michael on Mount Garganus which exists at the present day would never be considered as sufficient ground for instituting a feast for the Church universal, such as we find in the Kalendar on May 8? There are, then, some ancient feasts which no longer excite any perceptible degree of devotion on the part of the faithful, who would witness the diminution of their solemnity, or even their disappearance, without offence or grief. Without doubt, again, the Kalendar of the liturgy is not the martyrology: to suppress a festival is not to insult its subject or to deny its right to veneration. But for all that, to handle such matters successfully, what delicacy of perception is required! What dangers and difficulties surround their decision! On what solid principles must that decision be supported! Did the Congregation of Benedict XIV. possess all that tact, and had they got hold of the right criteria to guide them in their decisions? It is sufficient to read the preface of the Kalendar as reformed by them, and the discourse addressed to them in 1744 by Benedict XIV.,[1] to be convinced that such solid criteria were lacking to them. They retain in the Kalendar those saints whose festivals are ancient: where does antiquity end? They retain those who are dear to the devotion of the universal Church, or those on behalf of whom some special reason is alleged: what saint is there who could not be made to fit into one or other of these two categories? And as for tact, the list of saints eliminated from the Kalendar is sad reading. It is a melancholy exodus of saints, including the most venerable and the best beloved: S. Louis Gonzaga, S. Francis Borgia, S. John of the Cross, S. Placidus, S. Petronilla, S. Elizabeth of Hungary, not to mention S. Gregory VII.

[1] I allude to the reservations expressed by the Pope as to the principles formulated by the consultors.

and a host of others, more dear to universal devotion than many a name, venerable, no doubt, but well-nigh forgotten, whose only claim to retention in the Kalendar is its antiquity.

Here was the chief difficulty, in this business of the selection of saints to retain in the Kalendar, and in a lesser degree, in settling what rank should be assigned to each festival which was retained. Everybody was sensible that this difficulty existed; the thing was to resolve it: and it seems that in this the Congregation was far from successful: it left the work to Benedict XIV. to accomplish.

If we have the right to speak with some severity of the Kalendar proposed by the Congregation, it is only just to acknowledge the scrupulous care which it bestowed on purging the text of the Breviary from all errors. The lectionary required correction: it requires it still. Our Roman liturgists were well up in all the science of their time: they derived it from Cave, Tillemont, Baillet, Mabillon, the Bollandists, Ruinart, Tommasi, Fleury—most of all from Tillemont and Baillet, critics with scant indulgence for legends, but enlightened and scrupulous. The revisers, indeed, pushed their scruples too far, very much further than the liturgists of Urban VIII.; they rejected anything which was so much as controverted; they were unwilling that the letter of the Breviary should be in any degree open to question, and thus, along with the chaff, not a little good grain was thrown out. At the present time, there would be some room for correcting their corrections, for, if they were right in eliminating from the Breviary every trace of forged decretals, apocryphal Acts of Apostles, and unfounded legends of saints, it does not follow that we are to reject entirely all *Acta minus sincera*, any more than the '*Liber Pontificalis*,' for 'in the falsest of histories there is generally some truth for the foundation,' as Tillemont says somewhere, with great reason; besides which, the progress of archaeology and critical science, in adding to our information, so far from diminishing the area of certitude, has enlarged it. With greater enlightenment and experience, a more conservative spirit would now prevail in the editing of historical legends than the Congregation of Benedict XIV. were willing to show, and our Bollandists of the present day would make a better correction of the Breviary without throwing overboard so much.

So again, with less attachment to the principle so dear to the Gallican liturgists, in accordance with which the antiphons and responds should be exclusively derived from Holy Scripture, a principle to which our Roman liturgists felt themselves more than once compelled to be unfaithful, we, on the contrary, feel no repugnance to singing the antiphons and responds of S. Lucy, S. Agnes, S. Caecilia, S. Clement or S. Laurence, those compositions so deeply stamped with the authority of Roman liturgical tradition. And we should not be sorry to believe that the Congregation eventually shared this feeling, since in the end they retained in the Common of Saints antiphons and responds which, so far from being taken from Scripture, were, just as much as the responds of the office of S. Andrew, borrowed from Acts more or less historical, and even from apocryphal writings: such as the respond '*Lux perpetua lucebit sanctis tuis et aeternitas temporum*' of the Common of Martyrs, or the '*Quem vidi, quem amavi,*' of the Common of Widows.

Our readers will see from these remarks how far we are from considering the correction of the Breviary prepared by the Roman liturgists as being, on the whole, just or prudent. How far they were under the influence of the Gallican liturgists is for us only a secondary question. We know, on the one hand, that there was a fundamental difference between the views of De Vintimille and those of Valenti. And, on the other hand, as regards what they had in common, however true it may be that certain concessions were made in favour of the Gallican liturgy and in deference to Gallican erudition by a Pontifical Congregation at Rome, yet, if we entertained the idea of drawing thence any inferences in favour of that liturgy and that erudition, which some have been too eager to disparage, we should have to remember that the Holy See never resolved the doubts of its consultors or gave its decision on their propositions.

But we must beware of putting a bad construction on that silence, and making it a handle for charging the Pope with a dishonést reserve: it would be utterly false to say, as some have dared to say, that Benedict XIV. did not really desire the carrying out of that reform of the Breviary which he put in hand. His integrity is unquestionable. Benedict XIV., in the words of the splendid panegyric which Cardinal de Tencin pronounced on him, ' was incapable, not merely of deceit in his conduct, but of the least dissimulation.'[1] But he was too sagacious

[1] De Tencin to Amelot, Secretary of State, May 5, 1741 (*Corr. de Rome*, t. 785, f. 9).

a man not to see how great were the difficulties that attended any such reform.[1]

In 1743, Benedict XIV. had written to Cardinal de Tencin: 'As to a new Roman Breviary, we recognise not merely the advantage of it, but the necessity, and we are ready to set to work on it, being well accustomed to labour ever since we were in the world, and prepared, if need be, to die in the breach like a brave soldier. But, dear Cardinal, the whole world has arrived at such contempt of the authority of the Holy See, that, to hinder its execution of the most useful or the most pious designs, there is only needed, we will not say the opposition of a bishop, a nation, or a town, but the protest of a single monk. We have only too constant experience of it, not to speak of the murmurs of some who wear the same habit as your Eminence, who, when they hear of a projected new Breviary, rage against it just as if it was a question of making a new Creed. In spite of all this, and *non obstantibus quibuscumque*, we will devise with your Eminence what can be done to that end.'[2]

A few days later he writes: 'We do not lose sight of the notion of a new Roman Breviary, but we will candidly avow to your Eminence that we still fear the opposition which this great project is sure to encounter on the part of several persons here at Rome, besides what it will meet with in the countries beyond the Alps. Several people here whisper to one another that nothing

---

[1] See the letters of Benedict XIV. concerning the matter of Bellarmine's canonisation, a memorable example of his sagacity and prudence (*Études Religieuses*, 1896, t. lxxvii. p. 663).

[2] Benedict XIV. to De Tencin, April 26, 1743 (*Corr. de Rome*, t. 791, f. 215).

will be done in the matter of the Breviary of the Archbishop of Paris, on the pretext of waiting for ours; and that when we have worked hard at the latter, the French bishops will be the first to criticise it. It is all by way of saying something smart, but it annoys us all the same.'[1]

And again: 'The project of a new Roman Breviary is excellent, and the execution of it not at all impossible; but before undertaking it, much deliberation is necessary. The state of the world nowadays is such, that if the Pope does anything, those whom it happens to please are on his side, and those who don't like it go against him; and as it is impossible for the same thing to please everybody, mishaps and rebuffs are sure to be his share from one side or the other. Well-disposed persons urge the Pope to do this or that, and when it is done, even if they do not change their minds, they tell him at all events that they cannot give him any assistance. We have seen with our own eyes Clement XI. bite his nails more than once, when, after publishing the bull *Unigenitus*, he saw how Louis XIV. never kept the promise he had made him, of causing the bull to be accepted throughout his kingdom, and how Monsieur Amelot said to his very face, that the king had the best dispositions in the world, but could not do all he would wish. And we have experienced the same kind of thing ourselves.'[2]

Thus spoke Benedict XIV. in 1743, when the consultors, as we may say, were still only beginning their preliminary studies. When those studies are at last

---

[1] Benedict XIV. to De Tencin, May 3, 1743 (*Corr. de Rome*, t. 771, f. 227).

[2] The same to the same, February 8, 1743 (*Corr. de Rome*, t. 791, f. 52).

finished, when Valenti has put into the Pope's hands the resolutions finally arrived at by the Congregation—and we have seen what confidence Valenti felt in the excellence of the results achieved after those long and laborious discussions—the tone of the Sovereign Pontiff changes all at once: his disappointment is unmistakeable, but his determination is unshaken. The work of the Congregation is to his mind a failure, but he forms the plan of recasting it himself. In 1748, he writes:

'In reprinting here, by the request and at the cost of the King of Portugal, the Roman Martyrology, we have seized the opportunity to make certain additions to it, as your Eminence will see by the Preface, which we enclose. Would to God we had followed the same plan in regard to the correction of the Roman Breviary, and had worked at it by ourselves! It would have been completed long ago! But we started by appointing a Congregation, who, at last, have given in to us their conclusions, so confused, so obscure, and so contradictory, that it is a greater labour to correct them than to correct the Breviary. Yet, if God grants us life and health, we shall not fail yet to construct our new edition of the corrected Breviary.'[1]

And, in fact, Benedict XIV. set courageously to work. Anyone, he loved to say, who thinks he knows how to do a thing himself (*fare una cosa da se*), can hardly make up his mind to let others do it. And if he willingly left to

---

[1] Benedict XIV. to De Tencin, August 7, 1748 (*Corr. de Rome*, t. 796, f. 254): '*C' imbarcammo a deputare una Congregazione, che finalmente ci ha dati i suoi sentimenti tanto confusi e tanto imbrogliati, e tanto dissoni frà di loro, che vi vuole più fatica a correggere quelli, che il breviario. Se Iddio ci darà vita e sanità, non mancheremo di fare ancora la nuova edizione del breviario corretto.*'

others matters of ceremonial and politics, he felt he could handle by himself things involving positive theology and canon law. 'The Pope,' said Cardinal de Tencin too cavalierly, 'has an itching desire to make books and decrees.'[1] In reality, he was a learned man who knew no other recreation or consolation, in the midst of his thorny charge, than to get into his library and resume his dear old studies. With what care he touched and retouched the new editions of his treatises on Canonisation and on Diocesan Synods! He put the revision of the Breviary on the list of his personal undertakings. And in September 1748 he wrote: 'As to the Roman Breviary, we have taken up that matter ourselves. But to complete it we must have more time to devote to it than we have at present, being in truth not so much besieged as overwhelmed with work.'[2]

In 1755 he had not given up thinking of it. 'Two tasks,' he wrote, 'remain for us to accomplish. One about the sacraments, the administration of which in the Eastern Church demands new rules or new explanations; the other is a good honest correction of our Breviary (*l' altro è un' onesta correzione del nostro breviario*). We are not afraid of the work, having our storehouse already full of materials (*noi non recusiamo la fatica, avendo già il magazzino pieno di materiali*).' He had in mind, either the studies made by his consultors, or his own researches

---

[1] De Tencin to Fleury, October 20, 1741 (*Corr. de Rome*, t. 78 f. 117).

[2] Benedict XIV. to De Tencin, September 25, 1748 (*Corr. de Rome*, t. 796, f. 274): '*Rispetto al breviario, abbiamo ripigliata la materia. Ma per ridurla a capo, vi vorrebbe più tempo da impiegarci di quello che si ha, essendo veramente non che circondati, ma oppressi dalle fatiche.*'

on this subject. 'But,' he adds with sadness, 'some time would be needed, and one cannot easily find it: or if one does find it, the weight of years and infirmities makes itself felt.'[1]

On February 18, 1756, he writes again: 'If God grants us life and health, we shall write a little work which will contain all that concerns the matter and form of the sacraments in the Eastern Church. . . . We have revived here the study of Greek affairs, but without dispensing ourselves from working at them in person (*senza esentarci dal faticare personalmente*). Why are we at such an advanced age, made a prisoner by the gout, and so preoccupied with the grave affairs of the West?'[2]

Thus, in 1755, he still has thoughts of accomplishing the correction of the Breviary, of doing so himself, and after he has settled the question of the Greek ritual. In 1756 the latter question is in a way to be settled soon: the turn of the Breviary will come at last, and the Pope will give us that '*onesta correzione del breviario*' for which he has all the materials in hand. But the task is hard, and the age is one which it is difficult to satisfy ('*il secolo presente è di contentatura difficile*');[3] and on May 4, 1758, the Pope is dead.

---

[1] Benedict XIV. to Peggi, August 13, 1755 (*Briefe*, p. 115).
[2] The same to the same, February 18, 1756 (*ib.* p. 121).
[3] The same to the same, April 16, 1758 (*ib.* p. 134).

CONCLUSION

WE have never had that '*onesta correzione del nostro breviario*,' which the firm and loyal genius of Benedict XIV. would have given us, and which only his death prevented him from giving. Shall we have it some day, and will the world see those materials once more taken in hand which the great Pope collected for the correction of the blemishes of the Breviary, and the restoring of the equilibrium between the office of the Season and that of Saints, which is so greatly to be desired? It does not belong to us to answer this question, any more than to indicate here the corrections which are necessary, or to investigate the best means for re-establishing that equilibrium: this would be beyond the province of the historian. It is nevertheless of consequence, at the end of this History of the Roman Breviary, in which so many questions bearing on a possible reform of the Breviary, both in its text and in its rubrics, have been incidentally touched upon, to express as clearly as possible the only conclusions to which this study of liturgical archaeology and literary history unmistakeably lead us.[1]

---

[1] We leave on one side two developments. (1) Any account of the proposals made under Pius IX. for a reform of the Breviary. They did not amount to anything more than mere expressions of desire, and are not, it must be confessed, *secundum scientiam*. They will be found summed up by Schober, *op. cit.* pp. 78–80, and

We must reject the French liturgical Utopia of the eighteenth century, even as we rejected the Roman Utopia of the sixteenth. The liturgy of De Vintimille and that of Quignonez, of Coffin or of Ferreri, have to our mind, as archaeologians, no claim to take the place of the existing traditional liturgy.

For us, that traditional liturgy is represented by the Roman Breviary of Urban VIII., a book which constitutes for us a Vulgate of the Roman Office. That Vulgate, that *ne varietur* edition of 1632, is historic, and the Holy See has been well advised in showing itself unwilling to touch it without the exercise of the greatest caution and discretion. It would even be a desirable thing if all the additions made since 1632 could be printed separately, so that one would have a supplement containing all these added offices, while the Vulgate Breviary of 1632 remained permanently secured from alteration.

The thing which renders this Vulgate of 1632 precious to us is, that, thanks to the wisdom of Paul IV., Pius V., and Clement VIII., the differences between it and the Breviary of the Roman *Curia* of the thirteenth century are mere differences of detail : the substantial identity of the two is beyond dispute. The Breviary of Urban VIII. is the legitimate descendant of the Breviary of Innocent III.

And the latter, in its turn, is the legitimate descendant of the Roman canonical Office, as it was celebrated

---

by Bäumer, pp. 584-595. (2) The history of the suppression of the Gallican breviaries. On this point may be profitably consulted those pages of the Abbé Marcel's monograph, *Livres liturgiques du Diocèse de Langres* (Paris, 1892), which are devoted to 'Études d'histoire liturgique en France au XIXme Siècle.'

in the basilica of S. Peter at the end of the eighth century, such as it had gradually come to be in the course of the seventh and eighth centuries, a genuinely Roman combination of various elements, some of them Roman and some not, but of which some, at all events, go back to the very beginnings of the Catholic religion. The glory and the excellence of the Breviary of Urban VIII. is founded on its descent from such an august ancestor.

Undoubtedly it does not descend from it in a direct line: that is the chief fault we have to find with it. As archaeologians and historians, it is our grief not to be able to regard the office of the eighth century as the abiding canon of the Divine Office. We must be forgiven our scholarly predilections! In the breviary of Innocent. III. we have the abridgment, not of the ancient Roman Office as it was celebrated at S. Peter's in the eighth century, and even still in the thirteenth, but of that office as it was first adopted and then transformed, in France, Germany and Italy, from the ninth to the twelfth century, under the all-powerful influence of the religious Orders, and of Cluny more especially, thus becoming that 'Modern Office' which differed in so many respects from the pure Roman Office. The weak point about the correctors of the sixteenth century was their ignorance of that pure Roman Office, an ignorance which hindered them from drawing the text of the Divine Office from its true source.

Such as it is, let us count ourselves fortunate, as we should be if it had been our hap to see yet standing the old basilica of S. Peter at Rome, not indeed, as it was in the time of S. Damasus, not even as it was in the days of

Adrian I. and Leo III., the basilica which witnessed the coronation of Charlemagne, but just the basilica of the time of Nicolas V., decorated, furnished and blocked up as it was at that date, instead of having to go down into the Vatican crypts to see what small remains of that ancient and venerable sanctuary the vandalism of the Renaissance has allowed to survive. For in fact the Roman Breviary is, in its main lines, the old edifice which was completed in the eighth century. And if, from the ninth century to the thirteenth, from the thirteenth to the fifteenth, too many hands have been busy in decorating, modifying and encumbering it, at all events in the sixteenth century it was saved by the prudence of Paul IV., Pius V. and Clement VIII., from the plans of arbitrary restoration or disastrous reconstruction proposed by Leo X. and Clement VII., even though it did not afterwards escape the embellishments of Urban VIII. In this living work, still the rule and canon of our prayers, the edifice of the eighth century is standing yet.

And you, my pious readers, who have followed me thus far, when next you go on pilgrimage to the Eternal City, take the Appian Way, and follow it as far as the basilica of SS. Nereus and Achilles. In entering that church you will think of Pope Leo III., who constructed it on the traditional plan of the Roman basilicas, and decorated it with mosaics: you will be moved by the elegant simplicity, the austere and mystical beauty of that architecture. And if, remembering what manner of restorations were inflicted on the basilica of S. Gregory on the Caelian by Cardinal Borghese, on the basilica of S. Caecilia in the Trastevere by Cardinal Acquaviva, or on that of Holy Cross in Jerusalem by no less a personage than Benedict XIV., you wish to know by whose pious and enlightened care the work of Leo III. was preserved in such perfection, read the inscription in which Cardinal Baronius—for he it is—humbly claims the honour of this restoration of the basilica of his Title, and conjures his successors not to alter it:

> PRESBYTER CARD. SVCCESSOR QVISQVIS FVERIS
> ROGO TE PER GLORIAM DEI ET
> PER MERITA HORVM MARTYRVM
> NIHIL DEMITO NIHIL MINVITO NEC MVTATO
> RESTITVTAM ANTIQVITATEM PIE SERVATO.

That same love, that pious and well-instructed reverence, which Cardinal Baronius felt for his fair basilica, it is my wish to inspire in all my readers towards the ancient Roman Office, which the Breviary of the Council of Trent has preserved for us.

APPENDICES

APPENDIX A

EXTRACTS FROM THE *ORDO* OF MONTPELLIER [1]

THE text of the *Capitulare* has been copied from the MS., and carefully collated with it. The document appears to have assumed its present form before the year 800, and probably before 750, judging principally from what is said in it of the feasts of the Sanctorale.

[*Fol.* 87.] IN NOMINE DOMINI NOSTRI IHESU CHRISTI INCIPIT CAPITULARE ECCLESIASTICI ORDINIS QUALITER SANCTA ATQUE APOSTOLICA ECCLESIA ROMANA CELEBRATUR SICUT IBIDEM A SAPIENTIBUS ET VENERABILIBUS PATRIBUS NOBIS TRADITUM FUIT.

Primitus enim adventum Domini kalendis decembris incipiunt celebrare, et in ipsa nocte initiatur legi Isaia propheta, et usque Domini natalem repetendo a capite ipsum propheta legunt. Deinde una dominica ante natalem Domini incipiunt canere de conceptione sanctae Mariae. In ipsa vero ebdomada quarta et sexta feria seu et sabbatu stationes publicas faciunt: prima ad sanctam Mariam ad praesepe, secunda ad apostolos Iacobi et Iohannis, tertia cum XII lectionibus ad sanctum Petrum. Et in ipsa die sacerdotes et ceteri ministri ecclesiae si necesse fuerit ordinantur. Si autem evenerit ut vigiliae natalis Domini sabbato incurrant, precedente ebdomada omnem celebrationem vel ordinationem quam diximus usque in sabbato consummant. Quod si dominica contigerit, hora qua et reliquis

[1] Montpellier, *Bibliothèque de l'Ecole de Médecine*, No. 412 (ninth century).

diebus dominicis missarum solemnii celebrantur. In vigilia vero natalis Domini incipiente nocte mox ingrediuntur ad vigilias. Deinde expletis psalmis VIIII cum lectionibus vel responsuriis seu et matutinis cum antiphonis ad ipsum diem pertinentibus, expectantes domnum apostolicum modice requiescunt. Adpropinquante vero gallorum cantu, ipso domno apostolico cum episcopis vel reliquis sacerdotibus cum cereis vel multis luminibus procedente, surgentes preparant se qualiter ad missas ingrediantur. Et mox ut gallus [*fol.* 88] cantaverit domnus apostolicus cum omni ordine sacerdotum ad missas ingreditur. . . .

Post nativitatem vero Domini usque in octabas praeter sanctorum festivitatibus psalmi antiphonae responsuria seu lectiones in nocte et in die de ipso Domini natali sunt canendi. In octabas autem Domini quod est kal. januar. ordinem quo Domini natale in omnibus observant. Inde vero in teophania praeter dominicos dies vel nataliciis sanctorum de cotidianis diebus psallunt. Pridie theophaniae ieiunium publicum faciunt [*fol.* 94] et hora nona missas celebrant et laetaniam publicam ad missam faciant, et medio noctis tempore ingrediuntur ad vigilias. Psalmos quoque aut lectiones vel responsuria de ipsa die canentes tantum de muneribus magorum et baptismo, de nuptiis vero quae facta sunt in Chana Galileae octabas teophaniae celebrant. Sed et omni ebdomada usque in octabas semper de theophania canunt. Expletis igitur nocturnis seu et matutinis, mox cum cereis et candelabris seu et turibulis cantando TE DEUM LAUDAMUS ad fontes veniunt. Hoc finito incipiunt laetaniam id est CHRISTE AUDI NOS et reliqua. Ipsa expleta adstantibus episcopis presbiteris diaconibus subdiaconibus vel omni clero et cuncto populo in circuitu fontis cum multis luminibus statim episcopus benedicit fontes ; post benedictionem vero faciens de chrismate crucem in ipsis fontibus de ipsa chrisma spargit super cunctum populum. Hoc facto omnis populus accepit benedictionem unusquis in vasis suis de ipsa aqua ad spargendum tam in domos eorum quam et in vineis campis vel fructibus eorum. Deinde discalciati presbiteri aut diaconi induentes se aliis vestibus mundis vel candidis ingrediuntur in fontes et acceptis infantibus a parentibus baptizant eos ter mergentes in aquam in nomine Patris et Filii et Spiritus sancti, tantum sanctam trinitatem semel invocantes. Levatis ipsis infantibus offerunt eos in manibus suis uni presbitero. Ipse vero presbiter faciens de crisma crucem in vertice eorum invocatione sanctae trinitatis. Deinde sunt parati qui eos suscipere debeant cum lenteis in manibus eorum et traduntur eis a presbiteris vel diaconibus qui eos baptizant. Baptizati autem infantes mox deportantur ante episcopum et datur eis gratia Spiritus septiformis cum chrismate in fronte et invocatione sanctae trinitatis, id est confirmatio baptismi vel christianitatis. Missas vero in ipsa die ordine quo diximus [*fol.* 95] Domini natalem sequuntur.

Postea quidem die secundo mense februario quod est IIII non. ipsius mensis colliguntur omnes tam clerus romanae ecclesiae quam et omnes monachi monasteriorum cum omni populo suburbano seu et copiosa multitudo peregrinorum de quacunque provintia congregati venientes ad ecclesiam beati Adriani mane prima, et accipiunt de manu pontificis unusquis cereo uno omnes viri cum feminis et infantibus et accendunt eos portantes eos in manibus omnes una voce canentes unusquis in ordine suo quo militat, procedentibus ante domnum apostolicum septem candelabris cum cereis seu et turibulis cum timiamatibus, et accensis lampadibus ante uniuscuiusque domum, ante pontificem procedunt omnes cum magna reverentia ad sanctam Mariam maiorem, et ibidem devotissime missas celebrantur qualiter post purificationem beate Mariae dominus noster Ihesus Christus secundum legem Moysi representatus est in templo et accipiens eum beatus Simeon propheta in ulnis suis benedixit Deum.

Deinde septuagesimo die ante pascha dominica tamen ingrediente septuagesima apud eos celebratur. Hoc enim faciunt vel pro reverentia tantae festivitatis vel pro eruditione populi ut per numerum dierum cognoscant iam adpropinquare diem sanctum paschae et praeparet se unusquisque secundum devotionem et virtutem suam qualiter ad ipsum sanctum diem cum tremore et reverentia contrito corpore et mundo corde perveniant. Et non solum LXX sed et LX. L. XL. XXX. XX., XV et VIII semper ipso ordine celebrantur, ut quantum plus cognoverint adpropinquare sanctum diem paschae redemptionis nostrae tantum amplius ab omni inquinamento carnis vel immunditia se abstineant ut digni sint communicare corpus et sanguinem Domini [*fol.* 96]. Graeci autem a LX^{ma} de carne levant ieiunium, monachi vero et romani devoti vel boni christiani a L, rustici autem et reliquus vulgus a quadragesima. Primum autem ieiunium IIII et VI feria post L, id est una ebdomada ante quadragesima apud eos publicae agitur. Inde vero prima ebdomada in quadragesima iterum quarta et sexta feria seu et sabbato stationes publicas faciunt, et ieiunium cum XII lectionibus in ipso sabbato consummantur. Et si fuerit ipsum sabbatum de martio mense ordinationes sacerdotum faciunt, sin autem in alia ebdomada vel tertia quando pontifex iudicaverit iterum IIII et VI feria seu et sabbatum cum XII lectionibus sicut prius celebrare videntur et ordinantur qui ordinandi sunt. Quarta vero ebdomada ante pascha incipiunt scrutinium facere ad infantes qui in sabbato sancto baptizandi erunt. EXPLICIT.

APPENDIX B

EXTRACTS FROM THE *ORDO* OF S. AMAND[1]

QUALITER FERIA V CAENAE DOMINI AGENDUM SIT

MEDIA illa nocte surgendum, nec more solito *Deus in adiutorium meum* nec invitatorium, sed in primis cum antiphonis III psalmi secuntur; deinde versus; nec presbiter dat oracionem. Deinde surgit lector ad legendum, et non petat benedictionem, et non dicit *Tu autem Domine*, sed ex verbis leccionis iubet prior facere finem; III [lectiones] de tractatu sancti Augustini in psalmo *Exaudi Deus oracionem meam dum*

---

[1] Paris, *Bibliothèque Nationale*, No. 974, ninth century, from S. Amand-en-Puelle. This *Ordo* has been published by Duchesne, *Origines*, pp. 438 *sqq.* Only those passages are here quoted which relate to the Divine Office. The document is written in vernacular Latin, says M. Duchesne, which, if the author was a Frankish clerk, would take it back to a date somewhat earlier than A.D. 800. But if the writer was a *Roman* clerk the date might be a little later.

tribulor, III de Apostolo ubi ait ad Corinthios: *Et ego accepi a Domino quod et tradidi vobis*. VIIII [psalmi] cum antiphonis, VIIII lectiones, VIIII responsoria completi sunt; et non dicit *Gloria* nec in psalmis nec in responsoriis. Sequitur matutinum. Matutino completo non dicit *Chirie eleison*, sed vadunt per oratoria psalmis psallendo cum antiphonis. . . .

FERIA VI PARASCEVEN

Media nocte surgendum est; nec more solito *Deus in adiutorium meum* nec invitatorium dicuntur. VIIII psalmi cum antiphonis et responsoriis; lectiones III de lamentacione Hieremiae, III de tractatu sancti Augustini . . . de psalmo LXIII, tres de Apostolo ubi ait ad Aebreos: *Festinemus ergo ingredere in illam requiem*. Et non dicit *Gloria* nec in psalmis nec in responsoriis; nec lector petit benedictionem, sed sicut superius. Sed tantum inchoat ad matutinum antiphona in primo psalmo, tuta lampada de parte dextra, in secundo psalmo de parte sinistra; similiter per omnes psalmos usque VI aut VII, aut in finem evangelii, reservetur absconsa usque in Sabbato sancto. . . .

ORDO QUALITER IN SABBATO SANCTO AGENDUM EST

Media nocte surgendum est, et sicut superius taxavimus ita fiat, excepto in luminaribus, sed tantum una lampada accendatur propter legendum.

Post hoc vero die illa, octava hora diaei procedit ad ecclesiam omnis clerus seu et omnis populus, et ingreditur archidiaconus in sacrario cum aliis diaconibus et mutant se sicut in die sancta. Et aegrediuntur de sacrario et duae faculae ante ipsos accense portantes a subdiacono, et veniunt ante altare diaconi, osculantur ipsum et vadunt ad sedem pontificis, et ipsi subdiaconi stant retro altare, tenentes faculas usque dum complentur lectiones. Deinde annuit archidiaconus subdiacono regionario ut legatur lectio prima, in greco sive in latino. Deinde psallit sacerdos infra thronum in dextra parte altaris et dicit *Oremus*, et diaconus *Flectamus genua*, et post paululum dicit *Levate*. Et sequitur oracio *Deus qui mirabiliter creasti hominem*. Deinde secuntur lectiones et cantica seu et oraciones, tam grece quam latine, sicut ordinem habent.

Lectionibus expletis, egrediuntur de ecclesia quae apellatur Constantiniana et descendit archidiaconus cum aliis diaconibus, et ipsas faculas ante ipsos, usque in sacrarium qui est iuxta fontes, et ibi expectant pontificem.

[*Here follows the Baptism of the Catechumens, which we omit.*]

Deinde revertitur pontifex in sacrarium qui est iuxta thronum, et ipsas faculas ante ipsum. Et stat unus de scola ante eum, et dum ei placuerit, dicit: *Intrate*. Et inchoant letania hoc ordine, id est prima VII vicibus repetent. Similiter, facto intervallo, dum iusserit pontifex, dicunt tertia letania, ter repetant. Et dum dixerint *Agnus Dei*, egreditur pontifex de sacrario et diaconi cum ipso, hinc et inde, et duae faculae ante eum portantur ab eis qui eas portaverunt ad fontes. Et veniens ante altare, stat inclinato capite, usque dum repetunt *Kyrie eleison*; et osculatur altare et diaconi similiter, hinc et inde. Deinde revertit ad sedem suam, et ipsi subdiaconi regionarii tenent ipsas faculas retro altare, dextra levaque. Et dicit pontifex *Gloria in excelsis Deo*. Sequitur oratio, inde lectio et *Alleluia*, *Confitemini Domino* et tractus *Laudate Dominum*. Et ipsa nocte non psallit offertorium nec *Agnus Dei* nec antiphona ad communionem. Et communicat omnis populus, seu et infantes qui in ipsa nocte baptizati sunt, similiter usque in octavas paschae. . . .

[*The following illustrative passage is from a MS. little known, the Poitiers Pontifical in the Library of the Arsenal at Paris, No.* 227, *p.* 178 (10*th century*).]

Morem autem benedicendi cerei romana ecclesia frequentat, sed mane sancti sabbati sedente domno apostolico in consistorio lateranensi. . . . Omni autem sollicitudine procuretur ut GLORIA IN EXCELSIS DEO ea nocte ante non incipiatur quam stella appareat in coelum: quod tunc rationabiliter peragi poterit, si peracto baptismate hora consideretur, et, facto intervallo, secundum congruentiam temporis, laetania terna ad introitum ita inchoetur ut eadem finita . . . stella in coelo apparente GLORIA IN EXCELSIS DEO incipiatur: ea scilicet ratione ne populi ante medium noctis ab ecclesia dimittantur. Si quidem traditio apostolica est media nocte in huius sacratissimae noctis vigilia Dominum ad iudicium esse venturum. . . . Enimvero sicut veracium personarum relatione traditur, qui nostro tempore de Hierusalem advenerunt, hac auctoritate et traditione fideles populi illic instructi, in sabbato vigiliarum paschae in ecclesiam convenientes quasi Dominum excepturi ac velut ad eius iudicium properaturi, omni devotione et sollicitudine intenti cum silentio et tremore horam in evangelio designatam praestolantur. Clerus etiam ea nocte cum suo pontifice in ecclesia degens predictam cum pavore et devotione expectat horam : nec ante ingrediuntur ad missas quam una ex lampadibus in sepulchro Domini per angelicam illuminetur administrationem.]

In vigilia Pentecoste sicut in Sabbato sancto ita agendum est, sed tantum una letania ad fontem et alia pro int[roitu] ; offertorium seu Alleluia vel antiphona ad communionem sicut continet in antifonarium.

In ipsa nocte sancta Resurrectionis, post gallorum cantu surgendum est. Et dum venerint ad ecclesiam et oraverint, osculant se invicem cum silentio. Deinde dicit *Deus in adiutorium meum.* Sequitur invitatorium cum Alleluia; sequuntur III psalmi cum Alleluia : *Beatus vir, Quare fremuerunt gentes, Domine quid multiplicati sunt.* Sequitur versus, et orationem dat presbiter. Deinde secuntur III lectiones et responsoria totidem, prima lectio de Actibus apostolorum, inde secunda, tertia de omiliis ad ipsum diem pertinentium. Sequitur matutinum cum Alleluia.

Infra albas Paschae, tres psalmos per nocturno imponuntur per singulas noctes usque in octavas Paschae, id est, feria II*, *Cum invocarem, Verba mea, Domine ne in furore tuo;* feria III*, *Domine Deus meus, Domine Dominus noster, In Domino confido;* feria IIII*, *Salvum me fac Domine, Usquequo Domine, Dixit insipiens;* feria V*, *Domine quis habitabit, Conserva me Domine, Exaudi Domine;* feria VI*, *Caeli enarrant, Exaudiat te Dominus, Domine in virtute tua;* sabbato, *Domini est terra, Ad te Domine levavi, Iudica me Domine.* In dominica vero octabas Paschae vigiliam plenam faciunt, sicut mos est, cum VIIII lectionibus et totidem responsoriis.

ORDO QUALITER IN EBDOMADA PASCHE USQUE IN SABBATO DE ALBAS VESPERA CAELEBRABITUR

In primis dominica sancta, hora nona, convenit scola cum episcopis, presbiteris et diaconibus in ecclesia maiore quae est catholica, et a loco crucifixi incipiunt *Chyrie eleison* et veniunt usque ad altare. Ascendentibus diaconibus in poium, episcopi et presbiteri statuuntur locis suis in presbyterio et sancto ante altare stet. Finito *Chyrie eleison*, annuit archidiaconus primo scolae, et ille, inclinans se illi, incipit *Alleluia* cum psalmo *Dixit Dominus domino meo*. Hoc expleto, iterum annuit archidiaconus secundo vel cui voluerit de scola, sed et omnibus incipientibus hoc modo praecipit et dicit iterum *Alleluia* cum psalmo CX. Sequitur post hunc primus scolae cum paraphonistis instantibus *Alleluia* et respondent paraphoniste. Sequitur subdiaconus cum infantibus versum *Dominus regnavit decore induit*; et respondent paraphonistae *Alleluia*; item versum *Parata sedes tua Deus*, et sequitur *Alleluia* a paraphonistis; item versum *Elevaverunt flumina Domine*, et reliqua. Post hos versus salutat primus scolae archidiacono, et illo annuente incipit *Alleluia* cum melodias, simul cum infantibus. Qua expleta respondent paraphoniste prima *Alleluia* et finitur. Post hanc incipit *Alleluia* tercius de scola in psalmo CXI; post hunc sequitur *Alleluia* ordine quo supra: *Alleluia Pascha nostrum*; versus *Aepulemur*. Hanc expletam, ordinem quo supra, incipit archidiaconus in evangelio antiphonam *Scio quod Iesum queritis crucifixum*. Ipsa expleta, dicit sacerdos orationem.

Dein descendit ad fontes psallendo antiphonam *In die resurrectionis meae*, quam ut finierint inchoatur *Alleluia*; psallitur psalmus CXII. Ipso expleto, sequitur *Alleluia O Kyrios ebasileusen euprepian*, et sequitur *Alleluia* a cantoribus; item versus *Ke gar estereosen tin icummeni tis*; et finitur ordine quo supra. Post hanc sequitur diaconus secundus in evangelium antiphonam *Venite et videte locum*; deinde sequitur oratio a presbitero.

Et tunc vadunt ad sanctum Andream ad Crucem, canentes antiphonam *Vidi aquam egredientem de templo*. Post hanc dicitur *Alleluia* cum psalmo CXIII. Quo finito, primus scolae incipit *Alleluia, Venite exultemus Domino*, versus *Preoccupemus faciem eius*. Post hanc dicit diaconus in evangelio antiphonam *Cito euntes dicite discipulis eius*; deinde sequitur oratio a presbitero.

Deinde descendunt primatus ecclesiae ad accubita, invitante notario vicedomini, et bibet ter, de greco una, de pactisi una, de procumma [una]. Postquam biberint, omnes presbiteri et acholiti per singulos titulos redeunt ad faciendas vesperas, et ibi bibunt de dato presbitero.

Hec ratio per totam ebdomadam servabitur usque in dominica Albas.

APPENDIX C

EXTRACTS FROM THE ANONYMOUS LITURGICAL WORK PRINTED BY GERBERT [1]

I

CANTATUR autem omnis scriptura sancti canonis ab initio anni usque ad finem, et sic ordo est canonis decantandi in ecclesia sancti Petri. Quinque libri Moyse cum Iesu Nave et Iudicum in tempore veris. Septem diebus ante initium quadragesimae usque ad octavam diem ante pascha liber Isaiae prophetae, unde ad passionem Christi convenit. Et lamentationes Ieremiae. In diebus a pascha epistolae apostolorum et actus atque apocalypsin usque pentecosten. In tempore aestus libri Regum et Para-

---

[1] Saint-Gall, Stiftsbibliothek No. 349, fol. 49–118; among the anonymous fragments published by Gerbert, *Monumenta veteris liturgiae Alemannicae* (Saint-Blasien, 1779). Fol. 49, '*Cantatur autem omnis scriptura*,' ap. Gerbert, tom li. p. 181; fol. 50, '*Incipiunt capitula de libris novi ac veteri Testamenti*,' ib.; fol. 54, '*In Nomine S.D.N.I.C. incipit instructio*,' Gerb. pp. 175–177; fol. 67, '*Incipit capitulare ecclesiastici ordinis*,' and fol. 100, '*Item de curso divino*,' Gerb. pp. 168–175, fol. 104, '*Item incipit de convivio*, Gerb. pp. 188–185. The text of Gerbert's fragment will be found below, with the exception of the '*Capitula de libris N. ac V. Test.*,' which do not appear to be the work of the same writer, being written in more correct Latin, and being, besides of no special liturgical interest. We have also omitted the '*Capitulare ecclesiastici ordinis*,' which is merely an incorrect version of the *Ordo* of Montpellier. The text of the remainder, as given below, has been collated for us with the MS. by Dr. Füh, Curator of the Library of Saint-Gall.

lipomenon usque ad medium autumni, hoc est usque quinto decimo kalendas novembris. Deinde libri Salomonis, Mulierum atque Machabaeorum, et liber Tobi usque ad calendas decembris. Ante autem natale domini nostri Ihesu Christi Isaias Ieremias et Daniel usque ad epiphaniam. Postea Ezechiel et prophetae minores atque Iob usque in idus februarias. Psalmi omni tempore, evangelia et apostoli similiter, tractatus prout ordo poscit, passiones martyrum et vitae patrum catholicorum leguntur.

II

[1.] In nomine sancti domini nostri Ihesu Christi incipit instructio ecclesiastici ordinis qualiter in coenobiis fideliter Deo servientes, tam iuxta auctoritatem catholicae atque apostolicae romanae ecclesiae quam iuxta dispositionem ac regulam sancti Benedicti, missarum solemniis vel nataliciis sanctorum seu officiis divinis anni circuli die noctuque auxiliante Domino debeant celebrare, sicut in sancta ac romana ecclesia a sapientibus ac venerabilibus patribus nobis traditum.

[2.] Primitus enim adventum Domini cum omni officio divino tam lectionibus cum responsoriis vel antiphonis seu et versibus a cal. decembris incipiunt celebrare. Et initiantem legite Isaiam prophetam in vigiliis semper a capite repetendo usque in Dei natalem ipsum leguntur, responsoria vero usque octabas Domini praeter nataliciis sanctorum Hieremiam et Daniel leguntur. Postea quidem Hiezechiel et prophetae minores atque Iob in idus februarii. Epistolae Pauli apostoli omni tempore in posterioribus tribus lectionibus tam in die dominico ad vigiliis quam et in missarum solemniis leguntur, deinde vero quinque libri Moysi cum Iesu Nave et Iudicum in tempore veris iidem septem diebus ante initium quadragesimae usque ad octavum diem ante pascha leguntur, Et septem dies ante pascha liber Isaiae prophetae unde ad passionem Christi pertinent et lamentationes Ieremiae. In diebus autem paschae epistolae apostolorum et actus atque apocalypsis usque pentecosten. In tempore autem aestatis libri Regum et Paralipomenon usque ad medium autumni, hoc est quinto decimo calendas decembris. Tractatus vero sanctorum Hieronymi Ambrosii ceterorumque patrum prout ordo poscit leguntur.

[3.] In vigiliis omnium apostolorum vel ceterorum principalium omnes ieiunium faciunt, et hora nona natalitia eorum praevenientes absque GLORIA IN EXCELSIS DEO ET ALLELUIA missarum solemniis celebrantur, et ipsa nocte ad vigilias eorum passiones vel gesta leguntur. Quodsi in die dominica eorum natalitia evenerint tam in adventu domini quam in omni tempore, psalmi cum eorum passionibus vel gestis cum responsoriis et antiphonis de ipsis pertinentes canuntur. Si autem gesta eorum minor fuerit ut in novem lectionibus sufficere non possint, in tribus tantum posterioribus leccionibus leguntur. Et octabas eorum cum responsoria vel antiphonas seu et missarum solemniis sicut die primo festivitatis eorum celebrantur. Quod si octabas eorum natalitia aliorum evenerint, precedente die eorum octabas celebrantur.

[4.] Responsorius vero tercius secundum regulam sancti Benedicti cum GLORIA est canendus novissime, sed romana ecclesia omnia responsoria cum GLORIA semper cantatur. Secundum regulam sancti Benedicti omne tempore diebus dominicis legitur lectio sancti evangelii secundum tempus quo fuerit, et sequitur hymnum TE DEUM LAUDAMUS et versum cum KYRIE ELEISON a finiuntur vigiliae nocturnae. Matutinae vero laudes diebus dominicis praeter quadragesimam omni tempore cum ALLELUIA sunt canendae.

[5.] Una autem ebdomada ante natale Domini de Conceptione beatae Mariae incipiunt celebrare. In ipsa ebdomada quarta et sexta feria seu et sabbatum omnes ieiunium faciunt et missarum solemniis cum lectionibus vel responsoriis seu et antiphonis de ordine pertinentes celebrantur. Sabato vero cum duodecim leccionibus vel ordine missarum solemniis quae diximus celebrantur. Et ipsa die sacerdotes et ceteri ministri ecclesie si necesse fuerit ordinantur. Si autem evenerit ut vigiliae natalis Domini sabbato incurrunt, praecedente ebdomada omnem celebrationem vel ordinem quod diximus quae in sabbato celebrantur. Ipsam autem ordinationem sacerdotum quae diximus praeter quatuor tempora in annum, id est marcii iunii septembris et decembris mensis, non ordinantur, ità tamen ebdomada qua pontifex iudicaverit, ut et ieiunium quarta feria incipiente et sabbato omnia consummentur. Pridie natalis Domini, nisi forte dominica contigerit, omnes publicum ieiunium faciunt, et hora nona missas celebrantur. In vigilia pridie natalis Domini humiliae cum responsoriis suis vel antiphonis in matutinis laudibus de ipsa die pertinentes canuntur.

[6.] In vigilia natalis Domini tam psalmi novem cum antiphonis vel humilias cum responsoriis suis seu et versibus et matutinis laudibus expletis vel missarum solemniis ordine quo in priori capitulare memoravimus, cum magno decore celebrantur. Corpus autem Domini in ipsa nocte expletis missarum solemniis omnes communicant. De octabas Domini vel de epiphania superiore ordine invenitur qualiter celebrare debeamus. A quadragesima vero incipiente usque quinquagesimo die ante pascha ad vigiliis de aptatico unde leguntur, et responsoria inde canuntur. Quod si exinde minus responsoria habuerit, tam in die quam in nocte quadragesimalia responsoria canuntur.

[7.] In matutinis laudibus diebus dominicis sicut et cotidianis diebus a quinquagesimo incipiente id est MISERERE MEI DEUS, inde sequitur psalmus centesimus septimus decimus cum antiphonis suis, et sequitur ordo matutinorum solemnitas sicut et reliquis dominicis diebus. Et a quinto decimo die ante pascha tam responsoria quam et antiphonae cum versibus suis de passione Domini incipiunt celebrare.

[8.] Quinta vero feria ante pascha id est coena Domini ad missas antiphona ad introitum non psallitur, apostolum nec evangelium non legitur, nec responsorium cantatur, nec salutat presbyter, id est non dicit DOMINUS VOBISCUM, nec pacem faciunt usque in sabbato sancto, sed cum silentio ad missas ingrediuntur.

[9.] In paraceven autem quod est sexta feria passionis Domini hora nona colleguntur omnes in ecclesia et legunt duas lectiones, quas in capitulare vel in sacramentorum commemorat cum responsoriis de passione Domini, et legitur passio Domini secundum Iohannem, et dicuntur illas orationes presbytero quas in sacramentorum commemorat. Post unamquamque orationem admonentur omnes a diacono ut flectantur genua, et dicit diaconus FLECTAMUS GENUA, et prosternentes se omnes in terra cum lacrymis vel contritione cordis. Et iterum admonentur a diacono dicente LEVATE. Expletis autem ipsis orationibus dicit presbyter OREMUS, et dicit orationem PRAECEPTIS SALUTARIBUS cum oratione dominica, et sequitur oratio LIBERA NOS QUAESUMUS DOMINE AB OMNIBUS MALIS. Et accipit diaconus corpus Domini et sanguinem quod ante diem coenae Domini remansit et consecratum fuit et ponit super altare, et communicant omnes corpus et sanguinem Domini cum silentio nihil cantantes. Et ipsa nocte in ecclesia lumen non accenditur usque in sabbato. His autem expletis ingrediuntur ad vesperam. Et ipsa nocte abstinentes se ab omni delicia corporali, id est praeter tantum panem et aquam cum aceto mixtam non sumentes, cui autem Dominus virtutem dederit pertranseunt sine cibo usque in vigilia paschae, hoc autem apud religiosos ac venerabiles viros observantur.

[10.] In sabbato sancto paululum post hora nona ad vigilias, primitus autem vestiuntur se sacerdotes una cum diaconibus vestibus suis, et procedunt de sagrario cum cereis vel thuribulis, et intrant in ecclesiam cum silentio nihil canentes, stantes in ordine suo. Inde vero benedicentur cerei a diacono ordine quo in sacramentorum habetur, et statim accedunt et sedent sacerdotes in sedilia sua, diaconi vero tantum permanent stantes iuxta ordinem suum sive iuxta abbatem vel presbyterum qui missas celebratur. Et incipiunt legere lectiones de ipsa nocte una cum canticia eorum quas in sacramentorum commemorat. Expletis autem ipsis lectionibus omnes sacerdotes cum diaconibus revertuntur in sacrario ornantes se, qualiter ad missas ingrediuntur. Cum autem signum pulsatum fuerit procedunt de sacraria cum diaconibus accensis cereis cum thuribulis, sicut prius descripsimus, et intrant in ecclesia facientes litania. Expletas autem ipsa litania incipit abba aut presbyter qui missas celebrat GLORIA IN EXCELSIS DEO, et complebunt omnia missarum solemnia, sicut et reliquis diebus dominicis et ipsis septem diebus usque pascha, solita in omni officio divino.

[11.] Ita agitur sicut et diem sanctam paschae, praeter tantum psalmi qui de unamquamque diem psalluntur semper cum ALLELUIA, usque quinquagesimo die a pascha quod est pentecosten, tam psalmi vel responsoria cum versibus vel antiphonis omnes cum ALLELUIA sunt canenda.

[12.] Ascensionem vero Domini cum omni officio divino de ipsa die pertinente sicut et reliquis diebus dominicis celebrantur, responsoria vero vel antiphonis usque in sabbato pentecosten de ascensionem Domini canuntur.

[13.] Sabbato pentecosten omnes ieiunium faciunt et omni officio divino tam lectionibus quam et baptismum vel ordine sicut in sabbato sancto celebrantur. Tantum hora octava incipiente ingrediuntur ad vigilias vel missarum solemniis, ut hora nona diei expleta omnia consumentur. Diem sanctum pentecosten sicut et diem sanctum paschae celebrantur. In ipsa vero ebdomada post pentecosten quarta et sexta feria seu et sabbatum ieiunium faciunt et missarum solemniis cum omne officio divino sicut in sacramentorum commemorat celebrantur. Octabas autem pentecosten sicut et dominica praecedente ita celebrandum est.

[14.] Reliquo tempore in anni circuli praeter quod memoravimus de ipsis psalmis responsoria sunt canende, antiphonis vero tam matutinis quam et vespertinis laudibus de cotidianis diebus canuntur.

[15.] Ad agendas vero mortuorum ad vigilias tam psalmi quam et lectionibus cum responsoriis suis vel antiphonis in matutinis laudibus sine ALLELUIA de ipsis est canendum. In missas eorum nec GLORIA IN EXCELSIS DEO nec ALLELUIA non cantatur.

III

In nomine domini nostri Ihesu Christi incipit capitulare ecclesiastici ordinis qualiter a sancta atque apostolica romana ecclesia celebrantur, sicut ibidem a sapientibus et venerabilibus patribus nobis traditum fuit.

[1.] Primitus enim adventum Domini calendis decembris incipiente celebrare [*etc.*].

IV

Item de cursu diurno vel nocturno qualiter horas canonicas nuntiantur in sancta sedis romanae ecclesiae sive in monasteriis constitutis.

[1.] In primis prima sic temperantur ut sic canatur quando ora prima diei fuerit expleta si tamen necesse fuerit aliquam operam cum festinatione facere, sin autem quomodo ora diei secunda expleta fuerit. Sic cantatur apud eos prima, hoc est primitus dicit prior DEUS IN ADIUTORIUM MEUM INTENDE, et inde caeteri quod sequitur. Ista prima ibi cantatur ubi dormiunt et ibidem pro invicem capitulo dicto orant. Statim ibi sedeunt et prior cum ipsis et ibi legunt regulam sancti Benedicti, et a priore vel cui ipse iusserit per singulos sermones exponitur, ita ut omnes intelligant ut nullus frater se de ignorantiam regulae excusare possit. Inde accepta benedictione vadunt sive ad ciandum vel vestiendum atque lavandum, et abent spatium ad hoc faciendum usque ad oram terciam. Si est consuetudo apud ipsos ut ille archiclavus qui claves ecclesiae sive misterium sacrum sub cura sua habet, ipse custodit et oras canonicas ad cursum celebrandum quando signum pulsare debeat ut reddantur. Et neque ad tertiam nec ad sexta neque ad nonam vel ad vesperam nec ad completorio neque ad matutinis non dicit prior quando incipit apud illos DOMINE LABIA MEA APERIES, ni tantum ad nocturnas.

[2.] Completorio autem tempore aestatis quomodo sol occumbit colliguntur ad collecta. Tangit autem frater cui est cura iniuncta cymbalum aut tabula, et colliguntur fratres in unum locum et prior ipsorum cum ipsis sedens. Et omne sive estate sive hibernum tempore semper leccionem ad collectam leguntur, et ibi fructum quod eis Deus dederit manducantur et bibent. Postea pulsato signo canuntur completorio ubi dormiunt in dormitorio, et extremo versu dicuntur antequam dormiant, hoc est PONE DOMINE CUSTODIAM ORI MEO, et tunc vadunt cum silentio pausare in lectula sua.

[3.] Pausant autem usque nocte media si solemnitas praecipua non fuerit, si vero dominica vel alia grandis solemnitas evenerit temporius surgunt. Et habent positum ubi dormiunt tintinabulum talem qui ad excitandum eos pulsatur, et postea modico intervallo facto surgunt fratres. Cui autem opus exire ad necessaria seu urina digerendum, et ad introitum ecclesiae babeant vasculum positum cum aqua ubi lavent manus suas vel facies et tergant linteo iuxta posito. Et iterum cum pulsatum fuerit aliud signum ad psallendum parati ingrediuntur monaci, et prior statim dicit prolixe DOMINE LABIA MEA APERIES sub GLORIA PATRI lente decantantes et in fine ALLELUIA concludentes. Cantat statim cui iussum fuerit invitatorio, quod est VENITE EXULTEMUS DOMINO, cum antiphona ceteris respondentibus. Et omni officio suo quod supra scriptum est complebuntur. Nocturnis autem finitis si lux statim non supervenerit faciunt modicum intervallum ut superius dictum est propter necessitates fratrum, et iterum ingrediuntur ad matutinis laudibus explendas.

[4.] Si autem cottidianis dies fuerint tempore hyberni, post nocturnis finitis iterum pausantes usquequo lux apparere incipiat, et sic ingrediuntur ad celebrandum matutinorum laudibus. Sic autem est semper solicitus ille frater cui cura commissa est ut semper signum competenti ora insonare debeat. Si autem exinde aliqua negligentia ut adsolet fragilitate humana ei evenerit ut ante oram aut post oram pulsaverit, poenitentia ei exinde indicit prior suus. Et propterea vel reverentia Dei hoc semper metitatur et in his sit solicitus ut omnia semper oneste vel competenter et secundum ordinem explicantur, et Deus semper in omnibus magnifice laudetur.

V

Item incipit de convivio sive prandio atque coenis monachorum, qualiter in monasteria romanae ecclesiae constitutis est consuetudo.

[1.] Quando autem ad prandium accedunt dicit prior orationem cum fratribus, hoc est OCULI OMNIUM totam cum GLORIA PATRI subsequente prolixe dicuntur et postea in fine ALLELUIA canuntur. Et dicit sacerdos orationem talem vocem ut cuncti audiantur et respondeant AMEN HOC BENEDICANTUR NOBIS DOMINE DONA TUA, vel alias sunt plurimas quae ad hunc cibum sunt deputatas. Et sedeunt postea omnes in loco suo. Habent autem prope mensa abbatis cathedra tale ex alto stabilita cum analogio ubi librum ponitur, et sedeunt cum legunt. Et statim cum primum cibum ponunt ministri et signum insonuerit ut signetur a comedendum, respondent omnes DEO GRATIAS, priore signante aut presbytero vel cui iusserit, tali voce signatur ut universi audiant et respondent AMEN. In ipso inicio comedentium est praeparatus lector qui statim petit benedictionem dicit IUBE DOMNE BENEDICERE, senior autem dicit SALVET NOS DOMINUS, ei respondent omnes AMEN, et ingreditur ad legendum et legit quamdiu illum cibum manducant. Et postea si longo prandio habuerint ut diucius sedeant vel si alium ministrationem ministrentur, tangit prior mensa ut sileat ipse lector modicum. Et si fuerint pisces vel etiam si volatilia manducant, cum ministratur et insonuerit signum ut benedicatur, respondent omnes DEO GRATIAS, et benedicit prior aut cui iusserit dicente CREATURAM SUAM CREATOR OMNIUM DOMINUS BENEDICAT, et respondent omnes AMEN et manducantur. Si item alius cibus fuerit dicit orationem, hoc est PRECIBUS SANCTAE DEIGENITRICIS MARIAE ET NOS ET DONA SUA CHRISTUS FILIUS DEI BENEDICAT, respondent omnes AMEN.

[2.] Et ad aliam ministrationem iterum legit lector tamdiu quousque praecipiat ei abba ut finiatur, aut si ille congruam finem invenerit, si benedictio sonaverit, in extremo sermone repetit ipsum iterum secundum vicem prolixe, et respondent omnes DEO GRATIAS, et descendit. Si autem longa fuerit lectio et vel bene finierit sermonem, repetit ipsum et postea dicit TU AUTEM DOMINE DOMINE MISERERE NOBIS, et respondent omnes AMEN. Sic et ad nocturnis vel ad collecta vel ubi praeceptum legerint divinum ista est consuetudo ut semper quando incipit legere petita benedictione dicit IUBE DOMNE BENEDICERE. Quando finierit lector lectionem DEO GRATIAS respondent, et descendente eo vadit ante mensam abbatis et dat ei benedictionem unde manducat et bibit. Surgentibus autem fratribus dicent lente CONFITEANTUR TIBI DOMINE adiungentes GLORIA PATRI et ad finem ALLELUIA canentes. Et si maiorem refectionem habuerint ut eis exinde superfuerit, dicit prior vel cui cura commissa est orationem FRAGMENTA QUAE SUPERARUNT SERVIS SUIS CHRISTUS FILIUS DEI MULTIPLEXIT ET BENEDICAT ET ABUNDARE FACIAT QUI EST BENEDICTUS SAECULA SAECULORUM. Et respondentibus omnibus AMEN vadunt in oratorio ad orationem Dominium gratias agentes, et ibi dicent post finitam orationem DISPERSIT DEDIT completo officio sibi.

[3.] Item ad sera coenantibus cum ingressi fuerint ubi

reficiantur dicant subtrahendo moras orationem EDENT PAUPERES adiungentes GLORIA PATRI et in fine canentes ALLELUIA, et dicit senior orationem, sic tamen ut cuncti audiant et respondeant AMEN, hoc est TUA NOS DOMINE, vel alias sunt multas secundum tempus. Sedentes autem in sedilia sua faciunt similiter sicut et in prandio in die. Et si contigerit ut nox perveniet coenantibus et lumen necessse sit accendere, ille autem frater qui lumen adportat statim cum ingreditur in domo prope seniores dicit tali voce ut omnes audiant LUMEN CHRISTI, et dicunt omnes DEO GRATIAS, et iterum ipse incurvatus dicit IUBE DOMNE BENEDICERE, senior autem dicit IN NOMINE DOMINI SIT, et respondent AMEN, et sic ponit lumen in locum suum ut luceat omnibus in domo. Et si miscere iussum fuerit fratribus ut bibant, vadit minister ad ministerium et tangit digito suo calicem, et respondent omnes DEO GRATIAS, et signat et respondent omnes AMEN, et sic bibent cum benedictione. Et si fructum Dominus dederit dicit senior ita orationem FRUCTUS SUOS DOMINUS OMNIPOTENS BENEDICAT, et respondent omnes AMEN, sic fit de omnia administrationem cum autem refectio expleta fuerit, facto signo ut surgant, ille frater qui in quoquina septimanam facit quando fratres reficiunt semper cum aliis ministris ad mensam seniorum sive fratrum administrat, cum autem surgunt a mensa ille frater curvat se contra oriente super genua sua et rogat pro se orare dicens DOMNI ORATE PRO ME, et dicit senior SALVET NOS DOMINUS, ille frater surgens dicit prolixa voce DEO GRATIAS, statim omnes fratres incipiunt canere SEMPER TIBI DOMINE GRATIAS, ita finitum dicit prior cum fratribus MISERATOR ET MISERICORS DOMINUS prolixe cum GLORIA, adiungentes et in finem ALLELUIA sive QUI DAT ESCAM OMNI CARNI CONFITEMINI DOMINO COELI QUONIAM BONUS QUONIAM IN SAECULUM MISERICORDIA EIUS, et dicit sacerdos orationem hoc est SATIASTI NOS DOMINE, finita respondent omnes AMEN, et sic vadunt ad orationem et orant sicut supra scriptum est.

[4.] Ille autem septimanarius qui ingreditur quoquinam in die dominica ingreditur vel egreditur iuxta id quod in regula sancti Benedicti continetur scriptum, matutinis finitis statim in oratorio qui egreditur postulat pro se orare dicens DOMNI ORATE PRO ME, orantes autem dicit senior SALVUM FAC SERVUM TUUM, ille vero subsequens dicit cum omnibus fratribus BENEDICTUS ES

DOMINE DEUS, hoc usque tercio repetens accepta benedictione egreditur. Statim dicit qui ingreditur DEUS IN ADIUTORIUM MEUM INTENDE, et ista oratione tertia cum omnibus repetitur, et sic accepta benedictione intrat ad serviendum fratribus suis. Sic et in ecclesia beati Petri apostoli presbyter septimanam facit, vel mansionarii qui lumen vel ornatum ipsius ecclesiae custodiunt, die sabbati ora tercia consignant officia sua ad pares suos, et sic descendunt et vadunt in domos suas, et illi alii cum presbytero vel pares suos usque ad alio sabbato serviunt e faciunt similiter, et sic in omnibus officiis honeste vel ordinabiliter Deo conservantur.

[5.] Et si fortasse ista quae de multis pauca conscripsimus alicui displicuerit, non sit piger sed habeat prudentiam sic habent alii sacerdotes vel patres seu et monachi devoti qui recto ordine vivere atque custodire cum divina auctoritate desiderant, quomodo illi vadunt, istam sanctam doctrinam ad suam utilitatem vel suos seu et multorum aedificationem cum magno labore ipsam deferent, ut hic postmodum vel in futurum perpetualiter gaudeant atque letentur in conspectu Dei et angelorum vel omnium sanctorum eius. Vadat sibi ipsa Roma, aut si piget misso suo fideli in loco suo trasmittat et inquirat diligenter si est ita aut non est quod de pluribus parum conscripsimus, aut si non ita ibidem celebratur. Vel si bene cum sancta intentione vel devotione inquisierat, et adhuc in centuplum melias unde in opere Dei proficiat invenerit, tunc postmodum fortasse ista audiat despicere vel derogare vel etiam tantos et tales sanctos patres contra se adversare praesumat qui istam sanctam normam instituerunt.

[6.] Id est primus beatus Damasus papa adiuvante sancto Hieronymo presbytero vel ordinem ecclesiasticum descripto de Hierosolyma permissu sancti ipsius Damasi transmittentem instituit et ordinavit. Post hunc beatissimus Leo papa annalem cantum omnem instituit, atque opuscula in canonica institutione luculentissima edidit, quam si quis ea usque ad unum iota non receperit vel veneraverit anathema sit. Deinde beatus Gelasius papa similiter omnem annalem cantum seu et decretalia canonum honeste atque diligentissime facto in sede beati Petri apostoli conventu sacerdotum plurimorum conscripsit. Post hunc Simachus papa similiter et ipse annalem suum cantum edidit. Iterum post hunc Iohannes papa similiter et ipse annum circuli cantum vel omni ordine conscripsit. Post hunc Bonifacius papa, qui inspirante sancto spiritu et regulam conscripsit et cantilena anni circuli ordinavit, post hos quoque beatus Gregorius papa qui afflatu sancto Spiritu magnam atque altissimam gratiam ei Dominus contulit ut super librum beati Job moralia tibica investigatione tripliciter atque septiformem expositionem lucidaret, super Ezechiel quoque propheta prima parte seu et extrema luculentissima expositione declaravit, quid super evangelia quadraginta humiliarum expositione fecerit notum est omnibus christianis quam pulchre explanarit, quid inde aliquorum libris operante sancto Spiritu digessit vel aliarum multarum sanctarum scripturarum interpretatus est christianis in mundo tegentibus patefactum est, et cantum anni circuli nobile edidit. Post hunc Martinus papa similiter et ipse anni circuli cantum edidit. Post istos quoque Catalenus abbas ibi deserviens ad sepulcrum sancti Petri et ipse quidem annum circuli cantum diligentissime edidit. Post hunc quoque Maurianus abba ipsius sancti Petri apostoli serviens annalem suum cantum et ipse nobile ordinavit. Post hunc vero dominus Virbonus abba et omnem cantum anni circuli magnifice ordinavit.

[7.] Si quis postquam ista cognoverit custodire vel celebrare in quantum Deo iubente voluerit neglexerit, aut si melius aliunde scire vel accepisse exemplum fortasse iactaverit, dubium non est quod ipse sibi fallit et in caligine erroris semetipsum infeliciter demergit, qui tantos et tales patres sanctos auctores ausus sit despicere vel derogare. Nescio qua fronte vel temeritate praesumptuoso spiritu ausi sunt beatum Hilarium atque Martinum sive Germano vel Ambrosio seu plures sanctos Dei, quos scimus de sancto sede romana a beato Petro apostolum successoribus suis directos in terra ista occidentali et virtutibus atque miraculis coruscare, qui in nullo a sancta sede romana ... deviarint ... [*Conclusion abridged.*] Cum istos praeclaros confessores Christi quos superius nominavimus sciamus frequenter eos Romam ambulasse, et apud beatos papatus vel christianis imperatoribus colloquium habuisse, vel si qui a sancta romana sede deviabant saepe recorrexisse apud nos manifestum est. . . . Oportet eos diligenter inquirere et imitare atque custodire sicut et sancta romana ecclesia custodit ut teneant et ipsi unitatem catholicae fidei. Amen.

APPENDIX D

As much of the foregoing matter is exceedingly curious and interesting, the following English renderings of some passages are given, which must be taken for what they are worth, the original being in some places very obscure.

(I.) *Appendix A.*—On the Festival of Epiphany, here called *Theophania*

Nocturns therefore being finished, and also the Mattins [*i.e.* Lauds], forthwith, with candles and candlesticks, and also with censers, they proceed to the Font, singing *Te Deum*. And when this is ended they begin the Litany, viz. 'O Christ, hear us,' and the rest. When this also is finished the bishops, priests, deacons, and subdeacons, with the whole clergy and all the people, standing round the Font with many lights, forthwith the bishop blesses the Font; and after the benediction he makes a cross in the Font with chrism, and sprinkles some of the chrism on the people. And when this is done, all the people take some of the blessed water away in their own vessels, to sprinkle, not only in their hoases, but on their vines, fields, and fruit trees.[1] Then priests and deacons, having clad themselves in clean white robes, go barefoot into the Font, and, receiving the infants from their parents, they baptize them in the Name of the Father, and of the Son, and of the Holy Ghost, immersing them in the water thrice, but invoking the Holy Trinity once only. On raising the infants from the water, they offer them in their hands to a certain priest, who makes a cross on their heads with chrism, invoking

---

[1] [A long and elaborate service for this blessing of water on Epiphany may still be seen at the end of some editions of the *Rituale Romanum*. A.B.]

the Holy Trinity. And those who are to receive[1] the infants stand ready with towels in their hands, and the infants are handed to them by the priests and deacons who baptize them. Then the baptized infants are straightway carried to the bishop, and the grace of the Sevenfold Spirit is given them, with chrism on the forehead, and the invocation of the Holy Trinity, this being the Confirmation of their Baptism and admission into the flock of Christ.

(II.) *Appendix A.*—Observance of Candlemas

On the second of February, which is the fourth day before the nones of that month, all are gathered together, coming early in the morning to the Church of Blessed Adrian, both the clergy of the Roman Church, and all the monks of the monasteries, with all the people from the suburbs and a great multitude of foreigners collected from every province, and they each receive from the hand of the Pontiff a candle, both men, women, and children, and light them; and carrying them in their hands, all with one voice singing the while, each in his own place in which he marches, while before the Apostolic Lord there go seven candlesticks with candles, and also censers with incense, and lamps being lighted at everyone's door, they walk before the Pontiff with great reverence to S. Mary's the Greater, and there most devoutly celebrate the Mass, in honour of how our Lord Jesus Christ, after the Purification of Blessed Mary, was presented in the temple, and how the blessed prophet Simeon took Him up in his arms and blessed God.

(III.) *Appendix B.*—Passage from the Poitiers Pontifical

The Roman Church observes the custom of blessing the Paschal Candle, but it is done in the morning of Easter Eve, by the Apostolic Lord sitting in the consistory of the Lateran. . . . And with great care they contrive that 'Glory be to God on high' shall not be begun that night before one star can be seen

---

[1] [From its being their duty thus to receive (*suscipere*) the newly baptized infant from the priest at the Font, the god-parents or their proxies were said in Old English to 'huship' the child.—A.B.]

in the sky; which end will probably be secured if, when the baptisms are over, the time is taken note of, and a suitable interval having been made, according as the time requires, the triple Litany which is sung on entering the church is begun in such wise that when it is finished the *Gloria in excelsis* may be begun with a star already shining in the sky, to the end that the people may not be dismissed from the Church before midnight. For indeed it is an Apostolic tradition that at midnight on this most sacred night the Lord will come to judgment. . . . And as it is reported on the testimony of truthful persons who in our times have come from Jerusalem, the faithful there, being instructed in this authoritative tradition, assemble in the church for the vigil on Easter Eve, as if ready to receive the Lord, and hasting unto His judgment (II. S. Pet. iii. 12); and with minds filled with anxious devotion await the hour named in the Gospel in silence and fear. The clergy also, with their Pontiff, abiding in the church that night, wait for the predicted hour with fear and devotion; nor do they begin Mass until one of the lamps in the Sepulchre of our Lord has been lighted by Angelic ministration.

(IV.) *Appendix B.*—*After the description of solemn Vespers on Easter Day, as on pp.* 131-2, *the following passage occurs:*

Then the chief officers of the church go down to the Refectory, being invited by the Prior's Secretary (*invitante notario vicedomini*), and drink three cups, one of Greek wine, one of Pactisis, and one of Procumma. And after they have drunk, all the priests and acolytes of the various Titles go to their own churches to sing Vespers, and there they drink of the wine which has been given to their priest.

(V.) *Appendix C.*—Observance of Good Friday

On the Preparation, which is the Friday of our Lord's death, all are gathered together in the church at the ninth hour [3 P.M.], and they read two lessons which are set down in the *Capitulare* or the Sacramentary, with responds of the Passion, and the Passion of our Lord according to S. John is read, and those prayers are said by the priest which are set down in the

Sacramentary. After each prayer all are warned by the deacon to kneel, the deacon saying, 'Let us kneel,' and all prostrate themselves on the ground with tears and contrition of heart. And then again they are warned by the deacon, saying 'Rise.' And when these prayers are ended, the priest says 'Let us pray,' and he says the prayer 'Admonished by saving precepts,' with the Lord's Prayer, followed by 'Deliver us, O Lord, we beseech Thee, from all evils.' And the deacon takes the Body and Blood of the Lord, which had been consecrated and reserved on the previous day, which is the Supper of the Lord [Maundy Thursday], and places them on the altar, and all receive the Lord's Body and Blood in silence, without anything being sung. And on that night no lamp is lit in the church, until the Saturday. So, all this being finished, Vespers are begun.

And that night they abstain from all bodily refreshment: that is, they take nothing but bread only, and water mixed with vinegar. And those to whom God has given strength to do so remain without food over Easter Eve, this custom being observed by religious and reverend men.

(VI.) *Appendix C.*—Refectory customs

When they come to their morning repast the prior says the prayers with the brethren : that is, they recite slowly the whole of the *Oculi omnium*—Ps. cxliv. [cxlv.], verses 15 and 16—with *Gloria Patri* following it, and after that they sing Alleluya. Then the priest says the collect, in such a voice that all may hear, and respond 'Amen.' This collect is ' May these Thy gifts be blessed to us, O Lord,' or some other, there being many appointed for use at this meal. Then they sit down, each in his place. And they have, near the Abbot's table, a suitable pulpit raised on high, with a desk on which the book is laid, and there they sit when they read. And as soon as the serving brethren put on the first dish, and the bell sounds for grace to be said before eating, all respond 'Thanks be to God,' and the prior or the priest, or whoever is bidden, making the sign of the Cross, says grace so that all may hear, and respond 'Amen.' And as soon as they begin to eat, the reader is ready, and forthwith asks a blessing, saying 'Sir, bid a blessing,' and the senior brother says 'May the Lord save us,' and all respond 'Amen.' So he begins to read, and reads on for as long a time as they are eating that course. But if the repast is prolonged, so that they sit longer than usual, or if another course is to be served, the prior raps on the table for the reader to cease for a space. And there is fish or fowl for them to eat, when it is set on, and the bell rings for it to be blessed, all respond 'Thanks be to God,' and the prior, or whoever else is bidden by him, blesses it, saying 'May the Lord, the Creator of all things, bless these His creatures,' and all respond 'Amen,' and begin eating. But if it is some other food he says the prayer, 'Through the supplications of Mary, the Holy Mother of God, may the Lord bless us and these His gifts,' and all respond 'Amen.'

And when the second course is set on, the reader again reads, until such time as the Abbot tells him to finish; or if he finds a suitable point at which to conclude, and the bell for blessing has sounded, he repeats the last sentence over again slowly, and all respond 'Thanks be to God,' and he comes down from the pulpit. And if he has been reading a long time, or has finished what he is reading, he repeats the last words over again, and adds 'But Thou, O Lord, have mercy upon us,' and all respond 'Amen.' So both at nocturns and the evening reading, and whenever he reads the Divine law, such is the custom that he always, when he is to begin reading, asks a blessing, saying 'Sir, bid a blessing.' And when he has finished reading they respond 'Thanks be to God,' and the reader, coming down from the pulpit, goes to the Abbot's table and receives his blessing, that he also may eat and drink. And when the brethren rise from table they say slowly 'All Thy works praise Thee, O Lord'—Ps. cxliv. [cxlv.], verse 10—with *Gloria Patri*, and singing Alleluya at the end. And if they have a more abundant repast, so that some remains over, the prior, or he to whom this office is committed, says the prayer 'May Christ the Son of God multiply to His servants the fragments that remain, and may He bless them and make them to abound, Who is blessed for ever.' And when all have responded 'Amen,' they go into the oratory to pray to God and give thanks, and there, when these prayers are ended, they say ' He hath dispersed abroad '—Ps. cxi. [cxii.], verse 9—and so finish the grace after meat.

And for the evening meal, when they have entered the refectory, let them say without delay ' The poor shall eat '— Ps. xxi. [xxii.], verse 26—with *Gloria Patri*, and singing Alleluya at the end. Then the senior brother says the prayer, so that all may hear, and respond ' Amen,' viz. the prayer ' These Thy gifts, O Lord,' or some other, according to the season. Then sitting down in their seats they proceed in the same way as at the morning meal.

And if it happen that night comes on while they are at supper, and it is necessary to kindle a light, the brother who brings in the light, as soon as he enters and is near to the seniors, says, in such a voice that all may hear, ' The light of Christ,' and all respond ' Thanks be to God.'[1] Then, bowing, he says ' Sir, bid a blessing,' and the senior brother says ' In the Name of the Lord be it, &c.,' and they respond ' Amen,' and so he sets the light in its place, so that all in the house may see.

And if he has been ordered to pour out[2] wine for the brethren to drink, the serving brother goes to the sideboard and taps with his finger on the cup, and all respond ' Thanks be to God.' Then he signs it with the sign of the Cross, and all respond ' Amen,' and so they drink with a blessing.

And if the Lord has given them fruit, the senior brother says the prayer ' May the Almighty God bless these His fruits,' and all respond ' Amen.' And so is it done at every course.

And when refection is ended, and the signal given for rising

---

[1] ['Another old custom there is of saying, when light is brought in, "God sends us the light of heaven," and the Parson likes this very well : neither is he afraid of praising or praying to God at all times, but is rather glad of catching opportunities to do them. Light is a great blessing, and as great as food, for which we give thanks ; and those that think this superstitious, neither know superstition nor themselves. As for those that are ashamed to use this form as being old, and obsolete, and not the fashion, he reforms and teaches them, that at Baptism they professed not to be ashamed of Christ's Cross, or for any shame to leave that which is good. He that is ashamed in small things, will extend his pusillanimity to greater.'—George Herbert, *A Priest to the Temple*, chap. xxxv.]

[2] [Literally ' to mix,' the wine being commonly mixed with water.]

from table, the brother who is serving his week in the kitchen, and who, when the brethren take refection, always waits with the other serving brothers at the table of the seniors or brethren, on their rising from table goes down on his knees towards the East, and asks them to pray for him, saying ' Sirs, pray for me,' and the senior brother says ' The Lord save us, &c.' Then that brother rising up, says slowly ' Thanks be to God,' and forthwith all the brethren begin singing ' Thanks be always to Thee, O Lord,' and when this is finished the prior with the brethren says slowly ' The merciful and gracious Lord '—Ps. cx. [cxi.], verses 4 and 5—with *Gloria Patri*, and adding Alleluya : or else ' Who giveth food to all flesh,' and ' O give thanks to the God of Heaven, for He is gracious, and His mercy endureth for ever ' —Ps. cxxxv. [cxxxvi.], verses 25 and 26—and the priest says the prayer, viz. 'Thou hast filled us, O Lord, &c.,' and at the end all respond ' Amen,' and so they go to prayer, and pray as it has been already written.

The brother who enters on his week's service in the kitchen on the Sunday, enters on and leaves that service according to that which is written in the Rule of S. Benedict. As soon as Mattins are finished in the oratory, the brother who is ending his week of service asks the brethren to pray for him, saying ' Sirs, pray for me.' And they pray, the senior brother saying ' Save Thy servant, &c.,' and that brother responds, and says with all the brethren ' Blessed art Thou, Lord God, &c.,' and having repeated this thrice and received the blessing of the superior, he quits his service. And forthwith he who is entering on his week says ' O God, make speed, &c.,' and repeats this prayer thrice along with all the brethren, and so, having received the blessing, he enters on the service of his brethren. So also in the church of Blessed Peter the Apostle, the priest who serves his week, or the sacristans who attend to the lighting and decking of the church, give over their offices to their fellows at the third hour on the Saturday, and so quit their service and go to their own houses, and those others, both the priest and his fellows, serve until the next Saturday, and then do likewise, and thus, in all that pertains to His service, God is served decently and in order.

APPENDIX E

The following is a list of M. Batiffol's other contributions to the history of the Breviary:

(1) *Le Moyen Age*, July 1894: a review of M. Chevalier's 'Poésie Liturgique,' dealing with the question of the introduction of the Hymnary into the Divine Office. See above, p. 183.

(2) *Bulletin de la Société Nationale des Antiquaires de France*, 1893, pp. 147-152: a memoir on the rubrics found in a MS. Breviary (No. 468, Library of Lyons) of the end of the fifteenth century. This Breviary is from Avignon, and its rubrics bear the names of the following Popes: Boniface VIII. (1295-1303), John XXII. (1316-1334), Clement VI. (1342-1352), Gregory XI. (1371-1378), Clement VII. (1378-1394).

(3) In the same publication, pp. 222-224: on the rubrics in a MS. Breviary (No. 366, Mazarin Library), *circa* 1498. A Breviary of Venetian origin, whose rubrics bear the names of Popes Martin V. (1417-1431), Eugenius IV. (1431-1439), Calixtus III. (1455-1458). Also a discussion on the origin of the Feast of S. Joseph, founded on the rescript of the Cardinal Legate Alemannus Adimari, of July 29, 1414 (Latin MS. No. 3126, Bibliothèque Nationale).

(4) Same publication, 1894, p. 204: determination of the date of the Breviary of Innocent III.. See above, p. 207.

(5) Same publication, 1895, pp. 291-297: notice of the Breviary preserved at S. Clara d'Assisi, which is attributed to S. Francis, and may perhaps be a copy of the edition put forth by Innocent III.

(6) *Mélanges Julien Havet* (Paris, 1895), pp. 201-209: note on a Cassinensian Breviary of the eleventh century (MS. 364, Mazarin Library).

(7) *Revue des Questions historiques*, tom. lv. (Jan. 1, 1894), pp. 220-228: a memoir on the origin of the *Liber Responsalis* of the Roman Church, endeavouring to explain the legend of its supposed Gregorian origin. See above, p. 58.

(8) *Analecta Iuris Pontificii*, Feb. 1896: a memoir entitled 'Contribution à l'histoire du bréviaire. Le bréviaire Parisien de 1736 et le Pape Clément XII, d'après une correspondance diplomatique inédite.' See above, p. 297.

INDEX

ABELARD, 159, 175, 181
Ada of Treves, 139
Adrian I., Pope, 1, 71, 86, 354
Advent, services of, 114–118
Agatho, Pope, 75
Agde, Council at, 32, 183
Agimundus, 108
Agobard, Archbishop of Lyons, 187
Agulia, 66, 163
'Ακροστίχιον, 6, 100
Alanus, 108
Alaric, 82
Alcuin, 90, 108, 179, 204
Alexander II., Pope, 120, 180
Alexander III., Pope, 325
Alexander VI., Pope, 229
Alexis, S., 275, 277
All Souls, 200
Amalarius, 90, 91
Amand, S., Ordo of, 360
Ambrose, S., his chant, 27–29, 45
— — introduces daily vigils at Milan, 20
— — and the *Te Deum*, 109
— — his hymns, 182, 183, 276
— — a legend of, 276
Ambrosian Psalter, 101, 102
Amelot, 345 *note*, 347
Anastasis, at Jerusalem, 15, 21–24
Andrew, S., office of festival, 154
Anonymous Liturgist in Gerbert, 59, 99, 110, 113, 137, 365
Antioch, Church of, 19, 20
Antiphon, definition and use of word, 94, 95, 96 *note* 1
Antiphons of our Lady, 217
— new, 332, 333

Antiphons suppressed by Quignonez, 241
Antiphonal chanting, 26
Antiphonary, meaning of word, 59
— attributed to S. Gregory, 58–60
— of S. Peter's (12th cent.), 92, 159, 192, 196
Apollinaris, S., 337 *note* 2
Apparition of S. Michael, festival of, 224, 277, 310, 341
Appellants, 294, 296
Aquileia, 267
Architecture, development of, 14
Arevalo, 244
Ascetics, 15, 19, 20, 30, 31
Aspicicns a longe, 115–117
Assumption, festival of, 293, 308
Athanasian Creed, 190–192
Athanasius, S., his rule as to chanting, 6, 25, 46
Athenogenes, 10
Augsburg, 253, 254
Augustine, S., on chanting, 28–30
— — and the *Te Deum*, 109
— — and the Athanasian Creed, 190
Augustinus, 295
Aurelian, Bishop of Arles, 184
Autun, council at, 191
Ave Maria, 217
Avignon, 214, 215, 384
Aymo, 213
Azzoguidi, 302, 312–315, 322

BABYLAS, S., 6
Baillet, 334, 343
Baldwin, Emperor, 208

Bardesanes, 11
Baronius, 266, 272-279, 288, 292, 335 *note*, 355
Basilican monasteries, 63-73
— monks, influence of, on the office, 72
Basle, Council of, 226
Bede, 108, 179, 223 *note* 1
Beleth, John, 176, 177, 180
Bellarmine, 266, 272, 276 *note* 1, 278
Bembo, 230
Benedict Biscop, 75
Benedict II., Pope, 55
Benedict XII., Pope, 214
Benedict XIV., Pope, 266, 280, 297, 301-304, 312, 313 *note* 2, 318-322, 324, 326-329, 340-343, 345-351, 355
Benedict, Canon, 160, 192
Benedictine office, 34, 37, 48, 93, 94, 105-107, 109, 113, 185, 188
Benedictio Dei, 176
Bernard, S., 179, 276
Bernold, 170
Bible, distribution of, for lessons, 102, 103, 242, 265
Bonaventure, S., 210, 270
Books needed for the office, 201
Bouix, 287
Braga, Council at, 32, 185
Breviary, origin and meaning of word, 201-206
— arrangement and contents, 215-224
— of Alcuin, 204, 205
— — Quignonez, 238-248, 292
— — Pius V., 263-266
— — Paris, ancient, 268
— — Clement VIII., 275-280
— — Urban VIII., 281-287
— — De Harlay, 290-292
— — De Vintimille, 294-298, 326, 341
Breviaries, Gallican, suppressed, 352 *note*
— printed, 227
Bull, 'Quod a nobis,' 263, 269, 291
— 'Divinam Psalmodiam,' 287
— 'Unigenitus,' 294, 296 *note* 2, 347

CAESARIUS, Bishop of Arles, 33, 184
Candlemas, services of, 359, 378
Canisius, 243
Canones Hippolyti, 42-44
Canonisation, modes of, 325
Canterbury, 180
Capitulum, 102
Caracciolo, 249, 250
Cardinals, 40
Carthage, 13, 54
Cassian's account of monastic vigils, 7
Cassino, Monte, 103, 109, 188
Cassiodorus, 183
Catacombs, services in, 78, 79
— ruin of, 82, 83
Cencius, 160
Ceremonial of principal vigils at Rome, 161-166
Chant, primitive, 6
— development of, 27-30
— at Rome (in the 5th cent.), 46
— — development of, 54
Chapter, 112, 113
Charlemagne, confirms the Roman use, 88
— establishes Roman use at Lyons, 91, 187
Charles Borromeo, S., 225
Charles the Bald, 204
Charles V., Emperor, 237, 253
Christmas, services of, 118, 119, 368
Chrodegang, 69, 87
Chrysostom, S. John, establishes daily vigils at Constantinople, 20
— — introduces the Eastern chant, 28, 45
— — on devotion of the Ascetics, 16
Clement of Alexandria, 16, 179
Clement V., Pope, 207
Clement VII., Pope, 230-232, 236-238, 249-251
Clement VIII., Pope, 272, 275, 279
Clement XI., Pope, 347
Clement XII., Pope, 297
Cluny, 178-180, 189, 198, 200, 353
Coelestine I., Pope, orders Psalms to be sung before Mass, 47
Coelestine II., Pope, 160

INDEX 387

Coffin, Charles, 294, 295, 297
Collect supplants the Lord's Prayer in the office, 96
Cologne, 252
Compline, origin of, 36
— described, 98, 99, 371
Computus, 205
Conception of our Lady, festival of, 180, 308, 338 *note 3*
Confiteor introduced, 112 *note* 3
Congregations for reform of the Breviary, 255-258, 270, 271, 275, 281, 298, 299, 302, 321
Constantinople, 15, 28, 45, 62
Conversion of S. Paul, festival of, 311, 327
Corbey, 89, 91
Corpus Christi, festival of, 219, 307
Corsini, Cardinal, 300
Cubicularii, 63
Curia, 41, 160, 201, 232, 237, 238
— and the abridgment of the office, 207
Cyprian, S., 13

DAILY vigils, origin of, 15-17
— — established at Antioch, 19
— — — — Constantinople, Milan, Jerusalem, 20
— — — — Rome, 47, 48
— — form prescribed in fifth century, 51
Damasus, 46, 353
Deaconries, 40, 67
— churches of, 41, 78, 148
Deacons as chanters, 46
Decuriae, 101
Denis, S., 278, 291
Deusdedit, Pope, 54
Diodorus of Antioch, 19, 20, 26
Dominicum at Alexandria, 15
' Double office,' 136-138, 177
Durandus, 215 *note* 3, 217 *note* 1
Durham, 206

EASTER, vigil of, 3
— Eve, services of, 127, 128, 361-363, 369, 379

Easter Day, services of, 129-132, 364, 365, 379
Eastern Church, 349
Egbert of York, 58, 196
Egyptian monks, vigil services of, 7
Elizabeth of Schönau, 176
Epiphany, services of, 119, 358, 377
Epitaphs, 46, 54
Erasmus, 229

FERDINAND I., Emperor, 254
Ferial *Preces*, 97, 305
Ferreri, 231
Festivals, of our Lady, 150, 180, 308, 309
— local, 179, 180
— removed from the Kalendar, 221, 264, 295, 308-311, 315, 316.
— added to the Kalendar, 139-145, 222, 223, 269, 270, 280, 306
— rank of, 135, 136, 223, 224, 241, 264, 280, 317, 318
Flavian of Antioch, 28
Fleury, 298, 315 *note* 2
Foinard, 293, 341
Fons Avellanus, 194
Franciscans, 158, 209-214, 308 *note* 1
Fulda, 188, 189

GALL, Abbey of S., 205, 365
Galli, 302, 312, 323
Gallican Church, 288, 290, 315 *note* 2, 345
Gallican Version of Psalter, 101, 216
Gamugno, 194
Garganus, Mount, 277, 310, 341
Gavanto, 282
Gelasius, Pope, 50
German, S., of Paris, 186
Gesualdo, Cardinal, 271
Gloria Patri, 6, 105 *note*
Gondy, Peter de, 268
— John Francis de, 290
Good Friday, services of, 124, 361, 369, 380
Gradual, 28, 103, 104
Gradual Psalms, 93, 224, 260, 262, 305

Grancolas, 255 *note* 1, 267, 292, 293, 341
Gratian, 50, 57, 172, 174
Gregory, S., on choice of lessons, 53
— and the *Schola Cantorum*, 55-57
— and the Antiphonary, 58, 59
— favours monks, 61
Gregory II., Pope, 64, 67, 70
Gregory III., Pope, founds monasteries, 67, 69, 73
— — — institutes non-local observance of Saints' days, 85, 86
Gregory IV., Pope, 91
Gregory VII., Pope, and his supposed reform of the Breviary, 167-174
— — — his decrees, 171
— — — his festival, 315 *note* 2
Gregory IX., Pope, 158, 175, 213
Gregory XIII., Pope, 269
Gregory XIV., Pope, 271
Gregory of Tours, 101, 183, 276
Guardian Angels, festival of, 310
Guéranger, 167, 168, 267, 268, 289, 296
Guyet, 313

Harlay, Archbishop de, 290, 291, 294
Harnack, 190, 191
Hayto, Bishop of Basle, 191
Hilary of Poitiers, 182
Hincmar, Archbishop of Rheims, 191
Hippolytus, 42
Historia. 106
Holy Cross, festivals of, 307
— — in Jerusalem, basilica, 40, 114, 124, 237
Holy Name of Jesus, 308
— — — Mary, 309
Holy Week, services of, 123-127, 360-362, 368-370, 379, 380
Homiliaries, 108, 109
Honorius, Pope, 66, 71
Hormisdas, Pope, 49
Hymn, use of word, 183, 184
Hymns, metrical, 180-189, 232 235, 283, 284

Hymns corrected, 231, 251, 271, 275, 283-287
— of S. Ambrose, 182, 183, 276
— — Ferreri, 232-235
— — the Paris Breviary, 295

Innocent I., Pope, 61
Innocent III., Pope, 160, 207 209, 385
Innocent VIII., Pope, 229
Introit, 105 *note*
Invitatory, 6, 99
— not an antiphon, 100
Isachino, 251, 255
Ivo of Chartres, 170, 179

James the Greater, S., festival of, 277, 278
Jansenists, 296
Jerome, S., on Easter vigil, 3 *note* 3
— — his rules for Laeta, 44, 45
— — his translations of Holy Scripture, 100, 101, 216, 271
— — use of word 'hymn,' 183
Jerusalem, services at, 21-24
Jesuits, 244, 267, 283, 284
John VIII., Pope, 55, 189
John the Deacon, on foundation of *Schola Cantorum*, 56
John, Abbot, 75, 76
John of Avranches, 192, 193, 198, 217
John of Parma, 217
John de Arze, 244
Julius II., Pope, 229
Justinian, edict on the divine office, 31, 49
Justus, S., 80

Kalendar of Rome in eighth century, 139-145
— — — — thirteenth century, 221-224
— proposed in eighteenth century, 315, 316
— of Milan, 317 *note* 1

Lady, office for festivals of our, 15 156, 222 *note* 1, 338 *note* 2

INDEX 389

Laeta, 44, 45
Laodicea, 187
Lateran basilica, 15, 39, 55, 64-66, 71, 124, 159, 161, 207, 277, 311
Lauds, origin of, 9
— described, 110, 111
Lectors, 53, 54
Leidrad, Archbishop of Lyons, 91, 187
Lent, offices of, 121
— observance of, 120 *note* 3, 294, 306, 317, 360
Leo the Great, his homilies, 107
— — — establishes a monastery at S. Peter's, 63
Leo II., Pope, 55
Leo III., Pope, 91, 354
Leo IX., Pope, 168
Leo X., Pope, 229-232
Leonine Sacramentary, 82
— — on monks, 60
Leontius, Bishop of Antioch, 19
Lepanto, battle of, 269, 309
Lerins, 185
Lessons at Mattins, 53, 102, 103, 107-109, 366, 367
— — — introduced on ferias, 103
— — — abbreviated, 178, 240
— suppressed, 266, 276, 335, 337
— new, appointed, 242, 265, 266, 276, 330-339
— taken from various authors, 53, 107, 108, 179, 218-221
Liber Diurnus, 50, 134
Liber Responsalis, early MSS. of, 91, 92
Liège, 180, 207
Lombards, 83
Lord's Prayer, primitive use of, 96
— — at beginning of offices, 216, 217
Lorraine, Cardinal of, 254
Lorsch, 205
Louis le Débonnaire, 91
Louis XIV., 290, 347
Ludolf, Bishop of Eugubium, 194
Lyons, 91, 186, 187

Magnificat, 181
Marcion, 10

Marini, 258, 260, 262, 263
Martin, S., 276
Martin of Senging, 226
Martyrology, 113, 348
Martyrs, worship at tombs of, 78-81
— their relics moved into Rome, 84
— of Rome, 145-147
Mary Magdalene, S., 291, 331
Mary of the Snows, S., 243, 265, 266, 312, 334
Mary the Greater, S., basilica, 40, 65, 70, 114, 118, 119, 155, 312
Mattins at Jerusalem, 22
Maundy Thursday, 124, 360, 368
Melania, S., 24 *note* 2, 81 *note*
Memorials, 190, 192, 193, 217, 253
Methodius, on vigils, 5
Michael, S., Apparition of, 224, 277, 310, 341
Micrologus, 169, 170, 193
Milan, 20, 27, 45
Mombrizo, 242
Monachism, animosity towards, at Rome, 60-62
Monasteries, basilican, at Rome, 63-67
— — their character, 67-72
Monastic influence on form of office, 24, 60, 70, 72, 114
— offices, primitive, 7, 8
— — distinct from others, 31
Monazontes, 16, 22
Monti, 302, 312, 313, 321, 322
Montpellier, *Ordo* of, 85, 120 *note* 3, 357

Nepos, Bishop, 11
Nereus and Achilles, SS., church of, 354
Nicetas of Remesiana, 110
Nicolas III., Pope, 213, 214
Nicolas V., Pope, 229, 354
Nocturns described, 99-109, 372
— additional, 107
None, 17

O's, Great, 118
Odilo of Cluny, 200

Odo of Cluny, 95, 179
Office of sixth and eighth centuries contrasted, 133, 134
— double, 136–138, 177
— of Saints' days, 151
— of SS. Peter and Paul, 152–154
— of S. Andrew, 154
— of feasts of our Lady, 155, 156
— of Paschal Octave, short, 129, 172
— Little, of our Lady, 193–196, 224, 261, 262, 305
— of the dead, 196–200, 224, 261, 262, 305
Ordines Romani, 92, 159
Ordo of Montpellier, 85, 120 *note* 3, 357
— — S. Amand, 360
Origen, 179, 219, 251
Our Lady of Mercy, Order of, 310 *note* 1

Paris, Church of, 268, 290
Parthenae, 16, 22
Paschal, Pope, 68
Paschal candle, 127, 362
Paschal office, short, 129, 172
Passion-tide, offices of, 121–127, 360–362, 368–370
Pater noster, 96, 216, 217
Paul of Samosata, 10
Paul the Deacon, 109, 178, 188
Paul II., Pope, 229
Paul III., Pope, 238
Paul IV., Pope, 248–261
Paul, S., basilica of, 40, 64, 70, 81, 311
Pelagius, Pope, 50, 61
Pentecost, services of, 132, 133, 363, 370
Pepin, orders Roman use, 88
Peter, S., office of, 152–154
Peter, S., basilica of, 1, 40, 55, 63, 66, 72–77, 81, 85, 86, 92, 114, 120, 131, 152–154, 162–166, 312, 353
— — — Saints' days commemorated at, 85, 86
Peter Damian, S., 172 *note* 2, 176, 179, 194, 199
Peter Chrysologus, S., 337 *note* 2

Peter the Venerable, 180
Peter's, S., chains, 334
Petra Pertusa, 194
Philip II. of Spain, 267
Philocalus, 119 *note* 1
Pius II., Pope, 229
Pius V., Pope, 258, 259, 263, 267–270
Pius IX., Pope, 351 *note*
Platina, 242, 245
Pliny, on Sunday vigil, 4
Preces, 97, 305
Presentation of our Lady, festival of, 222, 264, 309
Pretiosa, 113
Prime, origin of, 35, 36
— described, 111–114, 371
— Sunday, length of, 211, 251, 261
Protestant Reformers, 237, 238, 247
Prudentius on observance of Saints' days, 78, 79
— hymns of, 188, 276
— of Troyes, 205
Psalmi Idiotici, 9–12, 109
Psalmody, primitive, 6, 7
Psalms, Latin versions of, 100, 101, 216
— few recited, 240, 306
— Penitential and Gradual, 224, 260–262, 305
Psalmus Responsorius, 6, 103
Psalter, distribution of, by Quignonez, 241
— — — in Paris Breviary, 295
— — — (Vespers) 93, 180 *note* 3, (Mattins) 101, 102, (Lauds) 110, 111, (Little Hours) 111, (Compline) 99, (Prime) 112, (Saints' days) 152, (general) 323
Puy, 206

Quicunque vult, 190–192
Quignonez, 236–250

Rank of festivals, 135, 136, 223, 224, 241, 264, 280, 317, 318
Raoul de Rivo, Provost of Tongres, 207, 225, 226, 228

Rationale,(Beleth)176; (Durandus) 216 *note* 3, 217 *note* 1
Readers, 53
Redemptus, 46
Refectory customs, 372–375, 380–384
Reformers, Protestant, 237, 238, 247
Relics of Martyrs translated into Rome, 84
Remigius, Bishop of Rouen, 88
Responds, 103–106
— curtailed, 117
Roman Church, local organisation of, 39–41
— Saints, local, 145–147
— use, when codified, 89
Rosary, festival of, 269, 309
Rubrics, 224, 264

Sabinian, Pope, 62
Sacramentary, Leonine, 60, 82
— Gregorian, 58, 59, 138, 139
Sadoleto, 230, 236
Saints' days, observance of, origin, 12
— — — originally local, 34, 82, 84
— — — introduced into monastic offices, 34
— — — in cemeteries, 77–82
— — — introduced into Rome, 83
— greater and lesser, 135, 136
— office of, its character, 151
— encroach on ferial office, 136, 137, 224, 225, 280, 306
Salimbenus, 199 *note* 2, 211, 212
Sannazar, 230
Santeuil, 295
Saragossa, 244
Sarum offices, 98 *note* 2, 132 *note* 1, 181 *note* 1, 253 *note* 1
Schola Cantorum, 55–57
Sens, Synod of, 252
Septuagesima, 120
Sergius, Pope, 55
Sessorium, 40 *note*
Sext, 17
Sidonius Apollinaris, 80
Silvia's account of services at Jerusalem, 21–24

Simplicius, Pope, 153
Sirleto, 255, 258, 272, 288
Sixtus IV., Pope, 229
Sixtus V., Pope, 269, 270, 274
Somaschi, 302
Sorbonne, 239
Southwell Minster, 226 *note* 1
Station days, 14
Stations, at Rome, 114, 160
Strada, 283
Subdeacons, 57
Suffragia Sanctorum, 190, 192, 193, 217, 253
Sunday office, privileged, 294
Syrian Churches, vigils of, 8

Tamburini, Cardinal, 321, 339
Te Deum, 109, 110
Tencin, Cardinal de, 297 *note*, 298, 319–321, 328, 345, 346, 349
Tenebrae, 124, 244
Terce, 17
Tertullian, on vigils, 5
— on hours of prayer, 17
Tertullianists, 80
Theatines, 249, 250, 256, 275
Theodemar, Abbot, 103
Theodore, Archdeacon of Rome, 91, 124
— Archbishop of Canterbury, 196
Theodosius, Emperor, 28
Thomas à Kempis, 181 *note* 2
— Aquinas, 219, 286
Thomassin, 300
Tillemont, 291, 333–337
' Titles,' 40, 58
— receive the names of Saints, 77, 83, 148
Toledo, Council at, 32, 186
Tours, 95, 186
— Council at, 33 *note* 1, 185
Tractus, 128 *note*
Transfiguration, festival of, 180, 251, 307
Trent, Council of, 252–257
Treves, Council at, 206
Triduum before Easter, services of, 123–127, 360–362, 368–370, 379, 380
Trinity Sunday, 180, 219, 251, 307

ULRIC of Cluny, 192, 193
Urban VIII., Pope, 233, 281–288, 295, 354

VAISON, Council of, 105 *note*
Valenti, 300, 302–305, 312–315, 318, 320, 323, 324, 326–330, 345
Vespers, origin of, 4, 97
— at Jerusalem, 21
— introduced late at Rome, 43
— in eighth century, described, 93–97
— on Easter Day, 130–132, 364, 379
Victor, Pope, 42
Victor Vitensis, 54
Vienne, 186
Vigier, 294, 297, 341
Vigil, origin of, 2, 3
— of Easter, 3, 362, 379
— of Sunday, 4
— the three original portions of, 5
— of festivals of Martyrs, 12
Vigils, daily, introduced at Antioch, 19

Vigils, daily, introduced at Constantinople, Milan, Jerusalem, 20
— — — — Rome, 47, 48
Vigil services, primitive, 7
— — at Rome in fifth century, 45, 51–53
— — at S. Peter's in twelfth century, 161–166
Vigilantius, condemns night services, 45
Vincent of Lerins, 190
Vintimille, Archbishop de, 294–298, 341, 345
Vision of S. Peter, 172 *note* 2
Vulgate, 264, 271, 272, 325

WALA, Abbot of Corbey, 89, 91
Walafrid Strabo, 189
Whitsun-tide, 132, 133, 363, 370
Worship, development of, 14

ZACHARY, Pope, 108
Zeno, Bishop of Maiuma, 19